"*Understanding Social Entrepreneurship* is one of the most comprehensive examinations of social entrepreneurship ever written. Kickul and Lyons completely capture both the essence and current surges in the field, covering every aspect from definition, opportunity, and scaling to funding, measurement, and ecosystems. For any scholar developing a course in social entrepreneurship, this is THE book!"

Donald F. Kuratko, Indiana University – Bloomington, USA

"The United States Association for Small Business and Entrepreneurship (USASBE) launched a teaching certificate in Social Entrepreneurship in 2012. Participants in the certificate program are faculty who are interested in creating and teaching courses in social entrepreneurship. *Understanding Social Entrepreneurship* is the recommended text for this certificate program and our participants value the up to date content and teaching tools provided. I personally use this text in courses I teach in Social Entrepreneurship and highly recommend it."

Tony Mendes, Former President USASBE, USA

Understanding Social Entrepreneurship

Understanding Social Entrepreneurship is the leading textbook that provides students with a comprehensive overview of the field. It brings the mindset, principles, strategies, tools, and techniques of entrepreneurship into the social sector to present innovative solutions to today's vexing social issues.

Kickul and Lyons cover all the key topics relevant to social entrepreneurship, including a detailed examination of each of the steps in the entrepreneurial process. This edition includes several new features:

- new international cases and examples—providing students with a broader understanding of social entrepreneurship globally;
- updated 'voices from the field' boxes—this popular feature shows how social entrepreneurship functions in the real world; and
- four new chapters—covering the emerging topics of lean start-up, support eco-systems, social intrapreneurship, and social entrepreneurship and environmental sustainability.

Bringing together a rigorous theoretical foundation and a strong practical focus, it is the go-to resource for students of social entrepreneurship. The companion website includes an instructor's manual, PowerPoint slides, and other tools to provide additional support for students and instructors.

Jill Kickul is Director of the Stern School of Business Program in Social Entrepreneurship at the Berkley Center for Entrepreneurship and Innovation, NYU, USA. As a Clinical Professor of Business and Society, she teaches courses in entrepreneurship, social entrepreneurship, and social impact strategies. She has published more than one hundred journal articles and books on the subject of entrepreneurship.

Thomas S. Lyons is the Lawrence N. Field Family Chair in Entrepreneurship, Professor of Management, and Field Mentor at Baruch College CUNY, USA. He has expertise in the following subjects: entrepreneurship, economic development, strategic planning, and public–private partnerships. He is co-author or editor of eleven books and has published over sixty articles and papers in scholarly outlets on entrepreneurial and economic strategy.

Understanding Social Entrepreneurship

The Relentless Pursuit of Mission in an Ever Changing World

Second Edition

Jill Kickul
Thomas S. Lyons

Routledge
Taylor & Francis Group

NEW YORK AND LONDON

For support material associated with Understanding Social Entrepreneurship, Second Edition, please go to www.routledge.com/cw/lyons

First edition published 2012
by Routledge
Second edition published 2016
by Routledge
711 Third Avenue, New York, NY 10017

and by Routledge
2 Park Square, Milton Park, Abingdon, Oxon OX14 4RN

Routledge is an imprint of the Taylor & Francis Group, an informa business

© 2016 Taylor & Francis

The right of Jill Kickul and Thomas S. Lyons to be identified as authors of this work has been asserted by them in accordance with sections 77 and 78 of the Copyright, Designs and Patents Act 1988.

Library of Congress Cataloging in Publication Data
A catalogue record for this book is available from the British Library

ISBN: 978-1-138-90383-8 (hbk)
ISBN: 978-1-138-90384-5 (pbk)
ISBN: 978-1-315-69597-6 (ebk)

Typeset in Berling Roman and Futura
by Keystroke, Station Road, Codsall, Wolverhampton

Brief Table of Contents

Detailed Table of Contents

Illustrations

FIGURES

TABLES

About the Authors

Jill Kickul, Ph.D., is the Director of New York University Stern School of Business Social Entrepreneurship Program in the Berkley Center for Entrepreneurship and Innovation. Prior to joining the faculty at Stern, Dr. Kickul was the Richard A. Forsythe Chair in Entrepreneurship in the Thomas C. Page Center for Entrepreneurship at Miami University (Ohio) and a Professor in the Management Department in the Farmer School of Business. Prior to joining the Miami University faculty, she was the Elizabeth J. McCandless Professor in Entrepreneurship at the Simmons School of Management. She has also taught entrepreneurship internationally for the Helsinki School of Economics and for the International Bank of Asia (Hong Kong MBA Program), and has delivered research seminars at the Stockholm School of Economics, the EM Lyon School of Business, Massey University Institute for Entrepreneurship and Social Innovation, the Aarhus Center for Organizational Renewal and Evolution (CORE), and the Jönköping International Business School.

Dr. Kickul has held a number of leadership positions in various well-respected entrepreneurship and management associations. She has been the Chair of the 2008 Internationalizing Entrepreneurship Education and Training (Eighteenth Annual Global IntEnt Conference). She has also served as Co-Chair of AOM Teaching Theme Committee (Academy-wide), President of the Midwest Academy of Management, Chair of the Individual Entrepreneurship division of USASBE, Chair of the inaugural USASBE Case Competition, and Chair of the Teaching Committee for the AOM Entrepreneurship division. Dr. Kickul also participates on a number of boards and organizations, most notably the European Microfinance Network (EMN), and is a Faculty Affiliate within the Center for Gender and Organizations (CGO).

As a scholar, she has been awarded the Cason Hall & Company Publishers Best Paper Award, Michael J. Driver Best Careers Paper, the Coleman Foundation Best Empirical Paper, the John Jack Award for Entrepreneurship Education, and the IntEnt Best Paper. She has more than one hundred publications in entrepreneurship and management journals, including *Entrepreneurship Theory and Practice*, *Small Business Economics*, the *Journal of Operations Management*, the *Journal of Management*, the *Journal of Small Business Management*, the *Journal of Organizational Behavior*, *Frontiers of Entrepreneurship Research*, the *International Journal of Entrepreneurship and Innovation*, the *International Journal of Entrepreneurial Behavior and Research*, the *Journal of Business Ethics*, *Decision Sciences*, the *Journal of Innovative Education*, and the *Academy of Management Learning and Education Journal*. She is a co-author (with Lisa Gundry) of the textbook *Entrepreneurship Strategy: Changing Patterns in New Venture Creation, Growth, and Reinvention* (Sage, 2007).

Finally, her work on entrepreneurship education development and curriculum design has been nationally recognized and supported through the Coleman Foundation Entrepreneurship Excellence in Teaching Colleges Grant and has been named by Fortune Small Business as one of the Top 10 Innovative Programs in Entrepreneurship Education.

Thomas S. Lyons, Ph.D., is the Lawrence N. Field Family Chair in Entrepreneurship and Professor of Management in the Zicklin School of Business at Baruch College of the City University of New York. He is also a Field Mentor in Baruch's Field Center for Entrepreneurship, offering counseling to New York City's entrepreneurs and small businesses and conducting seminars on strategic planning, financing social enterprises, marshaling resources for entrepreneurship, and refining and communicating market opportunities. Dr. Lyons has also served as a mentor to student teams in various business plan and case study competitions. He teaches courses in Social Entrepreneurship and Entrepreneurship and Community Development at Baruch College. Lyons also played a major role in developing Baruch's graduate major in Sustainable Business.

Lyons's research specialization is the relationship between entrepreneurship and community development. He is the co-author or editor of eleven books, among them *Investing in Entrepreneurs*, *Incubating New Enterprises*, *Creating an Economic Development Action Plan*, *Economy without Walls*, *Economic Development: Strategies for State and Local Practice*, *Financing Small Business in America*, and *Social Entrepreneurship: How Business Can Transform Society*. In addition, he has published over sixty articles and papers in scholarly and professional outlets, including *International Business Review*, *Economic Development Quarterly*, the *Journal of Developmental Entrepreneurship*, the *International Journal of Entrepreneurship and Innovation*, *Community Development*, *Evaluation and Program Planning*, and the *Journal of the American Planning Association*. He is the Guest Editor of a special issue of the *Entrepreneurship Research Journal* on "Entrepreneurship and the Community," published in early 2012. Dr. Lyons is also a member of Baruch College's research team, which serves as Babson College's US partner for the Global Entrepreneurship Monitor (GEM) Project.

Lyons is the original co-creator of the concept of the Entrepreneurial Development System (EDS), a framework for developing entrepreneurs and their enterprises as a community or regional economic development strategy. His ideas were the basis for the Kellogg Foundation's national Entrepreneurial Development Systems for Rural America: Promoting Vibrant Economies through Expanded Entrepreneurship competition in 2004, in celebration of the Foundation's seventy-fifth anniversary. He is also the co-creator of the Pipeline of Entrepreneurs and Enterprises framework, which helps communities and regions manage their portfolio of entrepreneurial assets in a more efficient, effective, and equitable way. Dr. Lyons is the recipient of the International Community Development Society's 2011 Ted K. Bradshaw Outstanding Research Award for his research contributions to the field of community development.

Dr. Lyons is a former chairman of the board of directors of the Rural Policy Research Institute's Center for Rural Entrepreneurship (CRE). He is a member of the advisory board of the National Executive Service Corps (NESC) in New York City. He has also served as a director or advisory board member of an empowerment business incubation program, a university-based technology commercialization incubation program, an urban microenterprise program, and several for-profit and nonprofit social ventures.

Lyons holds a doctorate in urban and regional planning from the University of Michigan, Ann Arbor. He has been a practicing entrepreneur and social entrepreneur.

Foreword

You *Can* Change the World

You *can* change the world—if you just give yourself permission. The biggest barrier by far to having all the satisfactions in life of being an effective social entrepreneur is paying attention to all the many people who will tell you: "You can't . . ."

Most people have this reaction because they didn't. If you go ahead and change the world, they will suffer a little regret that they did not give themselves permission, that they therefore spent their life in their law firm or wherever. Therefore, please be gentle and polite—but firmly ignore such advice.

Think of the social entrepreneurs whose stories you know—be it Florence Nightingale (who created the field of professional nursing), Jimmy Wales (Wikipedia), or Wendy Kopp (Teach for America). None of them required astrophysics to see a big problem and imagine a sensible answer.

Certainly you will have no problem spotting a problem!

Then, why couldn't you do what these and so many others have done: imagine a solution and then persist in refining that idea until it truly works and then until you have made it the new pattern for society?

The barrier is not intelligence. The chief question is: Will you give yourself permission to see a problem and then apply your native intelligence and what you have learned to find a solution and make it fly?

What is required is permission and persistence.

People who do not believe they can cause change do not want to see problems or opportunities. Why would they? Since they believe "I can't . . .," seeing a problem will only make them feel bad about themselves.

On the other hand, once you know that you *are* a changemaker, once you have core confidence in yourself and have given yourself the necessary skills, you will always be looking for a problem, preferably a big one. The problem then becomes an opportunity for you to express love and respect in action at the highest possible level. There is nothing that brings humans greater happiness in life—or that is more important to society. This is why Ashoka's central goal is an "everyone a changemaker™" world.

The central historical fact of our era is that the rate of change is still escalating exponentially—as are the number of changemakers and, even more important, the combinations of changemakers and also the combinations of these combinations.

Given this fact, the way the world has been organized since the agricultural revolution is coming to an end. Institutions have been designed for repetitive functioning. They are characterized by a very few people controlling everyone else, by limited and chiefly vertical nervous systems, and by walls. There is no way that such primitive organisms can survive in a world that is characterized by change on all sides, with each change stimulating more change widely across this new world.

Instead, we need teams of teams that shift fluidly to serve particular change opportunities. That is the ecosystem one increasingly sees in winning organizations and regions such as Bangalore and Silicon Valley. By contrast, fifty years ago Detroit was at the pinnacle of American technology and prosperity. Now it is not even in the game.

That is what will happen to any institution, community, or country that does not make the transition to "everyone a changemaker™"—only this time it will take ten to fifteen years at most. We do not have fifty years.

In this new team of teams world, the skills required are very different. One does not have a team unless everyone on it is an initiatory player. And in a world defined by change, one cannot be a player without being a changemaker.

The key factor for success for any group going forward will be: What percentage of its people are changemakers, at what skill level, and how well and how fluidly are they able to work together internally and externally?

In this world, social entrepreneurs are essential. The basic systems of society will be in constant and interacting change. Leading systems change is what entrepreneurs do. However, entrepreneurs who pursue their own or a particular group's interest can easily pull these changing systems off in dangerous directions. Thus, for example, many of the digital revolution entrepreneurs of today are following a business model of giving consumers something they want, getting information, and selling that information at a profit. This—along with the need for preventive surveillance in a world of terrorism and the fact that the cost of connecting the dots has all but disappeared—is devastating to privacy, which is critical for freedom and innovation.

Social entrepreneurs are the critical antidote. These are men and women who, from the core of their personality, are devoted to the good of all. Therefore, so is their work. The world needs many more.

Please give yourself permission and become one. This book will help.

Bill Drayton

Preface

Congratulations! Congratulations, we say . . . on beginning your journey in the field of social entrepreneurship! The future for social entrepreneurs is replete with opportunities to effectively address, and potentially solve, some of society's most pressing issues. It is our belief that social entrepreneurship involves the application of business practices in the pursuit of a social and/or environmental mission. It brings the mindset, principles, strategies, tools, and techniques of entrepreneurship to the social sector, yielding innovative solutions to society's vexing problems: poverty, hunger, inadequate housing and homelessness, unemployment and under-employment, illiteracy, disease, environmental degradation, and the like.

Because social entrepreneurs often operate in resource-scarce environments, they are compelled to use creative approaches to attract nontraditional resources and to apply those resources in novel ways to the challenges and problems that government and earlier private-sector efforts have failed to effectively remedy. Finally, it is often social entrepreneurs who encourage a heightened sense of accountability in the individuals and communities they serve, as well as instigating the outcomes and impacts that are created.

Our intriguing field of social entrepreneurship has captured the imaginations of thousands of business and public administration students around the world, leading to the creation of hundreds of courses and programs of study to meet this burgeoning demand. These programs are witnessing a surge of social consciousness among the incoming students. For example, the Aspen Institute's Center for Business Education (2008)[1] survey indicates that graduate students are thinking more broadly about the primary responsibilities of a company, considering "creating value for the communities in which they operate" to be a primary business responsibility.

---

1 Aspen Institute (2008). *Where will they lead? 2008 MBA student attitudes about business and society.* Washington, DC.

The Aspen Institute's biennial *Beyond Grey Pinstripes* reports a dramatic increase in the proportion (from 34 percent in 2001 to 63 percent in 2007) of Master's programs with required courses in business and society issues.

On the education front, the field has also increased, with over 350 professors teaching and researching social entrepreneurship in more than thirty-five countries and approximately 200 social entrepreneurship cases (Brock & Ashoka Global Academy for Social Entrepreneurship, 2008).[2] We believe that our textbook has a broad international appeal, given the nature of the social problems around the world and the focus on perspectives and examples for addressing social issues, including the other stakeholders in the field along the social value chain (government, public policy makers, customers, suppliers) to provide an additional lens and perspective into the complexity of making scalable progress in implementing new solutions.

AN INNOVATIVE LEARNING APPROACH TO UNDERSTANDING SOCIAL ENTREPRENEURSHIP

Within our book we explore both the theory and the practice of social entrepreneurship and blend these seamlessly through examples, case studies, the voices of practicing social entrepreneurs, and special features that put students in a position that requires creative thinking and strategic problem solving. Specifically, our approach is innovative in several ways. First, as suggested, our treatment is comprehensive, bridging theory and practice. Second, rather than employing lengthy case studies, we employ short problem-based cases in each chapter that both illustrate the principles conveyed and encourage deeper thinking.

Third, we include "voices from the field" segments that provide direct insights from practicing social entrepreneurs that reinforce the major points made in each chapter. Fourth, we include exercises to help make the direct connection between the theory of social entrepreneurship and its practice, as well as "connecting the dots" questions that test and challenge the student's learning and perspective in each of the chapters. We believe that, taken together, these unique features will provide you and your instructor with an effective tool for generating and sustaining social entrepreneurship interest and understanding. In turn, we hope that you will internalize the material, resulting in a deeper understanding of how and why social entrepreneurship works.

---

2 Brock, D. D., & Ashoka Global Academy for Social Entrepreneurship (2008). *Social entrepreneurship teaching resources handbook*. Arlington, VA: Ashoka.

THE ORGANIZATION AND FLOW OF OUR BOOK

As you begin reading, you will discover that we explore social entrepreneurship as a phenomenon and a field of practice in considerable depth. Our goal is to be comprehensive, fully exposing the theory of social entrepreneurship and linking theory to practice. We are often asked why, in a very practical field such as this one, it is necessary to discuss theory. The answer, of course, is that theory is the foundation upon which the house of practice is built. Theory tells us who social entrepreneurs are and why they are. It gives social entrepreneurs a "soul." To practice social entrepreneurship without understanding its essence is to be a professional automaton—one who masters the mechanics of the profession but has nothing upon which to reflect or from which to leverage higher levels of performance.[3]

That said, it should also be emphasized that theory without practice is ultimately an exercise in irrelevance as it pertains to a professional field like social entrepreneurship. One does not help people "in theory." Ultimately, the theory must translate into action for transformative change to occur. We are interested in imparting actionable knowledge—knowledge that can be acted upon. It is at this junction of theory and action that this textbook operates. We present theoretical underpinnings, to the extent they exist, to the field and we present "how-to" information.

After a brief introduction in Chapter 1, we begin our journey of understanding in Chapter 2 by attempting to define our terms, particularly "entrepreneurship" and "social entrepreneurship." This is not an easy task, as will be seen. There are many definitions of both terms and only grudging agreement as to their meanings. This is particularly true for social entrepreneurship, the newer of the two terms. Nevertheless, we will generate a working definition for the purposes of our discussion. The chapter then explores the relationship between business entrepreneurship and social entrepreneurship—how the two are similar and how they are different—and the implications for the practice of the latter. This chapter also discusses the ways in which this field stands at the nexus of the private, public, and voluntary sectors and how this fact has shaped its development.

In addition, Chapter 2 explores what underlies the motivations of social entrepreneurs—what some have called "intent."[4] It lays out the social entrepreneurship process, tracing its roots to business entrepreneurship and concludes with observations about beginning the social entrepreneurship journey from Tim McCollum, the co-founder of the social venture Madecasse.

Once this basic theoretical foundation for social entrepreneurship has been laid, attention can be paid to developing a social business concept and a vehicle for

---

3 Schön, D. A. (1963). *The reflective practitioner*. New York: Basic Books.

4 Mair, J., & Noboa, E. (2006). Social entrepreneurship: How intentions to create a social venture are formed. In J. Mair, J. Robinson, & K. Hockerts (Eds.). *Social entrepreneurship* (pp. 121–136). New York: Palgrave Macmillan.

taking that concept to its target "market." Chapter 3 looks at the important role of innovation in social entrepreneurship. The chapter explores the nature of innovation, its relationship to creativity, and how entrepreneurs perpetuate it. The difference between ideas and genuine opportunities to add social value is highlighted. A tool for assessing social ideas for their opportunity potential is introduced and sources of information for completing the assessment are discussed. The chapter concludes with an overview of the obstacles to innovation in the social sector that the social entrepreneur must acknowledge and overcome, and how this can be done.

When an opportunity to add social or environmental value has been identified and vetted, it is time to plan the vehicle that will take this opportunity to its "market" and the trajectory the vehicle will follow. Chapter 4 looks at this from the perspective of the "lean start-up" model, which involves customer-oriented, incremental innovation. This allows the social entrepreneur's "product" to be tailored to the needs of the people being served before a more elaborate plan is developed. This chapter details the process of lean start-up as it applies to social ventures and guides the student in the construction of a social business model canvas. It also provides examples of social entrepreneurs who have employed the lean start-up method. In Chapter 5 we focus on the alignment of the social venture's mission or vision with consideration of the necessary resources and operational strategy. The chapter introduces a strategic planning model that was specifically designed for the social sector, using elements of the best of both private and public planning frameworks. Special emphasis is placed on the development of mission and vision statements. The chapter also discusses the theory of change, with considerable emphasis placed on the action planning and implementation of the social venture's strategies. A sample plan for a social venture is provided to illustrate the application of the principles discussed in the chapter.

Chapter 6 then examines the options available to social entrepreneurs when designing and structuring the organization that will help them pursue their mission. Organizational structure has legal, managerial, and financial implications. This chapter takes an in-depth look at the various forms of legal structure that social ventures might adopt. These include nonprofit models, such as 501(c)(3) firms, popular in the United States, as well as other for-profit models. In between these two general approaches lie a set of models that blend aspects of the two—hybrids. These might include for-profits with nonprofit subsidiaries, nonprofits with for-profit subsidiaries, nonprofit–for-profit partnerships and private–public partnerships, among others. The chapter includes several examples of each structural model. The relationship between legal structure and models of management is discussed, as are the ways in which legal structure affects a social venture's ability to generate revenue. The chapter ends with a case study that stimulates thinking about the importance of organizational structure to the ability of a social venture to achieve its mission while ensuring its sustainability.

In Chapter 7 consideration is given to the many social venture funding alternatives available to social entrepreneurs, based on the previous chapter's discussion of structure. This is the fuel that powers the vehicle for achieving the social or environmental mission. Philanthropic, earned income, and hybrid approaches are explored. The emerging practice of "social enterprise," and the many forms it takes, is examined as well. The chapter also includes a section on financial sustainability that balances the social and economic considerations of the social venture. The chapter ends with a case study that poses challenges to financial sustainability and a set of reflections from a social entrepreneur on the vicissitudes of social venture finance.

The work of a social venture is greatly enhanced if it has in place a system for measuring its social impact. This is the subject of Chapter 8. It is best to identify and define measures of outputs, outcomes, and impacts before the launch of the venture. This permits the establishment of a baseline which allows the venture to identify more clearly those outcomes and impacts that are attributable to its efforts, making its claims to stakeholders more compelling. However, it is never too late to create an impact assessment methodology. Existing social ventures that do not have one should strive to develop and implement such an assessment tool. Chapter 8 also examines what an impact assessment process can do for a social venture and discusses how assessment can and should be closely tied to the mission and to the social value proposition. The chapter concludes with a case study designed to stimulate thinking regarding the challenges to social impact assessment and how those challenges might best be addressed.

In Chapter 9, entitled "Scaling the Social Venture," the issue of growth in the social entrepreneurship arena is examined. Much like commercial enterprises, at some point in their development social ventures are faced with a choice regarding growth. Depending upon their mission and goals, they can either choose to remain relatively small, with only a local impact, or they can elect to expand their reach to regional, national, or global markets. While there is nothing inherently wrong with a social entity that pursues its mission on a small scale, most experts in this field would argue that true social entrepreneurship involves a goal on the part of the entrepreneur to expand operations and maximize mission attainment, reaching as many target beneficiaries as possible. To achieve this scale of growth requires a change in the structure of the venture, if not multiple changes in structure over time.

Chapter 9 discusses what social ventures have to gain by pursuing growth and the obstacles that may stand in their way. It also explores the various structural mechanisms for achieving growth and argues that in order to grow the social venture, the entrepreneur must have the requisite skills to do so. The case of one entrepreneur's experiences in scaling his venture is studied.

Social entrepreneurship is not exclusive to the start-up of small enterprises. A social intrapreneur is one who pursues a social mission within a larger for-profit or nonprofit organization. This is the subject of Chapter 10. This chapter explores the concept of "shared value" and uses it as a frame for understanding social intrapreneurship, or corporate social entrepreneurship. It enumerates the skills required for success in this form of social entrepreneurship and discusses the role of environment, or context, in fostering such activity. In Chapter 11, the role of social entrepreneurship in environmental sustainability is examined. This chapter discusses the environmental aspects of social entrepreneurship, the challenges inherent in the environmental sustainability field, and the varieties of "green" opportunities. It offers guidance to constructing a strategic framework, known as an sSWOT, for developing a sustainability strategy for a social venture. It also includes a case study that documents the challenges faced by a fledgling environmental firm in commercializing its technologies.

Social entrepreneurs never have to work alone. Chapter 12 discusses the support ecosystem that has sprung up to nurture the work of social entrepreneurs. This includes social innovation incubators, co-working spaces, social entrepreneur networks, and other tools. The chapter looks at the needs of social entrepreneurs that such tools are designed to address. It also emphasizes the importance of systemic linkages between the various support tools and how to foster such linkages. This chapter features a detailed case study of an incubator located in New York City that is dedicated to fostering social innovation as well as many other examples.

With the essentials for launching, growing, and sustaining a social venture in hand, the book concludes with a look at the future of social entrepreneurship in Chapter 13. Future issues facing social entrepreneurs, such as increased resource scarcity, the emergence of new financing models, and the further need for systems of support, are discussed. Future opportunities stemming from these issues are identified. Opinions and insights regarding the future of the field from several practicing entrepreneurs are reported.

A FEW CONCLUDING WORDS AS YOU EMBARK ON THE JOURNEY . . .

We know that the field of social entrepreneurship creates a unique opportunity to continually integrate, challenge, and debate many traditional entrepreneurship assumptions in an effort to develop a cogent and unifying paradigm. We look forward to how the social entrepreneurs of tomorrow, like yourself, will not only find creative solutions but encourage others to take notice of these innovations and the impact they can have in driving long-term systemic change for broader social, political, and economic well-being. Let the journey begin . . .

Acknowledgments

Writing a textbook is not something its authors do alone. We have benefited greatly from the input and support of many people, and would like to take this opportunity to express our deep appreciation to all of them. First, we want to thank all the practitioners and scholars who came before us in the new, exciting, and rapidly growing field of social entrepreneurship. We walk in your pioneering footsteps.

We are indebted to the numerous anonymous individuals who reviewed the early drafts of this text and offered their insightful criticisms and very helpful suggestions for improvement. Thank you for your valuable time and effort. Any inaccuracies or misinterpretations that may remain are of our own making and not yours.

Thank you to the individuals who graciously shared their stories of social entrepreneurship with us so that we could include them in our "Voices from the Field" segments scattered throughout the text as well as those profiled in our cases and examples. Specifically, we would like to express our sincere appreciation to Ella Delio of World Resources Institute/New Ventures, Erica Dorn of Fair Reseources, Steve Godeke of Godeke Consulting, Mark Griffiths of Miami University, Stephanie Grodin, Bridges Ventures, Aaron Kinnari of Loyal Label, Allison Lynch of the New York Women's Social Entrepreneurship Incubator, Tim McCollum of Madecasse, Steve Rynn of the Mission of the Immaculate Virgin, Victor Salama, Network for Teaching Entrepreneurship (NFTE), Benjamin Stone and Matthew Mitro of Indego Africa, and Hans Taparia from TastyBite. We would also like to thank Joseph Townsend of the National Executive Service Corps in New York City for introducing us to Steve Rynn.

We want to express our gratitude to our respective institutions, New York University and Baruch College of the City University of New York, for their encouragement and support of this endeavor. A supportive environment is crucial to the success of any creative effort. In particular, we would like to thank our colleagues in the Berkley Center of Entrepreneurship and Innovation in the Stern

School of Business at NYU and the Lawrence N. Field Programs in Entrepreneurship in the Zicklin School of Business at Baruch College.

We are particularly indebted to our editor at Routledge, John Szilagyi, who shared our vision for this textbook, encouraged us throughout the process, and helped us over the rough spots with kindness and professionalism. We also want to thank John's assistant, Sara Werden, for all her efforts on our behalf. We add our thanks to Erin Arata, the editor of this Second Edition.

Introduction

AIM/PURPOSE

This chapter offers an introduction to the field of social entrepreneurship and a discussion of its importance to society. In addition, it lists online resources to help the student begin her or his journey of understanding.

LEARNING OBJECTIVES FOR THIS CHAPTER

1. To understand the economic considerations, particularly market failures, that make social entrepreneurship desirable and necessary.
2. To recognize why governments are sometimes unable to solve social and/or environmental problems.
3. To understand why private businesses are sometimes unwilling to address social and/or environmental problems.
4. To become familiar with the relatively recent developments that make social entrepreneurship possible.
5. To understand the characteristics of social entrepreneurship that position it as a powerful force for solving society's problems.

In Chapter 2 of this book we will explore in some detail what is meant by the term "social entrepreneurship." However, it is useful to have a working definition of this term as we examine its origins and importance. Put very simply, social entrepreneurship is the application of the mindset, processes, tools, and techniques of business entrepreneurship to the pursuit of a social and/or environmental mission. Thus, social entrepreneurship brings to bear the passion, ingenuity, innovativeness, perseverance, planning, bootstrapping abilities, and focus on growth characteristic of business entrepreneurs on the work of meeting our society's most pressing challenges. This is not intended as a complete definition but as a relatively easily understood place to start.

While social entrepreneurship as a field of study is relatively new, much has already been written on the subject (see Dees, Emerson, & Economy, 2001; Mair & Noboa, 2006; Wei-Skillern, Austin, Leonard, & Stevenson, 2007; Brooks, 2008; Elkington, Hartigan, & Schwab, 2008; Light, 2008; Nicholls, 2008; Welch, 2008; Bornstein & Davis, 2010, to name but a few). This is a direct reflection of the excitement it generates and the promise it is perceived to hold. Social entrepreneurs have captured our collective imagination with remarkable stories of their social innovations. These stories are uplifting and inspiring. Throughout this book, these social innovators are introduced and their innovations are explored. However, it is tempting to focus on the outcomes of social entrepreneurship and avoid thinking about why these innovations were needed in the first place and why social entrepreneurs are the logical providers of this service to society.

This chapter aims to lay this essential groundwork. In doing so, it ventures into territory that some people might find contentious; however, it is out of this very contentiousness that social entrepreneurship was forged.

We are a society that is frustrated by an overall lack of progress toward solving our most pressing social and environmental problems. Our governments and our private sector have disappointed us with their seeming inability or unwillingness to effectively address poverty, hunger, illiteracy, child abuse, domestic violence, teen pregnancy, global climate change, energy conservation, and many other challenges (Bornstein, 2007). We are eager for someone to step into the breach and meet these challenges head-on. Might that someone be the social entrepreneur?

Social entrepreneurs have been touted as the real-life superheroes of our society. Why? Why can't governments solve these problems? Why won't the private sector address them? Why entrepreneurship? The answers to these initial questions can help us to understand why the study of social entrepreneurship is important and worthwhile.

THE PUBLIC AND PRIVATE SECTORS AND OUR VEXING SOCIAL PROBLEMS

Many of the societal problems that we face have been with us for decades, if not centuries. While there has been an ebb and flow in our success in addressing these problems, the effect is that we have made surprisingly little net progress considering the time over which we have been working on them. Over the course of history, we have wavered between relying on private actors and relying on the government to help us to solve these problems. Neither sector has been consistently successful.

Despite the claims of neoclassical economists, markets are far from perfect. Adam Smith's "invisible hand"—the idea that if free markets are allowed to operate without interference, they will self-correct and benefit all members of society—has proven arthritic when it comes to addressing all segments of the economy. Market failures abound. They can be seen in situations where profits are insufficient to cause private developers to generate housing for low-income households; where banks refuse to invest in certain neighborhoods because of perceived risk, called redlining; where people go hungry in some parts of the world, while in other regions surplus food is destroyed or land is kept out of agricultural production; and where one community's pursuit of economic well-being pollutes the environment, thereby diminishing the ability of another community to provide for its residents. These are but a few examples. They are not isolated incidents. In fact, they are widespread and they are repeated on a regular basis around the world. Private markets help to create these problems and, if left to their own devices, have no incentive to reverse them.

Government, which is created to represent the interests of society as a whole and is in a position to address these issues, has not consistently been able to do so. This is due, in part, to inadequate resources; however, there are other factors at play as well. Politics is one of these.

There is too often a general lack of political will to sustain efforts to address societal problems. In democracies, short election cycles, term limits, and the propensity of newly elected officials to eschew the programs of their predecessors in favor of leaving their own mark tend to foster disjointed policy. Warring ideologies cause pendulum swings in attitudes and approaches as one regime replaces another, causing governments to "do and undo" their efforts rather than make steady forward progress. The well-documented breakdown in civil society (Milich, 2001; Putnam, 2001; Weiss & Gilani, 2001) has exacerbated this problem by radicalizing ideology and polarizing society. Because no ideology has a monopoly on truth, opportunities for the cross-pollination of ideas are being lost.

Authoritarian governments are no more successful at solving their society's problems, but for different reasons. One ideology dominates and eventually, and inevitably, reaches its point of diminishing returns for producing positive change. There are no checks on power, so corruption is common and counterproductive relative to focusing attention and resources on meeting the needs of the populace. Changes in government are often violent and the resulting instability creates still more social problems.

If our institutions are incapable of solving our social and environmental problems, then we must ask who, or what, is. How can we perfect imperfect markets without unintentionally destroying them? How can we circumvent the unproductive aspects of politics? How can we blend the best of the private and public sectors to address societal challenges? One seemingly viable answer to these questions is social entrepreneurship.

WHY THE TIME IS RIPE FOR SOCIAL ENTREPRENEURSHIP

While dissatisfaction with the relative inability of the public and private sectors to deal with society's problems helps to explain why social entrepreneurship represents an attractive option, it does not shed light on why this phenomenon is enjoying such a high level of popularity at this particular time in history. Bornstein (2007) makes a compelling case that major transformational changes worldwide over the past several decades have made it both possible and increasingly likely that citizens will take the lead in addressing social and environmental challenges.

Bornstein identifies several key changes that have made the social entrepreneurship phenomenon possible. One of these is the global increase in prosperity that brought the rise of the middle class and an increase in wealth that can be used to finance social ventures. Another is an increase in the number of democratic and semi-democratic societies, which has given citizens the freedom to pursue the correction of social and environmental wrongs outside of government and the business sector. A third is the proliferation of new communications technology that has increased people's level of awareness of global societal problems and their impacts. Fourth is the increased availability of formal education in general and the growth in the number of college-educated individuals in particular, which enhances wealth and heightens awareness as well. The final factor is the removal of many obstacles to the active participation of women and certain subjugated groups in societal affairs. As Bornstein (2007, p. 7) puts it, "To sum up, more people today have the freedom, time, wealth, health, exposure, social mobility, and confidence to address social problems in bold new ways."

SOCIAL ENTREPRENEURSHIP'S UNIQUE QUALIFICATIONS

Social entrepreneurship represents the best of the private and public sectors, while filtering out the limiting factors already discussed in ways that will be examined in this section. On the one hand, it embodies the enterprising spirit of the private sector and uses the power of economic markets to generate and deliver solutions to problems. On the other hand, it strives to intervene in broken markets in an effort to repair them and places the public interest ahead of private interests (Dees, 1998). As was noted at the beginning of this chapter, it brings the mindset, processes, tools, and techniques of business entrepreneurship to the solution of social and/or environmental problems.

Social entrepreneurship possesses unique qualifications that make it an attractive alternative to purely private or purely public approaches to social and environmental problem solving:

■ It is passionate and personal in that the social entrepreneur has chosen the problem to be addressed because it has deep meaning to her or him. Whether that meaning derives from personal experience, second-hand knowledge, or an avocation, it sparks an intense desire to pursue a solution to the identified problem. This is not to suggest that politicians and public officials are not passionate about certain issues, but their passion is often tempered by political realities that preclude a single-minded pursuit of an issue's resolution. Similarly, commercial entrepreneurs are typically quite passionate about their product or service, but that passion centers around the offering's ability to satisfy a customer need and thereby generate a profit for the business owner(s).

Thus, the difference between social entrepreneurs, government officials, and private business people relative to passion is the source of that passion; that is, the values that underlie it. Social entrepreneurship is often referred to as value-based (Cho, 2006; Brooks, 2008). This could be misleading, however. There are values that drive the actions of all three actors; these values merely differ from role to role. For the public official, it may be political expediency. For the commercial business person, it may be profit. For the social entrepreneur, the values are moral in nature, involving empathy for the plight of the beneficiaries of her or his efforts and some kind of judgment regarding the "rightness" of addressing the underlying problem (Mair & Noboa, 2006). Such morally based values have the power to drive the level of passion that is unique to social entrepreneurs.

■ It is not bureaucratic; it is nimble. Unlike governments or large companies, social entrepreneurship is not reactive or bound by cumbersome rules and processes. Like small commercial ventures, social ventures are nimble and strategic. They move quickly and decisively to address problems. Entrepreneurs recognize that there is a "window of opportunity" for capturing any market, which does not remain open indefinitely. Similarly, social entrepreneurs understand that social and environmental solutions have limited periods of effectiveness, which are always changing. This makes agility in adapting to changes crucial.

■ It enables transformation. Most of what is delivered to customers or clients or citizens by private businesses and by governments is conveyed by transaction. Goods and services are exchanged through short-term transactional relationships. This works as far as it goes, but it does not bring long-term change; it does not yield transformation.

Social and environmental problems are not solved through transactions. Giving a starving individual food does not end hunger in the world. Some people seem to think that piling up transactions can yield a transformation. However, giving 1,000 hungry individuals food will still not end world hunger. Not until the system that spawns hunger is permanently changed for the better will hunger be ended on a global scale. This kind of systemic change, yielding long-term benefits, is the focus of social entrepreneurs.

■ It builds, maintains, and utilizes social capital. A crucial factor in all entrepreneurship, and social entrepreneurship in particular, is networking. Bringing people and organizations together to focus attention on a problem, to marshal resources from a variety of places to implement solutions, and to effectively communicate outcomes is what gives social entrepreneurship its power. These networks of trust are built on a shared mission and vision for positive change. The public and private sectors are typically focused on adversarial relationships and competition. Political parties compete to control the policy agenda. Warring ideologies bludgeon each other over who is "right." Important decisions are reached using win–lose mechanisms that work for some and leave others out. Commercial businesses compete with others for market share, with the tacit, if not implicit, goal of putting the competition out of business.

Social entrepreneurs embrace the concept of "co-opetition" (Brandenburger & Nalebuff, 1997). They understand that, in their market ecosystem, sometimes they must compete with other social entrepreneurs, particularly for scarce resources. However, much of the time it makes sense to collaborate because it makes their ventures more effective, sustainable, and competitive.

■ It is mission focused, not profit driven. At the core of social entrepreneurship is the social or environmental mission. This is the compass that guides everything a social venture does. Even social ventures that are for-profit in their structure and those that are nonprofit but engaged in earned income activities put mission above revenue. This helps to ensure that society's interests will prevail over self-interest.

Its mission is the social venture's reason for existence. The mission reflects the values that gird the social entrepreneurship endeavor. As was noted earlier in this section, the nature of these values is what distinguishes social entrepreneurship from government and commercial activities.

■ It is accountable to society. Like government, social ventures are accountable to society, not to private shareholders. They operate in a "fish bowl." This brings with it both greater freedom and a higher level of responsibility. The freedom comes from not having to cater to the selfish interests of shareholders, who often tend to err on the side of ensuring their own benefit at the expense of the best interests of the venture and society as a whole. The private sector is rife with examples of companies whose pursuit of higher share value and dividends for shareholders has ultimately destroyed the business, resulted in the loss of jobs, and/or has left communities in economic, social, or environmental disarray.

The disaster caused by an accident involving a BP offshore oil rig located in the Gulf of Mexico in 2010 is a case in point. As the calamity unfolded, there was increasing evidence that BP was poorly prepared for such a scenario, looked the other way when confronted with safety issues concerning the rig prior to the accident, and was slow to react to the damage created by the spill (Langley, Weisman, & McDonald, 2010; Corkery, 2010; Casselman, 2010).

To take the necessary precautions required to ensure safe operation and to be prepared to act quickly in the face of a disaster are costly activities that reduce profit margins. This behavior suggests that the company placed its owners ahead of society in its decision-making process. While this is rational behavior for a commercial business, it clearly illustrates the kind of conflict that can arise between the private good and the common good.

The "shareholders" of social ventures are the people who are invested in the successful solution of the problem they address. This avoids misalignment between the goals of the venture and the goals of the segment of society it serves. Because of this, however, the social venture is held to a higher standard of accountability. It must document its impact on the problem, justify its existence, and freely share what it learns in the process with others.

■ It fosters social and environmental innovation. Whereas governments are often hamstrung by the never-ending struggle between those who want to preserve the status quo and those who advocate change, resulting in incrementalism at best, social ventures are exclusively built to foster positive change relative to a given challenge. To overcome that challenge requires a transformation. This automatically facilitates an environment in which creativity and innovation are welcomed and pursued. Social entrepreneurs take social inventions (the fruits of creativity), whether they are the creator or not, and implement them (innovation) as a means to problem solving and transformative change.

While this process is not unlike that followed by commercial entrepreneurs, there is a difference. The primary test of the value of a commercial innovation is its market potential. Despite the fact that a social innovation must have a market, the chief test of its value is its potential to solve a social or environmental problem.

■ It circumnavigates politics. While politics are a necessary factor in any endeavor with societal ramifications, by taking a more business-oriented approach social ventures avoid the most debilitating aspects of political wrangling. While governments are debating the problem, the social entrepreneur is working to solve it, or the social entrepreneur is showing leadership by bringing together the conflicted factions to negotiate a solution. In some cases, social entrepreneurs have helped to build public–private partnerships to address challenges mired in politics.

That said, we should point out that this should not be offered as an excuse for the social entrepreneur not communicating with her or his intended beneficiaries relative to what is needed. There have been cases in which, with the best of intentions, the social entrepreneur has made assumptions that led to actions that worsened the problem rather than solving it. Just as good business people first determine what customer need they are fulfilling and who their market is, good social entrepreneurs must first clearly define the problem they are attacking and who has that problem. In both cases, this involves communication with the prospective "customer" or community.

■ It facilitates development by lending equity and stability. Hamlin and Lyons (1996) identify six prerequisites to successful development: surplus, savings, investment, efficiency, equity, and stability. The first four are readily understood by business people and economic developers in a capitalist economy. A subsistence economy cannot develop because it generates no profit, or excess revenue; therefore, it can only cover its costs. Profit, or surplus, permits savings, which in turn can be invested in new development. Operating efficiently maximizes profit and return on investment. All of this perpetuates development over time.

What is less well understood is that none of this can take place in an economy that lacks equity and stability. Equity provides the balance that keeps a society together. For example, a so-called two-class society—rich and poor, with no middle class—is not an equitable society. The disparity in socio-economic status among the society's members is too great to be sustainable. A society that excludes certain of its members from access to opportunity is not equitable. Inequity can lead to protest, work disruption, and even violent revolt. All of these things undermine stability, which in turn precludes the society from developing its economy. There are other sources of instability. Incompetent governance and the resulting frequent turnover of leadership is one source. Natural disasters—earthquakes, floods, violent windstorms, etc.—are another source. Businesses require stability and predictability in order to function efficiently and effectively, allowing for the generation of surplus. In this way, we have come full circle in our explication of the required elements for successful development.

Social entrepreneurs address equity and stability through their efforts. When their work in the areas of education, health, poverty alleviation, community development, and so forth helps to create opportunities for socio-economic advancement, they are creating equity and enhancing stability. When they help to rebuild after natural disasters, they are fostering stability. In this way, social entrepreneurs are ensuring future development for the entire society. Business people sometimes do not understand this, or do not believe it is "their job." Governments can help with some aspects of ensuring equity and stability, but they are often constrained by the factors noted earlier in this chapter, rendering them unable to facilitate the requisite transformative change.

These characteristics give hope that social entrepreneurship can break the impasse often experienced by our traditional public and private institutions when it comes to solving society's most pressing problems. They also highlight the fact that social ventures are most valuable when they take on societal problems that neither government nor commercial business can solve. This is social entrepreneurship's market niche.

RESOURCES AND TOOLS TO BEGIN THE SOCIAL ENTREPRENEURSHIP JOURNEY

Before we begin our journey of understanding into the realm of social entrepreneurship, it is important to properly equip ourselves. The World Wide Web is full of resources for people who are just getting started. We highlight several such resources and tools here and encourage students to explore these before continuing on to Chapter 2 of this book.

The following is a list of websites that are rich with information on social entrepreneurship. Not only do they provide definitions, tools, and examples, but they profile organizations that are leaders in this movement as well. For example, Ashoka and Echoing Green are social venture philanthropies that provide social entrepreneurs with financial resources, technical assistance, and access to networks. Net Impact is a student organization that champions social entrepreneurship, corporate social responsibility, and sustainable business practices, and can be found on college campuses across the United States. We urge you to thoroughly explore these sites:

Ashoka: www.ashoka.org, www.changemakers.com, www.ashokau.org
Aspen Institute: www.aspeninstitute.org
Echoing Green: www.echoinggreen.org
Net Impact: www.netimpact.org
Next Billion: www.nextbillion.net
Skoll Foundation: www.skollfoundation.org/skoll-entrepreneurs
Social Enterprise Alliance: www.se-alliance.org

Another valuable Web-based resource is E-180, a website and blog that seeks to educate about social entrepreneurship and related topics. It abounds with information on what is happening in the field and where one can find training, fellowships, and other resources. In 2009, E-180 offered its ranking of the "Best Social Entrepreneurship News websites" (E-180, 2009). In rank order, they are:

1   E-180: www.e-180.com
2   CSR Wire: www.csrwire.com
3   Change.org: social entrepreneurship: www.change.org
4   Stanford Social Innovation Review: www.ssireview.org
5   Fast Company: social responsibility: www.fastcompany.com/topics/ethonomics
6   Social Edge: www.socialedge.org
7   Next Billion: www.nextbillion.net
8   Alltop: social entrepreneurship: http://social-entrepreneurship.alltop.com
9   Alltop: good: http://good.alltop.com

A perusal of these sites will provide an understanding of what is currently going on in the field of social entrepreneurship. It can, and should, be used as a source of real-world examples to which the theoretical material in Chapter 2 can be connected.

QUESTIONS FOR "CONNECTING THE DOTS"

1 Drawing on economic theory, what kinds of market failure underlie the world's most pressing problems? Examine three examples: hunger, groundwater contamination, and literacy.
2 Why is healthcare reform such a contentious issue in the United States? Why have public and private efforts been unsuccessful in fully addressing the challenge of affordable health care? What role(s) might social entrepreneurs play in solving the problem?
3 The chief goal of the private sector is efficiency. Why? The primary focus of the public sector is equity. Why? It is quite possible to be highly efficient yet ineffective. It is also possible to be very equitable but ineffective. How does social entrepreneurship blend efficiency, equity, and effectiveness?
4 Some have argued that social entrepreneurship is another form of commercial entrepreneurship with positive social or environmental change as its product. Do you agree with the accuracy of this observation? Why, or why not?

REFERENCES

Bornstein, D. (2007). *How to change the world: Social entrepreneurs and the power of new ideas.* New York: Oxford University Press.

Bornstein, D., & Davis, S. (2010). *Social entrepreneurship: What everyone needs to know.* New York: Oxford University Press.

Brandenburger, A. M., & Nalebuff, B. J. (1997). *Co-opetition.* New York: Broadway Business.

Brooks, A. C. (2008). *Social entrepreneurship: A modern approach to social value creation.* Upper Saddle River, NJ: Prentice Hall.

Casselman, B. (2010). Anadarko blames BP for rig disaster. *Wall Street Journal* (online), June 18.

Cho, A.H. (2006). Politics, values and social entrepreneurship: A critical appraisal. In J. Mair, J. Robinson, & K. Hockerts (Eds.). *Social entrepreneurship* (pp. 34–56). New York: Palgrave Macmillan.

Corkery, M. (2010, June 11). Deal journal/breaking insight from WSJ.com. *Wall Street Journal*, p. C3.

Dees, J. G. (1998). The meaning of "social entrepreneurship." Palo Alto, CA: Graduate School of Business, Stanford University. Retrieved from http://www.caseatduke.org/documents/dees_sedef.pdf (accessed June 22, 2010).

Dees, J. G., Emerson, J., & Economy, P. (2001). *Enterprising nonprofits.* New York: Wiley.

E-180 (2009). Best social entrepreneurship news websites. Retrieved from http://www.e-180.com (accessed July 10, 2010).

Elkington, J., Hartigan, P., & Schwab, K. (2008). *The power of unreasonable people: How social entrepreneurs create markets that change the world.* Cambridge, MA: Harvard Business School Press.

Hamlin, R. E., & Lyons, T. S. (1996). *Economy without walls*. Westport, CT: Praeger.

Langley, M., Weisman, J., & McDonald, A. (2010, June 11). BP weighs dividend cut: Estimate of spill's size is raised as Britain defends embattled oil giant. *Wall Street Journal* (Eastern edition), p. A1.

Light, P. C. (2008). *The search for social entrepreneurship*. Washington, DC: Brookings Institution Press.

Mair, J., & Noboa, E. (2006). Social entrepreneurship: How intentions to create a social venture are formed. In J. Mair, J. Robinson, & K. Hockerts (Eds.). *Social entrepreneurship*. New York: Palgrave Macmillan.

Milich, L. (2001). Civil society breakdown: Food security in the "new" Indonesia. *Development, 44*(4), 93–96.

Nicholls, A. (Ed.). (2008). *Social entrepreneurship: New models of sustainable social change*. New York: Oxford University Press.

Putnam, R. (2001). *Bowling alone: The collapse and revival of American community*. New York: Simon & Schuster.

Wei-Skillern, J. C., Austin, J. E., Leonard, H. B., & Stevenson, H.H.(2007). *Entrepreneurship in the social sector*. Thousand Oaks, CA: Sage.

Weiss, A. M. and Gilani, S. Z. (Eds.). (2001). *Power and civil society in Pakistan*. New York: Oxford University Press.

Welch, W. (2008). *Tactics of hope: How social entrepreneurs are changing our world*. San Rafael, CA: Earth Aware Editions.

Defining and Distinguishing Social Entrepreneurship

AIM/PURPOSE

This chapter seeks to define the field and distinguish between business and social entrepreneurship in useful ways. It explores the field's economic origins and examines the intentions of its practitioners. It also examines several models of the social entrepreneurship process, ultimately offering an original hybrid model as a guide for thinking about the field.

LEARNING OBJECTIVES FOR THIS CHAPTER

1. To comprehend the meaning and nature of entrepreneurship, in general.
2. To understand what constitutes social entrepreneurship.
3. To recognize the similarities and differences between business entrepreneurship and social entrepreneurship.
4. To understand what motivates social entrepreneurs to pursue their mission.
5. To envision and follow the social entrepreneurship process: who the actors are, what resources are required, what relationships must be developed, and which contextual factors are at play.

People have been engaged in the types of activities that today we include under the umbrella we call "social entrepreneurship" for centuries: ministering to the sick, feeding the hungry, teaching the illiterate to read, and so forth. Economic and social phenomena such as the spread of capitalism, the rise of the welfare state, and the decline of the traditional family support structure have served to make these activities more necessary and caused them to grow in scale and level of sophistication. As was suggested in Chapter 1, the problems at which these activities are targeted have also grown in intensity and scale to the point where existing governmental and private-sector institutions are no longer able to solve them, requiring a new approach to their alleviation which has taken on a life of its own.

Bill Drayton, the founder of the social venture philanthropic organization Ashoka, is widely credited with coining the term "social entrepreneurship" in the 1980s. However, it was J. Gregory Dees who first envisioned social entrepreneurship as a profession and a field of study in the late 1990s. Thus, it is clear that while many of the activities of social entrepreneurship have a long history, efforts to give it coherence as a body of knowledge and practice are quite recent. This is exciting in that we are delving into something very new. The reverse side of this coin, however, is that we, as students of this new field, have very little to work with in terms of theoretical background. In fact, there is still considerable disagreement as to how to define the term "social entrepreneurship." This situation presents both a challenge and an opportunity. We must navigate only partially charted waters; however, we have the unique chance to help shape this field and influence its innovation. What could be more entrepreneurial?

In this chapter we examine our current understanding of the terms "entrepreneurship" and "social entrepreneurship" and attempt to establish a working definition of the latter that will guide us as we continue our journey of understanding. We also endeavor to distinguish social entrepreneurship from its cousin, business entrepreneurship, in ways that are useful. We will discuss social entrepreneurship's economic origins and the role of individual intent and motivation in shaping efforts in the field. We will also look at several theoretical models of the entrepreneurship and social entrepreneurship processes to help us understand the roles, players, functions, and interrelationships involved.

As good scholars in all fields know, the best place to start one's inquiry into a subject is by defining what is meant by the terms being used. In this case, how do we define "social entrepreneurship"? The term is made up of two distinct words, each of which adds something to its meaning. An examination of each of these words separately, and then together, may prove useful.

DEFINING "SOCIAL"

"Social" derives from the Latin word *socialis*, meaning an associate, ally, or companion. The word suggests the organization of people, or confederates, into an interdependent group that lives and works together cooperatively—a community or society. Therefore, "social" has to do with anything that pertains to a community or society. By definition, it puts society ahead of the individual.

There is a tendency to think of the social aspect of life as being distinct from the economic. This conception of the world holds that the pursuit of economic advantage can, and should, be conducted in isolation from the affairs of society. In the United States, this is reflected in such time-honored ideas as *laissez-faire* (the government, as the representative of society, should keep its "hands off" private economic pursuits) and *caveat emptor* ("let the buyer beware," suggesting that it is society's responsibility to protect itself from unscrupulous business practices). Even the notion that it is the government's duty to provide a "safety net" for people who fall between the economy's cracks, which is common in many countries around the world, is another example of the perceived division between society and economy.

Fortunately, this view is shifting. As David Bornstein (2007, p. x) observes, "the conceptual firewalls that once divided the world into social and economic realms" are coming down. There are numerous examples of this all around us. The increasing interest in the areas of sustainable business and corporate social responsibility (CSR) offers numerous cases in point. PepsiCo measures and works to reduce its carbon footprint. NBC-Universal builds environmental sustainability into its practices and its brand. Highly successful entrepreneurs, like Bill Gates and Jeff Skoll, undertake massive philanthropic efforts that provide leadership in this arena and that support the work of social entrepreneurs. Private actors in the capital markets, such as the Shorebank model, bring financing to community development efforts (Wei-Skillern, Austin, Leonard, & Stevenson, 2007). Public–private partnerships and public–private–nonprofit partnerships abound (Hamlin & Lyons, 1996).

The fact is that the perceived partition between society and the economy is an artificial bifurcation. Society and the economy are inextricably linked. The economy is an invention of society and, as such, can and should be reinvented from time to time to make sure the two are in harmony. This reality is what makes addressing social issues through entrepreneurship a natural fit.

DEFINING "ENTREPRENEURSHIP"

"Social" is a relatively easy term to define. There may be, and is, disagreement about which should take precedence—the individual or society; the economy or the needs of society—but there is little or no disagreement about what "social" means. A widely agreed-upon definition of "entrepreneurship," on the other hand, is not nearly as uncomplicated to find. This is due to the wide variety of perspectives brought to bear on this subject.

There are purely economic definitions, like the one espoused by Terry (1995, p. 102), who describes an entrepreneur as "a production innovator who perceives the opportunity to provide a new product or implement a new production method and then organizes the needed production inputs and assumes financial risk." While this definition focuses on things that resonate for economists, such as means of production and production inputs, it also uses terms like "innovator" and "financial risk" that provide a glimpse into the characteristics that make entrepreneurs unique.

The economist Burton Klein (1977, p. 9) offers a broader perspective on the entrepreneur, calling her or him "a marriage broker between what is desirable from an economic point of view and what is possible from a technological (i.e., operational) point of view." This definition introduces the concept that entrepreneurship has to do with making connections and building networks that are essential to progress in solving problems and meeting needs. It also hints at a more romantic view of entrepreneurs as people who can help us make our economic dreams come true.

Entrepreneurship educators Timmons and Spinelli (2007, p. 79) provide yet another "take" on entrepreneurship, which they define as "a way of thinking, reasoning, and acting that is opportunity obsessed, holistic in approach, and leadership balanced." In so doing, they highlight the fact that entrepreneurship involves both cognitive processes and actual practice—it is a profession. Furthermore, they establish that entrepreneurs are perpetually focused on identifying viable business opportunities, are strategic or "big picture" thinkers, and are mindful of the fact that effective leadership is catalytic in nature, spreading responsibility and recognition evenly throughout the enterprise. Timmons and Spinelli describe this latter behavior as making "heroes" out of partners and employees.

Lichtenstein and Lyons (2010), entrepreneurship researchers and practitioners, offer yet another perspective. They maintain that an entrepreneur is anyone who innovates (by creating a new product or service, developing a new production process, or finding a new market) and who has a goal of growth and development for themselves and their business. This latter caveat refers to the idea that entrepreneurs seek to improve their own skills in order to more efficiently and effectively move their companies through the stages of the business life cycle.

While there are many other definitions of "entrepreneurship" that have been developed over the years, the aforementioned definitions are representative of the diversity among them. Despite this variation in thinking, there are some general aspects of entrepreneurship that appear to have at least some degree of universality. Entrepreneurs actively seek out opportunities to innovate in order to add value to the lives of their customers. They pursue a strategy of growth in order to expand their business's market reach and profits. They are strategic in the way they manage their enterprises, and they ably build networks among their investors, suppliers, and customers in order to achieve their business goals. While they are not necessarily risk takers, they are invariably risk managers. This skill at risk management enables them to bear greater risks than do most business people or members of the wider populace.

That said, there is still disagreement among entrepreneurship scholars on several of these points and related considerations. For example, Shane (2008) argues that successful entrepreneurs share genetic traits, while Lichtenstein and Lyons (2010) maintain that success in entrepreneurship rests with the mastery of a learned skill set. Shane states that business opportunities exist in the given context and must be found by the entrepreneur, while Sarasvathy (2008) asserts that entrepreneurs fabricate opportunities out of the stuff of their environments. Many entrepreneurship educators argue that the only true entrepreneurs are those who grow high-impact companies worthy of investment by venture capitalists; however, others include small business owners in their definition of entrepreneurs. These are ongoing debates that may never be resolved, but they need to be acknowledged because they have implications for the differences in the ways in which "social entrepreneurship" is defined and practiced.

DEFINING "SOCIAL ENTREPRENEURSHIP"

As is suggested at the end of the preceding section, finding a uniformly accepted definition of "social entrepreneurship" is just as problematic as getting agreement on a definition of "entrepreneurship." The latter impasse contributes to the former. As an example, Brock, Steinder, and Kim (2008) have identified thirteen different definitions of social entrepreneurship. Before taking up this issue, we review several of the definitions of social entrepreneurship that have been put forward.

Arguably the oldest and most cited definition of social entrepreneurship comes from Dees (1998, p. 4) in his seminal unpublished paper "The Meaning of 'Social Entrepreneurship.'" Dees draws upon definitions of entrepreneurship from Schumpeter, Say, Drucker, and Stevenson and adds a social twist. He states:

> Social entrepreneurs play the role of change agents in the social sector by:
>
> - Adopting a mission to create and sustain social value (not just private value),
> - Recognizing and relentlessly pursuing new opportunities to serve that mission,
> - Engaging in a process of continuous innovation, adaptation, and learning,
> - Acting boldly without being limited by resources currently in hand, and
> - Exhibiting a heightened sense of accountability to the constituencies served and for the outcomes created.

For Dees, social entrepreneurship is about applying what he perceives to be the best of business entrepreneurship to the pursuit of a social mission, or purpose. Thus, social entrepreneurship is a means to making nonprofit organizations less bureaucratic. Boschee's (1998, p. 2) definition of social entrepreneurs reinforces this idea:

Social entrepreneurs are not-for-profit executives who pay increasing attention to market forces *without* losing sight of their underlying missions, to somehow balance moral imperatives and the profit motives – and that balancing act is the heart and soul of the movement.

Mort, Weerawardena, and Carnegie (2003, p. 76) bring a more philosophical tone to the subject. They acknowledge the complexity of the field and the role that morality plays (a subject that will be addressed later in this chapter):

Social entrepreneurship is a multidimensional construct involving the expression of entrepreneurially virtuous behavior to achieve the social mission, a coherent unity of purpose and action in the face of moral complexity, the ability to recognize social value-creating opportunities and key decision-making characteristics of innovativeness, proactiveness and risk-taking.

Like Dees and Boschee, these scholars feature the use of entrepreneurial behaviors to achieve social mission; however, they do not expressly link this to a nonprofit organizational structure.

Alvord, Brown, and Letts (2004, p. 4) avoid the issue of organization structure as well and add the concepts of sustainability and transformation to their definition: "Social entrepreneurship creates innovative solutions to immediate social problems and mobilizes the ideas, capacities, resources, and social arrangements required for sustainable social transformations." This definition captures the entrepreneurial behaviors of innovation, the marshaling and mobilization of resources, and net-working ("social arrangements"), but it also highlights the idea that the ultimate product of these activities is long-term, deep social change. This is important because while earlier definitions attempted to link entrepreneurship to the solution of social problems, they did so in a way that implied short-term, transactional solutions. This is not surprising, given that business relationships are typically transactional—I give you $2 and you give me a loaf of bread. Growth in business is a result of amassing more transactions. Thus, when early social entrepreneurship thinkers were attempting to define the field, it was only natural for them to directly apply the basics of business entrepreneurship to social problem solving. Yet, the true solution of a social problem cannot be transactional; it cannot be superficial in that it treats only the symptoms. It must treat the root cause of the problem and seek to end the problem permanently (that is, it must be transformative and sustainable). As Bill Drayton has put it, "Social entrepreneurs are not content to give a fish or teach how to fish. They will not rest until they have revolutionized the fishing industry."

The preceding definitions of social entrepreneurship either make no stipulation about the nature of the organizational vehicle that social entrepreneurs use to pursue their social missions or clearly describe that vehicle as having a nonprofit structure. In this way, they represent two distinct approaches to thinking about social entrepreneurship: (1) as a set of practices that may or may not be associated with an organization; or (2) as the activities of nonprofit organizations that are seeking to enhance their effectiveness by behaving more like businesses, particularly entrepreneurial businesses.

Some scholars in this field see social entrepreneurship in another way: as for-profit entities that pursue a social mission. This has been called "social enterprise." Interestingly, Dees noted this phenomenon before he wrote his seminal paper on social entrepreneurship in 1998. In 1994 he observed that

> [s]ocial enterprises are private organizations dedicated to solving social problems, serving the disadvantaged and providing socially important goods that were not, in their judgment, adequately provided by public agencies or private markets. These organizations have pursued goals that could not be measured simply by profit generation, market penetration, or voter support.
>
> (Cited in Mair & Martí, 2006, p. 4)

Haugh and Tracey (2004) add to this perspective by noting that social enterprises

> trade for a social purpose. They combine innovation, entrepreneurship and social purpose and seek to be financially sustainable by generating revenue from trading. Their social mission prioritizes social benefits above financial profit, and if and when a surplus is made, this is used to further the social aims of the beneficiary group or community, and not distributed to those with a controlling interest in the enterprise.
>
> (Cited in Mair & Martí, 2006, p. 4)

This latter definition pushes the conception of social enterprise in the direction where it now stands.

Owing to increased interest in high-growth "gazelle" businesses in the commercial entrepreneurship arena and their ability to generate wealth quickly, a new focus has been placed on high-impact social ventures in the social entrepreneurship world because of their ability to rapidly scale up and maximize mission achievement. These "social entrepreneurship gazelles," however, could just as easily have nonprofit structures as for-profit structures. In this way, the term "social enterprise" has been broadened.

Still another use of "social enterprise" defines it as having to do with the earned income activities of nonprofit organizations (Lyons, Townsend, Sullivan, & Drago, 2010). While all of this can be confusing, it represents the evolution of the term toward encompassing the profit-making activities of organizations, regardless of their structure, that utilize their profits in the pursuit of a social mission.

A further evolution in the definition of social entrepreneurship has been taking place over the past few years. This is a movement toward viewing the field as pursuing its goals in multiple sectors, across sectors, or through hybrids combining sectors. Robinson (2006, p. 95) acknowledges that social entrepreneurship can take place via for-profit or nonprofit entities:

> I define social entrepreneurship as a *process* that includes: the identification of a specific social problem and a specific solution . . . to address it; the evaluation of the social impact, the business model and the sustainability of the venture; and the creation of a social mission-oriented *for-profit* or a business-oriented *nonprofit* entity that pursues the double (or triple) bottom line.

The triple bottom line referenced in this definition pertains to the pursuit of economic, social, and environmental outcomes by the for-profit or nonprofit organization.

Austin (2006, p. 22) introduces the idea that social entrepreneurship need not be confined to a single sector but can take place across multiple sectors: "Social entrepreneurship is innovative, social value creating activity that can occur within or across nonprofit, business, and public sectors." Wei-Skillern et al. (2007) echo this view in a very similar definition of the field.

However, as Hockerts (2006, p. 145) points out, there is a growing movement toward hybrid social enterprises. He gives these a name: "Social purpose business ventures are hybrid enterprises straddling the boundary between the for-profit business world and social mission-driven public and nonprofit organizations. Thus they do not fit completely in either sphere." These hybrid social enterprises are examined in more detail in Chapter 6.

These attempts at definition illustrate that social entrepreneurship is a rapidly growing and changing field. It is little wonder that there is no real agreement on a single definition, and this is not necessarily "bad." The definitions put forth to date are like the growth rings in a tree trunk: they mark the history of the field's development and help us to better understand how it has grown. This is precisely what theoretical consideration should do.

We have been given a snapshot of the latter-day social entrepreneur and her or his enterprise. Such a person is a social innovator who adds value to people's lives by pursuing a social mission, using the processes, tools, and techniques of business entrepreneurship. She or he puts societal benefit ahead of personal gain by using the "profits" generated by her or his enterprise to expand the reach of her or his mission. The social entrepreneur's vehicle for pursuing her or his mission could be for-profit, nonprofit, or public in its structure, or it could be a hybrid, or any or all of these. It should be emphasized that, as already stated, this is merely a snapshot, accurate only at this particular point in time. A future portrait of the social entrepreneur may look very different; however, this should not be a source of frustration or discomfort—quite the opposite: it reflects the excitement and dynamism of this field and is an ongoing challenge to those of us who would study it.

HOW ARE SOCIAL ENTREPRENEURSHIP AND BUSINESS ENTREPRENEURSHIP THE SAME AND DIFFERENT?

From time to time it is suggested to us by students in our social entrepreneurship courses (usually students with business backgrounds, or who are business majors) that there is really no difference between social entrepreneurship and business entrepreneurship—that a solution to a social problem is just another type of product that can be sold by a business entity. This is an interesting observation and, on its surface, seems to have merit. Yet, is it really that simple?

In reviewing the various definitions of "social entrepreneurship," "social entrepreneurs," and "social enterprise," a key similarity and a key difference between social entrepreneurship and business, or commercial, entrepreneurship become clear. Both types of entrepreneurship employ the behaviors, skills, processes, tools, and techniques of entrepreneurs: opportunity recognition (adding value by addressing needs), bootstrapping (being creative and efficient when assembling resources), risk tolerance through risk management, innovation, desire for control, network-building capability, and continuous learning (Dees, 1998; Perrini & Vurro, 2004). The chief difference appears to be the social entrepreneur's focus on social mission achievement as opposed to the commercial entrepreneur's focus on profits for the enterprise's owners. Put another way, the former serves stakeholders; the latter serves shareholders. A slight variation on this is the observation that social entrepreneurs use the pursuit of economic value as a tool for achieving social mission (Perrini & Vurro, 2004).

Dees makes this distinction clear in his 1998 definition of social entrepreneurship (see p. 16 of this chapter). Of his five bulleted activities of social entrepreneurs, three are drawn from the literature of commercial entrepreneurship: recognizing and pursuing opportunities; continuously innovating, learning, and adapting; and not being limited by current resources. The other two bullet points are specific to social entrepreneurship: creating and sustaining social value; and a higher level of accountability to multiple constituencies for the impacts achieved.

These are not the only distinctions drawn between social and business entrepreneurs in the literature, however. For example, Perrini and Vurro (2004) suggest that social entrepreneurs tend to have more democratic or participatory decision-making processes than do commercial entrepreneurs. Mair and Noboa (2003) argue that social entrepreneurs are particularly unsatisfied with the status quo, making them better positioned to recognize opportunities for social change. Prabhu

(1999) asserts that social entrepreneurs are more skilled than commercial entrepreneurs at building networks of support across diverse constituencies.

While these claims may bear some truth, they do not rest entirely on solid ground. There are commercial businesses that use participatory decision-making processes. This has become increasingly the case as the value of employee buy-in and more open strategic planning efforts have been recognized. Arguably, many business entrepreneurs build their enterprises around opportunities that stem from dissatisfaction with some aspect of the status quo. This might include the entrepreneur who starts his own business because he believes he can make the product better than his boss can, or the entrepreneur who identifies her business opportunity through frustration regarding an unmet need in her life that she shares with others. There is also merit in the contention that business entrepreneurs have become increasingly skilled at building networks along their supply chains because successful competition in the global economy demands it. Thus, a number of differences between social and business entrepreneurs appear to be differences of degree, not absolute differences.

This brings us back to a distinction based on social mission and accountability to stakeholders. Does this suggest, then, that social entrepreneurs are merely business entrepreneurs who happen to be selling social transformations? We think not. Social entrepreneurs are unique because they know how to operate at the nexus between the private, public, and nonprofit worlds from which their multiple stakeholders come. This is not easy to do. At the very least, it requires an understanding of the social sector that, in our experience, the average business person simply does not have, or does not care to have.

The business sector and the social sector use very different thought processes and equally different languages. The successful social entrepreneur must act as translator, ambassador, and facilitator between these two worlds. Social entrepreneurship is not about simply making the social sector more business-like, nor is it merely giving business a social conscience. These things may happen, but they are products of a more complex and sophisticated process. Social entrepreneurship is a blending of these two spheres in a way that adds social value in the most efficient, effective, equitable, and sustainable manner possible.

This suggests that social entrepreneurship involves both *agency* and *structure* (Granovetter, 1985). The individual entrepreneur can influence society in a positive way by using business strategies and tactics: *agency*. However, to believe that this can be done in a vacuum, while ignoring the social context, is elitist (CASE, 2008) and wrong. The successful social entrepreneur must do her or his work within the constraints of (and often empowered by) the cultural, political, legal, financial, and other infrastructures of the context: *structure* (Weerawardena & Sullivan Mort, 2006).

WHAT MOTIVATES SOCIAL ENTREPRENEURS?

Why do social entrepreneurs take on this challenge? What drives them to want to engage in the hard work of building an organization, marshaling resources, managing risk, building networks, and so forth? Does it have something to do with their background? Is it based in a reaction to something they have seen or heard about? Is it a product of their moral training?

Mair and Noboa (2006) maintain that what they call "background" and "content" are the major contributors to the motivation of social entrepreneurs. "Background" refers to how the individual entrepreneur was raised and socialized. This might include the influences of family, friends, religious leaders, and teachers. It may also reflect personal characteristics that heighten the individual's sensitivity to a particular social problem. Daryl Hammonds, founder of KaBOOM! (a nonprofit social enterprise that facilitates the building of children's playgrounds in underserved areas), had learning disabilities and was raised in a foster home (Wei-Skillern et al., 2007). Prospective social entrepreneurs may have had instilled into them strong beliefs about what is right and what is wrong. They likely have learned empathy for those who are less fortunate. They often have a strong sense of justice. This causes them to be altruistic, morally outraged by injustice, and sensitive to issues of equity (Anderson, 1998; Yujuico, 2008; Skoll Foundation, 2010).

Another aspect of background in social entrepreneurship is previous experience as an entrepreneur (Mair & Noboa, 2006). This gives the social entrepreneur the sense of self-efficacy that permits her or him the necessary comfort level to be able to proceed. Many successful social entrepreneurs were first successful business entrepreneurs. eBay founder Jeff Skoll, who created the Skoll Foundation, is often held up as an example. These individuals possess both self-confidence and the support of an established network of resource providers as they transition to launching and growing a social enterprise (Mair & Noboa, 2006).

"Content" provides the milieu in which the social entrepreneur's background interacts with the social sector. This is where they become exposed to social problems, for example seeing homeless people on the street, volunteering in a soup kitchen, watching a friend die of an incurable disease, or reading about war crimes. This causes them to exercise their altruism and focus their anger at social injustice. It also helps them in the process of recognizing an opportunity for adding social value and of developing a mission for delivering on that value proposition (Mair & Noboa, 2006).

Mair and Noboa (2006) take this a step further by creating a model that explains how a social entrepreneur moves from these motivating factors to perceptions that yield intentions which, ultimately, produce behaviors that result in the creation of a social venture (see Figure 2.1).

In this model, the social entrepreneur comes to believe that it is desirable, "right," and possible to create a social enterprise to address an identified social problem.

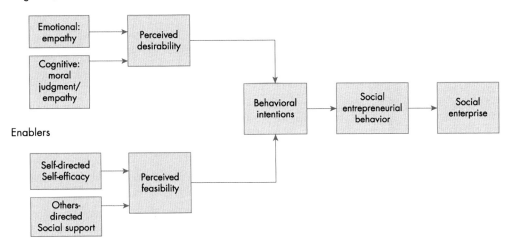

Cognitive/Emotional

Enablers

FIGURE 2.1 A Model of Social Entrepreneurial Intention Formation

Source: Mair, Robinson, & Hockerts (2006, p. 126).

This is driven by feelings of empathy for the disadvantaged members of society and the social entrepreneur's determination that their plight is morally "wrong." This is what drives social entrepreneurs' "perceived desirability" of creating the social enterprise. They are empowered by a belief that they can successfully accomplish what they seek to do and by the support of others who share their vision for a better situation. This gives them a sense of "perceived feasibility."

These perceptions underlie the social entrepreneur's intentions to move forward with the launch of a social enterprise. These intentions, in turn, allow her or him to engage in the necessary behavior for successful social entrepreneurship, which yields the actual creation of the enterprise.

Thus, social entrepreneurs are motivated by forces that are both internal and external to them. Internal motivation comes from personal values that foster empathy for the plight of others and from a self-confidence born of relevant experience. External motivation comes from an encounter with a social problem and from the support of others who share concern regarding that problem. Taken together, these forces give the social entrepreneur the impetus to act.

Case Study 2.1

Profile of a Social Entrepreneur: Peter Frampton, Manager, the Learning Enrichment Foundation

The Learning Enrichment Foundation's (LEF) mission is to provide community-responsive programs and services that enable individuals to become valued contributors to their community's social and economic development.

LEF, located in the most disadvantaged part of Toronto, serves thousands of people each year in programs ranging from community enterprises to childcare centers including employment counseling, career exploration, skills training, employer outreach, self-employment training, English for immigrants, and a business incubator. ACE, LEF's Action Centre for Employment, serves the recruitment needs of local employers and determines their training needs so that skill training at LEF remains targeted to opportunities. Thousands of people each year find employment through ACE.

LEF, whose mandate is community economic development, employs 235 people full time and 60 people part time, and has an annual budget of approximately $12 million.

What led you, Peter Frampton, to become a social entrepreneur?

The needs of our community, and most others, are far greater than can be met by government alone. For example, over 50 percent of the individuals we serve do not qualify for any of the "government" programs we operate. LEF, therefore, needs to weave together other opportunities that leverage that funding and enable us to serve everybody who comes to us for assistance. LEF has never had "core" funding. As a result, we have had to be innovative and develop other means of meeting the demands of our community.

For us, all of our programs are a response to local needs and make up what we call a "community economic development strategy." Within everything we do, there is an opportunity for skills training to take place. Each part of the organization works in an integrated fashion with the others, enabling us to propel literally many hundreds of people back to work each year.

How do you and your organization practice social entrepreneurship and social enterprise?

In a sense, you can look at all of our operation as a social enterprise. Over 60 percent of our budget is derived from fee-for-service operations. For example, our childcare centers operate on a fee-for-service basis. While most of the parents receive a subsidy, the subsidy travels with the parents and so we must earn their trust every day. In order to be able to offer a broad base of services in our childcare centers (from infant care to special support staff, parents, and children with special needs), we need to operate at a scale that enables us to sustain these essential services.

While training is available for those clients who qualify for government support (through Employment Insurance sometimes, and through Ontario Works), most individuals in our community do not qualify (new immigrants, reentry women, youth), and so we loan people the training and they agree to pay us back, based on a personal budget, what they can afford over an eighteen-month period once they start work.

Finally, at LEF we operate Community Enterprises: a woodworking shop for youth, a kitchen that makes about 1,500 meals a day, and a computer help desk that supports not only LEF but charities across Ontario and Manitoba as well. Each of these enterprises offers an important hands-on learning environment and a service that meets specific needs in our community. Each is an essential part of the integrated whole.

What successes have you and/or your organization enjoyed?

Our biggest success has been in being able to serve the whole community and not just those who qualify for narrowly defined government programs. This would not be possible if we did not take an entrepreneurial approach, effectively leveraging government support and constantly working toward a high degree of program integration. It is the leveraging and integration that, combined, enable us to have a local impact that far outweighs what any other program can achieve on its own.

What is the biggest challenge you have faced and how have you dealt with it?

Our biggest challenge has been, I believe, one of the keys to our success. Without ever having core funding, we have had to be entrepreneurial. While it remains a struggle to serve the whole community, especially within increasingly restrictive funding paradigms, understanding how to leverage and integrate activities has enabled us to continue to meet those needs.

The second biggest challenge is marketing. For marketing initiatives to be successful, they require a significant and ongoing investment. When one is surrounded by great need in a community, it is difficult to make that investment decision. (Do you increase the food in the food bank or market a social enterprise? The immediate needs win out every time— as they should.) The solution here is to build enterprises quietly over time.

What is the most important lesson you have learned about the work, and the field of social enterprise?

The key to success is to always ensure that one's "entrepreneurial activities" are aligned with one's mission and the needs of the community you serve. There are great ideas and opportunities that can be pursued, but do they enrich the local population and move them forward toward self-sufficiency? That is the key question. When looking at opportunities, we ask three questions:

1.   Does this opportunity meet local needs?
2.   Does this opportunity enhance and leverage our existing organizational capacity?
3.   Will we lose our shirt—or can we safely pull it off?

What does the field of social enterprise need most for its development in Canada?

Permission to fail and the ability to define success within a locally relevant context. For example, LEF's Wood Working Program loses money each year. By that definition, it is a failure. However, of 120 clients served each year (we receive our referrals from the courts and through schools), 72 percent return to school or find and keep employment. If this program were supported by the federal government, only 10 percent of the clients we serve would be allowed to participate. We see it as a huge success, and so do our private-sector funders and supporters.

Social enterprises exist to meet a local need that is not being met by either government or the private sector. They are, by definition, hard. Each failure makes the enterprise more bulletproof and enhances the working model. Organizations need an opportunity to fail quietly and an opportunity to share those failures with each other. They need an opportunity to test and retest market assumptions. Without flexible, multiyear support, the necessary learning cannot happen.

Peter Frampton joined LEF in 1993. As Manager of Development, Peter's role is to integrate enterprises, programs and initiatives that support the needs of the community and leverage the expertise of the organization. Peter is currently a member of the Board of Directors of the Canadian Community Economic Development Foundation (Chair of the Membership Committee), representative to the National Social Economy Round Table, Ontario Member & Chair of the Canadian CAP Association, and a member of IMIT Canada, a network of technology service providers dedicated to the voluntary sector.

Source: Used with the permission of the Canadian Social Entrepreneurs Network, www.csef.ca/organizations.php (accessed January 4, 2008)

THOUGHT QUESTIONS

1   What entrepreneurial behaviors are exhibited by Peter Frampton and LEF in this case?
2   What makes LEF a social enterprise?
3   Describe Frampton's motivation to be a social entrepreneur, in terms of his background and context.
4   How does LEF accomplish the social transformation called for by its mission?

MODELING THE SOCIAL ENTREPRENEURSHIP PROCESS

Social entrepreneurship can be looked at from the perspective of the individual entrepreneur, the enterprise, or the context within which the entrepreneur and her social enterprise operate. However, when all is said and done, social entrepreneurship is about a *process* that involves the interaction of all three of these elements (Mair & Martí, 2006; Wei-Skillern et al., 2007).

In its essence, a process is a flow of activity—what kinds of things take place and in what order. If the process is systematic, the right things are being done and in the right order. Mapping a process also clarifies the players in, or contributors to, the process and the nature of their relationships to each other.

In an effort to better articulate and understand the social entrepreneurship process, we introduce several process models for both business and social entrepreneurship. We examine each of these models for what they tell us and do not tell us. Along the way, we compare models. We then conclude this discussion with a process model that can guide our thinking about social entrepreneurship, and how it works, throughout the remainder of this text.

The Timmons Model of the Entrepreneurship Process

One of the simplest and most elegant models of the entrepreneurship process is the one developed by the late entrepreneurship educator Jeffrey Timmons. The Timmons model of the entrepreneurship process envisions the practice of entrepreneurship as a balancing act (see Figure 2.2). The lead entrepreneur, or founder, of an enterprise functions as the fulcrum of a seesaw. She or he must balance three weights that are variable in size. These weights represent the business opportunity that the enterprise is pursuing, the team that is assembled to do the work of the enterprise, and the resources required to pursue the opportunity.

The team of individuals with complementary skills assembled and the financial and physical resources marshaled must match the size of the opportunity that the enterprise is seeking to fulfill. If the opportunity is too big for the team and

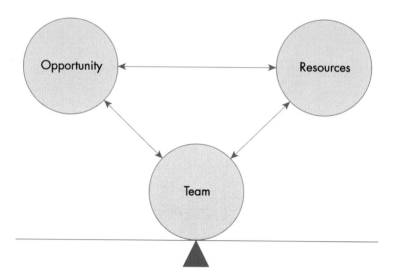

FIGURE 2.2 A Model of the Entrepreneurship Process
Source: Adapted from Timmons & Spinelli (2007, p. 89).

resources available, the seesaw collapses to the left, and the enterprise fails. If the team is too highly skilled and/or the resources are in excess of what is needed to pursue the given opportunity, the seesaw collapses to the right, killing the enterprise through inefficiency. The only way that the enterprise remains healthy and survives is if the entrepreneur successfully keeps these elements—opportunity, team, and resources—in balance. This is an ongoing process. As the opportunity grows over time, so must the team and resources grow commensurately. If, for whatever reason(s), the opportunity shrinks, the entrepreneur must "shrink" the team and resources in equal measure.

While this model provides a readily understandable picture of the role of the entrepreneur and the bare essence of the enterprise and its parts, it focuses solely on the entrepreneur and the enterprise, and leaves out the context in which this entrepreneurial activity takes place. In this way, it is helpful to our understanding of how the entrepreneurship part of social entrepreneurship works but not the social part.

The PCDO (People, Context, Deal, and Opportunity) Framework

Another model that was developed in order to explain the commercial entrepreneurship process is the PCDO framework (see Figure 2.3). It was created by four Harvard Business School professors: Stevenson, Roberts, Bhide, and Sahlman. PCDO is an abbreviation for People, Context, Deal, and Opportunity. "People"

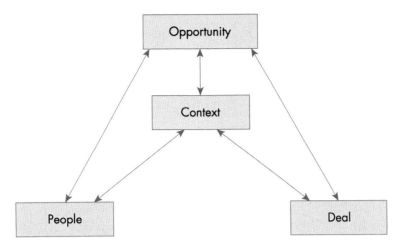

FIGURE 2.3 The PCDO (People, Context, Deal, Opportunity) Framework
Source: Sahlman, Stevenson, Roberts, & Bhide (1999).

represents the human capital necessary to successfully operate an enterprise. Similar to Timmons's "team," it acknowledges the complete, collective skill set necessary for successful entrepreneurship provided by the management team, employees, vendors, and external partners. In this model, the term "people" is also intended to include financial investors in the enterprise. This might include the entrepreneur her- or himself, family, friends, micro-lenders, bankers, mezzanine capitalists, angel investors, and venture capitalists. Thus, the PCDO model combines elements of the "team" and "resources" from the Timmons model under the "People" heading.

The term "Deal" denotes the transactions involved in determining how and to whom benefits of the entrepreneurial activity are dispersed. As Wei-Skillern et al. (2007, p. 11) put it, " 'Deal' is the substance of the bargain that defines who in a venture gives what, who gets what, and when those deliveries and receipts will take place." This incorporates into the model that which is the lifeblood of business: transactions among multiple parties. There is no counterpart for this element of the entrepreneurship process in the Timmons model; it is implied, and only for those transactions that take place inside the enterprise, as this model tends to leave the enterprise to operate in a vacuum.

"Context" signifies the elements of the environment or ecosystem in which entrepreneurship takes place and which are beyond the direct control of the entrepreneur. These might include political, legal, cultural, and economic elements. This is another way in which the PCDO framework is distinguished from the Timmons model.

As in the Timmons model, "Opportunity" plays an important role in the PCDO framework. This is the opportunity to add value to customers' lives by meeting a need they have. This is the essence of an enterprise.

The way in which these elements are structured in the PCDO framework is instructive of its designers' intent. Opportunity is at the top of the frame, symbolizing its vital importance and primacy in the entrepreneurship process. Context is used as a two-way filter. In one direction, the opportunity is sifted through the context, which may modify the former as it reaches the people and transactions that will put it in play. In the other direction, context filters the activities of the players and their interactions as they attempt to capture the opportunity. Thus, the entrepreneurship process is impacted by the context in which it takes place but is not constrained by it.

As has been noted already, these models were conceived to explain the commercial entrepreneurship process. How effective are they as conceptual frameworks for social entrepreneurship? Certainly, social entrepreneurs pursue opportunities. As was observed earlier in this chapter, these are opportunities to provide social value. Social entrepreneurs need human, financial, and physical capital in order to build and sustain their enterprises, just as do commercial entrepreneurs. Social entrepreneurs engage in deal making as they capture opportunities by building and growing their enterprises. However, this "deal making" is substantially more complex because the system of transactions must be systemic, and therefore synergistic, if the ultimate goal of social transformation is to be achieved. Simple business transactions will not accomplish the deep change desired. Furthermore, the context is of special importance to social entrepreneurs. It puts the "social" in social entrepreneurship by not only providing a source of opportunities to add social value but putting parameters of accountability on activities as well. Bryson (1995) calls these "formal and informal mandates." Formal mandates are those things that *must* be done, as required by law, societal mores, and so forth. Informal mandates stem from the expectations of stakeholders (not shareholders). They are what *should* be done. Therefore, context cannot be ignored, as in the Timmons model, nor can it be relegated to the role of a filter—something to be endured and adapted to—as in the PCDO framework. Context must be embraced as an essential part of the very fiber of social entrepreneurship, as something that encompasses all social entrepreneurship activity, impacting it and being impacted by it.

All of this suggests that social entrepreneurship is in need of its own process model, one that captures and emphasizes those aspects of its practice that are unique. There are two such models that warrant our attention: (1) a model developed by Güclü, Dees, and Anderson of the Center for the Advancement of Social Entrepreneurship (CASE); and (2) the Social Entrepreneurship Framework, created by Wei-Skillern, Austin, Leonard, and Stevenson of Harvard University. We will refer to these as the CASE Model and the Social Entrepreneurship Framework, respectively.

The CASE Model

The CASE Model focuses on the process of creating a social opportunity (see Figure 2.4). It is a two-stage model involving the generation of a promising idea in the first stage and the development of that idea into a viable opportunity in the second stage. The model holds that ideas are generated from unmet social needs and from the leveraging of existing social assets that, in turn, are influenced by the personal experiences of the social entrepreneur and by changes taking place in the context. In their current state, however, these ideas are not actionable. They must be developed into opportunities that are attractive to a variety of stakeholders (e.g., target beneficiaries, investors, and political supporters).

The opportunity will not be attractive unless a case can be made for its viability both as a feasible business model and as a strategy for effectuating a social transformation (i.e., achieving real social impact). The social impact theory must include a compelling working hypothesis regarding the social outputs, outcomes, and impacts that are achievable when the opportunity is actively pursued. As an example, suppose a social entrepreneur generates an idea for helping obese children to lose weight by teaching them how to cook with healthy, low-fat ingredients. She must then develop this into an opportunity by building a case for how many children she can serve (an output), what kind of weight loss they can anticipate (an outcome), and how this will change their self-image and lifestyle into adulthood (impact). The business model will need to describe how the enterprise will be operated in pursuit of the opportunity. That is, it must show the activities necessary and their proper order and flow—a systematic model. This

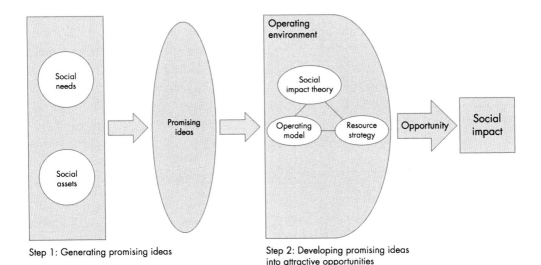

Step 1: Generating promising ideas   Step 2: Developing promising ideas into attractive opportunities

FIGURE 2.4   The CASE Model

Source: Adapted from Güclü, Dees, & Anderson (2002, p. 2).

operating model must be complemented by a strategy for marshaling and allocating resources that make operations possible.

Both of the principal elements—the social impact theory and the business model—operate within a context (operating environment) that will affect the successful implementation of the social venture idea. This context includes market, industry structure, cultural, and political factors (Güclü, Dees, & Anderson, 2002). Also in the mix are the entrepreneur's motivation, skill level, and personal networks necessary for success, or what the CASE Model calls "personal fit." If the social impact theory and business model are compelling, the operating environment is favorable, and the personal fit is good, then the social entrepreneur has a viable social opportunity that can generate true social impact.

The CASE Model takes us from idea to opportunity to social impact. Along the way, it introduces the elements of social needs, social assets, impact logic, operations, resources, and individual entrepreneur capability as well as context. It captures much of what we have learned from the commercial entrepreneurship models and adds a social aspect. It uses context as a frame within which the process for developing opportunities takes place.

The Social Entrepreneurship Framework

The Social Entrepreneurship Framework, which is a modification of the PCDO framework introduced earlier in this section, presents another way of thinking about how social entrepreneurship comes about (see Figure 2.5). It identifies three major elements: opportunity, people, and capital. "Opportunity" and "People" represent essentially the same variables as they do in the PCDO framework, with the exception that financing providers are no longer included in the "People" category. Instead, "Capital" includes all sources of capital, including financial capital. These three major elements are brought together in a Venn diagram ("Opportunity" is placed intentionally at the top), with the area of overlap labeled "Social Value Proposition" (SVP). The SVP is the reason(s) why target beneficiaries (customers) of a social venture should choose that venture's services over those of competitors. This model's developers are placing the SVP at the heart of the social entrepreneurship process because not only does it represent the product of the coming together of opportunity, people, and capital, but it also lies at the core of the social venture's purpose—its mission.

The Venn diagram is an interesting graphic choice because it captures the synergy embedded in the social entrepreneurship process, which makes social transformation—the manifestation, or delivery, of the SVP—possible. Another interesting feature of this model is the way in which it represents context. The latter is a porous (as indicated by the dotted lines) envelope within which all social entrepreneurship activity takes place. Its non-impervious nature allows it both to

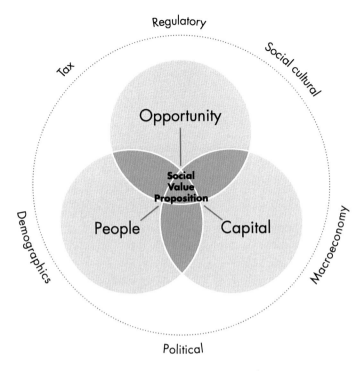

FIGURE 2.5 Social Entrepreneurship Framework

Source: Wei-Skillern et al. (2007, p. 23). © 2007.

affect the process and to be affected by it. This is a significant departure from the PCDO model, which suggests that context is merely a filter for this activity.

In many respects the Social Entrepreneurship Framework captures the same process as is found in the opportunity development portion of the CASE Model. The latter is more explicit, but, essentially, both models are attempting to portray the process by which an enterprise is formed and sustained to pursue a viable opportunity to generate social impact. The key difference between these models is that the CASE Model takes into account the process by which the idea that underlies the opportunity is created, while the Social Entrepreneurship Framework assumes this.

Each of these models offers important insights about the social entrepreneurship process. The Social Entrepreneurship Framework captures the synergy of opportunity, people, and capital necessary to fulfill the SVP. It also effectively highlights the importance of context as both an influencer of the process and that which is impacted by it. The CASE Model reminds us that social opportunities have their origins in ideas that reflect both a social need and the capacity of society to meet that need. In addition, it emphasizes the importance of having a theory of change leading to social impact.

Yet neither of these models is complete. As noted, the Social Entrepreneurship Framework leaves out the crucial idea-generation process. The CASE Model provides only superficial treatment of the context, relegating it to the role of an "operating environment" in which opportunity development takes place. While the Social Entrepreneurship Framework errs on the side of simplicity, the CASE Model is a bit too complex, relying heavily on an accompanying narrative to clarify its sometimes opaque elements.

The Social Entrepreneurship Process Model

With the understanding that models are merely attempts to make that which is complex more manageable, we attempt to create a hybrid process model of social entrepreneurship that reflects both the need for simplicity and the desire for completeness. Our model seeks to capture the best of both the CASE Model and the Social Entrepreneurship Framework (see Figure 2.6) in a streamlined manner.

In our model, the social entrepreneurship process takes place in two stages, similar to the CASE Model. Stage 1 is Idea Creation, where an idea is generated by the coming together of the entrepreneur's individual motivation, the social need to be addressed, and the current capacity of the community or society to fulfill that need (i.e., current assets available for use in addressing the need). As was discussed earlier in this chapter, the entrepreneur's motivation is influenced by her or his background and context. If properly motivated, the entrepreneur will be able to conduct a cursory assessment of both the need she or he seeks to fulfill and the resources available to meet that need.

This yields an idea for changing the world in a positive way. However, it is as yet an untested idea. The social entrepreneur does not know whether a viable social

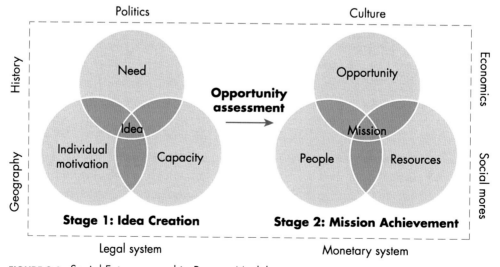

FIGURE 2.6 Social Entrepreneurship Process Model

venture can be built around it. Therefore, the idea must be thoroughly vetted to determine its feasibility. Will it garner the needed societal acceptance as a legitimate social issue? Can it attract adequate human, social, financial, and physical capital to address the need over time? Is there a market for this proposed social innovation? Does it have the potential to achieve scale? If the answers to these questions are "yes," then the idea is indeed a social opportunity, and a social venture can be created to pursue a mission that stems from this opportunity.

Stage 2 is the Mission Achievement phase, which brings together this newly confirmed opportunity and the human and other resources to pursue it. At the core of this convergence is the mission, or purpose, of the social venture. This stage is so named because the focus is on the social venture's performance in attaining its mission—in achieving positive impact.

Both stages represent synergistic interactions of elements that result in the two key components of any social entrepreneurship endeavor: the idea for meeting a societal need and an opportunity-driven, mission-based vehicle for fulfilling the identified need. These two synergistic stages make transformational impact possible.

All of this activity takes place within a context that brings its own politics, culture, economic environment, social norms, geography, history, and legal and monetary systems to bear. As with the Social Entrepreneurship Framework, this context is permeable, permitting interaction between it and the social entrepreneurship effort.

This model, which we have labeled the Social Entrepreneurship Process Model, will be used to guide our thinking throughout the remainder of this book.

VOICES FROM THE FIELD

Tim McCollum, the co-founder of Madecasse, does not think of himself as a social entrepreneur, nor does he use the term "social entrepreneurship" when he talks about his company. However, he is aware that other people do. Because of this, he has a ready response when asked what "social entrepreneurship" means to him. He defines the term as "the idea of using business, markets and capitalism to create a for-profit enterprise to solve a social need." He contrasts this to corporate social responsibility (CSR) by noting that CSR involves a business model for a profitable business that allows the owner to donate a portion of her or his profits to charity, while in social entrepreneurship the social good is embedded in the operations of the company.

One can easily understand McCollum's perspective when Madecasse's story is unfolded. Madecasse is a company that makes chocolate in the African country of Madagascar. Madagascar is an island off the coast of East Africa. With 587,041 square kilometers of land area, it is the fourth largest island in the world. Fifty percent of its population lives below the poverty line. It has a predominantly agricultural economy, with vanilla, cocoa, coffee, cloves, sugarcane, and rice among its major export crops (CIA, 2010).

Since its launch in 2006, Madecasse has worked with cocoa farmers in northern Madagascar to grow, ferment, and dry their cocoa beans in a manner that greatly enhances their flavor and, thereby, their value for making chocolate. This value-added process has doubled the income of the farmers with whom Madecasse works. Madecasse provides equipment and technical training to the farmers. It also buys the cured beans they produce and uses them to make chocolate through a partnership with an in-country chocolate factory. Tim McCollum points out that the process of fermenting and drying the cocoa beans takes about two weeks. Cocoa farmers in Madagascar are accustomed to selling their beans immediately, as a commodity for export, because of their subsistence-based economic lives. Madecasse offers them incentive to undertake the value-added process by paying them in advance at double the amount they would receive from cocoa importers.

The chocolate produced by Madecasse is a rival to the finest chocolates made in Europe. Three team members located in the United States are responsible for the marketing, promotion, and distribution of the Madagascar-made chocolate in the United States and Europe.

When asked about the original idea behind the creation of Madecasse, McCollum admits that he and co-founder Brett Beach never had an "aha moment." Instead, the emergence of the social venture was evolutionary in nature. The two social entrepreneurs served together in Madagascar while in the Peace Corps. They came to love the island nation and its people, and resolved to continue helping Madagascar even after their Peace Corps stint ended. Brett started by importing vanilla beans from Madagascar and, in so doing, became increasingly familiar with the world's high-end chocolate industry. Africa produces 85 percent of the world's cocoa, and Madagascar is widely recognized as having the best cocoa in the world. However, less than 1 percent of the world's chocolate is produced in Africa. McCollum and Beach came to realize that an opportunity existed to begin moving Africa in general, and Madagascar in particular, into the high-end chocolate market and away from selling cocoa as a commodity. In doing so, they could generate social change, as the value of chocolate is five times that of cocoa beans. They could achieve a double bottom line, allowing the market to drive social change.

McCollum freely admits that had they had any idea how difficult this effort would turn out to be, they might not have undertaken it. He cites as an example the challenge presented by the fact that Madagascar has a very warm climate, chocolate melts, and they are working in a very isolated part of the country with no electricity. Yet, their motivation to help Madagascar drove them forward past such obstacles. His advice to would-be social entrepreneurs: "Don't let the feasibility assessment discourage you. You can overcome any obstacle if you believe strongly enough in what you are doing."

Madecasse's approach to assembling the financial and physical resources they needed reflects this philosophy. In the beginning, they did not really know what they would need. If they had known, the resource-marshaling task would have been daunting. Instead, they bootstrapped, using money from their own savings, McCollum's paychecks from American Express, and the prize money they won in a business plan competition at New York University. Later, as they demonstrated what could be done, they attracted money from family and friends. As an indication of how far they have come over their first several years, they were recently able to raise a substantial amount of money from an equity investor.

Another manifestation of the bootstrapping strategy is the pro bono help they have received with trademarking and other intellectual property (IP) considerations from a law firm. They also received pro bono help with their website and with branding from a marketing firm. Together, this assistance represents at least $80,000 that they did not have to spend from their own resources.

Tim McCollum feels that the connection to Madagascar is what brings unity to the Madecasse team. Besides his and Brett Beach's connection, the third U.S.-based member of the team was also a Peace Corps volunteer there (at a later time). McCollum notes that the fact that the Peace Corps tour of duty is only two years in length and that some people want to stay connected to the country after this time creates a pool of ability upon which Madecasse can draw for future talent.

The Madagascar context has played and continues to play an important role in Madecasse's growth and development. As Tim McCollum observes, the context has presented its challenges, but these have not dissuaded the Madecasse team. A 2009 coup highlighted the political instability in the country; however, the team's experience and in-country connections helped them to weather that storm. When Madagascar lost its status under the African Growth and Opportunities Act, all aid to the country stopped and many of the local NGOs failed. Madecasse stepped in and took over some of the work of these organizations, which affected the enterprise's financial resources. Despite all of this instability, Madecasse was still able to attract the equity financing noted earlier in this discussion. As McCollum puts it, "You can do anything if you have a good opportunity and the right people behind it."

Through its perseverance and good work, Madecasse has had a very positive impact on Madagascar. In addition to making the country a viable chocolate exporter and doubling the income of twenty farm families in the bargain, the social venture has helped the farmers' cooperative to establish a bank account and has taught them how to balance it. McCollum likes to tell a story that epitomizes the improvement in local quality of life that Madecasse's efforts have brought. The village of about 800 households where the cocoa farmers live is located 50 kilometers from the nearest source of electricity. Despite this, the village leader has established "movie night" in that community. Using an electrical generator that he purchased with profits from the sale of value-added cocoa, he shows a movie on DVD once a week to the villagers at no cost to them. While this may seem like a small thing, it is a wonderful example of how tapping private markets can generate surplus in what is otherwise a subsistence economy, allowing for savings that can, in turn, be invested in the community's quality of life.

QUESTIONS FOR "CONNECTING THE DOTS"

1   Theory is the foundation upon which the house of practice is built. How would you interpret this statement and relate it to social entrepreneurship?
2   Which model of the social entrepreneurship process presented in this chapter resonates for you? Why?
3   Which do you think is more important to a social entrepreneur's intention: perceived desirability or perceived feasibility? Explain your answer.
4   Is a venture that offers dry-cleaning services using environmentally friendly processes and cleaning products a social venture? Why, or why not?

REFERENCES

Alvord, S. H., Brown, L.D., & Letts, C. W. (2004). Social entrepreneurship and societal transformation. *Journal of Applied Behavioral Science, 40*(3), 260–282.

Anderson, A. R. (1998). Cultivating the Garden of Eden: Environmental entrepreneuring. *Journal of Organizational Change Management, 11*(2), 135.

Austin, J. (2006). Three avenues for social entrepreneurship research. In J. Mair, J. Robinson, & K. Hockerts (Eds.). *Social entrepreneurship* (pp. 22–33). New York: Palgrave Macmillan.

Bornstein, D. (2007). *How to change the world: Social entrepreneurs and the power of new ideas.* New York: Oxford University Press.

Boschee, J. (1998). Merging mission and money: A board member's guide to social entrepreneurship. Retrieved from http://www.socialent.org/pdfs/MergingMission.pdf (accessed June 24, 2010).

Brock, D. D., Steinder, S. D., & Kim, M. (2008). Social entrepreneurship education: Is it achieving the desired aims? *United States Association of Small Business & Entrepreneurship (USASBE) 2008 Conference Proceedings.*

Center for the Advancement of Social Entrepreneurship (CASE) (2008). Developing the field of social entrepreneurship. Durham, NC: Fuqua School of Business, Duke University. Retrieved from http://www.caseatduke.org/documents/CASE_Field-Building_Report_June08.pdf.

Central Intelligence Agency (CIA). *The world factbook.* Retrieved from www,cia.gov/library/publications/the-world-factbook/geos/ma.html (accessed July 16, 2010).

Dees, J. G. (1994). Social enterprise: Private initiatives for the common good. Working Paper Series No. 9-395-116. Cambridge, MA: Harvard Business School.

Dees, J. G. (1998). The meaning of "social entrepreneurship." Palo Alto, CA: Graduate School of Business, Stanford University. Retrieved from http://www.caseatduke.org/documents/dees_sedef. pdf.

Granovetter, M. (1985). Economic action and social structure: The problem of embeddedness. *American Journal of Sociology*, *91*(3), 481–510.

Güclü, A., Dees, J. G., & Anderson, B. B. (2002). The process of social entrepreneurship: Creating opportunities worthy of serious pursuit. Durham, NC: Center for the Advancement of Social Entrepreneurship, Duke University.

Hamlin, R. E., & Lyons, T. S. (1996). *Economy without walls*. Westport, CT: Praeger.

Haugh, H., & Tracey, P. (2004). The role of social enterprise in regional development. Paper presented at the Social Enterprise and Regional Development Conference, Cambridge-MIT Institute, University of Cambridge.

Hockerts, K. (2006). Entrepreneurial opportunity in social purpose business ventures. In J. Mair, J. Robinson, & K. Hockerts (Eds.). *Social entrepreneurship* (pp. 142–154). New York: Palgrave Macmillan.

Klein, B. (1977). *Dynamic Economics*. Cambridge, MA: Harvard University Press.

Lichtenstein, G. A., & Lyons, T. S. (2010). *Investing in entrepreneurs: A strategic approach for strengthening your regional and community economy*. Santa Barbara, CA: Praeger/ABC-CLIO.

Lyons, T. S., Townsend, J., Sullivan, A.M., & Drago, T. (2010). *Social enterprise's expanding position in the nonprofit landscape*. New York: National Executive Service Corps.

Mair, J., & Martí, I. (2006). Social entrepreneurship research: A source of explanation, prediction, and delight. *Journal of World Business*, *41*, 36–44.

Mair, J., & Noboa, E. (2003). Social entrepreneurship: How intentions to create a social enterprise get formed. Working Paper No. 521. Barcelona: IESE Business School, University of Navarra, September.

Mair, J., & Noboa, E. (2006). Social entrepreneurship: How intentions to create a social venture are formed. In J. Mair, J. Robinson, & K. Hockerts (Eds.). *Social entrepreneurship* (pp. 121–136). New York: Palgrave Macmillan.

Mair, J., Robinson, J., & Hockerts, K. (2006). *Social entrepreneurship*. New York: Palgrave Macmillan.

Mort, G. S., Weerawardena, J., & Carnegie, K. (2003). Social entrepreneurship: Towards conceptualization. *International Journal of Nonprofit and Voluntary Sector Marketing*, *8*(1), 76–88.

Perrini, F., & Vurro, C. (2004). Social entrepreneurship: Innovation and social change across theory and practice. In J. Mair, J. Robinson, & K. Hockerts (Eds.). *Social entrepreneurship* (pp. 57–86). New York: Palgrave Macmillan.

Prabhu, G. N. (1999). Social entrepreneurial leadership. *Career Development International*, *4*(3), 140–145.

Robinson, J. (2006). Navigating social and institutional barriers to markets: How social entrepreneurs identify and evaluate opportunities. In J. Mair, J. Robinson, & K. Hockerts (Eds.). *Social entrepreneurship* (pp. 95–120). New York: Palgrave Macmillan.

Sahlman, W. A., Stevenson, H. H., Roberts, M. J., & Bhide, A. V. (Eds.). (1999). *The entrepreneurial venture*. Boston, MA: Harvard Business School Press.

Sarasvathy, S. D. (2009). *Effectuation: Elements of entrepreneurial experience*. Cheltenham, UK: Edward Elgar.

Shane, S. (2008). *The illusions of entrepreneurship*. New Haven, CT: Yale University Press.

Skoll Foundation (2010). What is a social entrepreneur? Retrieved from http://www.skollfoundation. org/aboutsocialentrepreneurship/whatis.asp (accessed June 29, 2010).

Stevenson, H. H., Roberts, M. J., Bhidé, A., & Sahlman, W. A. (1999). Some thoughts on business plans. In W. A. Sahlman, H. H. Stevenson, M. J. Roberts, & A. Bhidé (Eds.). *The entrepreneurial venture* (pp. 138–176). Boston, MA: Harvard Business School Press.

Terry, J. V. (1995). *Dictionary for business finance* (3rd edn). Fayetteville, AR: University of Arkansas Press.

Timmons, J., & Spinelli, S. (2007). *New venture creation: Entrepreneurship for the 21st century.* New York: McGraw-Hill/Irwin.

Weerawardena, J., & Sullivan Mort, G. (2006). Investigating social entrepreneurship: A multi-dimemensional model. *Journal of World Business, 41*, 21–35.

Wei-Skillern, J., Austin, J. E., Leonard, H., & Stevenson, H. (2007). *Entrepreneurship in the social sector.* Thousand Oaks, CA: Sage.

Yujuico, E. (2008). Connecting the dots in social entrepreneurship through the capabilities approach. *Socio-Economic Review, 6*(3), 493–513.

Recognizing Social Opportunities

AIM/PURPOSE

Generating ideas for a social venture and assessing those ideas for their potential to be true opportunities is the focus of this chapter. As part of this discussion, the chapter explores the role of innovation in social entrepreneurship and presents several tools for assessing social opportunities.

LEARNING OBJECTIVES FOR THIS CHAPTER

1. To recognize the sources of ideas for social entrepreneurship.
2. To be able to assess an idea for its viability as a true opportunity to add social value.
3. To understand the forms innovation takes and the role it plays in opportunity recognition and implementation.
4. To recognize forms of resistance to social innovation and to devise strategies for overcoming them.
5. To grasp the nature and importance of a social value proposition (SVP).
6. To understand the function of mission in social entrepreneurship and how to write an effective mission statement.

In Chapter 2 the process of generating ideas for pursuit as a social entrepreneur is touched upon and placed in the larger context of a complete social entrepreneurship process. It is also emphasized that if a social entrepreneur is to be successful, he or she must assess their initial idea's potential as a viable opportunity to address a social or environmental need—a process that is known in the entrepreneurship field as opportunity recognition. This is to say that good ideas are not necessarily true opportunities to add social value. Each idea must be intentionally examined to ascertain the likelihood that it can produce positive social change, that there is a market for it, and that a social venture built to pursue the idea is sustainable over time (Dees, Emerson, & Economy, 2001). Even if this is not done formally, successful social entrepreneurs informally evaluate their opportunities—they think them through—as was the case with Allison Lynch of the New York Women's Social Entrepreneurship Incubator featured in the "Voices from the Field" section at the end of this chapter.

In this chapter we discuss social ideas and where they come from. We explore the process of assessing an idea to determine whether or not it represents a genuine opportunity. Along the way, we introduce the concept of innovation and the role it plays in opportunity recognition and implementation. We also discuss typical forms of resistance to innovation and how those might be addressed and overcome. We conclude with a discussion of the social value proposition (SVP) and the mission of the social venture that pursues the identified opportunity.

SOCIAL IDEAS

Every social venture begins with an idea for improving society in some way. *Webster's New Collegiate Dictionary* defines an idea as "an indefinite or unformed conception." It is important to understand that ideas are merely "grist for the mill" of entrepreneurship. They represent a starting place but they lack the finish to build an enterprise around. Timmons and Spinelli (2007, pp. 116–122) assert that ideas are "inert" and have no real value, in and of themselves. This may be a bit of an overstatement, but it is certainly true that ideas represent unrealized potential value in their original state. They are the "commodities" of the entrepreneurship process. Just as is the case with commodities, ideas have a value as the raw materials from which opportunities are made and ventures are launched. In this way, they are important and worthy of our deeper consideration.

Entrepreneurs are often credited for their creativity and ability to generate new ideas for meeting customer needs. One of the authors of this text knew an entrepreneur operating in a city in the southern United States who came up with 100 new business ideas every month. There is the often-told story of Anita Roddick, founder of The Body Shop, who generated new ideas every time she walked down the street, observing her surroundings. But where and how do ideas for meeting needs actually originate for most entrepreneurs?

The following are general sources of ideas. Most of these apply to both business and social entrepreneurs (Fiet, 2002; Longenecker, Moore, Petty, & Palich, 2006; Timmons & Spinelli, 2007):

- personal experiences—these may include experiences at work or at home;
- hobbies or avocations—activities people enjoy engaging with during their free time;

- serendipity or accidental discovery—something that is identified in the course of seeking something else;
- systematic or intentional search—a deliberate effort to find an idea through research;
- awareness generated by media, personal and professional networks, etc., with the prospective entrepreneur learning about an issue or a problem through a newspaper account, a television report, or a session at a conference.

Personal experiences are a common source of entrepreneurial ideas. The would-be entrepreneur encounters a problem or need in her or his life that she or he believes is common to many people and in need of addressing. An example from social entrepreneurship might be a mother whose child suffers from a learning disability and is not getting the help he needs from the local public school, so the mother founds an organization that provides specialized assistance to children who share this particular disability. The case of Madecasse, presented in the "Voices from the Field" section of Chapter 2, is another good example of a social idea generated from personal experience. In that case the founding entre-preneurs got their idea for making chocolate in Madagascar through their Peace Corps experience in that country and their professional knowledge of the chocolate industry.

Sometimes, social entrepreneurs draw their ideas from their own hobbies. One of our former students was an avid rock climber. She loved the sport for the healthy way it made her feel and for the opportunity it gave her to interact with nature. It struck her that many inner-city youth never got the chance to enjoy an experience like this and that it could benefit them. She proposed to build an enterprise that would provide equipment, training, and transportation to disadvantaged youth who wanted to experience rock climbing.

There are numerous stories in the business world about entrepreneurs whose ideas came to them purely by a lucky accident. The inventors of a blood coagulant called Quick Relief originally set out to develop a method for purifying water. By accident, they created a product that is now widely used to stop bleeding caused by sports injuries. Its customers include several professional sports franchises (Longenecker et al., 2006, p. 530). In the social entrepreneurship arena, Kate Davenport, who is currently the Green Business-Green Jobs Program Director for Eco-Ventures International (a group that assists green enterprises), went to an event several years ago with the express purpose of hearing Nelson Mandela speak. When she got to the venue, however, she became absorbed in some informational literature she just happened to see on environmental sustainability, which inspired her so much that she went on to found a recycling business in Washington, DC.

Some entrepreneurs generate their ideas very intentionally; they search for them. Some look through lists of unused patents. Others immerse themselves in what are sometimes called "idea baths." These are gatherings of experts in a particular field or industry who discuss trends and, in so doing, tease out ideas that might be pursued by value-adding enterprises (Lichtenstein & Lyons, 1996).

Prospective entrepreneurs can emulate the results of an idea bath by engaging in their own trends analysis. They can look for what Timmons and Spinelli (2007) have called "sea changes." This is a nautical reference going back to the days when sailors did not have elaborate navigational systems at their disposal. Instead, they had to rely on the diligent monitoring of changes in wind patterns and velocity, the color of the sky, wave action, and so forth. These "sea changes" were the precursors of the challenges they would face to charting their course, maintaining it, and keeping their ship upright in a storm. This is a useful metaphor for thinking about trend or pattern analysis.

If entrepreneurs carefully monitor changes in their environment, they will see patterns that will help them to predict arising challenges or needs to be addressed. When the "window of opportunity" for acting on an identified need opens, they will be positioned to take maximum advantage of the timing. But what do entrepreneurs look for?

Strategic planners talk about four major areas of society to monitor when looking for sea changes, which they have given the acronym PEST (Bryson, 1995). The "P" stands for the political arena—changes in regime, ideology, leadership, and so forth. "E" is economic and involves changes in structure, monetary policy, trade policy, etc. The "S" stands for social, which may include demographic and cultural shifts. The "T" is technology, which accounts for a host of changes stemming from the development and implementation of new technologies. Within these major areas the entrepreneur is looking for shifts in perception, process, structure, or new knowledge (Longenecker et al., 2006). Embedded within any of these changes may be an idea for a new product, service, process, and so forth.

Social entrepreneurs, in particular, may find the media to be a source of ideas. Hearing about or seeing a social problem elsewhere in the world can trigger thinking about what might be done to solve that problem. Professional and social networks may also be sources of ideas, as word of social needs is widely spread. In short, vehicles of mass communication have shrunk the world and helped to make a problem in one corner of the world everyone's problem. An individual in the United States who hears about human rights abuses somewhere in Africa may become a social entrepreneur who builds a venture to bring a solution to that problem to its source.

Longenecker et al. (2006) offer another perspective on the generation of entrepreneurial ideas. They classify ideas as falling into three categories. Type A ideas are those that involve identifying a new market for an existing product or service. Type B ideas are those that represent the creation of an entirely new product or service, often through a technological breakthrough. Ideas that involve creating new processes for producing and/or delivering existing products or services are called Type C ideas. This conceptual framework for thinking about the creation of enterprise ideas is rooted in the field of innovation, which we take up next.

THE ROLE OF INNOVATION

A discussion of the ideas that underlie entrepreneurial ventures, and social enterprises in particular, would not be complete without a discussion of innovation. In order to fully understand innovation, an important distinction must be made between the terms "creativity" and "innovation." These terms are often used as synonyms, but they are not. Creativity is the development of original ideas, or inventions. Innovation is the *implementation* of those inventions. Entrepreneurs, by definition, are innovators, but they are not always inventors (though some are). The social entrepreneurs behind Madecasse (Chapter 2) did not invent chocolate, nor did they invent the process for curing cocoa beans that they teach the cocoa farmers with whom they work. They did, however, find a way to produce chocolate in a developing African country that can compete in a global marketplace; this is their innovation.

Dees et al. (2001, p. 162) observe that "innovation involves establishing new and better ways for accomplishing a worthwhile objective." In social entrepreneurship the identified "worthwhile objective" is the creative idea; the innovation is the implementation of that idea.

The Austrian economist Joseph Schumpeter identified five types of innovation, and Dees has added two more that are specific to social entrepreneurship (Dees et al., 2001):

- The creation of new products or services. In social entrepreneurship this might also include new programs or projects. This is a bit confusing because it blurs the line between creativity and innovation. It might more usefully be stated as the *implementation* of new products, services, programs or projects—that is, the delivery to market of things that had not previously been conceived of.
- A new process for producing or delivering an existing product, service, program, or project. For example, throughout much of the twentieth century, affordable housing for low-income households was delivered by government through the construction of public housing projects, which employed multiple family dwelling units for rental. Habitat for Humanity introduced a new process model by which low-income households, with the help of volunteers, could build their own detached, single-family dwelling, which they then owned.
- Delivering an existing product, service, program, or project to a new or previously underserved market. When Muhammad Yunus created the idea of micro-lending, he implemented it with low-income entrepreneurs in his native Bangladesh. The concept has since been exported to countries around the

world. In the United States it has undergone substantial adaptation to accommodate itself to a very different economy (e.g., the need for much larger loan amounts).

- Utilizing a new source of labor or other production inputs. Greyston Bakery of Yonkers, New York, operates a bakery that produces high-quality baked goods for restaurants and hotels using ex-convicts and other "unemployable" individuals as bakery workers. In a social entrepreneurship situation such as this one, the focus is on putting unemployed people to work, as opposed to a business entrepreneurship model that might seek to hire these individuals as inexpensive labor or, more commonly, not to hire them at all. As Greyston Bakery puts it, "We don't hire people to bake brownies; we bake brownies to hire people."

- Implementing a new organizational or industrial structure. Community development banks are private banks, like their commercial banking cousins; however, they do not offer checking accounts or access to safe deposit boxes. Instead, they sell certificates of deposit to their investors and use the money to invest in the development of their communities in a variety of ways. They typically invest where private banks will not (e.g., loans for the creation of minority-owned small businesses and for projects that benefit disadvantaged members of the community). As an example, the Louisville [Kentucky] Community Development Bank made a substantial loan to a nursing home for elderly, low-income, minority individuals so that the home could make major repairs to its leaky roof.

- Implementing new ways of engaging "customers" or target beneficiaries. A relatively new nonprofit social venture in New York City called Blue Skies (now part of the Robin Hood Foundation) uses the Internet to consolidate information on social service programs in the area and streamline the application process for its users. This system engages social service beneficiaries in very different ways than the highly fragmented traditional system has.

- The utilization of new funding models. As is discussed in Chapter 7, the funding of nonprofit social ventures, in particular, has departed dramatically from a dependence on the traditional philanthropic sources to a greater reliance on the generation of earned income.

Innovation provides the link between ideas and opportunities. Innovation involves the implementation of ideas. This implies, of course, that those ideas are implementable. Opportunities are implementable ideas. But how do we know whether an idea is implementable? The short answer to this question is that we test the idea in advance of pursuing it further. This reduces the chance of failure and its consequent wasting of resources—financial, physical, human, and social. The longer answer follows.

OPPORTUNITY RECOGNITION

Clearly, opportunity recognition involves movement from an idea to an opportunity. Timmons and Spinelli (2007, p. 116) describe this process as "transforming caterpillars into butterflies." We know what an idea is, but what is an opportunity? If opportunities are implementable ideas, what makes them implementable?

To begin to answer these questions, we attempt to establish a working definition of "opportunity." Timmons and Spinelli (2007) describe the key characteristics of a business opportunity as including:

- the ability to add value for the customer;
- adding value by solving a customer problem or fulfilling a customer need;
- the ability to capture a market and generate profits; and
- compatibility with the skill set of the entrepreneurs who pursue them.

Mariotti (2007, p. 18) simply defines an opportunity as "an idea that is based on what customers need or want." Barringer and Ireland (2008, p. 38) state that "[a]n opportunity is a favorable set of circumstances that creates a need for a new product service, or business." These latter authors go on to identify the "essential qualities" of an opportunity: attractiveness, timeliness, durability and basis in a product that adds value for the customer (Barringer & Ireland, 2008, p. 39).

Common to all of these definitions is the idea of adding value for the customer. Marketing experts call this the value proposition—that aspect of the product or service that causes customers to choose to buy it over its competitors. This, in turn, suggests that the product or service in question is addressing a need or want of the customer that the competition is not attending to. While crucial, adding value for the customer is not the only criterion that must be satisfied in order to judge an idea to be a true opportunity, however. The ability to financially sustain the enterprise must be apparent (i.e., a large enough market that it can cover its costs and generate a profit) and the timing must be right (an open "window of opportunity").

With these things in mind, our working definition of *opportunity* might look something like this:

> An opportunity is a business concept for a product or service that adds value to the lives of its customers by uniquely addressing an identified need or desire in a way that takes advantage of existing market conditions and the skill set of the entrepreneur(s) and ensures the financial viability of the enterprise delivering the product or service.

To this point, we have been discussing opportunity from the perspective of business entrepreneurship. How might this be translated for the social entrepreneurship world? Like business entrepreneurs, social entrepreneurs need to identify the needs and wants of their "customers"—the target beneficiaries of their efforts. Clayton Christensen, a Harvard business professor, refers to this as a "job" that the customer needs to have done for them (Christensen & Raynor, 2003). Presumably, this is a job that the customer is either unable or unwilling to do for themselves. In social entrepreneurship it is most likely the former; therefore, the question for the social entrepreneur is "How can I do this job for this target beneficiary in a unique way that improves her or his life?"

Like business opportunities, social opportunities have a "window of opportunity." This is the time period within which the social entrepreneur can provide maximum benefit to her or his customer before circumstances change, diminishing the value of the service. A window of opportunity might be opened by an event, a change in political regime and accompanying policy, a demographic shift, or an emerging trend. The earthquake in Haiti in January 2010 was a single event that opened the window of opportunity for social entrepreneurs who sought to help the victims of that disaster. The Reagan administration's decision to close government-funded facilities for the mentally ill and effectively put many of them on the streets in the 1980s presented an opportunity for social entrepreneurs to devise new ways to help these individuals. The trend toward an increasing number of single-parent households in the United States has created opportunities to fulfill the needs of both these parents and their children through social entrepreneurship. Windows of social opportunity may be closed when the given need has been fulfilled and new needs emerge, when an identified trend ends or is reversed, when a political regime changes, or when a particular idea or perspective is no longer in good currency.

Social opportunities are also like business opportunities in that they must be financially sustainable for the enterprise that pursues them. While social ventures that are nonprofit in structure do not need to turn a profit, they do need to at least break even and, better still, generate excess revenue. With the rise of for-profit social enterprise, there really is no difference between social and business entrepreneurship in this regard. Thus, our working definition of opportunity would seem to work for both types of entrepreneurship.

Having defined opportunity, we can now turn our attention to "recognizing" it. In fact, a big part of recognition lies in knowing what it is that you are looking for. The real challenge lies in systematizing the recognition process so that it can be repeated with some measure of consistency in its predictive power. This must be done with the understanding, however, that there is no foolproof way to forecast the success of an entrepreneurial endeavor before it begins. This is due to the fact that entrepreneurship is an organic process, not a mechanistic one. The road from point A to point B is not a straight line but a circuitous path. An entrepreneur is laying the tracks just ahead of the train (Lichtenstein & Lyons, 2010). With this acknowledged, we will look at some of the tools that have been created for helping entrepreneurs to reduce their risk in their efforts to ascertain whether or not an idea is an opportunity.

Opportunity Recognition Tools

Tools for the purpose of assessing ideas to determine their potential as an opportunity tend to fall into two broad categories: (1) tools that evaluate the internal and external contexts within which the enterprise pursuing the opportunity operates and the tangible and intangible resources necessary and available; and (2) tools that attempt to comprehensively evaluate the attractiveness of the idea relative to criteria such as industry, market, economics, competition, management, and the personal goals of the entrepreneur. We explore each of these types of tools for assessing business opportunities in turn, and then apply them to social opportunities.

The environmental scan, more commonly referred to as the SWOT analysis, from strategic planning is a common tool for evaluating ideas. It is commonly prescribed in books on business planning as a way of offering a rationale for a business concept being proposed in the plan. It permits the entrepreneur to examine the implementation of the idea by strengths and weaknesses that are internal to the operations of the enterprise that will pursue the idea and by threats and opportunities presented by the external environment in which the enterprise operates.

Strengths and weaknesses may include a wide variety of factors: the skill set of the entrepreneur and/or her or his team, organizational structure, available financial and physical resources, and so forth. These are current strengths and weaknesses. Strengths and weaknesses are often two sides of the same coin—as the ancient Greeks observed, one's greatest strength may also be one's "Achilles heel." Listing an idea's strengths and weaknesses helps the entrepreneur to think these things through systematically, reducing the probability that an important consideration will be missed.

Similarly, a list of the future threats and opportunities potentially afforded by the context can be quite varied: changes in the industry, changes in the economy, changes in the political landscape and resultant policy and regulatory alterations, market shifts, and the like. Accounting for these forces the entrepreneur needs to think about contingencies and whether or not the enterprise could survive the contextual shift. Again, certain events may harbor both an opportunity and a threat.

A complete SWOT analysis must not stop with a mere listing of strengths, weaknesses, opportunities, and threats. It must also examine the interactions. For example, how might a particular strength be used to thwart an impending threat or leverage an emerging opportunity? If an idea holds up to this scrutiny and still looks viable, it may well be an opportunity.

Drawing extensively on the SWOT analysis model is the Outside-In/Inside-Out Analysis model (Longenecker et al., 2006). This latter model assesses ideas for their potential as opportunities by looking at the prospective impact of the outside context (defined as the "general environment" and the "industry environment") on the proposed enterprise and at the internal capacity of the enterprise to act (Longenecker et al., 2006).

In the Outside-In Analysis the general environment includes the following factors: political/legal, socio-cultural, macroeconomic, global, and technological (Longenecker et al., 2006, p. 56). The industry environment takes into account Porter's five competitive factors: new competitors in the industry, products or services that can be substituted for those of the enterprise under analysis, rivalry among competitors, the influence of suppliers, and the influence of buyers (Porter, 2008). All of these things will either positively or negatively influence the ability of an idea to be attractive and sustainable.

Outside-In Analysis tells us how opportunities might be shaped, but this is only half of the assessment. It is also important to understand how capable the entrepreneur and the enterprise are of carrying the idea forward to the market. Such an understanding involves an assessment of internal resources (tangible and intangible) and capabilities (skills and core competencies). The results of the Outside-In and the Inside-Out analyses can then be blended and assessed using a standard SWOT analysis (described above).

The more comprehensive opportunity assessment tools seem to find their origins in the work of entrepreneurship educator and researcher William D. Bygrave. Bygrave (Bygrave & Zacharakis, 2004) established a set of criteria to be evaluated relative to the "attractiveness" of the idea being assessed. For each criterion, he provided a brief profile of what that criterion would look like if it were to achieve either its highest potential or its lowest potential. In this way, Bygrave created a spectrum within which to assess each criterion within a comprehensive evaluation of an idea. For example, one of his market criteria was "Customers." He identified the highest potential of this criterion to be "Reachable; purchase orders" and the lowest to be "Loyal to others or unreachable." Presumably, many ideas will fall somewhere between these two end points, where the customer base is not entirely reachable but not without hope of being reached.

Bygrave identified seven major areas for assessment: Industry and Market, Economics, Harvest Issues, Competitive Advantage Issues, Management Team, Personal Criteria, and Strategic Differentiation. He broke each of these areas down into several specific criteria. As an example, Industry and Market comprised the criteria Market (which was further disaggregated into Customers, User Benefits, Value Added, and Product Life), Market Structure, Market Size, Growth Rate, Market Capacity, Market Share Attainable (Year 5), and Cost Structure (Bygrave & Zacharakis, 2004). Thus, he provided a very thorough tool for assessing a business opportunity.

Timmons and Spinelli (2007, pp. 170–171) adapted Bygrave's model into a tool they called QuickScreen. QuickScreen follows the Bygrave approach of nested criteria, with a higher potential to lower potential range for each. However, QuickScreen, as its names implies, takes a more streamlined approach. There are only three major assessment areas: "Market and Margin Related Issues," "Competitive Advantages: Relative to the Current and Evolving Set of Competitors," and "Value

Creation and Realization Issues." The parameters on each criterion are more concise and sharper. For example, one of the Market and Margin Related Issues criteria is "Need/want/problem/pain-point." It is considered higher potential if the Need is "Identified" and lower potential if the Need is "Unfocused." QuickScreen also offers higher average/lower ranges for some criteria (e.g., "Exit/Liquidity," "Timing," and "Barriers to Entry"). Finally, QuickScreen allows the entrepreneur doing the assessment to consider the idea's "Overall Potential" and make "Go," "No Go," and "Go, If" decisions.

Bygrave and Zacharakis (2008) offer another variation on the Bygrave model, which they call the Opportunity Checklist. They use many of the same criteria but add a few unique ones of their own: "Psychographics" (under "Customer"), "Stealth Competitors" (under "Competition"), and major assessment areas of "Government" and "Global Environment." Another interesting feature of the Opportunity Checklist is the scale for assessment for each criterion. Rather than providing a range from higher to lower, Bygrave and Zacharakis simply permit the entrepreneur to evaluate the idea as a "Better Opportunity" or a "Weaker Opportunity."

While business entrepreneurs have several opportunity recognition, or assessment, tools from which to choose, social entrepreneurs have substantially less guidance in this area. Kitzi provides an opportunity assessment model for nonprofit social ventures (Dees et al., 2001, pp. 53–54). It is a version of Bygrave's model that has been substantially stripped down, in terms of the number of criteria, and modified to reflect a focus on social mission. The Kitzi model evaluates social ideas on three broad dimensions: social value potential, market potential, and sustainability potential. It assesses each criterion as falling in a range of high to low. While the model is very useful for assessing opportunities for social ventures with a nonprofit structure, it no longer reflects the rapidly changing nature of social entrepreneurship, which places a new emphasis on for-profit ventures and earned income activities by nonprofits.

In light of this reality, we offer a new opportunity assessment model that reflects both Kitzi's and Bygrave's thinking as well as insights from other models based on Bygrave's. Our model attempts to capture both the pursuit of social value and the market-driven aspects of business opportunities. This model, which we call the Social Opportunity Assessment Tool, can be found in Figure 3.1.

USING THE SOCIAL OPPORTUNITY ASSESSMENT TOOL

A quick perusal of the Social Opportunity Assessment Tool reveals that it has four major assessment categories: Social Value Potential, Market Potential, Competitive Advantage Potential, and Sustainability Potential. Within each of these categories are five criteria by which to evaluate the idea under study. The tool then permits the prospective social entrepreneur to develop composite ratings for each

Social Value Potential

Criterion	Strong Opportunity	Weak Opportunity
Social need	Service or product directly addresses an identified need	Service or product addresses need only indirectly
Mission alignment	Service or product is in direct alignment with mission	Service or product is only indirectly aligned or is misaligned with mission
Achievable impact	Service or product can fulfill identified social need in a measurable way	Service or product will only minimally address the need
Social return on investment (SROI)	A strong effectiveness to cost ratio	A weak effectiveness to cost ratio, or costs exceed impact
Community support	Service or product will be positively perceived and endorsed by the community	Service or product will not be well accepted by the community

Market Potential

Criterion	Strong Opportunity	Weak Opportunity
Customer need or want	Target beneficiary both needs and wants the service or product	Target beneficiary is indifferent to the service or product
Window of opportunity	Timing is good	Timing is poor
Investor interest	Evidence of philanthropic, government, or private-sector financial interest	Evidence of little or no interest by philanthropic, governmental, or private investors
Market size	Large	Small
Market share attainable	An open market, with little or no competition	Very competitive market, with several substitutors

Competitive Advantage Potential

Criterion	Strong Opportunity	Weak Opportunity
Barriers to entry	High, many	Low or nonexistent
Prospective partnerships or alliances	Many potential partners	Few potential partners
Control over costs	Substantial control	Little or no control
Compelling mission	Highly compelling; widespread sympathy	Less compelling; little understanding or sympathy
Management team	Strong, complete skill set	Incomplete skill set

Sustainability Potential

Criterion	Strong Opportunity	Weak Opportunity
Venture capacity	Sufficient physical resources to start and maintain the venture	Insufficient physical resources to start and maintain the venture
Venture capability	Sufficiently skilled entrepreneur(s), staff, and board	Insufficiently skilled entrepreneur(s), staff, and board
Investor interest	Evidence of philanthropic, government, or private-sector financial interest	Evidence of little or no interest by philanthropic, governmental, or private investors
Ability to generate earned income	High potential for charging user fees and/or selling goods or services	Low potential for charging user fees and/or selling goods or services
Compelling mission	Highly compelling; widespread sympathy	Less compelling; little understanding or sympathy

Overall Potential

Social value potential	High	Medium	Low
Market potential	High	Medium	Low
Competitive advantage potential	High	Medium	Low
Sustainability potential	High	Medium	Low
Composite potential	High	Medium	Low

FIGURE 3.1 The Social Opportunity Assessment Tool

assessment category and for the four categories combined. This should provide ample guidance for deciding whether or not to proceed with creating the social venture.

Before we look more closely at the tool, interpret the assessment criteria, and discuss where to find or develop the data for conducting the assessment, we would emphasize that this is intended to be a pre-launch test. Therefore, the idea is being assessed in advance of any action being taken on it. It is intended to force entrepreneurs to think through their idea before investing time and resources on it. If the assessment yields a positive result, they can proceed with relative confidence to pursue their genuine opportunity. If the results of the assessment are negative, they can abandon the idea before incurring any losses. In order for this to work, however, a social entrepreneur must be willing to be honest with her- or himself in carrying out the assessment. It is very easy for entrepreneurs to fall in love with their idea and delude themselves into believing that it will work despite strong evidence to the contrary.

That said, it is entirely possible to derive a "false negative" from this process. This could, in turn, scare an entrepreneur away from a social opportunity the weaknesses of which might be overcome through motivation and resourcefulness. As Tim McCullum of Madecasse observed in Chapter 2, sometimes it's better not to know what you can't do. Nevertheless, we urge prospective social entrepreneurs to put their ideas through an opportunity assessment because the systematic process will likely open their eyes to unanticipated strengths and weaknesses. The choice as to whether or not to proceed is the prospective entrepreneur's alone.

Whenever we ask a class of our social entrepreneurship students to put a social idea through an opportunity assessment, we have observed an interesting and recurring phenomenon. Invariably, one or more students in the class will express frustration with the assignment. They will ask the following question: Because my idea is about something new that no one has ever done before, how can I be expected to predict how it will work, and where will I be able to find data to test it? This is a fair question.

The answer lies in understanding that such an assessment must be handled as a "what if" scenario. If I pursue this idea, what is likely to happen? Is it likely to have customers? Will investors want to put their money behind it? Will the community in which it is implemented support it? Will it have a measurable social impact? Obviously, none of these questions can be answered definitively; however, by examining the experiences and outcomes of comparable efforts, we can draw some preliminary conclusions about their likely answers.

Where can this kind of information be found? It can be discovered in articles and books about the social problem(s) to be addressed; in case studies of similar social ventures; from relevant industry associations (e.g., housing groups, education associations, literacy groups, associations of foster children); from the financial records of nonprofits (which are a matter of public record and can be found on the Internet); from other social ventures in the same industry that are not competitors; by conducting interviews with prospective customers; in directories of foundations and other philanthropic sources; and so forth.

While most of this information will not be a precise fit with the situation of the proposed social venture, it will be close enough to allow informed assumptions to be made and to permit interpolation and extrapolation of data to better fit the circumstances being tested. The important idea here is that prospective entrepreneurs who engage in opportunity assessment should perceive themselves not as describing the present but, instead, as predicting the future based on a comparable past. When this latter mind-frame is accepted and adopted, the work becomes easier.

What follows is an examination of the Social Opportunity Assessment Tool itself. This examination is broken down by major assessment factors, with a discussion of the criteria within each factor.

Social Value Potential

In order for an idea to be a viable social opportunity, it must have the potential to create social value for the customers, or target beneficiaries. The five criteria for assessing the social value potential of an idea are social need, mission alignment, achievable impact, social return on investment, and community support.

First, the idea must meet a true social need. This is a need that has been clearly identified as such. One way to determine the relevance of a perceived need is to survey the prospective target beneficiaries. Their response can help to determine whether or not to move forward with an idea. For example, one of our students had an idea for a social venture that would help to prepare economically disadvantaged urban youth for college. She proposed to start her efforts in a particular neighborhood in New York City. She conducted a survey of a representative sample of high school students in that neighborhood. The response of the high school students was strongly supportive of this idea, which suggested to our student that her idea, if implemented, would be addressing a true social need. A word of caution is appropriate here, however. Target beneficiaries' responses to anything that may be of benefit to them tend to be skewed to the positive. A more accurate determination of need in this case involved surveying high school teachers and administrators and college admissions officers as well.

Another way to determine customer need is to study the results of secondary research on the subject. Books, articles in academic and professional journals, and technical reports can all be sources of information on a given need. A prospective social entrepreneur who is assessing an idea for a system to address illiteracy in the rural United States could look at studies of literacy in rural communities or regions to determine how many people are affected by the problem, their attitudes toward learning to read, and efforts to date to address the issue.

Another measure of social potential is alignment with the social venture's mission. This is probably most germane to social ventures that are already in operation and are exploring new opportunities to pursue. The rule of thumb is that if an idea will not distract the venture from its mission (i.e., will not result in what is referred to as "mission creep"), it is worth exploring as an opportunity. If it will draw human, financial, and physical resources away from the mission, it should be approached with considerable caution.

Mission alignment for start-up social ventures works in the opposite direction. Once an idea is determined to be a genuine opportunity, a mission can be clearly articulated for a venture whose purpose is to pursue that opportunity (or fulfill the identified need). That is, a mission can be created that aligns with the initial opportunity. We discuss mission and the mission statement in more detail later in this chapter.

An idea for a social venture cannot be a viable opportunity if it will not yield an achievable impact. It must produce a transformation—a deep and lasting social change of some kind. This performance must be demonstrable in some way. It is not enough to say that it is your intention to end homelessness; you must be able to show that your efforts as a social entrepreneur can be directly linked to a lower rate of homelessness in your community and that the people you remove from the street do not return.

Obviously, there is no way to guarantee that an idea will have impact before it is pursued, but, at the least, there should be the ability to put a system in place to measure and report on progress toward the stated goal. There should also be a reasonable expectation that the idea, once implemented, can have a positive impact on fulfilling the identified need. Looking at comparable social entrepreneurship efforts with an eye to understanding how and why they did or did not succeed is one approach to determining the reasonableness of your own expectations relative to your idea. If, for example, the idea under consideration is a program for teaching obese children how to cook, using healthy ingredients, as a way to address the problem of childhood obesity in the United States, the prospective social entrepreneur will want to do some research on the impacts of other programs that address childhood obesity as well as the efficacy of cooking classes for children.

Going hand in hand with achievable impact as a criterion for social value potential is social return on investment (SROI). In business entrepreneurship, every investor in an enterprise expects a return on investment (ROI). That is, for each dollar they invest, they do so with the hope that they will receive more than a dollar in return. This is the incentive to invest. No investor in a business invests with the idea of breaking even or of losing money. The same should be true for social investments; they should "pay off" by producing social gains that exceed the value of the initial investment.

The difficult aspect of SROI is that, unlike ROI, it cannot always be measured in dollars. How does one accurately monetize lives saved or quality of lives improved? Nevertheless, there must be a return to the social investor, or the idea being assessed must be considered to lack an important element of social value. It is a major challenge for social entrepreneurs to demonstrate the return that their value propositions can produce, especially in advance of putting their ideas into action (Austin, 2006). Much thought has been, and continues to be, given to how to think about and measure SROI (Sawhill & Williamson, 2001; Campbell, 2003; Emerson & Bonini, 2004; Wei-Skillern, Austin, Leonard, & Stevenson, 2007). See Chapter 8 for a more detailed discussion of both measuring impact and SROI.

The final criterion for determining an idea's social value potential is community support. A true social opportunity has the support of the community (however this term is defined) where it is being pursued. The community must believe in the idea philosophically, must believe in its ability to be effective, and must be willing to, at least, provide political support. This is because the community is a stakeholder in the opportunity in the sense that the social entrepreneur's success in addressing the need will impact quality of life in the community. The social entrepreneur should research the history of the community's support for similar social opportunities and may want to survey community leaders for their reactions to the idea under evaluation. Community resistance will, at best, make pursuing the idea difficult and, at worst, destroy the idea and divide the community. For example, an idea for addressing teen pregnancy through birth control is unlikely to receive support from a community where the majority of residents believe in abstinence for religious and ideological reasons.

Market Potential

The first criterion for determining the market potential of a social idea is its ability to address a customer need or want. As was noted earlier in this chapter, in business an important aspect of a viable opportunity is the ability of the product or service to add value to its customers by satisfying a need they have. This is no less true for a social opportunity. If the real need of the youth in a particular community is for better access to training for the skilled trades, a would-be social entrepreneur with an idea for helping these youth go to college does not have a genuine opportunity because she or he would not be meeting the needs of the intended customers.

Even meeting a customer *need* may not be enough if the customers do not *want*, or desire, the service being offered. In the case of the social entrepreneur with an idea for addressing childhood obesity through cooking classes for children, noted previously, there may be clear evidence that obesity among children in the community is a problem. Experts may agree that there is a need for viable ways to address this problem. The parents of obese children in the community may even agree that something should be done. However, if the children don't want to attend cooking classes, or if their parents want to try managing their diets at home rather than sending them to cooking classes, the idea has failed this test.

This latter example raises another level of complexity in assessing this criterion. Who is the actual customer in this case? Is it the parents, who make the ultimate decision as to what is best for their child? Is it the child, who has a sense of what she or he likes or dislikes? The answer: the customers, in this case, include both the parent and the child. The child may be the one who directly benefits from the service, but the parent is an indirect beneficiary. Thus, both must need and want this service in order for it to represent a true social opportunity.

There have been too many instances of would-be social entrepreneurs attempting to ride to the rescue of people who they perceived needed and wanted what they were offering, only to find that this was not the case. Just like a business person who tries to sell a product for which there are no customers, a social entrepreneur who does the same will soon be out of business.

An important concept in entrepreneurship is that of the window of opportunity. Every opportunity has one—a specific period of time in which conditions are ideal for a favorable reception of the good or service. The window may be opened by a specific event or pattern shift. The 2010 oil spill in the Gulf of Mexico was a catastrophe that opened a window of opportunity for social entrepreneurs seeking to help natural wildlife, businesses, and entire communities negatively affected by it. How long this window will be open is presently unknown; however, as life along the Gulf returns to normal, the window will surely close. The trick is to enter this market space as close to the time the window of opportunity opens as possible. This will maximize the impact of your social venture.

In order for a social idea to have market potential, it must be able to attract investor interest. This is because social investors represent a market as well. Social entrepreneurs must be capable of selling investors on their product's or service's ability to meet the needs and desires of its intended customers. This is true whether the investors are philanthropic organizations, government agencies, or private entities.

Market size is another important consideration when evaluating market potential. True social entrepreneurs, like business entrepreneurs, must "think big" about their opportunities. They should seek to maximize mission achievement by reaching as many customers as possible. As was noted in Chapter 2, a goal of growth for her or his venture is a hallmark of a serious entrepreneur. The larger the market, the greater the SROI will be, in most cases. This will, in turn, attract more investors.

A large market does not necessarily ensure a large market share for the social venture, however. How much of that large market the venture captures will depend on how open the market is and how much competition exists in the market ecosystem. These two factors generally work together. In some markets a strong competitor may dominate the market, with many customers who are loyal to that competitor and unlikely to change their allegiance. An example from the world of business is what sometimes happens among competing automobile manufacturers. Many people in the market may develop a loyalty to a particular make of car because of considerations like cost, reliability, and appearance. Thus, a large segment of the market becomes loyal to a particular manufacturer—say Honda. It is very hard for Ford, Nissan, Toyota, or Hyundai to take that market share away from Honda. An example from social entrepreneurship might be the dominance of Habitat for Humanity in the market for providing affordable housing for low-income households through homeownership. If a social entrepreneur was seeking to enter this market with a new offering, she or he might find it very difficult to capture market share because of loyalty to Habitat's mission and model by prospective customers and investors.

Sometimes there are so many competitors in a given market that no matter how open the market is to new entrants, there is very little, or no market share left to be had. In business entrepreneurship such a situation would likely result in fierce competition among companies to take market share away from each other. This is problematic in social entrepreneurship, however, because competitors typically share similar social missions. Running another social venture out of business in order to corner the market on helping the homeless is hardly in keeping with the ethos of social entrepreneurship. It is much more likely that competitors would find ways to pool resources and work together to help the homeless in the given community. Of course, for most social problems there is far more demand than there is supply; therefore, markets overcrowded by competition are a rarity. Prospective social entrepreneurs simply should be sure that they can capture adequate market share to sustain their ventures.

Competitive Advantage Potential

Pursuant to the discussion of market potential, including an assessment of competitive advantage may seem redundant. However, carefully examining the criteria relative to competitive advantage can prove very useful to a better understanding of one's opportunity.

A very important competitive advantage criterion is barriers to entry. As the name implies, these are obstacles that make it difficult for new ventures to enter a market. This acts as an advantage for those ventures that have already entered the same market; the higher the barriers to entry, the longer the venture already in the market has to capture market share before competition emerges. This is why being "first to market" is a highly sought-after position among ventures serving a given customer segment. This suggests, of course, that the early entrants to a market have the ability both to overcome existing market barriers and to use those barriers as a weapon, of sorts, to thwart competition.

Robinson (2006) identifies five types of barriers to entry that have relevance to both business and social entrepreneurship: economic, social, institutional, formal (public), and cultural. Economic barriers to entry usually involve not having access to resources that can build a company up to a place where it can thwart the competition. Such barriers might include not having access to certain intellectual property (e.g., patented technology), sufficient financial capital, or specialized equipment, and so forth.

Social barriers to entry prevent an entrepreneur from having access to social networks in the market that are crucial to success. In particular, these include such resources as labor markets, civic organizations, business organizations, political networks, and other business owners (Robinson, 2006, p. 101).

Barriers to entry that are institutional in nature involve not having access to knowledge about the norms, rules, and values of the community in which business is to be done. This precludes necessary relationships between the business entering the market and public and private actors in the community (Robinson, 2006).

Formal barriers to entry are those that involve the lack of formal institutions for governance, legal interactions, market interactions, and financial capital provision in the context that the company is trying to enter (Robinson, 2006, p. 103). Most developed countries have these institutions in place; however, many developing countries do not.

While formal barriers to entry are created by a lack of formalized institutions, cultural barriers are characterized by informal institutions in the context to be entered that present obstacles to the entrepreneur. These include cultural norms, such as dress, etiquette, legends, superstitions, and language and slang, that affect the ability to establish trust (Robinson, 2006, p. 103). These things must be learned and understood if the entrepreneur is to successfully enter the market—something that is extremely difficult.

Prospective social entrepreneurs should research the barriers to entry in their proposed opportunity's market. What are these barriers? What is the entrepreneur's capability for overcoming them? Information for this analysis can be derived from sources that cover the market and context in which the entrepreneur would be operating. If, for example, the idea being assessed involves creating an organization that facilitates the adoption of orphaned children in Nepal by parents from other countries, the would-be social entrepreneur must understand Nepalese adoption laws, cultural norms regarding orphaned children and adoption, the language of the country, international laws regarding adoption, the human capital (skill sets) required to operate such an organization, physical facilities required, and many other barriers to entering this market. The social entrepreneur must then attempt to realistically determine whether or not she or he can overcome these barriers and establish a venture in this market.

As is discussed in the subsection "Market Potential" (pp. 57–59), social entrepreneurs are not typically engaged in direct competition for market share. In fact, competition in this world is more often for resources. Because of this, successful social entrepreneurs are more likely to collaborate to compete by sharing resources. Therefore, competitive advantage might be thought of, at least in part, as the ability of the social venture to attract and build strategic partnerships. Prospective social entrepreneurs should ask themselves what the likelihood of developing partnerships and alliances in their market is. If alliance building is likely, that bodes well for their competitive advantage.

Social entrepreneurs' ability to compete also will be affected by the amount of control over costs they have, including control over costs, prices, and distribution channels (Bygrave & Zacharakis, 2004). The more control the better, because that allows them to make favorable deals with their suppliers and raise or reduce their prices as necessary. However, many social entrepreneurs are limited in their control. For those whose customers are low-income, pricing options are limited, which means that they must rely heavily on subsidy to cover their costs. This puts them in direct competition with those seeking the same kind of philanthropic investment. Those who operate in a market with a dominant competitor may be at a disadvantage in developing favorable supplier relationships equivalent to those of the major competitor, resulting in higher relative costs. This factor of competitive advantage is closely linked to that of prospective partnerships or alliances noted above. For many social ventures, being able to maximize their control over costs and prices is a function of their ability to develop strong networks with suppliers and other social ventures.

Because competition in social entrepreneurship is often over resources, the ability of the social venture's mission to attract investors, suppliers and customers is very important. A mission that is highly compelling can be a powerful competitive advantage. Memorial Sloan-Kettering Cancer Center in New York City is a large nonprofit cancer research hospital. It has been very successful in its ability to attract donors, partners, and customers because of its mission aimed at cancer research and treatment, a social issue that touches the lives of millions of people around the world.

In the case of for-profit social ventures, competition is most likely to be for customers. Newman's Own, Inc., a food distribution company founded by the late actor Paul Newman that gives all of its after-tax profits to charity, is a good example. Newman's Own makes a concerted effort to let its customers know that when they purchase one of its products, they are making a contribution to charity in addition to acquiring a high-quality food item. This allows Newman's Own to compete effectively in a crowded and challenging market (Wei-Skillern et al., 2007).

The ability to effectively articulate and communicate the social venture's mission to the other players in its market—customers, investors, suppliers, partners—is crucial to success in that market. This can be done by crafting a clear and compelling mission statement. We will discuss this later in this chapter.

The final factor in determining the competitive advantage potential of an opportunity is the management team of the social venture. A strong team that represents the complete skill set necessary to effectively operate the venture can be a decided competitive advantage. Lichtenstein and Lyons (2001) describe the skills necessary for successful entrepreneurship as lying within four dimensions: technical, managerial, entrepreneurial, and personal maturity skills. Technical skills are those needed to effectively operate in a given industry. For example, social entrepreneurs who provide affordable housing to low-income households must possess skills in real estate development and law, building construction, finance, and other relevant areas. Managerial skills permit the daily operation of the venture on a successful basis: administrative, management, bookkeeping, marketing, and related skills. Entrepreneurial skills include those addressed in this text: the ability to recognize and act on opportunities, bootstrapping, and risk management skills, among others. Personal maturity includes such skills as the ability and willingness to take responsibility, self-awareness, the management of emotions, and creativity. A competitive management team will embody all of these skills. While no individual is likely to possess all of them, the individuals on the team each will bring some of them and, in so doing, complement each other.

Sustainability Potential

Starting a social venture is of little use if it cannot be sustained over time. Therefore, an idea is not an opportunity unless its financial sustainability is likely. There are five factors that can be assessed to determine an idea's sustainability potential.

The proposed venture's capacity is an important consideration regarding its sustainability. Capacity refers to the physical resources necessary to operate the venture over time. Physical resources might include facilities, equipment, inventory, and the like, depending on the industry in which the venture is operating (Dees et al., 2001). The question here is whether or not these resources are sufficient for starting and maintaining the venture. Answering this question will require the prospective social entrepreneur to think through the activities necessary to accomplishing her or his mission and the physical resources required to carry out each activity (Dees et al., 2001).

Another important factor in determining sustainability potential is venture capability, which represents the combined skills of the entrepreneurial team, the staff, and the board of directors and/or board of advisors. Does the entire organization have a sufficient skill set to start and maintain itself over time? In a similar way to the assessment of capacity, the would-be social entrepreneur must ascertain the activities necessary to launching and maintaining the venture and link those to the skills required to carry out those activities.

Just as it was important to assessing market potential, investor interest is a useful indicator of sustainability potential. It is one factor in the financial sustainability of the proposed venture. There must be sufficient evidence of philanthropic, governmental, and/or private-sector financial interest if the venture is to be sustainable. The findings of the assessment of investor interest relative to an investor market for the venture can be applied here, with a shift of focus from merely ascertaining whether potential investors exist to estimating how much they might be expected to invest. This can be determined by looking at what a particular prospective investor has put into similar efforts in the past. This information can be gathered from a variety of sources including foundation and corporate giving directories, the *Federal Register*, and the websites of social venture philanthropic organizations.

An increasingly important indicator of the financial sustainability of an opportunity is its ability to generate earned income, a phenomenon that is frequently referred to as "social enterprise." This is an issue for both for-profit and nonprofit social ventures. Obviously, for-profits must have an opportunity that produces earned income through sales or they do not have a viable business model. For these social ventures, assessing financial sustainability using this factor is a matter of determining whether or not there is an adequate market that is willing to pay for their product or service to the extent that they can cover their costs and generate a profit. This is no different than for a commercial business.

For a nonprofit social venture, however, the issues are slightly different. Non-profits can draw upon both philanthropic financing sources and earned income. Traditionally, these kinds of social ventures have relied heavily on the former, rarely or never drawing upon the latter. As philanthropic dollars have become harder to come by, a clear shift is under way toward the pursuit of earned income by nonprofits. This is becoming viewed as a necessity. Nevertheless, earned income strategies represent uncharted waters for most nonprofits, with considerable concern about the impact of these activities on the tax-exempt status of these ventures. This latter issue will be discussed in more detail in Chapter 6.

Suffice it to say that generating earned income has become an important sustainability issue for all social ventures, be they for-profit or nonprofit. If a social venture cannot generate at least some earned income, its likelihood of survival is greatly reduced. Prospective nonprofit social entrepreneurs, in particular, now need to give serious thought to how they might generate earned income through fees and/or the sale of goods and services before they try to launch their ventures. Some of these social entrepreneurs are now creating hybrid organizations—part for-profit, part nonprofit—to address this issue (see Chapter 6 for a discussion of this option).

A crucial factor in sustainability potential, just as it was in competitive advantage potential, is having a compelling mission. The more compelling a social venture's mission, the more likely it is that it will be able to attract financial investment for start-up and ongoing maintenance as well as for growth.

Overall Potential

Once the factors within each major assessment category of the Social Opportunity Assessment Tool have been researched and evaluated, an overall assessment of that category can be made on a high–medium–low scale. Then, a composite assessment can be made for the idea under scrutiny. If the idea has a "high" composite rating, it is likely to be a true opportunity and worth pursuing. If it is scored as having "medium" potential, it may be worth further consideration and, with modification, may yet be a viable opportunity. A "low" score suggests that the prospective social entrepreneur should seriously consider moving on to another idea. However, it does not necessarily preclude major modification to the original idea that may improve its potential.

Of course, all of this is merely suggestive. There are many examples of ideas for social change that have been successfully pursued in spite of their perceived low potential for success. The entrepreneur's motivation and relentlessness can carry a social venture a long way. Because the development of a social venture is an organic process, making adjustments along the way to counter arising obstacles is entirely possible. Nevertheless, thinking through a social idea before running with it does no harm and may prevent the waste of valuable time and resources.

FROM OPPORTUNITY TO MISSION

As was noted earlier in this chapter, existing social ventures already have a mission and will assess arising opportunities in light of this mission, in part. However, new, start-up social ventures need an initial opportunity with which to work before they can understand what their mission is. For them, the opportunity recognition process, just described, comes first and the clarification of a mission and development of a mission statement follows.

For those start-up social ventures that have undertaken the opportunity assessment process and have a viable opportunity with which to work, the next step is to begin the process of building a venture that will serve as the vehicle for the pursuit of that social opportunity. An important piece of this venture-building process is the identification of a mission for that venture. Johnston (2001, p. 20) defines mission as "why we do what we do, a reason for being, purpose."

It is important that a social venture should have a very clearly articulated mission because that is what attracts customers, investors, suppliers, partners, and community supporters to the venture. The written expression of the mission is called a mission statement. There are two competing schools of thought about the nature of a mission statement. One calls for a short, concise statement of purpose. This stems from the thinking of the late management guru Peter Drucker. A good example of such a mission statement is that of the social venture Common Ground, whose statement simply reads, "To end homelessness." The other school of thought holds that mission statements should be longer and convey a complete message about the venture's purpose, often including bullet points offering detailed information on the various activities of the venture. The mission statement of the French Broad Food Co-op (located in North Carolina) epitomizes this model and reads as follows:

> We are dedicated to serving our members and the Western North Carolina community by providing high quality natural foods and personal care products through a mutually beneficial exchange.
>
> We support consumption of healthful and organic foods grown or produced locally with ecological and social responsibility.
>
> We encourage informed choice and consumer empowerment, with an emphasis on education and customer assistance.
>
> We are committed to use our profits to strengthen and improve the Co-op community, and to provide a livable wage to our employees.
>
> We pledge to maintain a pleasant environment that fosters goodwill, cooperation and participation.

No matter what approach to writing a mission statement is used, having such a statement for a social venture is essential. Not only can a compelling mission statement attract customers and resources, but it can act as a guiding light for the social entrepreneur as well. It keeps the focus on the venture and what it exists to do. As new potential opportunities arise, it must be asked, "Is this opportunity in keeping with our mission?" When potential partnerships present themselves, the appropriate first question is, "Will entering into this partnership further our mission?" While having a mission can be valuable to commercial ventures, the mission drives everything in a social venture. The mission will be discussed in the context of strategic planning in Chapter 5.

Case Study 3.1

The Case of the Intel Computer Clubhouse Network

The mission of the Computer Clubhouse is to provide "a creative and safe out-of-school learning environment where young people from underserved communities work with adult mentors to explore their own ideas, develop skills, and build confidence in themselves through the use of technology" (http://www.computerclubhouse.org, 2010). From humble beginnings in a space in the Computer Museum in Boston, which is now part of the Museum of Science, it has grown to include 100 locations in twenty countries, which serve a total of over 25,000 youth per year: the Intel Computer Clubhouse Network (http://www.computerclubhouse.org, 2010).

The Computer Clubhouse was co-founded in 1993 by Natalie Rusk of the Computer Museum and Mitchel Resnick of the MIT Media Lab (Garr, 1998). Their idea had two major sources (Garr, 1998; Resnick, Rusk, & Cooke, 1998): (1) an interactive exhibit at the museum that allowed for computer-controlled manipulation of LEGO blocks, which was wildly popular with children; and (2) a concern that disadvantaged urban youth have less access to computers than their suburban counterparts because most do not have a computer at home and because inner-city public schools are under-resourced.

Rusk and Resnick wanted to harness the creativity of the children who visited the museum exhibit on an ongoing basis, while addressing the special needs of urban youth for computer literacy. To accomplish this, they set aside a room in the Computer Museum that was well equipped with hardware and software. Unlike most computer labs for children, however, the Computer Clubhouse chose not to install software that only permitted its users to work with programs designed by others. Instead, it installed programming software that allowed participating youth to design their own applications. This decision was a conscious one that is very much in keeping with the learning philosophy adopted by the Clubhouse (Garr, 1998; Resnick et al., 1998).

This learning philosophy is based on the concept that Clubhouse founders call "technology fluency." It holds that learning to be fluent in the use of technology is similar to learning how to become fluent in a language. Fluency does not come from rote memorization or formal classroom learning. It is developed by immersing oneself in the culture in which the language is spoken. Thus, the Clubhouse aims to immerse youth in the culture of computer use by bringing them together with adult mentors to engage in creative processes that involve the use of computer hardware and software (Resnick et al., 1998).

This broad philosophy has been translated into four learning principles that comprise the Computer Clubhouse's learning model (Resnick et al., 1998):

1. Focus on a learning experience that features learning through creating and designing, not passive, hands-off of knowledge.
2. Let youth work on projects that are of personal interest to them, which will cause them to truly immerse themselves in those projects.
3. Create a diverse learning community that includes individuals of different ages, gender, cultures, and experiences in which the technology can be mastered in a collaborative way.
4. Foster trust and respect among the members of the community, which enables creativity and innovation in a safe environment.

These principles are reflected in the programs that the Computer Clubhouse offers to the youth it serves. The Adobe Youth Voices (AYV) program is funded by the Adobe Foundation and provides money, equipment, and training to Clubhouse youth to create multimedia projects that let them reach out to their communities about issues of interest and importance to the young people. The Clubhouse-to-College/Clubhouse-to-Career (C2C) program aims to help Clubhouse youth develop marketable skills through the use of equipment and software that are also used in the professional world. The goals of this program include developing proficiency in using these tools, engendering a love for learning and scholarship, placing motivated participants in college, preparing youth for placement in professional technology-related jobs, and stimulating interest in careers in technology fields (Computer Clubhouse, 2010).

C2C engages its participating youth in a variety of activities. These include college visits, field trips to local technology companies, visits from technology-related professionals, internships, shadowing experiences with technology professionals, and career development workshops (Computer Clubhouse, 2010).

The Hear Our Voices program supports young women and girls in their use of technology to combat the underrepresentation of women in the technology fields. It was initially funded by the National Science Foundation and picked up by some local Clubhouses. Today, about one-third of all the Clubhouses around the world have adopted this program.

The idea behind Hear Our Voices is to make using technology an enjoyable experience and to encourage female youth to express themselves through computer technology. Girls in the program work with women mentors to create computer-generated projects, science projects, and original video and movie productions. They also participate in relevant field trips and workshops (Computer Clubhouse, 2010).

Another of the Clubhouse's programs is the biennial Teen Summit. This gathering includes youth selected from local Clubhouses around the world and is held in Boston on a college campus. The summits are designed to allow the participants to learn about each other's cultures, explore career opportunities in technology fields, work together on computer-based projects, and discover life on a college campus. Each summit has its own theme(s) around which activities revolve (Computer Clubhouse, 2010).

At the 2010 summit, 250 youth, representing nineteen countries, were in attendance. The summit was held on the campus of Northeastern University. The themes were "reducing urban violence" and "the environment." Among the activities at the summit were a career fair and work on projects directed at the summit's themes. The summit culminated in a "Project Showcase" that gave participants a chance to share their work with others. Funders of the 2010 Summit included Adobe Systems, Autodesk, Boys & Girls Clubs of Boston, the Equal Footing Foundation, Intel, MIT, the Museum of Science of Boston, the New York City Department of Housing Preservation, and the New Zealand Computer Clubhouse Trust (Computer Clubhouse, 2010).

The management team of the Intel Computer Clubhouse Network has an impressive combined résumé. There is a Director, two Program Managers, a Community Liaison, a Knowledge Manager, a Program Coordinator, a Technology Manager, and a Communications & Marketing Manager. Their skills are in such fields as organization management, strategic management, youth outreach and development, case management, programming, elementary education, early childhood development, entrepreneurship, music, urban renewal, social policy, women's studies, information technology, Web design, digital art, psychology, and communications.

As the Intel Computer Clubhouse Network has grown, it has continued to attract major funding support. In the beginning, support came from the founding institutions – the Boston Computer Museum and the MIT Media Lab. In 2000, Intel became the title sponsor. That same year, Adobe Systems, Autodesk, Macromedia, Hewlett-Packard, LEGO Systems, and Haworth Furniture, Inc. came on board as sponsors. Since that time, Corel, Harmony Line, the National Science Foundation, and Staples have joined in supporting the Network's efforts (Computer Clubhouse, 2010).

THOUGHT QUESTIONS

1 Was the original idea underlying the Computer Clubhouse a Type A, Type B, or Type C idea? Explain.

2 Are the programs adopted over the years by the Computer Clubhouse in alignment with this social venture's mission? Why or why not?

3 Clearly, the opportunity pursued by the founders of the Computer Clubhouse was a viable one. In hindsight, assess the original idea's social value, market, competitive advantage, sustainability, and overall potential.

4 What is it about this opportunity that has permitted it to grow from a single site to a global network?

VOICES FROM THE FIELD

Allison Lynch, Founder, New York Women's Social Entrepreneurship (NYWSE) Incubator

Allison Lynch had a long-time interest in social entrepreneurship and had on several occasions sought to start her own social venture. Yet, she could never seem to quite get to the point of actually launching one. She holds an MBA and is an otherwise self-assured person; so, what was holding her back? She puzzled over this situation and came to the conclusion that she felt alone, lacking in the support she needed to undertake this kind of endeavor. In her words,

> I had previously been interested in starting several socially oriented enterprises (including leaving a job to investigate such a possibility), but had not taken the final plunge. I wondered why I was hesitating. Was it a lack of gumption? Were the ideas not compelling enough to move me to undertake them fully? Was there another factor? Ultimately, I felt that perhaps the reason was because I felt isolated and lacking connections to information, capital/fundraising sources, legal/tax support, and was uncertain about how I could survive financially in a start-up phase. I also realized that most of my colleagues in graduate business classes were men; I didn't know any women who had started their own social ventures. And I thought—maybe launching a social enterprise could be a better experience for women like me.

These observations led Lynch to her idea: an incubator for women social entrepreneurs. This incubator would empower women to launch social ventures by providing them with knowledge and skills and a support structure within which to work. She pitched the idea to Natalia Oberti Noguera, who leads New York Women Social Entrepreneurs (NYWSE), which is a community of several hundred socially entrepreneurial women in New York City. Noguera liked Lynch's idea and proposed that it be set up as a pilot program under the auspices of NYWSE. Within four months the NYWSE Incubator was born, in January 2009. Allison Lynch had her own social venture and a support structure for launching and building it. Now she could turn her attention to helping other women who found themselves in the same position she had been in before she talked to Noguera.

The NYWSE Incubator's first "class" of social entrepreneurs consisted of six women pursuing opportunities ranging from helping obese women in New York City to lose and keep off weight to providing enhanced educational opportunities for women in India. The six were chosen from a pool of approximately twenty applicants by a panel assembled by Lynch that was tasked with assessing each applicant relative to such criteria as the quality of the opportunity, the entrepreneur's background and projected capability to successfully pursue the opportunity, potential social impact, and so forth.

Each of these social entrepreneurs was matched with a leading female mentor in their field and with a female student apprentice, or "junior partner." This group of three made up the enterprise team for that social venture. This multigenerational approach provides the social entrepreneur with opportunities to mentor and be mentored. It also affords stable, long-term support in an encouraging and safe environment as the entrepreneur pursues her goals.

The Incubator also provided clients with technical training in business and in social entrepreneurship. This training was provided by three partners with whom Lynch developed a relationship: Baruch College's Lawrence N. Field Center for Entrepreneurship and its Small Business Development Center (SBDC); Angela Jia Kim, co-founder of Savor the Success, an online women's entrepreneurship network and successful entrepreneur; and Geri Stengel, adjunct professor of social entrepreneurship at the New School of Social Research, co-founder of the Women's Leadership Exchange, and a successful entrepreneur.

Baruch College provided training in topics such as social enterprise business models, organizational structure (nonprofit, for-profit, hybrid), opportunity assessment, social value proposition, marketing and market research, financing and funding, operations planning, financial statements, impact and scalability, evaluation, key personnel and responsibilities, and assembling advisory boards and boards of directors. Kim provided Savor the Success training. Stengel conducted training in marketing-related topics.

Because these partnerships permitted a volunteer-based program and because the Incubator was launched as a pilot, start-up costs were exceptionally low. This made it possible for the NYWSE Incubator to charge a symbolic participation fee of only $150 per entrepreneur.

The outputs and outcomes of the Incubator's pilot year are impressive. The services of the six social ventures benefited sixty-eight new individuals. Twenty-one new organizations had entered into partnerships with these ventures. A total investment of $15,000 in these ventures had yielded $55,000 in new funding. The participating social ventures had completed business plans, assembled boards of directors, and attracted new paid staff, volunteers, and partners. Two of the client ventures had created first demonstration websites for their Internet-based activities. Allison Lynch expects that these initial successes will multiply over time.

When Lynch reflects on her idea to create an incubator for women social entrepreneurs, she attributes it to her personal experience, her recognition that there were other women who shared that experience, and the support of Natalia Oberti Noguera and the NYWSE. As for Lynch's assessment of the idea as an opportunity, she acknowledges that it was more informal than formal. As she puts it,

> The decision to launch the Incubator came primarily from gut instinct—a strong belief in the need and impact of a women's social entrepreneurship incubator; an impulse of excitement; a trust in my own instincts; and my observations of the dynamics in the target community of women.

Thus, she knew that there was social value to be added in this arena and that a market existed. Through her contacts she knew that nothing like this was being done elsewhere in New York City. At least in the pilot year, financial sustainability was not really an issue. So, in effect, she conducted an opportunity assessment in her head, if not on paper. A strong belief in the "rightness" of the cause and motivation to right the "wrong" should not be discounted, however.

QUESTIONS FOR "CONNECTING THE DOTS"

1   The protocols for assessing ideas as opportunities discussed in this chapter follow a linear, mechanistic approach to problem solving favored by Western societies. In essence, they assume that ideas *exist* in the entrepreneur's environment and must be *found*. An emerging competing school of thought holds that entrepreneurs *create* ideas from the relationships, resources, and experiences resident in their environments—a more organic approach. In your opinion, which of these schools of thought better describes reality, and why?

2   Which opportunity recognition tool discussed in this chapter resonates most for you, and why?

3   If you were to guess, what percentage of social entrepreneurs engage in formal assessment of their ideas as compared with those who do so informally? Explain your reasoning. What are the advantages of each approach? What are the disadvantages?

4   What is the relationship between the social value proposition of a social venture and its mission?

REFERENCES

Austin, J. E. (2006). Three avenues for social entrepreneurship research. In J. Mair, J. Robinson, & K. Hockerts (Eds.). *Social entrepreneurship* (pp. 22–33). New York: Palgrave Macmillan.

Barringer, B. R., & Ireland, R. D. (2008). *Entrepreneurship: Successfully launching new ventures*. Upper Saddle River, NJ: Pearson Prentice Hall.

Bryson, J. M. (1995). *Strategic planning for public and nonprofit organizations*. San Francisco, CA: Jossey-Bass.

Bygrave, W. D., & Zacharakis, A. (2004). *The portable MBA in entrepreneurship* (3rd edn). New York: Wiley.

Bygrave, W. D., & Zacharakis, A. (2008). *Entrepreneurship*. New York: Wiley.

Campbell, D. (2003). Outcomes assessment and the paradox of nonprofit accountability. *Nonprofit Management and Leadership, 12*(3), 243–260.

Christensen, C. M., & Raynor, M. E. (2003). *The innovator's solution: Creating and sustaining successful growth*. Boston, MA: Harvard Business School Press.

Dees, J. G., Emerson, J., & Economy, P. (2001). *Enterprising nonprofits: A toolkit for social entrepreneurs*. New York: Wiley.

Emerson, J., & Bonini, S. (2004). Blended value map. Retrieved from http://www.blendedvalue.org (accessed July 28, 2010).

Fiet, J. O. (2002). *The systematic search for entrepreneurial discoveries*. Westport, CT: Quorum Books.

Garr, R. (1998). Groups that change communities: The computer clubhouse. Retrieved from http://www.grass-roots.org/usa/cluhous.shtml (accessed January 9, 2009).

Johnston, R. (2001). Defining your mission. In J. G. Dees, J. Emerson, & P. Economy (Eds.). *Enterprising nonprofits: A toolkit for social entrepreneurs* (pp. 19–42). New York: Wiley.

Lichtenstein, G. A., & Lyons, T. S. (1996). *Incubating new enterprises: A guide to successful practice*. Washington, DC: Aspen Institute.

Lichtenstein, G. A., & Lyons, T. S. (2001). The entrepreneurial development system: Transforming business talent and community economies. *Economic Development Quarterly, 15*(1), 3–20.

Lichtenstein, G. A., & Lyons, T. S. (2010). *Investing in entrepreneurs: A strategic approach for strengthening your regional and community economy*. Santa Barbara, CA: Praeger/ABC-CLIO.

Longenecker, J. J. G., Moore, C. W., Petty, J. W., & Palich, L. E. (2006). *Small business management: An entrepreneurial emphasis* (13th edn). Mason, OH: Thomson South-Western.

Mariotti, S. (2007). *Entrepreneurship: Starting and operating a small business*. Upper Saddle River, NJ: Pearson Prentice Hall.

Porter, M. E. (2008). The five competitive forces that shape strategy. *Harvard Business Review*, January, p. 86.

Resnick, M., Rusk, N., & Cooke, S. (1999). The computer clubhouse: Technological fluency in the inner city. In D. Schön, B. Sanyal, & W. J. Mitchell (Eds.). *High technology and low-income communities: Prospects for the positive use of advanced information technology* (pp. 263–286). Cambridge, MA: MIT Press.

Robinson, J. (2006). Navigating social and institutional barriers to markets: How social entrepreneurs identify and evaluate opportunities. In J. Mair, J. Robinson, & K. Hockerts (Eds.). *Social entrepreneurship* (pp. 95–120). New York: Palgrave Macmillan.

Sawhill, J. C., & Williamson, D. (2001). Mission impossible? Measuring success in nonprofit organizations. *Nonprofit Management and Leadership, 11*(3), 371–387.

Timmons, J. A., & Spinelli, S. (2007). *New venture creation: Entrepreneurship for the 21st century* (7th edn). New York: McGraw-Hill/Irwin.

Wei-Skillern, J., Austin, J. E., Leonard, H., & Stevenson, H. (2007). *Entrepreneurship in the social sector*. Thousand Oaks, CA: Sage.

Lean Start-up for Social Enterprises

AIM/PURPOSE

This chapter provides an overview of the lean start-up method in relationship to traditional business planning. It highlights the key principles and tools of the lean start-up approach, with a specific focus on the business model canvas. It also examines how two start-ups (Kinvolved and Farmerline) applied the lean start-up approach to their current ventures.

LEARNING OBJECTIVES OF THIS CHAPTER

1. To learn about the key elements of the lean start-up approach compared to traditional business planning.
2. To understand the lean start-up process and construct a business model canvas and/ or lean canvas to develop your venture's hypotheses.
3. To provide examples of entrepreneurs in the field using the lean start-up method to understand their customers and inform their long-term strategy and business plan.

The goal of all successful entrepreneurs is to identify and deliver opportunities that are successful, financially sustainable, and have an impact on the customers and communities they serve. An increasingly popular approach to achieving this goal is the "lean start-up" approach.

The lean start-up phenomenon has gone global and is at the heart of a revolution not only in the realm of business start-up but also new product development and innovation (Blank, 2013). The key to the lean start-up model (and most business modeling tools) is vigorous, ruthless, continuous questioning of the venture's most cherished assumptions (Ries, 2011). Absent very strong market forces, it falls to the entrepreneur, for-profit or non-profit, to keep testing and re-testing what lies beneath their value propositions—if they wish to continue identifying and delivering great value to their stakeholders.

At the beginning of a discussion of the lean start-up model, it is important to clarify what is meant by the term "business model." Business models are the "recipes" for how a venture becomes sustainable economically. They typically have three critical components:

1   *Value identification*—identifying genuine value desired by customers and/or other stakeholders, from their perspective and not that of the entrepreneur.
2   *Value delivery*—figuring out how to deliver that value, once identified, to intended recipients.
3   *Value capture*—if significant value is identified and delivered, rents accrue to the venture and other stakeholders (i.e., who gets paid and how?). The venture's revenue model(s) is usually at the heart of this.

A successful venture needs to develop all three, almost always iteratively through experimentation. The interplay of the three is most likely to evolve, making this a seemingly complex process. Also note that financial and environmental "sustainability" is easily extended to many types of ventures (for profit and non-profit) and makes the process still more complex on the surface but actually offers increased opportunities to design a viable venture.

Entrepreneurship is at the leading edge of teaching, practice, and research in business modeling. These innovative lean start-up tools are practically essential for identifying and validating business opportunities. We expect that this is just the start of developing an even more comprehensive "entrepreneurial" toolkit to promote innovation and to help you start your own venture. However, many aspiring entrepreneurs are thus far surprisingly under-informed about these tools, despite fast-growing interest. Many nascent student entrepreneurs are "winging it" and are hesitant to break away from current conventional business plans and strategic thinking. That said, the new focus on business models is not only popular, it seems to be a powerful strategy.

Steve Blank's new online (and free) *Lean Launchpad* course (check out Udacity, specifically https://www.udacity.com/course/ep245) has already led to multiple successful sustainable technology and customer-driven launches for entrepreneurs globally. In particular, the obsessive focus with creating value for stakeholders seems apt for all types of ventures. As social entrepreneurs look toward this phenomenon, it is clear that there are equally powerful implications for them. However, it remains to be seen how those implications may differ. We next offer a quick overview of the key differences between traditional business planning and the lean start-up process.

THE LEAN START-UP PROCESS VS. TRADITIONAL BUSINESS PLANNING

According to Steve Blank, "No business model survives the first contact with customers." The lean start-up approach asserts the idea that elaborate business plans are an inefficient use of time during the start-up phase. First, lean start-ups use the *business model canvas*[1] to define their new venture with little emphasis on the formal business plan process. Second, while traditional financial accounting was used as a baseline to assess venture value, metrics based on customer acquisition, *churn rate*,[2] and *viralness*[3] are more key indicators. Third, failure is expected and used to help the firm iterate and pivot (referring to a shift in strategy) their ideas to create value within the lean start-up process; whereas, failure in the traditional models means going out of business and ceasing implementation. Finally, lean start-ups iterate their ideas rapidly with the focus on good-enough data while the traditional process relies on measured, complete data, even before the building and testing of the venture's prototype (Blank, 2013).

KEY ELEMENTS OF THE LEAN START-UP

The lean start-up is an approach coined by Eric Ries to build companies and launch products quicker. This method aims to be more in line with customer needs while eliminating long development times and large amounts of funding needed to launch a venture. According to Ries, the lean start-up method rests on five key principles and three key elements:

Key Principles

1 Entrepreneurs are everywhere: Entrepreneurs can come from large established companies or a tiny garage. There is no prerequisite to start your own venture.
2 Entrepreneurship is management: Think of a start-up as an institution that requires management specifically geared to its context.
3 Validated learning: Start-ups exist to learn how to build a sustainable business. This learning can be validated scientifically by running experiments that allow us to test each element of our vision.
4 Innovation accounting: To improve entrepreneurial outcomes, and to hold entrepreneurs accountable, we need to focus on how to measure progress,

---

1 **Business model canvas** is a tool for describing, analyzing, and designing business models.
2 **Churn rate** is the turnover rate of customers who purchase a business's products or services over a specified time period.
3 **Viralness** refers to how rapidly and widely knowledge or purchase of a product or service spreads.

how to setup milestones, how to prioritize work, specific to the start-up context.

5   Build–measure–learn: The fundamental activity of a start-up is to turn ideas into products, measure how customers respond, and then learn whether to *pivot* or *persevere*. All successful start-up processes should be geared to accelerate that feedback loop.

Key Tenets

The lean start-up method addresses the problem that many companies spend months, if not years, building and perfecting robust products and services only to learn that customers want something different. Without customer feedback and input at critical points of development, start-ups risk missing key elements of what customers really want.

Business Modeling

The first step of the lean start-up focuses on the search for the right business model by developing hypotheses. One of the fundamental tools of this approach is the business model canvas. The best way to build a great business model is to ruthlessly identify every possible assumption that underpins the model, drilling down as deeply as possible—then testing each assumption equally ruthlessly and rigorously. If the assumption passes muster, then proceed; if not, pivot. The business model will change dramatically (and swiftly), hence the business model itself is far less important than its evolution, as the entrepreneur works through each section/block of the business model canvas. For a full tutorial on how to use the business model canvas see http://theleanstartup.com/.

Agile Development

When it comes to understanding the venture's potential customers, lean start-ups adopt a "get out of the building" philosophy that enables the entrepreneur to test many of the core assumptions and hypotheses they have about their idea in the marketplace.

Customer Development[4]

Customer development is completed almost entirely outside of the building, in front of customers, stakeholders, and partners as you test your hypotheses with a series of experiments. These tests help you understand and refine who your

---

4 **Customer development:** the formal process of testing your hypotheses.

customers are, what are the problems and potential solutions, and what specific types of changes are needed to improve your product or service based on direct feedback. According to Steve Blank, the founder(s) should be heavily involved in this process in order to change the core of your venture quickly if needed.

Early on, entrepreneurs develop their *MVP*,[5] or *minimum viable product*. It builds on the reality that successful ventures launch "too early" (i.e., fail early, fail fast, learn even faster). By building an MVP, new ventures with their existing, and often limited, resources can test their product and/or service in the marketplace with potential customers, suppliers, and funders, and make iterative and incremental changes. Typically early adopters are the first testers of your MVP. This type of "agile development" enables the start-up to pivot (adapt your business model) and create value for the business and its customers that is further developed as the firm rolls out its business model canvas (Blank, 2013).

"The fundamental activity of a startup is to turn ideas into products, measure how customers respond, and then learn whether to pivot or persevere. All successful startup processes should be geared to accelerate that feedback loop" (Ries, 2011, p. 32). The *build–measure–learn*[6] approach shortens product development cycles and builds products and services that directly meet customers' needs by applying learning, experimentation and iterative product releases.

BUSINESS MODEL CANVAS

In today's rapidly changing business environment, entrepreneurs are now turning to tools such as the business model canvas to cut down on elaborate planning without customer feedback. This alternative to a business plan, which Steve Blank (2013, p. 62) refers to as "a document investors make you read that they don't read," is a visual representation of how a business works to create value. In this section, we will outline the traditional business model canvas and an adaptation called the lean canvas.

The Traditional Canvas

The original business model canvas was developed by Alexander Osterwalder in 2008 to "make strategy, innovation, and entrepreneurship simple, practical and applicable." The canvas is a tool for describing, analyzing, and designing business models (Osterwalder, 2010, p. 18).

---

5 **MVP:** the most basic version of the product or service that has just enough features to provide value to your customers.

6 **Build–measure–learn:** the continuous cycle in which the learning received from customers determines whether you change, tweak, or continue to build your product.

This simple-to-use tool can be described using nine basic building blocks. Mapping these elements out on a pre-structured canvas helps you map, discuss, and design your venture.

1   **Customer Segment:** You start with your customer segments that you want to create value for including paying customers and simple users.
2   **Value Proposition:** For each customer segment, you have a specific value proposition—which are the bundles of products and services that directly create value for your customers.
3   **Channels:** Describe how you interact with your customers and deliver that value.
4   **Customer Relationships:** What type of relationship are you developing with your customers?
5   **Revenue Streams**: How and through which pricing mechanisms are you capturing value?
6   **Key Resources:** What is the infrastructure that you are using to create, deliver, and capture value? Which assets are indispensable in your business model?
7   **Key Activities:** What things do you really need to perform well?
8   **Key Partnerships:** Who can help you leverage your business model? You won't have all resources and be able to perform all activities yourself.
9   **Cost Structure:** Once you understand the other elements of your business and its infrastructure that will help inform the pricing and cost structure.

The Lean Canvas

The lean canvas, developed by Ash Maurya in 2010, is an adaptation of the original business model canvas with a more actionable focus. According to Maurya, "My approach to making the canvas actionable was capturing that which was most uncertain, or more accurately, that which was most risky" (http://leanstack.com/why-lean-canvas/, 2012). Because time is our scarcest resource, the lean canvas recommends that you spend even less time developing the model and focus on empirical testing. The overarching purpose of the canvas is to take a snapshot of your current thinking in order to test and refine it.

Many entrepreneurs have found this variation useful, particularly for social enterprises and/or non-profits, who need to specifically identify their problem statement, mission (solution), and key metrics. There are four boxes that are different in the lean canvas adaptation:

1   **Problem** replaces Key Partners
2   **Solution** replaces Key Activities
3   **Key Metrics** replaces Key Resources
4   **Unfair Advantage** (competitive advantage) replaces Customer Relationships

The Business Model Canvas

Key Partners

Who are our Key Partners?
Who are our key suppliers?
Which Key Resources are we acquiring from partners?
Which Key Activities do partners perform?

MOTIVATIONS FOR PARTNERSHIPS:
Optimization and economy
Reduction of risk and uncertainty
Acquisition of particular resources and activities

Key Activities

What Key Activities do our Value Propositions require?
Our Distribution Channels?
Customer Relationships?
Revenue streams?

CATEGORIES
Production
Problem solving
Platform/network

Key Resources

What Key Resources do our Value Propositions require?
Our Distribution Channels?
Customer Relationships?
Revenue Streams?

TYPES OF RESOURCES
Physical
Intellectual (brand patents, copyrights, data)
Human
Financial

Value Propositions

What value do we deliver to the customer?
Which one of our customer's problems are we helping to solve?
What bundles of products and services are we offering to each Customer Segment?
Which customer needs are we satisfying?

CHARACTERISTICS
Newness
Performance
Customization
"Getting the job done"
Design
Brand/status
Price
Cost reduction
Risk reduction
Accessibility
Convenience/usability

Customer Relationships

What type of relationship does each of our Customer Segments expect us to establish and maintain with them?
Which ones have we established?
How are they integrated with the rest of our business model?
How costly are they?

EXAMPLES
Personal assistance
Dedicated personal assistance
Self-service
Automated services
Communities
Co-creation

Channels

Through which Channels do our Customer Segments want to be reached?
How are we reaching them now?
How are our Channels integrated?
Which ones work best?
Which ones are most cost-efficient?
How are we integrating them with customer routines?

CHANNEL PHASES:
1. Awareness
   How do we raise awareness about our company's products and services?
2. Evaluation
   How do we help customers evaluate our organization's Value Propositions?
3. Purchase
   How do we allow customers to purchase specific products and services?
4. Delivery
   How do we deliver a Value Proposition to customer?
5. After sales
   How do we provide post-purchase customer support?

Customer Segments

For whom are we creating value?
Who are our most important customers?

Mass market
Niche market
Segmented
Diversified
Multi-sided platform

Cost Structure

What are the most important costs inherent in our business model?
Which Key Resources are most expensive?
Which Key Activities are most expensive?

IS YOUR BUSINESS MORE:
Cost Driven (leanest cost structure, low price value proposition, maximum automation, extensive outsourcing)
Value Driven (focused on value creation, premium value proposition)

SAMPLE CHARACTERISTICS:
Fixed costs (salaries, rents, utilities)
Variable costs
Economies of scale
Economies of scope

Revenue Streams

For what value are our customers really willing to pay?
For what do they currently pay?
How are they currently paying?
How would they prefer to pay?
How much does each Revenue Stream contribute to overall revenues?

TYPES:
Asset sale
Usage fee
Subscription fees
Lending/renting/leasing
Licensing
Brokerage fees
Advertising

FIXED PRICING
List price
Product feature dependent
Customer segment dependent
Volume dependent

DYNAMIC PRICING
Negotiation (bargaining)
Yield management
Real-time market

WWW.BUSINESSMODELGENERATION.COM

FIGURE 4.1 The Business Model Canvas

Source: from Wikimedia Common (free to share).

The lean canvas can be filled out in any order, but the recommended chronology follows:

1 **Customer Segment:** The customer segment box drives the rest of the canvas. First, you split the customer box into specific customer segments. It is much easier to target customer attributes when you understand their nuances and preferences. Next, you pick the strongest customer segment to focus on for the canvas, while making sure to make the distinction between customers and users (customers pay and users do not). It is also useful to consider who the early adopters of your product might be. The order in which you fill out the Problem and Customer Segment boxes can be switched.

2 **Problem:** Determine what the top three problems are that your product or service addresses. It is helpful to refine your list of problems by continuously drilling down to the root cause of the problem to ensure that you are targeting something specific. You can also think about what the current possible alternatives are without your product and how do customers currently deal with this problem.

3 **Solution:** This box helps you determine what your MVP is, which is the most basic solution that creates value for the customer. In this box, focus on the top three simple things that the MVP does.

FIGURE 4.2 The Lean Canvas

Source: Lean Canvas is adapted from The Business Model Canvas (http://www.businessmodelgeneration.com) and is licensed under the Creative Commons Attribution-Share Alike 3.0 Un-ported License.

4   **Unique Value Proposition (UVP):** This section is considered the most difficult because you should determine what makes your product or service stand out to customers. Maurya recommends crafting your UVP around the top problem and how the customer can immediately understand how it creates value in the most concrete and specific way possible.

5   **Revenue Streams:** When determining your revenue streams, it is helpful to think about value-based pricing against existing alternatives. It is also useful to understand how the way you price your product determines what types of customers you want to attract.

6   **Channels:** This box is the most risky section because you need to have access to your customers in order to gain any momentum. Think through what your immediate versus scalable channels are.

7   **Key Metrics:** This section explains how you are measuring success in two ways. First, what key activity/action will you use to measure your value proposition? Second, how do you define success and what do you need to achieve to make your product or venture worthwhile?

8   **Cost Structure:** When developing your cost structure, outline your fixed and variable costs, key resources, and all other relevant start-up costs. It is useful to consider your break-even point based on your pricing structure and how many customers you would need to be "successful" based on your key metrics.

9   **Unfair Advantage:** This box is also called your competitive advantage and helps you identify how you would defend against competition. What is something about your product, service, or venture that cannot be easily copied or bought?

VOICES FROM THE FIELD

The Lean Start-up in Action with Kinvolved

To gain a closer look at the lean start-up approach in action, we interviewed one of our entrepreneurial teams in New York University's inaugural 2013 (NYU) Summer Launchpad Accelerator program about their venture, Kinvolved. Summer Launchpad is a ten-week intensive program that supports start-up ventures through the notoriously difficult stage of early development and provides them with resources, personalized instruction, guidance, and connections to increase the likelihood of their success. Participating teams are steeped in lean start-up principles using techniques for testing hypotheses, experimentation, and iteration as they search for a commercially viable business model. The Kinvolved team's responses to our questions follow.

1.   *What is Kinvolved? What customer problem does it solve? What success have you had so far?*

Kinvolved, a New York-based social venture, provides a hybrid model of technology and human capital to help schools better engage families to drive student impact. The company has developed an app to enable instant communication between schools and families, complemented with intensive training and coaching to ensure the technology is used to inform interventions that drive measurable improvement in attendance, behavior, and academics for students.

Kinvolved helps save teachers time communicating essential information to families about student progress by enabling instant one-to-one or mass text messaging. Through the app, school staff can collaboratively keep parent contact information updated. In the high-need communities in which Kinvolved's customers exist, parents routinely change phone plans, and become unreachable. Kinvolved's app can help (1) detect invalid numbers, and (2) enable educators and administrators to collaborate by consistently updating parent contact information shared by all users. Finally, Kinvolved goes above competitive products, by providing clients with the training and coaching they need to use the technology effectively and efficiently, and to strategize communication that creates positive relationships with families, rather than continuing the status quo, which is often hostile relationships between the two parties.

Research shows that parent engagement is the best way to keep students in school, but 53 percent of dropouts report that their schools never informed their families when they missed class, failed class, or even dropped out.[i] Attendance is the top indicator of graduation, but more than 7.5M[ii] students miss a month of school annually, and many parents don't even know if their children have shown up to class. It is essential that schools have effective communications tools and the training and support to use these tools to drive outcomes. Kinvolved is starting by helping schools increase student attendance.

i   Bridgeland, John, et al. (2006). The Bill & Melinda Gates Foundation. The Silent Epidemic: Perspectives of High School Dropouts. https://docs.gatesfoundation.org/Documents/thesilentepidemic3-06final.pdf
ii Toppo, Greg. (2010). *USA Today*. Study: 7.5 million students miss a month of school each year. http://usatoday30.usatoday.com/news/education/story/2012-05-17/study-chronic-school-absenteeism/55030638/1

Since launching its first beta test in an NYC public elementary school in early 2013, Kinvolved has grown to work with more than 200 schools and youth programs serving high-need, urban communities nationwide, as of August 2015. To date, Kinvolved has *proven results*, including 90 percent of teachers reporting better communication with families, 75 percent higher parent attendance at school conferences, and a 12 percent increase in homework completion. In addition, the team and founders have won the Teach for America Social Innovation Award, Milken PennGSE Grand Prize, Robin Hood College Success Prize, NYU Berkeley Center Social Innovation Competition, and University of Pennsylvania Policy Challenge. Co-founders Miriam Altman and Alexandra Meis have been named 30 Under 30 most influential in Education by *Forbes* in 2015, company covered in *Forbes*, *Business Insider*, on NPR's Marketplace, Fox National News, PBS, and named on the list of 30 Female Saas Founders in NYC You Should Know.

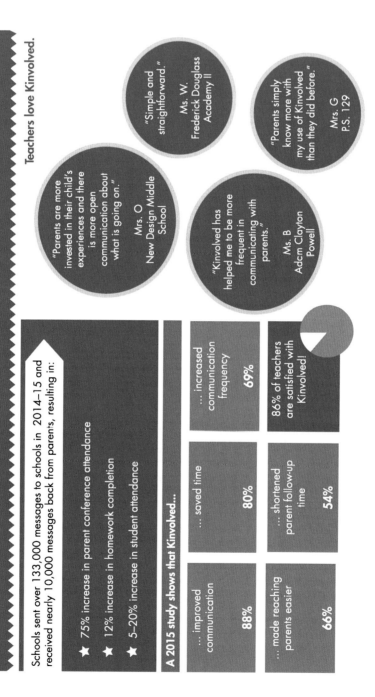

Teachers love Kinvolved.

Schools sent over 133,000 messages to schools in 2014–15 and received nearly 10,000 messages back from parents, resulting in:

★ 75% increase in parent conference attendance
★ 12% increase in homework completion
★ 5–20% increase in student attendance

A 2015 study shows that Kinvolved...

... improved communication
88%

... saved time
80%

... increased communication frequency
69%

... made reaching parents easier
66%

... shortened parent follow-up time
54%

86% of teachers are satisfied with Kinvolved!

"Parents are more invested in their child's experiences and there is more open communication about what is going on."
Mrs. O
New Design Middle School

"Simple and straightforward."
Ms. W.
Frederick Douglass Academy II

"Parents simply know more with my use of Kinvolved than they did before."
Mrs. G
P.S. 129

"Kinvolved has helped me to be more frequent in communicating with parents."
Ms. B
Adcm Clayton Powell

FIGURE 4.3 Why Does Attendance Matter?

2. *How have you initially benefited from learning the lean start-up process?*

Kinvolved has consistently interviewed customers and watched them use the apps to identify user challenges and identify new features that would improve their satisfaction with the product. We have developed a new role, titled Community Specialist, for which we hire individuals to work with our clients to gather and report feedback to our Product Team. Our Product Team develops our product roadmap, including prioritization of new features, based on the volume of feedback we gather from users about a specific function list. This process enables the company to remain competitive and to retain our customer base.

3. *Which lean start-up principles and methodologies have you already implemented in your business planning and strategy?*

Kinvolved relies on customer feedback to consistently innovate and improve its software program and three-part model according to consumer and user desires. Kinvolved's cycle is: build the program, test it with users and consumers, then innovate and iterate based upon the feedback to continually develop the best program at the lowest cost by bypassing development of features that consumers do not directly request.

The Launchpad has allowed Kinvolved to consider and focus on the strongest value propositions, consider target customer segments, and develop a customer profile and the process of getting the program into the hands of customers and users in the simplest way possible.

4. *What recommendations would you offer aspiring entrepreneurs based on what you have learned in starting Kinvolved?*

Kinvolved has been successful because the team has built and deeply engaged with its strong networks to meet mentors, potential customers, and fellow entrepreneurs. Relationship building has been key to Kinvolved's preliminary success, and sets Kinvolved apart from potential competitors. The Kinvolved team has taken every opportunity to meet with advisors and mentors to acquire the knowledge of the business sector that the co-founding team lacks. Kinvolved is never afraid to ask for advice from seasoned professionals, and this has served the team very well. There are many opportunities for entrepreneurs to gain knowledge and services at a free or reduced cost, and part of finding these opportunities is through strong networks and relationships.

CONCLUSION

An exciting, and highly effective, alternative to the traditional business planning approach to business start-up is the lean start-up model. It focuses on developing the product and the enterprise through experimentation in the marketplace that allows the entrepreneur to fine-tune her/his offering to the needs and desires of the customer. In doing so, it emphasizes business models over business plans. What could be more truly entrepreneurial than challenging assumptions, experimentation, learning from failure, and adding value in a sustainable way?

QUESTIONS FOR "CONNECTING THE DOTS"

1   In this chapter, what is meant by the term "business model"?
2   What are the three components of a business model?
3   How does the lean start-up process differ from traditional business planning?
4   What are the core principles of the lean start-up?
5   Describe some of the elements of the traditional canvas? How does the lean canvas differ from the traditional canvas?

Case Study 4.1

Farmerline

FIGURE 4.4   Weather Forecast

For a classic example of the effective use of the business model canvas, we interviewed the Founder and CEO of Farmerline, an award-winning social enterprise based in Ghana that empowers rural farmers with critical weather, market, and farming information. Farmerline's long-term mission is to empower small-scale farmers to become more prosperous by using technology and increased information access to improve their harvest and income. From 2012 to 2013, Farmerline served over 4,000 farmers and planned to reach over 10,000 by the spring of 2015. In addition, Farmerline has received international recognition and awards from the World Bank, the U.S. State Department Apps4Africa Competition, the Bill and Melinda Gates Foundation, Echoing Green, and many other global social impact organizations.

In the early stages of Farmerline's business development in 2012, Laura Manley worked with Farmerline to begin testing their business model canvas hypotheses and refine their implementation strategy. The interview with Farmerline's Founder and CEO Mr. Alloysius Attah follows.

VOICES FROM THE FIELD

Introduction to the Business Model Canvas

In the beginning, we weren't comfortable writing a business plan because we thought it was a waste of time and, on top of that, very difficult. I had just graduated from college with a degree in natural resource management and my teammates were specialized in computer programming and engineering. We decided to take a training on creating sustainable business models from the World Wide Web Foundation and there we were introduced to the business model canvas. During the training, we spent less than an hour putting our first draft of the canvas together. Since then, we have iterated on it hundreds of times. The canvas really helped us think about the company in a new way that other tools hadn't. It also helped us get additional funding because it prompted us with questions that funders and competitions usually ask for such as: How do you make money? Who are your partners? How do you keep in touch with your customers?

Understanding Your Customer Segments

One key part is knowing your various customer segments and your key value proposition for each type of customer. In the beginning, we were really motivated to sell to farmers directly. We came to realize that this actually takes a very long time and that we needed to start somewhere else. We decided that our customers could actually be the businesses that work with the farmers, instead of the farmers directly. We also realized that farmers were a beneficiary of the work that we did, instead of a direct customer. By redefining our customer segment, we made significant changes to the rest of our strategy and where we wanted to focus our energies in the first years. We would like to work directly with farmers as a long-term strategy, but for now we are building the capacity to serve them through our current customers. As of now, we are selling our technologies and content to agricultural companies, NGOs, and food dealers that work directly with farmers.

Refining Your Unique Value Proposition

The business model canvas helped us match our customer segments with our unique value proposition. As a result of having to think through the key attributes of our customer segments, we were able to think about what would add unique value to our customers on a more granular level. After several iterations of our unique value proposition, we decided we want to do two specific things: (1) create better mobile communication channels for businesses that interact with illiterate communities, and (2) develop services to help farmers increase their yield and profits.

Leveraging Partners

The business model canvas made us think about our partners in a different way. When we started, we thought about doing everything ourselves, in most cases. We found out very quickly that this was going to be impossible if we wanted to scale and hit our goals. When we completed the business model canvas, it was the first time we thought seriously about the partnerships box and what that meant for our work. What were the more efficient gateways we could work through?

We now have a partnership with the Ghanaian Ministry of Food and Agriculture using their open data, instead of making it ourselves. We have partnerships with NGOs, research institutions, and USAID-funded projects that we exchange experience, skills, and information with. The incentive for them is that they get our technology to help them do their work better and in turn, we get free content and best practices for farmers. We also have good connections with agricultural extension agents and agricultural businesses, so we are able to work with a pre-existing delivery and distribution system, instead of establishing one by ourselves. All of these partnerships save us a lot of time, energy, and money.

Over the past year, we have worked with approximately 2500 farmers that produce maize, rice, and fish. We would like to expand and begin reaching cocoa farmers, and this is only possible through a partnership. We are developing a plan with another organization to serve 10,000 cocoa farmers over two years with 50 percent switching to paying customers by the end of the twenty-four months. That is the power of partnerships—we can't go at this by ourselves if we want to achieve big goals. We can scale quicker and faster when we align our visions.

Using the Business Model Canvas for Projects

The business model canvas has been very helpful to us as an organization; so, we teach our team members how to use it for our various projects inside the company as well. We are currently working on a project with the European Union to provide more accurate weather data for farmers across Sub-Saharan Africa in their local language. We are asking each team to develop their own canvas for their project with a solid unique value proposition that fits in with the general goals and objectives of the overall company. For example, we have specific goals for each quarter (i.e., reach X number of famers and X organizations use our services). We use the canvas to develop the moving parts to make sure we hit our goals. It also really encourages the team members to think through all parts of their project.

Recommendations for Social Entrepreneurs

Building a company is a continuous process. You have to keep changing every day and every week. Even if you spend a lot of time on something, you have to be willing to change it. That is the iterative process of a start-up. For example, you will meet new partners and find out that there is a better channel for you to connect with customers through. You may change who your customers are and that changes everything. The business model canvas made us think about all the different parts of Farmerline in ways that add value to each area. This is a very important step. We thought about new ways of interacting with customers and partners; we thought about how to go to market faster through the most efficient and appropriate channels; we thought about how to get a higher return on investment by leveraging available resources. At the end of the day, the most important thing is to listen and learn from the field.

REFERENCES

Blank, S. (2013). Why the lean start-up changes everything. *Harvard Business Review* 91(5), 63–72.

Maurya, A. (2012). *Running lean: Iterate from plan A to a plan that works* (revised/expanded ed.). Sebastopol, CA: O'Reilly.

Ries, E. (2011). *The lean startup: How today's entrepreneurs use continuous innovation to create radically successful businesses*. New York: Crown Publishing.

Developing a Strategic Plan for a Social Venture

AIM/PURPOSE

The central point of the chapter is the focus and alignment of the social venture's mission or vision with its consideration of its resources and operational strategy. A discussion of the implementation and action planning of the social firm's strategy from initial concept summary and opportunity to financial plan is presented. Additionally, a firm's development of its theory of change and its elements are also discussed. Finally, an example of a social venture plan to review and critique is presented.

LEARNING OBJECTIVES FOR THIS CHAPTER

1. To learn about the importance of strategic planning to a new social venture.
2. To gain an understanding of the relevant information needed within a social venture plan.
3. To understand how to develop an initial concept summary for a social venture.
4. To construct a framework and steps for structuring a social venture plan.
5. To learn how to put all the social venture plan sections together in a compelling and concise manner.
6. To provide an example of a social venture plan to review and critique.

THE IMPORTANCE OF SOCIAL VENTURE PLANNING

As highlighted in our previous chapter and the lean start-up approach, most social entrepreneurs will agree that the value of developing a social venture strategy does not necessarily lie in having a finished plan in hand; rather, the real value comes from the process of thinking about and researching the social venture in a strategic and systematic way. The process of planning can assist you in thoroughly understanding the social problem you hope to solve and the resources you need to launch, develop, and sustain your business.

Strategic planning requires taking a long-range view of the social venture and developing the vision to guide operations (Brinkerhoff, 2000; Bryson, 2004). It involves identifying opportunities and threats in the external environment, and assessing how the venture's internal and external strengths and weaknesses can be leveraged to take advantage of the opportunities and minimize the threats. Although a comprehensive plan may be written, such a plan does not take the place of strategic planning—an activity that should be ongoing throughout the life cycle of the new social venture (Bryson, 1995, 2004). Many of the same components and framework on the lean start-up approach can be integrated into the social venture plan itself.

Research has shown that new social ventures that have a strategy and formal plan outperform those firms that do not (Miller & Cardinal, 1994; Rogers, Miller, & Judge, 1999). There are four major reasons why entrepreneurs and managers of new social ventures should embrace planning:

1   The probability for success and sustainability increases.
2   Managerial leaders can more effectively adapt to change.
3   Planning helps provide a meaningful context and direction for employee and volunteer work.
4   Planning helps align controls to key social and economic objectives.

Like most strategic planning, it also assists social entrepreneurs in developing their social venture business plan in meeting the demands of the social venture market, potential investors, and employees. Despite the critiques of business plans, either traditional or social (Honig, 2004), numerous practitioners expound the benefits behind using them (Sherman, 2007). "Good intentions without rigorous analysis and smart strategy lead to a waste of scarce resources" (Brock & Ashoka, 2008). In addition to information found in a typical business plan, social venture business plans should include:

- Social or environmental innovation: A clear understanding of the social or environmental need or problem it seeks to address, the feasibility of the innovation, and the economic and social or environmental drivers of the business model.
- Social or environmental impact: A practicable approach to measuring organizational outcomes and long-term impact. A social return on investment (SROI) should be demonstrated with a framework that assesses the double or triple bottom-line impact (social, economic and/or environmental).
- Sustainability/scale: The concept business model and how likely it is to make a substantial contribution toward the solution of the need or problem that can

be sustained for a period of time consistent with achieving its social or environmental impact.

To initially begin thinking about the formal plan itself, it is useful to consider first the overall concept and define the social venture opportunity. As is shown in Figure 5.1, we have a number of core questions that social entrepreneurs may follow as they embark on defining their social venture concept.

1. New social venture idea

   a. The big idea/your solution: Describe the service or product, its unique social value benefit.
   b. What social innovation(s) is this venture leveraging? How does this social innovation address the problem or need?
   c. Who is your customer that is in need of your service or product? Is there more than one customer group? (Remember to differentiate between the customer who pays, and the end user of your service or product.)

2. Social venture (sustainability) model

   a. What are your potential sources of revenue and initial funding?
   b. What are your cash needs for the first year of operations? How can you get there?
   c. What are your initial financial projections? Provide a simple income statement with revenue, cost of goods sold, other expenses, and projected margins.
   d. How do you plan to scale and grow the venture?

3. Market analysis

   a. Who is the present competition and possible new entrants? Consider other solutions that exist and already solve your problem/need.
   b. What is your competitive advantage? Is this advantage sustainable?
   c. What are the critical success factors?
   d. What are the critical risks and how, if possible, will you manage them?
   e. What is the appropriate segment of customers?
   f. What is the marketing plan?

4. Operations and social impact measurement

   a. How does this business work? Identify: development/logistics/human resources/physical facilities/operating and sales cycle necessary to fulfill the strategy and mission of the venture.
   b. Articulate milestones and longer-term goals for your new venture. What is your current status?

5. Management

   a. What are the current team's qualifications for executing this plan successfully? (Consider personal connection to mission, background, experience, expertise, network, and advisors.)
   b. What is your initial management and governance structure?
   c. Who are the necessary key hires? Key partnerships?

FIGURE 5.1   Writing a Concept Summary for Your Social Venture: Questions to Consider before Writing Your Plan

DEVELOPING A SOCIAL VENTURE PLAN FOR A SOCIAL VENTURE: FROM OPPORTUNITY TO FINANCIAL PLAN

Once the social entrepreneur has thought about her or his concept, many of the answers can be integrated within the process and steps for writing a social venture business plan. As the social entrepreneur embarks on this process, she or he can follow the following steps and questions in developing a coherent, concise, and compelling strategy. These steps and process can then be used to customize the social venture plan, as shown later in the chapter with the Loyal Label business plan.

1   What is the social problem your social venture would like to solve?
2   What is your vision and mission?
3   What is your theory of change—your social impact theory?
4   What is your business model?
5   Who is your competition?
6   Who is on your team and your operational plan?
7   What is your growth strategy (how do you plan to scale and replicate your operations)?
8   How will you assess and measure your social impact?
9   What is your financial plan?

We shall discuss each of these steps in further detail, starting with the problem and opportunity.

1. What Is the Social Problem Your Social Venture Would Like to Solve?

What specific problem does your idea solve? Why is it important? What is the scale of the problem? What are the contributing factors to the problem? Why is it solvable? Zahra, Rawhouser, Bhawe, Neubaum, and Hayton (2008) have identified these five core areas that make a promising social opportunity (as shown in Figure 5.2), which overlap with many of the features discussed in Chapter 3.
    More specifically, these dimensions include:

- Prevalence—how rampant is the social problem or need in society?
- Relevance—does the aspiring entrepreneur have the necessary knowledge, skills, and abilities (KSAs) to effectively solve the problem and launch the social venture?
- Radicalness—how creative and innovative is the solution to solve the social problem?

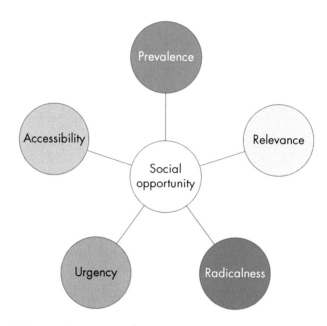

FIGURE 5.2 Social Venture Opportunity Characteristics

■ Urgency—does the social problem need a quick, immediate response by the social venture team?

■ Accessibility—what is the level of difficulty in addressing a social need through traditional welfare mechanisms, including government interventions or foundation support? For example, if the government has difficulty in effectively solving a social problem, there is a need and opportunity for outside assistance on the part of the social entrepreneur to arrive at a new solution through the social venture.

VOICES FROM THE FIELD

From Prevalence to Accessibility: A Social Venture Opportunity: Greening the Desert

"It is not possible to know what is possible," says Frances Moore Lappé, author of the best-seller *Diet for a Small Planet* and eighteen other books on hunger, poverty, and environmental crises. The story of Yacouba Sawadogo, an indefatigable farmer in Burkina Faso in West Africa, is a striking testimony to this notion. Burkina Faso lies in a region of Africa known as the Sahel, a semi-arid zone between the Sahara

Desert and the lush savannas of Central and Southern Africa. From the late 1960s to the early 1980s this region experienced rapid encroachment by the Sahara Desert. This resulted in a famine that killed 100,000 people and left another 750,000 people on food aid. Millions of residents in Niger, Mali, Burkina Faso, Chad, and Mauritania abandoned their engulfed farms and moved to nearby cities, putting further pressures on resources.

Yacouba Sawadogo was among the few who decided to remain on his farm and dedicate his life to "greening the desert." In 1981, he, along with a small group of farmers, began experimenting with ancient techniques to restore the soil. There were two simple techniques at the core of their approach. The first was called *cordons pierreux*, which involved laying long lines of stones (each about the size of a fist) on the field. These cordons would cause rainfall to pause long enough to percolate through the soil. Seeds would be sowed along these lines of stones, and growing plants would slow the water flow even further. Within a few years, a simple line of rocks could restore an entire field. The second approach was to hack thousands of foot-deep holes (*zaï*) in the fields during the dry season. Each *zaï* would be pitted with manure, which attracts termites. The termites would digest the manure, making nutrients more available. In each hole, Sawadogo would plant a tree. Within three years, Sawadogo had transformed a piece of barren land into a 12-hectare productive farm and forest with a large variety of species.

While Sawadogo was initially dismissed by his peers, his success did not go unnoticed, and his approach went viral. Sawadogo went on a campaign to educate farmers across the region on his approach. It is estimated that in less than twenty years, over half a million hectares of desert has been converted to fertile fields by indigenous methods in Burkina Faso and Niger, affecting over 3 million lives. Desertification is still often viewed by experts as an irreversible process triggered by declining rainfall and destructive farming methods. However, teams of researchers from University College London, the University of Copenhagen, and the Free University, Amsterdam, assert that satellite images indicate that there has been a steady reduction in "bare ground" with "vegetation cover, including bushes and trees, on the rise in the dunes." This is being witnessed across the Sahel from the Atlantic Ocean to the Red Sea, 6,000 kilometers away. Today, a variety of aid organizations ranging from the World Wide Web Foundation to the United Nations are studying these ancient greening techniques and working with farmers across the region to help implement them. There is little question that stories like that of Yacouba Sawadogo are what Margaret Mead had in mind when she said, "Never doubt that a small group of thoughtful, committed citizens can change the world; indeed, it's the only thing that ever has."

Source: Hans Taparia, March 28, 2010 (used with permission).

2. What Is Your Vision and Mission?

Once the social problem has been identified and the opportunity to create a venture is seen as innovative and sustainable, and can potentially be scaled to other regions, the social entrepreneur will want to develop both the vision and the mission of what her or his social venture does. As discussed in Chapter 3, developing a vision can also give an image of the change the social entrepreneur seeks to create through the business. Consider what the world could be if the idea or solution were implemented. Ultimately, a vision should motivate and drive the social entrepreneur and the team in the same direction. An example of a vision from the Network for Teaching Entrepreneurship (NFTE), an organization dedicated to offering entrepreneurship education to underserved youth, is "Every young person will find a pathway to prosperity." A vision also helps the social entrepreneur think about the overall mission of the social venture. It more specifically addresses how she or he can implement the vision and objectives that reinforce how the social venture will operate in solving a pressing social problem. Carrying the NFTE example forward, its mission is as follows:

> NFTE provides entrepreneurship education programs to young people from low-income communities.
>
> *How We Do It . . . NFTE achieves its mission by:*
>
> - Creating engaging, experiential curricula and tools to improve academic, business, and life skills
> - Training and supporting teachers and youth professionals
> - Partnering with schools, community-based organizations, and post-secondary institutions
> - Offering volunteers meaningful opportunities that connect students to real world experiences
> - Linking the educational and business worlds in the classroom and beyond
> - Providing services to program graduates
> - Demonstrating outcomes of entrepreneurship education through research
> - Building public awareness to expand entrepreneurship education.

3. What Is the Theory of Change—the Social Impact Theory?

Based on the understanding of the problem and the vision or mission, what is the theory about which actions will lead to the results the social entrepreneur wants to achieve? A theory of change offers a clear road map to achieving results by identifying the preconditions, pathways, and interventions necessary for an initiative's success. It is a statement about causality. Some examples from social ventures include the following:

- habitat for humanity: providing families with simple, decent, affordable housing will break the cycle of generational poverty;
- low-cost eyeglasses: delivering affordable corrective eyewear to the 1 billion people in the developing world who need it and can't get it will raise the standard of living in those countries through enhanced educational and employment opportunities for the wearers;
- charter schools: offering parents and students choice in public schools creates competition, which will spur innovation and lead to higher performing schools and better educational outcomes.

Placing the Social Venture's Theory of Change into a Logic Model

In conveying a venture's theory of change, it is helpful to articulate it with a logic model that involves all key stakeholders, including your team, employees, volunteers, advisors, and investors (Anderson, 2004; Clark & Anderson, 2004). Developing a theory of change and a logic model is a process of aligning stakeholder goals and expectations with the strategic planning process and business strategy by (1) making underlying assumptions about cause and effect explicit, and (2) examining the dynamics that make the social venture successful on a blended value basis.

Essentially, a logic model places the social venture's theory of change into action by communicating what are the key resources needed to begin solving the social problem and what are the core activities that need to be in place in order to solve the problem (Anderson, 2004; Clark & Anderson, 2004). Once the resources and activities have been articulated, the social entrepreneur and her or his team can begin examining what the short-term outputs (immediate results that will be realized by the social venture) and the short- and long-term outcomes (what specific changes they hope to see after one to three years and four to six years) as well as overall impact (changes that the social entrepreneur would like to see seven to ten years after the solution and venture has been launched). The following steps as well as Figure 5.3 show the framework of the logic model that can be utilized by social entrepreneurs as they communicate their own theory of change to their stakeholders and community.

1   Resources. Consider: in order to accomplish our set of activities, we will need the following: This can include finding your management team, employees, volunteers as well as securing financial capital to launch the social venture.

2   Activities. Consider: in order to address our problem, we will accomplish all of the following activities: This is basically your operating model or your working business plan in action. Consider all the strategic planning and processes, marketing, operations, personnel, etc. that need to be implemented for the launch of the social venture.

3   Outputs. Consider: we expect that once accomplished, these activities will produce the following evidence of service delivery. This could include number of graduates from an adult literacy program; number of solar panels installed in homes and businesses; number of workers trained in basic accounting and financial skills.

4   Short- and long-term outcomes. Consider: we expect that if accomplished, these activities will lead to the following changes in one to three years, then four to six years. This could include: greater likelihood of securing employment, higher intentions in launching own business, and improved emotional well-being and social behavior.

5   Impact. Consider: we expect that if accomplished, these activities will lead to the following changes in seven to ten years. This could include: lifelong employment and job security, increased pay and healthcare coverage, and less dependence on the government welfare system.

Resources (Resource Strategy)	Activities (Operating Model)	Outputs	Short- and Long-Term Outcomes	Impact
In order to accomplish our set of activities we will need the following:	In order to address our problem, we will accomplish the following activities:	We expect that once accomplished these activities will produce the following evidence of service delivery	We expect that if accomplished, these activities will lead to the following changes in 1–3 then 4–6 years	We expect if accomplished these activities will lead to the following changes in 7–10 years
Tangibles: ■ Funding Intangibles ■ People (social capital)	Assembling the Business Plan Itself: ■ Vision & Mission ■ Strategy (includes Go-to-market strategy, marketing plan ■ Team and Operational Plan ■ Growth Strategy ■ Measuring Results ■ Financial Plan			

FIGURE 5.3 The Logic Model Framework

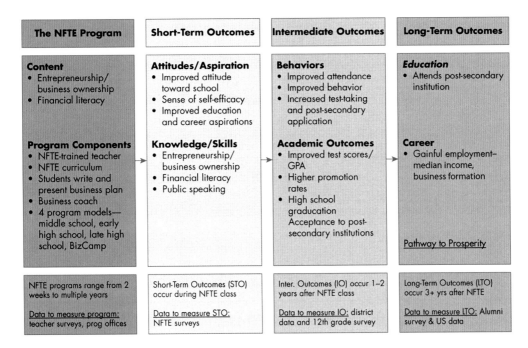

The NFTE Program	Short-Term Outcomes	Intermediate Outcomes	Long-Term Outcomes
Content • Entrepreneurship/ business ownership • Financial literacy	**Attitudes/Aspiration** • Improved attitude toward school • Sense of self-efficacy • Improved education and career aspirations	**Behaviors** • Improved attendance • Improved behavior • Increased test-taking and post-secondary application	**Education** • Attends post-secondary institution
Program Components • NFTE-trained teacher • NFTE curriculum • Students write and present business plan • Business coach • 4 program models—middle school, early high school, late high school, BizCamp	**Knowledge/Skills** • Entrepreneurship/ business ownership • Financial literacy • Public speaking	**Academic Outcomes** • Improved test scores/ GPA • Higher promotion rates • High school graduacation Acceptance to post-secondary institutions	**Career** • Gainful employment– median income, business formation Pathway to Prosperity
NFTE programs range from 2 weeks to multiple years Data to measure program: teacher surveys, prog offices	Short-Term Outcomes (STO) occur during NFTE class Data to measure STO: NFTE surveys	Inter. Outcomes (IO) occur 1–2 years after NFTE class Data to measure IO: district data and 12th grade survey	Long-Term Outcomes (LTO) occur 3+ yrs after NFTE Data to measure LTO: Alumni survey & US data

FIGURE 5.4   An Example of NFTE's Logic Model from Activities to Long-Term Outcomes

Source: NFTE

Finally, referring back to NFTE, Figure 5.4 displays NFTE's own theory of change and their logic model. Under the NFTE program they include components of their resources and activities leading to their short-term outcomes (many of these are outputs) as well as intermediate outcomes and long-term outcomes (in this case, their impact).

4. What Is the Social Venture's Business Model?

In this next step in developing the social venture plan, considerations should be made as to how the social entrepreneur will put her or his theory into action and develop the firm's business model (Magretta, 2002; Seelos & Mair, 2005). Is there an earned revenue stream? In what ways can the social venture sustain itself financially beyond just donations and philanthropic support? Careful attention should be paid to how the venture can generate revenue to support all of the various expenses and costs involved in implementing and pursuing its mission and strategy. The following is an example of the business model for a T-shirt company with a social mission called Loyal Label (see the full case study at the end of this chapter):

> Loyal Label will operate primarily as an e-commerce business, making most of our revenues through our website www.loyallabel.org. After

products are produced, they will be shipped to our storage facilities in Atlanta, Georgia, where a Loyal Label staff member will manage shipping and order fulfillment. Additionally, we will generate revenue through product sales during our T-Shirt Truck Tour, a three month long tour visiting college campuses across the country. The Truck Tour will put our products in the hands of consumers, build brand awareness, create a connection between consumers and the company's founders who will be on the tour, and literally, drive sales. Finally, a portion of our revenue will come from larger orders from environmentally friendly retailers, both online and brick and mortar, and eventually, larger department stores and our own Loyal Label retail outlets.

Moreover, part of developing the business model is formulating the social venture's go-to-market (GTM) strategy (Gundry & Kickul, 2007). It has been said, "If you don't know where you are going, any road can take you there." To eliminate such disorientation and provide direction, a social entrepreneur should create a go-to-market strategy to prepare for the social firm's launch. A full GTM strategy encompasses the channels that a venture uses to connect with its customers and the organizational processes it develops to guide customer interactions from initial contact through fulfillment. The right GTM strategy has a significant impact on a social firm's ability to cost-effectively deliver its value solution to each of its target segments. Social ventures are becoming increasingly focused and sophisticated in the way in which they compete to create superior customer value at an affordable rate. As social entrepreneurs tailor their value solutions to better address customers' needs and problems beyond product specifications and to better align their cost of sales and fulfillment relative to those needs, the go-to-market strategy plays a central role.

Once the GTM strategy has been developed, identification of the partners that are needed to assist in maximizing success and social impact should be made (Austin, 2000).These partners are aligned and understand the vision or mission and have similar social venture goals. They may have a needed competency or resource that the social entrepreneur does not have, and together will be able to assist the social venture in achieving its full potential and social goals. The following considerations can be taken into account in the search for partners:

- Identify the partners that will be needed to achieve your vision or mission in terms of competency and knowledge needs in particular.
- Explain the value that each partner will bring to the partnership. What is the contribution each partner is making? Are they highly competent, connected, or experienced? Essentially, why does your social venture need them?
- Why will they need or want to work with you? What is the value your social venture has for each of them? What is the synergy between you and your partner?

Partner	Value Contribution Why we need them?	Strategic Fit Why work with us?	Potential Partners to Contact
Social organizations dedicated to hunger relief	• Provide advice on most critical hunger issues for us to address • Provide a network for contributing to hunger relief projects	• Donation revenue • Raise awareness of hunger issue among new market	The Hunger Project Action Against Hunger International Food Policy Research Institute
Independent music labels	• Expand our presence and network in the independent music scene • Recruit new artists	• Bring social activism element to their marketing	Verge Records Ryko
Music schools	• Recruit new artists • Endorsements as a go-to source for new music	• Provide promotion and source of revenue for their students	Julliard Berklee College of Music Tisch
Live music venues	• Showcase our artists through live performance • Fundraising events	• Bring new patrons • Promotion	Bower Ballroom Mercury Lounge Arlene's Grocery Knitting Factory

FIGURE 5.5   Hungry Musician's Partnership Model

■ Finally, describe the status of the partnership. Have you contacted them and do they agree to work as a partner? Do you have their leadership and management support?

Figure 5.5 offers an example from a social venture called Hungry Musician. The goal of Hungry Musician is to provide an online platform where up-and-coming musicians can sell their music in exchange for income, with a portion of the proceeds also going to feed hunger throughout the world.

5. Who Is the Social Venture's Competition?

It is likely that there will be competitors who are providing a similar type of program or service. In consideration of launching the social venture, the social entrepreneurship should be aware of competitors and understand who is providing similar value to its customers. Conducting a competitor analysis helps the social venture position itself in relation to others in the marketplace and create new strategies and value to its customer groups. The competition can include those that directly compete with venture (direct competitors) or substitutes that also solve the same problem or need as is being addressed through the social business (indirect competitors). Several questions that the social venture should address in this regard include:

- What other solutions exist and what are the implications for your team?
- What other service providers or models are there?
- What's distinctive about yours?
- How much money flows to your "issue" annually and how is it distributed? How will you capture some of those dollars or attract others?

6. Who Is on the Management Team and the Operational Plan?

One of the most crucial components of venture planning is deciding on the team that will be executing the vision or mission of the new venture (Amason, Shrader, & Tompson, 2006). Specifically, the social entrepreneur will want to address what it is about this team that makes it likely that they can execute this plan. What is their personal connection to the vision or mission? What background, experience, leadership, and expertise do they bring to the social venture? Also, consider the expertise that they do not have and think about how they can obtain it. As the social venture grows and develops over time, consider how the team composition will change over time. As the social venture scales, a different type of skill set, experience, and leadership may be needed to grow the social business to other regions of the world and to other customer groups and their expectations and needs.

Along with identifying your management team, the social entrepreneur will also want to define an operational plan for the launch and development of the firm. An operational plan details (1) the processes that must be performed to serve customers every day (short-term processes); and (2) the overall business milestones that the company must attain to be successful (long-term processes). In looking at both the short-term and long-term milestones that need to be in place, consider developing a timeline or using a Gantt chart to demonstrate ramp-up to launch and beyond. Figure 5.6 affords an example of such a timeline, detailing key activities of a new social venture called Seeding Change.

7. What Is the Social Venture's Growth Strategy? How Will the Venture Scale?

While it may be difficult in the beginning of the planning stages to foresee where the social venture may be after several years of operation, it is important to convey

Seeding Change – Business Plan	Cost	Months													Years				
		0	1	2	3	4	5	6	7	8	9	10	11	12	2	3	4	5	6
• Identify mechanisms to reach social entrepreneurs	$200k																		
• Identify target social entrepreneurs																			
• Develop and refine criteria to pre-screen entrepreneurs for participation																			
• Identify business partners looking to engage in meaningful social impact																			
• Engage with social entrepreneurs	$50k																		
• Select candidate social entrepreneurs																			
• Establish relationships with business partners																			
• Develop contracts and terms of agreement for social entrepreneurs and business partners' collaboration	$200k– $500k p.a.																		
• Establish partnerships between social entrepreneurs and business partners																			
• Actively monitor and review the partnerships																			
• Engage the social capital markets																			
• Undertake analysis and review of partnerships and changes in the social sector, developing reports on the findings																			
• Serve as a primary source of information to the social capital market																			

FIGURE 5.6 An Example of a Social Venture's Gantt Chart

to the team, employees, volunteer, donors, and investors what the potential of the social business can be for other customer groups and locations around the world (Bloom & Chatterji, 2009: Bradach, 2003). What will be the replication of your organization or your model? That is, will the social entrepreneur launch more sites or make your model available for others to implement? As the venture grows, considerations should be made of the value the social entrepreneur is trying to create and the level of quality needed to perform in order to continue to create value as the social venture grows (Dees, Anderson, & Wei-Skillern, 2004). Given this, how should the social entrepreneur balance the "need for speed" with the quality hurdle to maximize social value creation? Chapter 9 discusses the issue of scaling in more detail.

8. How Will the Social Venture Assess and Measure Its Social Impact?

Although the social entrepreneurship field has matured, our ability to measure the impact of a venture's efforts still remains a significant challenge for most organizations. Despite noteworthy advancements in the field, there are still no standard measures of success, and impact data remain quite challenging and costly for social ventures to collect and share. That said, there are a number of ways that the social entrepreneur can communicate the value of their social impact to the community.

We will more fully discuss tools, resources, and best practices for measuring social impact in Chapter 8, but all social ventures should relate their venture's outcomes and impact to their theory of change (Paton, 2003; Sharir & Lerner, 2005). All indicators should link back to your theory of change and strategy, and should take into account the time horizon it makes sense to measure. Figure 5.7 provides an example of how those running the social venture Seeding Change can convey their plans to assess and measure their firm's social outcomes.

9. What Is the Social Venture's Financial Plan?

The last step in the social venture strategic planning process involves the development of the financial plan and resources needed to effectively launch and sustain the firm (Zietlow, Hankin, & Seidner, 2007). In this last stage, the development of the pro forma financial documents can assist the social entrepreneur in understanding the amount of start-up capital the firm needs, how the funding will be used, and what sources are available to provide initial seed capital. As a baseline, the social entrepreneur should develop a profit and loss statement, a balance sheet,

Critical Success Factor	Primary Measure	Evaluation	Target Outcome
Social entrepreneurs gain access to much-needed business resources	Number of social entrepreneurs in partnerships	Seeding Change's records	Yr 1 ~ 10 partnerships Yr 2 ~ 30 partnerships Yr 3 ~ 100 partnerships
	Social entrepreneurs achieve outputs and outcomes outlined in terms of agreements	Monitoring and evaluation undertaken by Seeding Change	LT: 80% of social entrepreneurs in partnerships achieved agreed outputs
	Satisfaction with Seeding Change	1. Satisfaction score on customer service survey 2. Number of referrals to other social entrepreneurs	LT: 90% of social entrepreneurs would use Seeding Change's services again and would refer to a peer organization

Business partners contribute meaningfully to the achievement of social change	Number of businesses in partnerships	Seeding Change's records	Yr 1 ~ 10 partnerships Yr 2 ~ 30 partnerships Yr 3 ~ 100 partnerships
	Number of businesses returning to undertake subsequent partnerships	Seeding Change's records	LT: 80% of business partners return to participate in additional partnerships
	Businesses deliver services as outlined in terms of agreement	Monitoring and evaluation undertaken by Seeding Change	LT: 90% of businesses in partnerships delivered agreed outputs
	Satisfaction with Seeding Change	1. Satisfaction score on customer service survey 2. Number of referrals to other business partners	LT: 90% of business partners would use Seeding Change's services again and would refer to peer organization
Individuals involved in Partnerships achieve a sense of personal fulfillment and job satisfaction	Individual sense of satisfaction and fulfillment	Monitoring and evaluation undertaken by Seeding Change Business partners' reports on staff satisfaction and retention	80% of individuals rate the experience as highly satisfying and would be willing to commit to another partnership Business individual metrics on staff satisfaction and retention show a significant impact
	Active advocacy and promotion of Seeding Change and social entrepreneurs	Monitoring and evaluation undertaken by Seeding Change	80% of individuals participate in actively promoting the social entrepreneur and partnership opportunities through Seeding Change
Social capital markets gain access to a screened pool of high-impact social entrepreneurs, and make investments in social entrepreneurs involved in Seeding Change's partnership program	Number of social venture capitalists purchasing Seeding Change's reports	Seeding Change's records	30 – SVC purchasing the reports from Seeding Change within 5 years
	Satisfaction with Seeding Change	1. Satisfaction score on customer service survey 2. Number of referrals to other SVCs	LT: 90% of SVC partners would use Seeding Change's services again and would refer to a peer organization

FIGURE 5.7   Seeding Change's Assessment Plan

and cash flow analysis. In Chapter 7, "Funding Social Ventures," the case study of PODER provides an example of such statements as well as an opportunity to analyze each statement in assisting the social entrepreneur in making decisions regarding the financial sustainability of the social venture.

QUESTIONS FOR "CONNECTING THE DOTS"

1   What role, if any, does strategic planning have for a nascent social venture? What role does it have for a social venture you would like to launch, given the social sector you are entering?

2   What are some initial first steps that social entrepreneurs should be aware of as they embark on writing their social venture plan?

3   From your understanding, how does a social venture plan differ from the traditional business plan?

4   Of all the various sections of the social venture plan, which do you think is the most difficult to write? What suggestions would you offer to overcome some of the difficulties and challenges in writing such a plan?

Case Study 5.1
Loyal Label Business Plan

TABLE OF CONTENTS

EXECUTIVE SUMMARY

Loyal Label is a socially conscious lifestyle brand that redefines the way that consumers view the products they buy. Our company provides a unique retail concept combining design, activism, and sustainability and brings these things right to the consumer. We focus on connecting people to causes they care about through sustainable and stylish apparel. We believe that giving people a concrete way to make a difference will empower them to change the world.

Loyal Label as a company characterizes what is now being called the fourth sector. It is a for-benefit corporation, a hybrid between the for-profit and nonprofit sectors. For-benefit corporations are "driven by both social purpose and financial promise [and] fall somewhere between traditional companies and charities." The term 'fourth sector' derives from the fact that participants are creating hybrid organizations distinct from those operating in the government, business and nonprofit sectors.

Loyal Label will appeal to ordinary consumers as well as those seeking ways to effectively contribute to causes they care about. As information becomes more widely available and cultures become more globally connected, consumers are becoming increasingly aware of how their actions affect the bigger picture. They are looking for convenient and efficient ways of providing aid to and benefiting others. However, existing retail-based charities are unclear about how and where their proceeds are being allocated, and consumers are left unsatisfied and skeptical. Loyal Label provides consumers with a straightforward solution to this problem, offering complete transparency and maintaining close relationships with various charitable causes.

The product mix consists of seven lines, each connected to a different cause. The first six lines are Water, Hunger, Life, Earth, Learning, and Peace. Revenues from each of these lines will fund initiatives with relevant partner charities. The last line, the Loyal line, is tied to the company's own not-for-profit, The Loyal Foundation. This foundation offers grants to young and aspiring social entrepreneurs with novel ideas to impact and improve our world. By factoring the donations into the price, Loyal Label guarantees that every product makes a contribution to the relevant charity.

The key differentiator for Loyal Label is that every item in each line will be tied to a direct action. For example, a t-shirt from the Hunger line has the potential to provide a child with 20 meals, while one from the Earth line could cover the cost to plant five trees. This model of creating a connection between a customer and a solution is what distinguishes Loyal Label from other companies in the apparel market. We call it the "Consumer/Cause Connection."

Each line will have its own original "Loyal Ts," featuring fashionable designs printed on organic cotton t-shirts. Loyal Label will initially sell through the website loyallabel.org. As the company grows and adds new products to the mix, we will explore new avenues for sales. The Loyal Label brand will always strive to be sustainable and socially conscious in every aspect from the supply chain to its partner charities to the product itself. It will stand for fairness in the manufacturing and distribution of all products. In the future, Loyal Label also looks forward to having a real economic impact in emerging markets by vertically integrating its own Fair Factories. These factories will offer livable wages, health care and education to employees and their families in underprivileged communities around the world.

As soon-to-be college graduates, the founders of Loyal Label recognize the strength and impact that young individuals have on their peers. Hence, Loyal Label's marketing strategy focuses initially on college students, who will engage with the brand through our nationwide campus T-Shirt Truck Tour. This tour will simultaneously build awareness, create buzz and drive sales. Additionally, Loyal Label will actively use social networks, events marketing, the Impact Quarterly magazine and other media to connect the consumer to the company.

With low start-up costs, the company is expected to grow 20 times within the next five years. Loyal Label has great potential to be profitable and sustainable while providing solutions that produce real change around the world. The satisfaction of being able to advance the lives of those in need with a simple purchase will generate tremendous loyalty to the brand.

COMPANY OVERVIEW

OUR MISSION

In a world that is more connected and interdependent than ever before, two very different stories still exist. In one corner of the world, a young woman is thirsty and hungry, lacking access to clean drinking water or enough food to be healthy. Like millions of other refugees, she has been uprooted from her home because of war, and is unable to work to support her family. Her children don't have a school to attend or access to medicine to cure their illnesses.

In another part of the world, a young woman is full of energy and optimism. Like millions of others from her generation, she is concerned about social issues affecting people around the globe, including everything from extreme poverty to environmental sustainability, and she has a strong desire to express her passion. She is willing to support causes she cares about, but she lacks confidence in many of the traditional forms of community giving and questions her ability to make a real impact.

Our mission for Loyal Label is to unite these two people, through a model we call the Consumer/Cause Connection. Working with partner charities, we will use direct proceeds from every clothing item we sell to fund a specific social outcome. We will communicate this outcome to consumers, so that the socially conscious consumer knows that a t-shirt she bought will ultimately result in 20 school meals for a child in a developing country, or medical supplies for a refugee in need. Throughout the entire process, we will use modern technology to enhance the transparency, and will keep consumers engaged with updates about their social impact.

OUR HISTORY

Loyal Label was started by three college students from the Stern School of Business at New York University. The company's founders noticed that a growing number of individuals from their generation were becoming increasingly more civicly engaged and were interested in giving back to their communities and the world at large. Harnessing the energy of this movement, one of Loyal Label's founders, Aaron Kinnari, started The World Water Project to engage his fellow classmates in efforts to provide clean water to

people in need. The Water Project's main initiative involved selling stainless steel water bottles, with the model that for every bottle sold, The World Water Project would fund projects with partner organizations to provide a child with clean water for an entire year. This direct connection between the bottle and a child getting clean water was very popular on the NYU campus, and Aaron believed the same approach could work with other products and causes. Working with classmates Edlin Choi and Stephanie Huang, he started to develop the idea for Loyal Label.

OUR PRODUCTS

Loyal Label is made up of seven lines, each connected to a different cause. The first six lines – *Hunger, Water, Earth, Learning, Life,* and *Peace* – each generate proceeds from product sales to fund specific projects with partner charities. Our last line, the *Loyal Line,* funds initiatives with our company's non-profit Loyal Foundation, which distributes grants to young social entrepreneurs and supports service projects.

Initially, we will offer seven different t-shirts, which we call Loyal Ts, one for each line, with each shirt connected to a specific outcome. For example, purchasing a Loyal T from our *Water Line* would supply an individual with clean water for five years, while one from our *Earth Line* would cover the cost to plant five trees.

As our company grows, so will our product offerings. Other products that we have in the pipeline include a line of Hoodies Against Hunger, with each hoodie sold funding 40 schools meals for children in need. Additionally, we will explore the potential of developing higher-end products for limited edition runs, such as a Loyal Label Laptop Bag, that when purchased, provides a child a laptop for educational purposes from the One Laptop Per Child organization.

Our products are produced using environmentally sustainable processes, including the use of organic cotton as our primary material. Additionally, we only work with manufacturers that meet high levels of labor conditions. We have already identified the manufacturer Anvil and the screener Jakprints as strong partners. As a future goal, once we reach a critical mass, we plan to build our own Fair Factories in developing countries, to encourage economic development in communities that need it most.

OUR BUSINESS MODEL

Loyal Label will operate primarily as an e-commerce business, making most of our revenues through our website www.loyallabel.org. After products are produced, they will be shipped to our storage facilities in Atlanta, Georgia, where a Loyal Label staff member will manage shipping and order fulfillment. Additionally, we will generate revenue through product sales during our T-Shirt Truck Tour, a three month long tour visiting college campuses across the country. The Truck Tour will put our products in the hands of consumers, build brand awareness, create a connection between consumers and the company's founders who will be on the tour, and literally, drive sales. Finally, a portion of our revenue will come from larger orders from environmentally friendly retailers, both online and brick and mortar, and eventually, larger department stores and our own Loyal Label retail outlets.

OUR TARGET MARKET

Our primary target market consists of socially conscious young adults, primarily college students, who care about certain social causes and have a desire to support those causes and share their concerns with others. Research has shown this market to be genuinely interested in global issues, ranging from climate change to world hunger. These consumers tend to support companies that are actively pursuing social causes and are often times willing to pay a premium for these company's products. Additionally, we will target parents of these consumers, marketing our products as the perfect gifts for their younger children. Studies have shown that large percentages of these older consumers are increasingly more concerned about social issues, and are also willing to pay a premium to support companies who give back to their communities.

OUR MARKETING STRATEGY

Our marketing strategy will focus on developing a strong story about our brand and a personal connection with our consumers. As fellow college students, we will connect with our target market as we share our own experiences building our company. We'll use tools like the T-Shirt Truck Tour, well developed blogs, a strong social networking presence, our Campus Brand Manager Program and other marketing efforts to generate awareness about our brand. And post-purchase, we'll continue to engage consumers, sending them personalized thank-you notes and giving them options to share their impact with friends via Facebook and Twitter. We will be completely transparent about where we send proceeds from clothing sales, allowing consumers to click a link on electronic receipts from their purchases to "track their impact" and see when funds are disbursed to partner charities and where this money is used. We will also hold ourselves accountable to high standards for producing our products, and will communicate to consumers where we still need to make improvements, such as in the color and dying process of producing the t-shirts. This will help to reduce the potential for negative feedback about "greenwashing" consumers, typically associated with companies who are not entirely honest about their environmental actions. We will seek to reduce energy and resource usage, even going as far as using recycled paper grocery bags to make the hangtags for our t-shirts. All of these efforts will add to the credibility of our brand, and turn potential customers into Loyal customers.

OUR CURRENT STATUS

As of April 2010, we have launched the blog, www.followthestartup.com (see appendix exhibit 1), which chronicles our experiences starting the company and serves as a way to build a following prior to launching the brand. The blog has had over 1,000 unique visits in a few short weeks. Additionally, we have launched a Twitter account, twitter. com/tweetthestartup, which has attracted over 500 followers. We are currently in the middle of working with designers to produce the first seven *Loyal Ts*, and have already chosen several designs (see appendix exhibit 2). Once all seven designs are developed, we will begin production on our first run of Loyal Ts through our supplier JakPrints. These will go on sale through our website, www.loyallabel. org, which we are currently in final phases of development. Lastly, we are in the process of trademarking our name, which is available, and establishing a S-Corporation.

OUR SOCIAL MISSION

OUR MODEL FOR SOCIAL IMPACT

Loyal Label is made up of seven clothing lines, each connected to a different cause. The seven lines are *Water, Hunger, Earth, Life, Learning, Peace, and Loyal*. Profits from the first six lines will benefit partner charities and not-for-profits associated with each cause. The following map demonstrates the various social impacts that the production and sale of a t-shirt from our *Hunger Line*, which gives 20 meals to school children, will have through the product's life cycle.

SUSTAINABLE PRODUCTION WITH ORGANIC COTTON & FAIR LABOR PRACTICES

Production of our *Hunger Loyal T* with organic cotton will:

- Comply with Global Organic Textitle Standard (GOTS) and SA8000 Labor Standards
- Reduce the amount of pesticides used in farming and dyes in clothing production which will lower the amount of greenhouse gases and pollution
- Invest in farmers in developing countries to boost economies
- Provide employment in under-privileged communities and education & health services

WFP

FUNDS SENT TO UN WORLD FOOD PROGRAM TO PAY FOR MEALS FOR SCHOOLS

Giving 20 nutritious school meals to children in need will:

- Reduce the number of deaths caused by malnutrition
- Encourage school attendance, most especially by young girls, which will further education attainment
- Create economic opportunities for farmers in developing countries who produce the WFP school meals
- Advance overall health and productivity of the receiving country over the long term

CONSUMERS ARE ENGAGED THROUGOUT THE ENTIRE PRODUCT LIFE CYCLE

By continuously sharing information and updates, we will:

- Educate our customers about world hunger and provide opportunities for them to help bring an end to the global crisis
- Empower people to share solutions with friends & family
- Build our brand's credibility by clearly tracking and demonstrating how our work is having an impact in people's lives around the world
- Encourage consumers to participate in "slow fashion" and recyle their *Hunger Loyal T* when they are finished wearing it

7 LINES. 7 CAUSES. 7 ORIGINAL LOYAL Ts.

Loyal Label will launch with seven original Loyal Ts – one for each of the seven lines. The purchase of every t-shirt will be tied directly to a tangible outcome, as outlined below. As sales grow, so will the product lines with the introduction of additional t-shirts and other items, each connected to new tangible outcomes. Other future products in the mix include *Hoodies Against Hunger* as part of the *Hunger Line* and *Good Well* bags as an extension of the *Water Line*. The chart below explains our seven lines, the problem each one addresses, and the initial impact the the original Loyal T will provide (see the appendix exhibit 1 for a few example t-shirt designs).

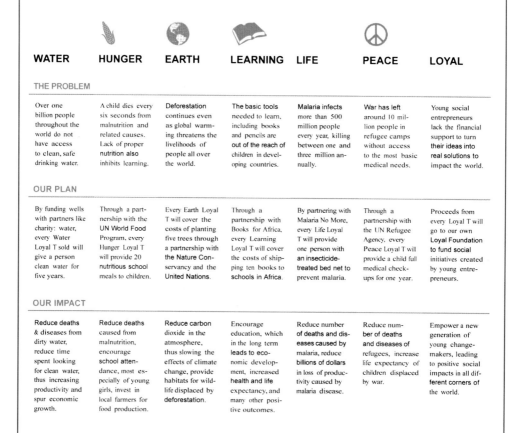

	WATER	HUNGER	EARTH	LEARNING	LIFE	PEACE	LOYAL
THE PROBLEM	Over one billion people throughout the world do not have access to clean, safe drinking water.	A child dies every six seconds from malnutrition and related causes. Lack of proper nutrition also inhibits learning.	Deforestation continues even as global warming threatens the livelihoods of people all over the world.	The basic tools needed to learn, including books and pencils are out of the reach of children in developing countries.	Malaria infects more than 500 million people every year, killing between one and three million annually.	War has left around 10 million people in refugee camps without access to the most basic medical needs.	Young social entrepreneurs lack the financial support to turn their ideas into real solutions to impact the world.
OUR PLAN	By funding wells with partners like charity: water, every Water Loyal T sold will give a person clean water for five years.	Through a partnership with the UN World Food Program, every Hunger Loyal T will provide 20 nutritious school meals to children.	Every Earth Loyal T will cover the costs of planting five trees through a partnership with the Nature Conservancy and the United Nations.	Through a partnership with Books for Africa, every Learning Loyal T will cover the costs of shipping ten books to schools in Africa.	By partnering with Malaria No More, every Life Loyal T will provide one person with an insecticide-treated bed net to prevent malaria.	Through a partnership with the UN Refugee Agency, every Peace Loyal T will provide a child full medical check-ups for one year.	Proceeds from every Loyal T will go to our own Loyal Foundation to fund social initiatives created by young entrepreneurs.
OUR IMPACT	Reduce deaths & diseases from dirty water, reduce time spent looking for clean water, thus increasing productivity and spur economic growth.	Reduce deaths caused from malnutrition, encourage school attendance, most especially of young girls, invest in local farmers for food production.	Reduce carbon dioxide in the atmosphere, thus slowing the effects of climate change, provide habitats for wildlife displaced by deforestation.	Encourage education, which in the long term leads to economic development, increased health and life expectancy, and many other positive outcomes.	Reduce number of deaths and diseases caused by malaria, reduce billions of dollars in loss of productivity caused by malaria disease.	Reduce number of deaths and diseases of refugees, increase life expectancy of children displaced by war.	Empower a new generation of young changemakers, leading to positive social impacts in all different corners of the world.

MARKET AND CONSUMER ANALYSIS

A MARKET WITH EXPLOSIVE GROWTH

Loyal Label will be a player in the apparel industry, which had a market size of over $480 billion in 2005,[1] and is expected to surpass $800 billion in sales by 2015.[2] More specifically, the company will compete in the rapidly growing sustainable apparel market, which includes products made from environmentally friendly materials, such as organic cotton and bamboo. In 2007, sales of sustainable apparel exceeded $3 billion,[3] and analysts predict the industry to grow to over $11 billion by 2012.[4]

Even if the industry quadruples in size, it will still be a small island in the vast ocean of the apparel industry. But we believe there is even greater potential for growth. In a survey of 22,000 consumers conducted in December of 2007, half of the respondents said they consider at least one sustainability factor when making a purchase, with 20% considering more than one factor.[5] More specifically, in our target segment of Generation Y, a Maritz Research poll found that 47% of respondents were willing to pay more for eco-friendly products.[6] Currently, there are simply not enough apparel options available to this huge market of socially conscious consumers, and we believe that we can capitalize on their unmet needs.

Furthermore, this shift in the market towards environmentally sustainable products is even more pronounced in the explosion of media coverage of this movement. Top publications from O Magazine to Vogue to numerous blogs online are all covering this shift towards green manufacturing. Additionally, several non-profits are actively building awareness about this small industry. One of these organizations, Earth Pledge, lead a "Future Fashion Show" highlighting sustainable apparel at the 2008 New York Fashion Week with the support of the popular department store Barney's New York and Lexus Hybrid. The media coverage and attention of the sustainable apparel industry far outstretches its market size, and foreshadows its future success in coming years.

OUR MARKET RESEARCH

To better understand the consumer, we designed a simple online survey that was completed by 216 participants ranging across all age groups. Almost all respondents, 92.1%, signified "quality material" as an attribute that would influence them to pay a premium for a clothing item, followed by 77.3% choosing a "cool design" as important. "Association with a cause" and "sustainable production" both had sizable response rates with 25.9% and 24.1% respectively.

When asked to list their favorite charities, respondents provided a broad range of answers, supporting our decision to have multiple product lines connected to distinct and separate causes. Additionally, 40.2% of respondents were more likely to buy a cause-related t-shirt that had a more tangible outcome. The scenario was described as follows: "By purchasing this t-shirt, one meal will be served at a local soup kitchen." In contrast, another choice was "By purchasing this t-shirt, $5 of the proceeds will be given to a local soup kitchen," which was selected by only 25.7% of respondents. Willingness to pay for organic cotton t-shirts clustered around $15–25 and most respondents estimated their monthly expenditure on clothing to be $50–100. In our sample size of 216 respondents, 84.2% fell within our target age demographic of 18–24. We believe the numbers support our concept and business model.

THE TARGET MARKET

Our main target market will focus on Generation Y, which consists of 40 million Americans between the ages of 18 and 29, most especially the younger half of this generation, the 23.7 million adults ages 18–24.[7] Furthermore, as we will focus heavily on the 43% of Generation Y that is still in college, we will also target their Baby Boomer parents, who often provide financial support. Studies show Baby Boomers to be highly environmentally and socially conscious, and we believe Loyal Label will be a perfect option for this market to consider when looking for gifts for their younger children.

Geographically, we will focus heavily on northern states, for their affluence, brand-consciousness, high levels of education attainment and metropolitan populations, as well as pacific states, known for their youthful populations, experience and comfort with e-commerce, and high interest in social issues.

PRIMARY TARGET MARKET

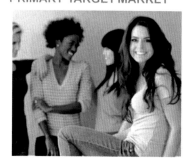

Our primary customer is a socially conscious, 18 to 24 year old college student. This consumer is part of Generation Y, which is characterized by the following traits:[8]

- 77% are "seriously concerned about the environment"
- 43% more likely than adult average to pay more for eco-products.

85%	**70%**	**68%**	**47%**
of consumers have better opinions about companies that support causes they care about	of Baby Boomers feel a responsibility to make a positive impact in the world	of consumers would remain loyal to a brand during a recession if it supports a good cause	of Generation Y is willing to pay a premium for a product if it is environmentally friendly

SECONDARY TARGET MARKETS

Our secondary target market will consist of young, working professionals, ages 25 to 34, who have a high level of discretionary income, are socially conscious about global issues, and have a desire to express themselves through casual clothing when they are not in business attire for work. This age group places a high value on brand names and is willing to pay extra for better quality products.

Additionally, Loyal Label can provide a great gift option for the Baby Boomer generation to choose for their college age children. This generation is very socially conscious, with 35% actively looking for green products & services. Furthermore, AARP recently estimated that 40 million Boomers are involved in socially minded consumerism, including buying "from companies that give back to their communities."[10]

PACIFIC AND NORTHEAST MARKETS COMPARED TO NATIONAL AVERAGES

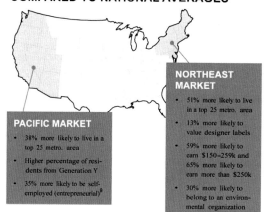

NORTHEAST MARKET

- 51% more likely to live in a top 25 metro. area
- 13% more likely to value designer labels
- 59% more likely to earn $150–259k and 65% more likely to earn more than $250k
- 30% more likely to belong to an environmental organization

PACIFIC MARKET

- 38% more likely to live in a top 25 metro. area
- Higher percentage of residents from Generation Y
- 35% more likely to be self-employed (entrepreneurial)[9]

THE COMPETITION

Several companies have a presence in the sustainable apparel market or have some version of cause-branded apparel lines. Mass marketers, such as Wal-Mart and Target, as well as department stores, including Barneys New York and JCPenney, have introduced clothing lines made from organic cotton and other environmentally friendly materials. Others have participated in cause-branded campaigns, probably the most widely known being the partnership between Gap and (PRODUCT)Red, in part due to the campaign's high-profile spokesman, Bono from U2. But the campaign has struggled to communicate its mission and the impact of its efforts, leaving many consumers unfamiliar with the cause of the campaign and where specifically proceeds are having an impact.

Smaller socially conscious brands like TOMS Shoes and Stella McCartney have also been tremendously successful. Their success proves that consumers are willing to pay a premium for design and support brands that aid causes they care about. American Apparel, known for its practice of using domestic labor and paying fair wages, has also been extremely successful. However, the company has suffered recently from their attempts to cut corners, suggesting the need for more accountability in the industry.

Lastly, there are several brands that compete primarily online in the sustainable apparel market. This includes WeAreOverlooked.com, which most closely resembles our model of creating direct connections between consumers and causes. This company has struggled with successfully marketing its brand, and does not go nearly as far as Loyal Label in providing transparency of impact.

400,000 SHOES IN 3 YEARS: A STUDY OF THE COMPETITION

Blake Mycoskie founded TOMS Shoes in 2006 after a trip to Argentina where he witnessed the large number of children without shoes to protect their feet, which led to diseases and the children being unable to attend school. TOMS functions on a "one for one" model – for every pair of TOMS shoes sold, the company donates an identical pair to a child in need.

In the first few weeks of TOMS, an article about the company was published in the *Los Angeles Times* and 2,000 pairs of the canvas shoes sold overnight. Since its launch just three years ago, TOMS has sold over 400,000 pairs of shoes, and given away the same amount of pairs to kids in need. Mycoskie contributes much of the brand's success to the "one for one" model that TOMS uses.

OUR COMPETITIVE ADVANTAGE: THE CONSUMER/CAUSE CONNECTION

Much of the competition focuses only on manufacturing sustainable apparel from organic products or advertises that they give a percentage of their revenue to a certain cause. Loyal Label will take this a step further and combine both aspects. Furthermore, rather than simply saying we give a percentage of our revenues to a charity, Loyal Label clearly identifies a specific outcome of a product purchase, and will work with partner organizations to ensure transparency along the way. This model of creating a direct connection between a consumer and a cause is unique to the industry, and we believe it will build the credibility of our brand and the willingness of customers to continue to purchase our products.

To further illustrate how the Consumer/Cause Connection works, consider our Loyal T from the *Water Line*. First, it is produced with organic cotton in fair labor conditions. Then, by working closely with a partner organization like charity: water, who is able to build wells and provide clean water to a person for an average of $1 per year, we can guarantee that every shirt sold will give an individual clean water access for five years. And using a system that charity: water already has in place, which tracks donations and posts photos of newly developed wells on a Google map, we can prove that proceeds from shirts are actually having a direct impact for communities in need. Post-purchase, we will follow up with consumers, and encourage them to "track their impact" online, further connecting them to the cause and the Loyal Label brand. This kind of direct connection is unprecedented in the apparel industry, and is even advance for many non-profits that seek donations, but we know that transparency and accountability is crucial to our success.

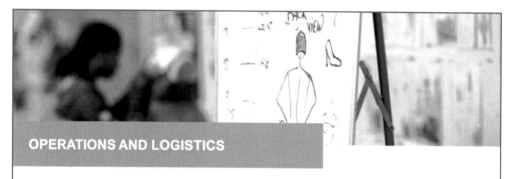

OPERATIONS AND LOGISTICS

Loyal Label will focus on environmental sustainability and fairness in all aspects of the manufacturing process while we strive to contain costs. We will do this successfully by building strong partnerships along every step of the process, from the beginning stages with young, freelance designers to the very end, with our delivery support.

DEVELOPING A DESIGN

Loyal Label will work with young, aspiring designers to develop the graphics for the seven original Loyal Ts. Designers will be paid a royalty per shirt sold featuring their graphic, up to a negotiated capped amount, agreed to by contract. This model reduces the costs associated with high salaries for full-time design staff. Additionally, it promotes young designers, who will, in turn, market our products to their own friends and families. As the company grows, we will also look towards design interns to develop graphics for additional products.

PRODUCING OUR PRODUCTS

Initially, our t-shirts will be sourced from Anvil, an American manufacturer whose eco-friendly and socially responsible practices have received extensive attention. The partnership will allow us to buy 100% organic cotton material in bulk with complete assurances that production is fair. We have also identified several other potential partners, including Edun Live, a company that produces organic cotton shirts in Uganda, which would be a great partner in the future to produce t-shirts with a higher price point.

Screen printing will be sourced to the online vendor JakPrints. The company already works extensively with Anvil, and offers great pricing for wholesale orders. Because of the chemicals used, screen printing is the one aspect of production that still needs to make a lot of progress to become fully environmentally friendly. As the sustainable apparel industry grows, we will seek addtional sources for Screen-printing that uses eco-safe dyes.

STORING AND SHIPPING OUR SHIRTS

From the screen-printing location, our Loyal Ts will be shipped to a location we have already secured from a family member for free in Atlanta, Georgia. This location will serve as a storage facility during the intitial phases of the company. We will also store some products in our New York offices to have on hand for events and local sales. Additionally, during our T-Shirt Truck Tour, we will strategically locate supplies of products across the country at the homes of family and friends so that we may continuously restock our product as we sell shirts throughout the tour. As our company grows, we will seek larger facilities, in either upstate New York or New Jersey, as the close proximity to our headquarters and main sales location will keep transportation costs low.

When products are ordered on our website, we will ship to customers directly from our storage facilities in Atlanta using the United States Post Office. We have an individual who will handle shipping, and we will pay this person per package sent, a cost that will be covered by the shipping and handling fee that we charge customers. Additionally, working with this individual, we will track supply levels using a simple inventory management software program. As the company grows, we will also look towards FedEx Small Business for larger order fulfillment.

FRUGAL AND FAIR FOCUS

Throughout the entire process, we will focus our efforts on containing costs by implementing efficient policies and harnessing strong supplier relationships. One example of these efforts will include offering some designs in limited edition runs, which creates an incentive for consumers to act quickly and reduces the potential for high storage costs for excess supplies and cuts in margins for selling excess products at a discount. However, unlike some other companies, we will not sacrifice integrity to save money, and will continue to act in the most socially responsible ways, even if they are not always the cheapest.

SEVEN SIMPLE STEPS FROM THE CONCEPT TO THE CONSUMER

ONE	**TWO**	**THREE**	**FOUR**	**FIVE**	**SIX**	**SEVEN**
New product is developed and designed with social outcome in mind	Suppliers produce new product using sustainable practices	Finished product is shipped in batches to our storage facilities in Atlanta, GA	New product is advertised and posted for sale on our website LoyalLabel.org	Consumers purchase product using PayPal online merchant system	Product is shipped by Loyal Label staff member through the USPS	Consumer receives follow-ups regarding satisfaction and proof of social impact

HUMAN RESOURCES

For the first year, Loyal Label will be maintained primarily by members of the management team. The Chief Executive Officer will be responsible for building relationships with partner organizations receiving funding from the sales of our clothing, which will include ensuring accountability and transparency of our social impact. Additionally, the CEO will be responsible for managing relationships with all outisde parties, except manufacturers, including legal counsel, accountants, retail buyers, contractors, advisory board members, and all other major partners. The Chief Operations Officer will oversee all aspects of the production process, including ensuring product quality, working with freelance designers to develop products, and delivery of customer orders. Furthermore, the COO will be responsible for managing relationships with all suppliers. Lastly, the Chief Marketing Officer will oversee all corporate communication, including advertising and public relations campaigns and online media. The CMO will also be responsible for managing the Campus Brand Manager Program and the T-Shirt Truck Tour.

To contain costs and reduce the amount of full time staff during the first year, we will also rely on independent contractors. Though these individuals often times cost more per hour, costs associated with their work will still be much lower than full time employees. We will rely on contractors to further develop our website, produce marketing material, and assist in other tasks. We will also seek outside counsel for legal and accounting activities.

We will also recruit college students to serve as Campus Brand Managers (CBMs) and interns for the company. CBMs will be recruited through a network of contacts that we have developed from past work experience. They will be engaged throughout the year in conference calls with top management and and given marketing material to distribute on their college campus. They will be tasked with monthly intitiatives, and will report back on progress through an online, internal network. CBMs will be compensated with credit for company purchases tied to performance, and will have access to employee discounts.

As for the interns, during the summer, design and business students will have the opportunity to work with the Loyal Label team on a rotation through several steps of the production process. Interns will be invited to attend key meetings with top management and be involved in many of the decision-making processes. At the end of the summer, they will be expected to present ideas and designs for new products and potential partnerships. Furthermore, at the end of their term, interns will be great ambassadors for the brand on their college campuses and will also serve as a great resource in gauging the youngest, freshest minds. For their efforts, interns will enjoy clothing samples, as well as employee discounts.

KEY HIRES

As Loyal Label grows, we will look to hire additional employees to manage many aspects of the growing company. Many of these new employees will come in the second year of operation, and will be contingent on our company reaching sales and revenue targets that will allow for this personnel expansion. As of now, we will look for individuals to fill the following positions, in this specific order:

- Chief Financial Officer: oversees all finances, seeks new opportunities for additional funding, would be offered shares of the company

- Webmaster: develops and maintains LoyalLabel.org, works with the CMO to update social networking sites

- Director of Product Development: an individual with fashion experience who can assist the Chief Operating Officer in overseeing product development (allowing the COO more time to oversee HR)

- Director of Communications: assists CMO on developing communications, maintains public relations

- Director of Social Impact: works with partner organizations to track social impact and ensure accountability, assists CMO in communicating social impact.

CRITICAL RISKS

1. Costs exceed estimates

If actual operating costs exceed our expected numbers, we would reevaluate our pricing strategy. Within the sustainable apparel industry, our items are priced at about average to below average. To make up for unexpectedly high costs, we may adopt a premium price strategy instead.

2. Sales forecasts are not reached

To address sales that do not reach our forecasts, we would scale down our marketing. The goal here would not necessarily be to reduce marketing, but just its costs, through the adoption of even more cost-effective marketing strategies. Additionally, the product designs would be reevaluated and the sales strategy would need to be thoroughly examined to identify improvement areas.

3. Product development schedules are not met

Addressing the third critical risk requires more preemptive action than adjusting reaction. We will strive to maintain close and open communication with suppliers to avoid surprises. We will also work with suppliers beforehand to set clearly defined stipulations regarding consequences of missed deadlines or scheduling delays. If product delays still transpire, Loyal Label would push back product releases. This reaction could prove to be costly, and if scheduling problems were to become frequent, we would change suppliers. Again, this is a tedious measure, so the best way to manage this risk factor is to create cooperative dialogue with suppliers and proactively prevent the problem.

OUR "GO TO MARKET" STRATEGY

Even with limited resources, Loyal Label has the potential to start generating revenue in a very short period of time. The following process, which we believe can be completed over six to eight weeks, explains our strategy for producing products and initiating sales should the company only have limited resources to begin operations:

- Continue to work with freelance designers to complete the designs for the seven original Loyal Ts

- Order 1,000 organic Anvil t-shirts from JakPrints, to be split evenly between all seven original Loyal Ts, and have the designs screen printed

- Market t-shirts for sale on our website LoyalLabel.org and start advertising via social networking sites and our blog, FollowTheStartUp.com

- Participate in local events, including New York City street fairs and student club events, to continue sales and build brand awareness

BUILDING AN ONLINE MARKETPLACE

Despite unfavorable economic conditions, the e-commerce apparel industry still experienced a growth rate of 11% in early 2009.[11] Loyal Label will be a player in this industry, as many of our intitial sales will be made through our website LoyalLabel.org. This will require a strong online presence. We have past experience developing many basic websites, including one that has operated as a platform for online sales. We are already in the process of developing a website that will be adequate for the initial stages of our company. However, we will look to outside contractors, and eventually an internal webmaster, to develop a more interactive website that will allow consumers to customize their own homepage, share information about Loyal Label with their friends on social networks, and continously interact with the company.

GLOBAL SUSTAINABLE APPAREL AND FAIR LABOR STANDARDS

Currently, there is not a universally accepted standard for sustainable apparel. However, many non-profits in the green movement are pushing for an industry standard, which would include a recognizable stamp to be placed on apparel made from organic material, much like the stamps placed on organic food. The most popular option is the Global Organic Textile Standard (GOTS). If this measure is adopted by the industry, consumers will be able to easily recognize organic apparel, and have greater confidence in retailers and more acceptance of the industry. Loyal Label will manufacture our products to meet these standards.

Additionally, there are currently universal standards regarding fair labor practices in the apparel industry. These standards, known as SA8000, stipulate requirements for labor used in manufacturing, including the prohibition of child labor and oppressive working conditions. When we look to foreign manufacturers for our clothing, we will only work with suppliers that meet these conditions.

LEGAL STRUCTURE

Certain tax benefits exist for making large donations, and we will seek legal counsel in the creation of contracts and subsequent compliance with contract law. Loyal Label will operate as a for-profit corporation, and will enjoy tax deductions on subsequent donations to charitable causes. For-profit and S-Corp status are significant benefits to Loyal Label, as resources can then be more freely leveraged and reinvested into the growth and development of the company as a fashion merchandiser.

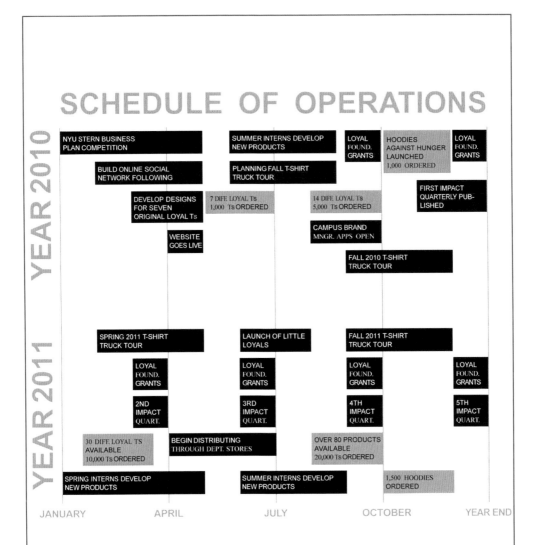

SCHEDULE OF OPERATIONS

YEAR 2010

NYU STERN BUSINESS PLAN COMPETITION	SUMMER INTERNS DEVELOP NEW PRODUCTS	LOYAL FOUND. GRANTS
BUILD ONLINE SOCIAL NETWORK FOLLOWING	PLANNING FALL T-SHIRT TRUCK TOUR	HOODIES AGAINST HUNGER LAUNCHED 1,000 ORDERED
DEVELOP DESIGNS FOR SEVEN ORIGINAL LOYAL Ts	7 DIFF. LOYAL Ts 1,000 Ts ORDERED	14 DIFF. LOYAL Ts 5,000 Ts ORDERED

LOYAL FOUND. GRANTS

FIRST IMPACT QUARTERLY PUBLISHED

WEBSITE GOES LIVE

CAMPUS BRAND MNGR. APPS OPEN

FALL 2010 T-SHIRT TRUCK TOUR

YEAR 2011

SPRING 2011 T-SHIRT TRUCK TOUR

LAUNCH OF LITTLE LOYALS

FALL 2011 T-SHIRT TRUCK TOUR

LOYAL FOUND. GRANTS

LOYAL FOUND. GRANTS

LOYAL FOUND. GRANTS

LOYAL FOUND. GRANTS

2ND IMPACT QUART.

3RD IMPACT QUART.

4TH IMPACT QUART.

5TH IMPACT QUART.

30 DIFF. LOYAL TS AVAILABLE 10,000 Ts ORDERED

BEGIN DISTRIBUTING THROUGH DEPT. STORES

OVER 80 PRODUCTS AVAILABLE 20,000 Ts ORDERED

SPRING INTERNS DEVELOP NEW PRODUCTS

SUMMER INTERNS DEVELOP NEW PRODUCTS

1,500 HOODIES ORDERED

JANUARY   APRIL   JULY   OCTOBER   YEAR END

DISTRIBUTING THROUGH SPECIALTY RETAILERS & DEPARTMENT STORES

A percentage of our sales will come from smaller, specialty retail stores, and ultimately, larger department stores. Sales meetings with these parties will be led by our management team. We will target primarily retail outlets in the vicinity of New York City. Additionally, we will meet with specialty retailers in larger cities during our T-Shirt Truck Tour. We will negotiate pricing strategies with these retailers, but based on industry norms, we can expect to lose between 30 and 50% of the final sales prices to these retailers.

However, this still allows us to make sufficient profit on each item, especially our higher priced products, and gives us an opportunity to expand the reach of our brand.

MILESTONES FOR 2012–2014

Major milestones for 2012 will include the launch of our first "Summer Service Tour," which will be a national community service tour sponsored by our own Loyal Foundation. 2013 will include the opening of our first flagship store in New York. 2014 will bring an additional west coast store, in either Los Angeles or San Francisco.

MARKETING AND COMMUNICATIONS

CAMPUS BRAND MANAGERS

Loyal Label will create a collegiate marketing program with one Campus Brand Manager for each major university throughout the country. These Campus Brand Managers (CBMs) will be charged with spreading awareness of the brand and communicating our values to the opinion leaders on their campuses. Because Loyal Label is a fun, hip, and socially conscious company, the mainstay of collegiate marketing efforts will be guerilla and experiential marketing campaigns to create buzz, capture social media mentions, and generate word-of-mouth. Campus Brand Managers will be compensated with employee discounts, valuable work experience, and the chance to influence the growth of a start-up.

T-SHIRT TRUCK TOUR

At the heart of the Campus Brand Manager program will be the T-Shirt Truck Tour. The T-Shirt Truck will visit major campuses across the country, selling Loyal Ts from a modified ice cream truck and educating students about the Loyal Label concept. This tour will be activated around community service projects close to the universities. In this way, Loyal Label can have a positive impact with an immediate effect in the community, generate good publicity, and humanize the brand by connecting with consumers in a very personal way.

IMPACT QUARTERLY

Four times a year, Loyal Label will publish the Impact Quarterly (IQ) The IQ will serve as a venue to engage our consumers and create a level of accountability and transparency for Loyal Label. The report will include a detailed analysis of projects that are supported by proceeds from our company and will feature young social entrepreneurs who have received support from The Loyal Foundation. Additionally, the report will serve as an outlet to announce upcoming product releases and specials to the existing consumer base. The report would be printed for distribution throughout our T-Shirt Truck Tours and in participating retailers, and it will be available electronically online.

A CLOSER LOOK AT THE T-SHIRT TRUCK TOUR

The Loyal Label T-Shirt Truck Tour will occur once every collegiate semester for about three months. Our aim is to spread awareness of the brand, connect with our customers, and bolster revenues by making sales along the way. With a different selection of universities spread across the country on each tour, Loyal Label can effectively promote its brand and its values.

The operating costs include financing for the truck ($414.58 per month), maintenance and insurance ($236.42 per month), fuel costs ($2,847.55 per tour), marketing and events costs ($10,000 per tour), and staff salary ($13,500 per tour for two additional staff members). We believe the tour can be profitable given our assumptions outlined in the appendix, including visiting 5 medium-sized universities per month. Our goal, however, is to visit over 12 campuses per month with medium- to large-sized student populations (for a more detailed look at the tour, see appendix exhibit 2).

OUR PRICING STRATEGY

Our products are priced competitive to popular, higher end retailers targeted towards young adults, such as Abercrombie & Fitch and American Apparel. Our price point of $26 for our Loyal Ts is averagely priced compared to other sustainable apparel manufacturers, and we offer the additional benefit of donating to a charitable cause. We believe we have flexibility to increase our prices in the future as our brand grows.

ONLINE MARKETING

To gain maximum exposure, we will leverage the power and reach of online social networks. Our journey in starting Loyal Label, especially with the T-Shirt Truck Tour, will be documented into webisodes for social media platforms, the Loyal Label blog, and our website FollowTheStartup.com, which recently launched and has received over 1,000 unique hits. Web presence will serve the dual purpose of broadening our reach and humanizing the brand, ultimately creating personal connections with as many consumers as possible. In this light, we have made a Twitter account, twitter.com/tweetthestartup, which has over 500 followers, and we plan to launch a Loyal Label fan page on Facebook.

Additionally, we will utilize e-mail as an inexpensive and effective way to engage consumers. E-mails will build awareness about new products and special promotions offered on our website. Furthermore, it will serve as a way to continue to connect with consumers post-purchase, as we will use e-mail to update consumers about the progress of the social impact that their purchase made possible.

EVENTS MARKETING

To build brand awareness and increase our interactions with our consumers, Loyal Label will host several events around the country. We will utilize our relationships with our Campus Brand Managers, partner charities, and Loyal Foundation beneficiaries to promote events that increase our presence while promoting various causes. Events that we will participate in will include fashion shows, film festivals, and concerts. With every event, we will focus on documenting the experience to share online.

PUBLIC RELATIONS

Loyal Label will actively pursue strong relationships with members of the press and media industries. By garnering their support, we hope to benefit from additional press coverage, which will ultimately strengthen our brand awareness at a low cost to our company. We will participate in forums and discussions whenever possible and seek out opportunities to be included in editorials targeted towards our primary market segment.

CONSUMER ENGAGEMENT

We will continue to engage consumers in several ways. First, individuals will be able to set up their own personalized Loyal Label homepages. These individual profiles can be customized to reflect whichever of the seven Loyal Label causes the consumer is most concerned about. Furthermore, we will enhance the personal connection consumers feel towards the brand through efforts that connect consumers to management from our company. For example, consumers making large purchases will receive personalized thank-you notes from a member of our management team.

ONE YEAR TIMELINE FOR OUR MARKETING STRATEGY

April–July 2010:

- Marketing efforts focused on online media, including advertisements on Facebook, Google, and environmental blogs, as well as e-mail campaigns
- Build a following on our own company blogs (follow The Startup and the Loyal Blog) as well as our social network pages

August–September 2010:

- Targeted efforts on Facebook towards students at universities that the T-Shirt Truck Tour (TTT) is visiting
- Public relations campaign building awareness and hype about the TTT

September–November 2010:

- Fliers and marketing material produced for distribution by Campus Brand Managers at TTT universities
- T-Shirt Truck Tour takes place and numerous events are held on university campuses across the country

December 2010:

- Heavy e-mail campaign leading into Holiday 2010, with "Season of Giving" messaging
- Branded community service campaign in New York coupled with PR outreach

January 2011:

- Announcement and advertising of our Spring 2011 T-Shirt Truck Tour schedule
- Marketing campaign geared towards buyers for sustainable apparel retailers

February–April 2011:

- Spring 2011 T-Shirt Truck Tour and associated campaigns
- Spring collection marketing

April–May 2011:

- Heavy sales and marketing campaign targeted at buyers for department stores

MANAGEMENT TEAM

The Loyal Label team consists of three seniors at New York University's Stern School of Business. Aaron Kinnari, Edlin Choi, and Stephanie Huang each have great experience, and bring diverse and crucial skill sets to the company.

AARON KINNARI
CHIEF EXECUTIVE OFFICER

Aaron has always been committed to creating a positive impact in the world. He has worked for many non-profit organizations including the Clinton Foundation and the Clinton Global Initiative, both founded by Former President Bill Clinton, and the Council on Foreign Relations. Additionally, Aaron worked for the New York City Mayor's Office and in several marketing-related positions with companies like TBWA/Chiat Media Arts Lab and David and Goliath, working with various clients including Apple, Universal Studios, and Kia Motors. In 2009, Aaron founded The World Water Project, an organization committed to building awareness about the global water crisis and funding projects to deliver clean water to people in need. Under his leadership, the organization developed a strong online presence, raised funds for water delivery programs, and established contacts with partners from the for-profit and non-profit sectors. He is currently the president of Stern Cares, the community service and social entrepreneurship club at NYU Stern. Aaron will use all of his experience to successfully lead the Loyal Label team as the Chief Executive Officer.

STEPHANIE HUANG
CHIEF OPERATIONS OFFICER

Stephanie brings a valuable point of view to the team. She has studied abroad in London and traveled to all corners of Europe, observing first-hand the differences in fashion and culture that characterize each region. Triple majoring in Finance, Marketing, and Art History, she is also focused and hardworking. Her broad experience within the fashion industry includes work as a Marketing Associate at adidas, an Accounting and Finance Intern at Calvin Klein, an Inventory Management Intern at Gucci, and a Buying Intern at Macy's. Along with fashion, new ventures have long been an interest of hers. The Aronsson Group and J. Christopher Capital have been exciting work experiences for her to pique this interest and learn about venture capital. She will serve as the Chief Operations Officer and use her keen and holistic industry knowledge to drive the company forward, building Loyal Label into a formidable player in the world of fashion.

EDLIN CHOI
CHIEF MARKETING OFFICER

Edlin inititially became interested in social enterprise during an exchange program in Sydney, Australia. In a class called The Marine Environment, he learned about the Great Pacific Garbage Patch, a whirlpool of litter in the North Pacific Ocean that is twice the size of Texas. Hoping to help solve this problem, his ambition is to create businesses that will empower people to be proactive and generate positive change. This interest led Edlin to become a founding member and Marketing Director of NYU Stern's undergraduate chapter of Net Impact, a global network that equips students to leverage business to effect social and environmental sustainability. Edlin has worked with Red Bull, building brand awareness in a campus setting and designing word of mouth marketing campaigns. Edlin is also adept at leveraging social media to magnify the reach of these efforts. His work with HBO gave him experience in navigating online social networks and search engine optimization. Majoring in Marketing and Finance, with a specialization in Entrepreneurship, Edlin's financial know-how will help ensure that Loyal Label is a profitable venture while he builds the brand as the Chief Marketing Officer.

ADVISORY BOARD

There are several experienced individuals from the fashion, marketing, finance, legal and technology sectors that we have consulted throughout various steps of producing our business plan. We will continue to consult each of these individuals, and plan to offer them formal positions on an advisory board as we grow our company.

FINANCIALS

FINANCIAL SUMMARY

Our vision is to create a profitable retail company that allows for extra margins to be donated to causes that our consumers care about. We believe that we can achieve this with an approach based on low overhead costs, competitive prices and a unique sales and marketing strategy. Already, we have built critical relationships with key partners beneficial to the progress of our company. After examining comparable companies and averages for apparel start-ups, we believe that our costs are relatively conservative, and we have presented a realistic estimation for our revenues and profits over the next five years. In our appendix, we provide an even more detailed explanation of how we reached our estimated revenues, based on a forecast of sales from our online marketplace, T-Shirt Truck Tour, and third party retailers.

We believe that our sales and marketing strategies are essential to differentiating ourselves from our competitors and generating profits. After identifying a niche sector of the retail industry and an unmet desire in our consumers, we found ourselves able to take advantage of this opportunity while simultaneously benefitting people in all corners of the world. Our main marketing tool is the T-Shirt Truck Tour, which increases brand awareness and customer loyalty directly with our target consumer. In addition, our multi-faceted sales distribution allows us to reach a larger audience to further increase our donations and impact on others.

The retail industry has relatively high start-up costs, with heavy investments for initial inventory. Therefore, we acknowledge that we will realize some losses during the first few years. In the last six months of 2010, which will be our first six months of business, we expect to have losses of just over $15,000. In 2011, we estimate a slightly smaller net loss of around $6,000. However, because of increased sales from expanded product lines and brand awareness, by 2012 we expect to see profits exceeding $26,000. Furthermore, because of the additional sales from our own Loyal Label retail outlets, we predict future sales to lead to revenue growth of a healthy rate of about 80 percent per year after year 2012, reaching about $3.5 million in revenues and just under $300,000 in profits by 2014. Refer to the following pages for our revenue and profits, cash flows, and social return on investment, and our appendix for a more detailed look at our financial analysis.

COST BREAKDOWN
HOW WE'LL SPEND $100,000

MANUFACTURING PRODUCT – *$36,000*
A good part of the funds will go to producing our original Loyal Ts. The allocated amount will allow us to produce 7,000 t-shirts at the price of $5.12 each. We will order these in separate batches to reduce storage costs.

LEGAL & ACCOUNTING FEES – *$3,000*

MARKETING EXPENSES – *$27,400*
To boost our brand presence, we will use a part of the seed funding to fund some of our marketing costs, including costs associated with printing materials, hosting events, online ad buys, public relations consulting, and other initiatives. See "Revenues and Profits" for more details.

TECHNOLOGY COSTS – *$6,000*
A part of the funds will go towards covering technology costs associated with developing www.loyallabel.org and equipment for office operations.

T-SHIRT TRUCK TOUR – *$27,600*
A portion of the seed funding will be used to purchase and remodel the truck for the T-Shirt Truck Tour. This investment in the truck will yield an increase in sales and brand awareness.

REVENUES & PROFITS

	2010	2011	2012	2013	2014
Revenue:[1]					
E-commerce sales	$33,325	$275,500	$644,500	$1,421,500	$2,336,000
T-Shirt Truck sales[2]	$106,125	$391,500	$506,500	$592,750	$679,000
Sales to retailers	$0	$51,000	$153,900	$344,550	$545,700
Less returns	$5,578	$28,720	$52,196	$94,352	$142,428
NET REVENUES	**$133,872**	**$689,280**	**$1,252,704**	**$2,264,448**	**$3,418,272**
Cost of revenue:[3]					
Cost of e-commerce sales	$12,800	$55,456	$131,990	$290,660	$475,972
Cost T-Shirt Truck sales	$17,920	$79,725	$103,423	$121,197	$138,970
Cost of sales to retailers	$0	$17,269	$53,096	$116,653	$183,450
Cost of outgoing donations[4]	$22,300	$119,000	$226,100	$420,450	$640,700
TOTAL COSTS OF REVENUE	**$53,020**	**$271,450**	**$514,609**	**$948,960**	**$1,439,092**
GROSS PROFIT	**$80,852**	**$417,830**	**$738,095**	**$1,315,488**	**$1,979,180**
Operating Expenses:					
Sales and marketing:					
Discounts and rebates[5]	$5,355	$27,571	$37,581	$45,289	$68,365
Printing and mailing costs	$2,000	$3,000	$5,000	$8,000	$9,000
Website and online ads	$3,000	$3,000	$4,000	$5,000	$7,000
Events	$5,000	$6,000	$8,000	$10,000	$14,000
Giveaways/promotions	$2,000	$4,800	$4,000	$4,000	$5,000
Transaction fees[6]	$1,647	$11,077	$23,725	$49,297	$79,171
Legal and accounting fees	$3,000	$6,000	$8,000	$8,000	$10,000
Insurance	$2,790	$4,008	$5,000	$6,000	$8,000
Store and office space[7]	$0	$0	$0	$48,000	$72,000
T-Shirt Truck Tour:					
Financing payments	$12,437[8]	$4,975	$4,975	$4,975	$4,975
Maintenance and insurance	$1,419	$2,837	$2,837	$2,837	$2,837
Fuel costs	$2,848	$5,695	$5,695	$5,695	$5,695
Marketing and events	$10,000	$20,000	$20,000	$20,000	$20,000
Staff salary	$13,500	$27,000	$27,000	$40,500	$40,500
Travel expenses[9]	$7,200	$21,600	$21,600	$32,400	$32,400
Sales, general & administrative[10]	$16,740	$256,960	$520,000	$800,000	$1,140,000
TOTAL OPERATING EXPENSES	**$88,936**	**$404,523**	**$697,413**	**$1,089,993**	**$1,518,943**
OPERATING INCOME	**$(8,084)**	**$13,307**	**$40,682**	**$225,495**	**$460,237**
Income tax expense (35%)	$0	$4,657	$14,239	$78,923	$161,083
NET INCOME (LOSS)	**($8,084)**	**$8,650**	**$26,443**	**$146,571**	**$299,154**

NOTES AND ASSUMPTIONS

[1]Based off of sales projections, which are enumerated in the appendix exhibit 4
[2]Assumes 35 Loyal Ts sold on average per day, over 100 days of the tour, for the first three tours. Two tours per year (spring and fall semesters) starting in 2011
[3]Cost of Goods Sold (COGS) includes all costs associated with product manufacturing, including shipping from manufacturer and packaging. Costs based on quotes from selected manufacturers. Includes special price discounts
[4]Refers to donations given to partner charities to support social outcome
[5]Accounts for 20% of our merchandise receiving a 20% discount first 2 years, 15% discount for third year, and a 10% discount last 2 years
[6]PayPal charges 2.5% on transaction totals, plus $0.35 on each transaction; we expect that the average total for each transaction will be $60, meaning a $0.35 cost is incurred for every $60 in revenue, plus 2.5% of all sales from credit cards (T-Shirt Truck Tour sales with credit cards will also be processed through PayPal)
[7]Estimated rent of $6,000/month ($70/sqf/year, ~1,000 sqf)
[8]Expresses down-payment on truck
[9]Covers costs for food and occasional hotel fares
[10]Includes founder salaries

Additional notes:
Refer to appendix for breakdown of revenues and profits for first 18 months.

CASH FLOWS

	2010, Q3	2010, Q4	2011, Q1	2011, Q2	2011, Q3	2011, Q4	Year Ended December 31 2012	2013	2014
AVERAGE SALES	$28,054	$105,818	$178,574	$156,662	$109,661	$244,382	$1,252,704	$2,264,448	$3,418,272
Revenue growth	-	277%	69%	-12%	-30%	123%	82%	81%	51%
Cost of goods sold	$18,280	$34,740	$68,166	$59,416	$42,958	$100,911	$514,609	$948,960	$1,439,092
% of Sales	65%	33%	38%	38%	39%	41%	41%	42%	42%
GROSS PROFIT	$9,774	$71,078	$110,408	$97,247	$66,703	$143,471	$738,095	$1,315,488	$1,979,180
Gross margin	35%	67%	62%	62%	61%	59%	59%	58%	58%
Operating Expense	$33,934	$35,560	$49,603	$22,155	$33,571	$38,987	$179,507	$254,507	$310,507
SG&A Expense	$2,370	$2,370	$75,990	$75,990	$75,990	$75,990	$580,000	$800,000	$1,140,000
TOTAL OPER. EXP.	$36,304	$37,930	$125,593	$98,145	$109,561	$114,977	$759,507	$1,054,507	$1,450,507
% of Sales	129%	36%	70%	63%	100%	47%	61%	47%	42%
EBIT (TAX-EFFECT.)	$(26,530)	$33,148	$(15,185)	$(898)	$(42,858)	$28,494	$(21,412)	$260,981	$528,673
Operating Margin	-95%	31%	-9%	-1%	-39%	12%	-2%	12%	15%
Change in NWC (1% of Sales)	$281	$1,058	$1,786	$1,567	$1,097	$2,444	$12,527	$22,644	$34,183
UNLEVERED FREE CASH FLOW	($26,810)	$32,090	($16,970)	($2,465)	($43,954)	$26,051	$(33,939)	$238,337	$494,490
Optimistic (+3%)	$(26,526)	$34,190	$(13,712)	$406	$(41,986)	$30,281	$(11,796)	$277,801	$553,866
Pessimistic (-5%)	$(27,285)	$28,589	$(22,401)	$(7,249)	$(47,235)	$18,999	$(70,844)	$172,562	$395,531

SOCIAL RETURN ON INVESTMENT

Much of our success will rely on our ability to analyze our social return on investment, ensure that we continuously maximize out impact, and effectively share our results with our consumers. We have identified a list of eight tools from a list compiled by McKinsey & Company and The Foundation Center, collectively titled "Tools for Researching and Assessing Social Impact" (TRASI). These eight tools will be used in various aspects of our business progression, including developing our products using sustainable practices, identifying potential charity partners, selecting projects for social impact, and analyzing our internal management processes.

Our production process will use Cradle to Cradle ceritfication standards to ensure the life cycle of our products meet the highest standards of sustainability. This includes such aspects of using organic cotton and other raw materials, reducing our use of chemicals in the production process, and encouraging our consumers to retain our products for longer periods of time, thus reducing the amount of waste and turnover of our products.

We will utilize two tools from the Bill and Melinda Gates Foundation to identify and rate potential charitable partners. These tools, known as the Cost Benefit Analysis and Cost Effectiveness Analysis, which collectively measure the return on investment of different social initiatives. Using these tools, we will be able to successfully identify the most promising opportunities for new partnerships. After identifying partners, we will use the Acumen Fund Scorecard to continue to measure our results working on different initiatives. Additionally, the Ashoka Measuring Effectiveness Questionnaire will be used to identify strong, young social entrepreneurs to receive grants from our Loyal Foundation.

Lastly, to internally measure our effectiveness in implementing our mission, we will use the five assessment tools from B-Ratings Systems. This will help us to ensure that we are using our internal resources to the best extent. All of these tools will help us evaluate our impact, and the following demonstrates results from our donations that we expect in three and five years from the start of our company.

RESULTS BY THE END OF YEAR 3

10,497 Kids with clean water for five years.
209,942 School meals for hungry children.
52,485 Trees planted throughout the country.
20,994 People with mosquito nets to stop malaria.
524,857 Books sent to Africa for kids to read.
52,485 Refugees with medical checkups for one year.
52 Young entrepreneurs with $1,000 to change the world.

RESULTS BY THE END OF YEAR 5

40,816 Kids with clean water for five years.
816,314 School meals for hungry children.
204,078 Trees planted throughout the country.
81,631 People with mosquito nets to stop malaria.
2,040,786 Books sent to Africa for kids to read.
204,078 Refugees with medical checkups for one year.
204 Young entrepreneurs with $1,000 to change the world.

While the above results and impacts are compiled from relationships with organizations from our seven original Loyal Ts, our actual results may vary as we add new partners and products as the company grows.

FUTURE

FUTURE OUTLOOK FOR LOYAL LABEL

Loyal Label has identified four future growth opportunities that we believe offer great up-side potential for our company. Each of these will help diversify our products, increase revenues, and further our mission.

Expanding the Product Line: To increase revenue and appeal to a larger audience, Loyal Label will introduce additional products including hoodies, bags, and other accessories. We will experiment with offering higher priced items offered in limited edition runs, and invite well-known guest designers to develop a few products. One possible item includes a designer bag priced at $6,000, that when purchased, will fund the entire cost of construction for a water well for a community in need.

Developing "Little Loyals" Youth Line: We will introduce the "Little Loyals" line, a line of clothing specifically for kids. In creating children's clothing, we hope to attract their young, thirty-something parents, who are at the higher end of our target age group. We believe that our products, which use less chemicals and organic materials in production, will be especially of interest to new parents worried about selecting the highest quality products for their children.

Setting up Regional Retail Outlets: By establishing physical retail outlets, we hope to mitigate some of the fears of buying from a relatively unknown brand and increase brand awareness throughout the country. These Loyal Label stores will add to the customer experience as we integrate information about our causes into our store. We plan to launch our first retail store in New York City in July of 2013, and will expand to a second west coast store in 2014.

Investing in Fair Factories in Developing Countries: By building fair factories in developing nations, Loyal Label will directly aid communities in need through sustainable investments. All fair factories will pay livable wages to employees, offer health benefits, and provide education services to children in the local communities. With our Fair Factories, we believe we can truly revolutionize the retail industry, which has historically negative perceptions regarding labor practices.

All four of our future goals help further Loyal Label's mission of positively impacting the world. We believe that each of them offer great potential for our company and our global community.

APPENDIX

EXHIBIT 1 - EXAMPLES OF SHIRT DESIGNS

PEACE LINE
Proceeds from this shirt will be given to the UN Refugee Agency to provide a child with full medical checkups for one year.

WATER LINE
Proceeds from this shirt will be given to charity: water to fund well construction and provide a person with clean water for five years.

LOYAL LINE
Proceeds from this shirt support the mission of our own Loyal Foundation, which gives grants to young social entrepreneurs.

EARTH LINE
Proceeds from this shirt will be given to the Nature Conservancy to cover the costs of planting five trees in the United States.

EXHIBIT 2 - T-SHIRT TRUCK TOUR SCHEDULE

Date	School	State	Approximate Size
Aug 29–30	New York University	New York	41,700
Aug 31	Columbia	New York	22,600
Sep 1	Marist College	New York	5,700
Sep 2	Cornell	New York	19,800
Sep 5	Syracuse	New York	19,000
Sep 7–8	Harvard	Massachusetts	25,600
Sep 8	Tufts	Massachusetts	9,700
Sep 9–10	Northeastern	Massachusetts	24,400
Sep 12–13	Boston College	Massachusetts	14,600
Sep 13–14	Boston University	Massachusetts	32,000
Sep 15	University of New Hampshire	New Hampshire	15,000
Sep 16	Plymouth State University	New Hampshire	6,500
Sep 19–21	Penn State, Park Campus	Pennsylvania	43,200
Sep 21	Bucknell	Pennsylvania	3,600
Sep 22	Villanova	Pennsylvania	10,400
Sep 23–24	University of Pennsylvania	Pennsylvania	23,900
Sep 27	Lehigh	Pennsylvania	6,800
Sep 28	University of Pittsburgh-Pittsburgh Campus	Pennsylvania	27,000
Sep 29–30	University of Akron	Ohio	23,000
Oct 1–4	Ohio State University, Main Campus	Ohio	52,500
Oct 5–7	University of Michigan-Ann Arbor	Michigan	41,000
Oct 8–11	Michigan State	Michigan	46,000
Oct 12	University of Notre Dame	Indiana	11,700
Oct 13	Chicago State	Illinois	6,800
Oct 14–15	University of Chicago	Illinois	14,500
Oct 18–19	Northwestern	Illinois	19,000
Oct 20	Loyola	Illinois	15,500
Oct 21	Marquette	Wisconsin	11,500
Oct 22–25	University of Wisconsin-Madison	Wisconsin	41,500
Oct 26	Illinois State	Illinois	20,200
Oct 27–28	Indiana University Bloomington	Indiana	38,900
Oct 30–31	Miami University	Ohio	15,900
Nov 2–3	Georgia State	Georgia	27,100
Nov 4	Georgia Institute of Technology	Georgia	18,700
Nov 5–8	University of Georgia	Georgia	33,800
Nov 10	University of North Florida	Florida	16,400
Nov 11	Florida Atlantic University	Florida	26,100
Nov 12–13	University of Miami	Florida	15,400
Nov 15	University of Tampa	Florida	5,600
Nov 16–18	University of Florida	Florida	51,700
Nov 20–22	Florida State University	Florida	40,500

EXHIBIT 3 - REVENUES & PROFITS BY MONTH (1 OF 3)

	Jul-10	Aug-10	Sep-10	Oct-10	Nov-10	Dec-10
Revenue:						
E-commerce sales	$1,333	$2,333	$4,332	$6,665	$8,665	$9,998
T-Shirt Truck sales	$0	$0	$21,225	$31,838	$39,266	$13,796
Sales to retailers	$0	$0	$0	$0	$0	$0
Less returns	$53	$93	$1,022	$1,540	$1,917	$952
NET REVENUES	$1,280	$2,239	$24,535	$36,962	$46,014	$22,842
Cost of revenue:						
Cost of e-commerce sales	$512	$896	$1,664	$2,560	$3,328	$3,840
Cost of T-Shirt Truck sales	$0	$3,584	$6,272	$6,272	$1,792	$0
Cost of sales to retailers	$0	$0	$0	$0	$0	$0
Cost of outgoing donations	$892	$1,561	$2,899	$4,460	$5,798	$6,690
TOTAL COSTS OF REVENUE	$1,404	$6,041	$10,835	$13,292	$10,918	$10,530
GROSS PROFIT	$(124)	$(3,802)	$13,700	$23,670	$35,096	$12,312
Operating Expenses:						
Sales and marketing:						
Discounts and rebates	$51	$90	$981	$1,478	$1,841	$914
Printing and mailing costs	$200	$760	$400	$0	$640	$0
Website and online ads	$200	$400	$400	$0	$640	$1,360
Events	$1,000	$0	$1,000	$1,000	$1,000	$1,000
Giveaways/promotions	$0	$400	$400	$400	$400	$400
Transaction fees	$41	$72	$257	$391	$496	$389
Legal and accounting fees	$500	$500	$500	$500	$500	$500
Insurance	$465	$465	$465	$465	$465	$465
Store and office space	$0	$0	$0	$0	$0	$0
T-Shirt Truck Tour:						
Financing payments	$10,365	$415	$415	$415	$415	$415
Maintenance and insurance	$236	$236	$236	$236	$236	$236
Fuel costs	$0	$0	$949	$949	$949	$0
Marketing and events	$0	$0	$3,333	$3,333	$3,333	$0
Staff salary	$0	$0	$4,500	$4,500	$4,500	$0
Travel expenses	$0	$0	$0	$3,600	$3,600	$0
Sales, general & administrative	$2,790	$2,790	$2,790	$2,790	$2,790	$2,790
TOTAL OPERATING EXPENSES	$15,849	$6,128	$16,627	$20,058	$21,805	$8,469
OPERATING INCOME	($15,973)	($9,929)	($2,927)	$3,612	$13,290	$3,843
Income tax expense (35%)	-	-	-	$1,264	$4,652	$1,345
NET INCOME (LOSS)	($15,973)	($9,929)	($2,927)	$2,348	$8,639	$2,498

EXHIBIT 3 - REVENUES & PROFITS BY MONTH (2 OF 3)

	Jan-11	Feb-11	Mar-11	Apr-11	May-11	Jun-11
Revenue:						
E-commerce sales	$13,775	$16,530	$27,550	$33,060	$22,040	$16,530
T-Shirt Truck sales	$19,575	$39,150	$58,725	$58,725	$19,575	$0
Sales to retailers	$2,550	$3,060	$5,100	$6,120	$4,080	$3,060
Less returns	$1,436	$2,350	$3,655	$3,916	$1,828	$784
NET REVENUES	$34,464	$56,390	$87,720	$93,989	$43,867	$18,806
Cost of revenue:						
Cost of e-commerce sales	$2,773	$3,327	$5,546	$6,655	$4,436	$3,327
Cost T-Shirt Truck sales	$3,986	$11,162	$12,756	$9,567	$0	$0
Cost of sales to retailers	$863	$1,036	$1,727	$2,072	$1,382	$1,036
Cost of outgoing donations	$5,950	$7,140	$11,900	$14,280	$9,520	$7,140
TOTAL COSTS OF REVENUE	$13,573	$22,665	$31,929	$32,574	$15,338	$11,504
GROSS PROFIT	$20,892	$33,725	$55,792	$61,415	$28,529	$7,303
Operating Expenses:						
Sales and marketing:						
Discounts and rebates	$1,379	$2,256	$3,509	$3,760	$1,755	$752
Printing and mailing costs	$500	$500	$100	$100	$100	$100
Website and online ads	$500	$500	$100	$100	$100	$100
Events	$0	$600	$800	$0	$600	$800
Giveaways/promotions	$400	$400	$400	$400	$400	$400
Transaction fees	$554	$756	$1,222	$1,398	$818	$528
Legal and accounting fees	$500	$500	$500	$500	$500	$500
Insurance	$334	$334	$334	$334	$334	$334
Store and office space	$0	$0	$0	$0	$0	$0
T-Shirt Truck Tour:						
Financing payments	$415	$415	$415	$415	$415	$415
Maintenance and insurance	$236	$236	$236	$236	$236	$236
Fuel costs	$949	$949	$949	$0	$0	$0
Marketing and events	$3,333	$3,333	$3,333	$0	$0	$0
Staff salary	$4,500	$4,500	$4,500	$0	$0	$0
Travel expenses	$3,600	$3,600	$3,600	$0	$0	$0
Sales, general & administrative	$12,330	$18,330	$18,330	$18,330	$18,330	$22,330
TOTAL OPERATING EXPENSES	$29,530	$37,209	$38,328	$25,572	$23,587	$26,495
OPERATING INCOME	($8,639)	($3,484)	$17,463	$35,843	$4,942	($19,192)
Income tax expense (35%)	$0	$0	$6,112	$12,545	$1,730	$0
NET INCOME (LOSS)	($8,639)	($3,484)	$11,351	$23,298	$3,212	($19,192)

EXHIBIT 3 - REVENUES & PROFITS BY MONTH (3 OF 3)

	Jul-11	Aug-11	Sep-11	Oct-11	Nov-11	Dec-11
Revenue:						
E-commerce sales	$11,020	$16,530	$19,285	$27,550	$33,060	$38,570
T-Shirt Truck sales	$0	$0	$58,725	$58,725	$58,725	$19,575
Sales to retailers	$2,040	$3,060	$3,570	$5,100	$6,120	$7,140
Less returns	$522	$784	$3,263	$3,655	$3,916	$2,611
NET REVENUES	$12,538	$18,806	$78,317	$87,720	$93,989	$62,674
Cost of revenue:						
Cost of e-commerce sales	$2,218	$3,327	$3,882	$5,546	$6,655	$7,764
Cost T-Shirt Truck sales	$0	$0	$10,364	$11,162	$20,729	$0
Cost of sales to retailers	$691	$1,036	$1,209	$1,727	$2,072	$2,418
Cost of outgoing donations	$4,760	$7,140	$8,330	$11,900	$14,280	$16,660
TOTAL COSTS OF REVENUE	$7,669	$11,504	$23,785	$30,334	$43,736	$26,842
GROSS PROFIT	$4,869	$7,303	$54,532	$57,386	$50,253	$35,832
Operating Expenses:						
Sales and marketing:						
Discounts and rebates	$502	$752	$3,133	$3,509	$3,760	$2,507
Printing and mailing costs	$100	$500	$200	$200	$500	$100
Website and online ads	$100	$500	$200	$200	$500	$100
Events	$800	$400	$1,000	$0	$0	$1,000
Giveaways/promotions	$400	$400	$400	$400	$400	$400
Transaction fees	$352	$528	$958	$1,222	$1,398	$1,345
Legal and accounting fees	$500	$500	$500	$500	$500	$500
Insurance	$334	$334	$334	$334	$334	$334
Store and office space	$0	$0	$0	$0	$0	$0
T-Shirt Truck Tour:						
Financing payments	$415	$415	$415	$415	$415	$415
Maintenance and insurance	$236	$236	$236	$236	$236	$236
Fuel costs	$0	$0	$949	$949	$949	$0
Marketing and events	$0	$0	$3,333	$3,333	$3,333	$0
Staff salary	$0	$0	$4,500	$4,500	$4,500	$0
Travel expenses	$0	$0	$3,600	$3,600	$3,600	$0
Sales, general & administrative	$22,330	$22,330	$22,330	$26,330	$26,330	$29,330
TOTAL OPERATING EXPENSES	$26,068	$26,895	$42,088	$45,728	$46,755	$36,267
OPERATING INCOME	$(21,200)	$(19,592)	$12,443	$11,658	$3,499	$(435)
Income tax expense (35%)	$0	$0	$4,355	$4,080	$1,224	$0
NET INCOME (LOSS)	$(21,200)	$(19,592)	$8,088	$7,578	$2,274	$(435)

EXHIBIT 4 - SALES FORECAST (CONT. ON NEXT PAGE)

Item/Avenue of Sale	COGS	Outgoing Donation	Sales Price	2010	2011	2012	2013	2014
				Realistic	Realistic	Realistic	Realistic	Realistic
LOYAL Ts								
LoyalLabel.org & LL Retail	$5.12	$4.00	$26	$18,200	$234,000	$520,000	$1,144,000	$1,846,000
Units				700	9,000	20,000	44,000	71,000
T-Shirt Truck Tour	$5.12	$4.00	$26	$91,000	$364,000	$468,000	$546,000	$624,000
Units				3,500	14,000	18,000	21,000	24,000
Third Party Retailers	$5.12	$4.00	$15.60	$0	$46,800	$124,800	$265,200	$436,800
Units				0	3,000	8,000	17,000	28,000
Revenue				$109,200	$644,800	$1,112,800	$1,955,200	$2,906,800
Total Units				4200	26000	46000	82000	123000
COGS				$21,504	$133,120	$235,520	$419,840	$629,760
Outgoing Donations				$16,800	$104,000	$184,000	$328,000	$492,000
Profit				$70,896	$407,680	$693,280	$1,207,360	$1,785,040
Hoodies Against Hunger								
LoyalLabel.org & LL Retail	$16.09	$10.00	$55	$15,125	$22,000	$55,000	$110,000	$154,000
Units				275	400	1000	2000	2800
T-Shirt Truck Tour	$16.09	$10.00	$55	$15,125	$27,500	$38,500	$46,750	$55,000
Units				275	500	700	850	1000
Third Party Retailers	$16.09	$10.00	$33.00	$0	$3,300	$13,200	$23,100	$33,000
Units				0	100	400	700	1000
Revenue				$30,250	$52,800	$106,700	$179,850	$242,000
Total Units				550	1000	2100	3550	4800
COGS				$8,850	$16,090	$33,789	$57,120	$77,232
Outgoing Donations				$5,500	$10,000	$21,000	$35,500	$48,000
Profit				$15,901	$26,710	$51,911	$87,231	$116,768
$25 or Less Products								
LoyalLabel.org & LL Retail	$3.00	$3.00	$15	$0	$7,500	$13,500	$24,000	$34,500
Units				0	500	900	1600	2300
T-Shirt Truck Tour	$3.00	$3.00	$15	$0	$0	$0	$0	$0
Units				0	0	0	0	0
Third Party Retailers	$3.00	$3.00	$9.00	$0	$900	$3,600	$7,650	$12,600
Units				0	100	400	850	1400
Revenue				$0	$8,400	$17,100	$31,650	$47,100
Total Units				0	600	1300	2450	3700
COGS				$0	$1,800	$3,900	$7,350	$11,100
Outgoing Donations				$0	$1,800	$3,900	$7,350	$11,100
Profit				$0	$4,800	$9,300	$16,950	$24,900

Item/Avenue of Sale	COGS	Outgoing Donation	Sales Price	2010	2011	2012	2013	2014
				Realistic	Realistic	Realistic	Realistic	Realistic
$25 - $100 Products								
LoyalLabel.org & LL Retail	$18.00	$12.00	$65	$0	$0	$26,000	$58,500	$104,000
Units				0	0	400	900	1600
T-Shirt Truck Tour	$18.00	$12.00	$65	$0	$0	$0	$0	$0
Units				0	0	0	0	0
Third Party Retailers	$18.00	$12.00	$39.00	$0	$0	$7,800	$15,600	$27,300
Units				0	0	200	400	700
Revenue				$0	$0	$33,800	$74,100	$131,300
Total Units				0	0	600	1300	2300
COGS				$0	$0	$10,800	$23,400	$41,400
Outgoing Donations				$0	$0	$7,200	$15,600	$27,600
Profit				$0	$0	$15,800	$35,100	$62,300
$100 or More Products								
LoyalLabel.org & LL Retail	$18.00	$40.00	$150	$0	$12,000	$30,000	$60,000	$97,500
Units				0	80	200	400	650
T-Shirt Truck Tour	$18.00	$40.00	$150	$0	$0	$0	$0	$0
Units				0	0	0	0	0
Third Party Retailers	$18.00	$40.00	$90.00	$0	$0	$4,500	$18,000	$36,000
Units				0	0	50	200	400
Revenue				$0	$12,000	$34,500	$78,000	$133,500
Total Units				0	80	250	600	1050
COGS				$0	$1,440	$4,500	$10,800	$18,900
Outgoing Donations				$0	$3,200	$10,000	$24,000	$42,000
Profit				$0	$7,360	$20,000	$43,200	$72,600
$1000 Specialty Products								
LoyalLabel.org & LL Retail	$200.00	$200.00	$1,000	$0	$0	$0	$25,000	$100,000
Units				0	0	0	25	100
T-Shirt Truck Tour	$200.00	$200.00	$1,000	$0	$0	$0	$0	$0
Units				0	0	0	0	0
Third Party Retailers	$200.00	$200.00	$600.00	$0	$0	$0	$15,000	$0
Units				0	0	0	25	0
Revenue				$0	$0	$0	$40,000	$100,000
Total Units				0	0	0	50	100
COGS				$0	$0	$0	$10,000	$20,000
Outgoing Donations				$0	$0	$0	$10,000	$20,000
Profit				$0	$0	$0	$20,000	$60,000
Total Revenue				$139,450	$718,000	$1,304,900	$2,358,800	$3,560,700
Total Revenue Less Returns				$133,872	$689,280	$1,252,704	$2,264,448	$3,418,272
Total COGS				$30,354	$152,450	$288,509	$528,510	$798,392
Total Outgoing Donations				$22,300	$119,000	$226,100	$420,450	$640,700
Gross Profit				$81,219	$417,830	$738,095	$1,315,489	$1,979,180

ENDNOTES

1. International Market for Sustainable Apparel, May 2008, Packaged Facts, Page 71.

2. International Market for Sustainable Apparel, May 2008, Packaged Facts, Page 71.

3. International Market for Sustainable Apparel, May 2008, Packaged Facts, Page 1.

4. International Market for Sustainable Apparel, May 2008, Packaged Facts, Page 75.

5. Times and Trends: Sustainability 2007, Information Resources Inc.

6. Maritz Research, September 12, 2007 Press Release.

7. Generational Market Research Bundle: Baby Boomers, Gen X and Gen Y, December 2008, Packaged Facts.

8. Generational Market Research Bundle: Baby Boomers, Gen X and Gen Y, December 2008, Packaged Facts.

9. U.S. Regional Trends: Demographics, Attitudes, and Consumer Behavior, February 2008, Packaged Facts.

10. AARP and Focalyst Survey, www.focalyst.com.

11. U.S. Retail E-Commerce Sales, February 9, 2010, www.emarketer.com.

THOUGHT QUESTIONS

1   Assume that you are one of the founders of Loyal Label. What would be your three-minute pitch to investors and stakeholders (employees, new team members, volunteers, etc.)?

2   How well does Loyal Label explain its Social/Innovation, Social Impact, and Sustainability/Scale? What could be improved?

3   In your own words, what is Loyal Label's theory of change? How compelling is it?

4   Has Loyal Label clearly defined its go-to-market strategy? If you were in its founders' shoes, what would you do differently?

5   In what ways other than those described in the plan can Loyal Label measure its social impact?

6   How well has Loyal Label outlined its marketing plan and competition? What additional information would you like it to present?

7   If you were a social investor, would you invest in Loyal Label? Why, or why not? What are your major concerns? How could Loyal Label resolve them?

REFERENCES

Amason, A., Shrader, R., & Tompson, G. (2006). Newness and novelty: Relating top management team composition to new venture performance. *Journal of Business Venturing, 21*, 125–148.

Anderson, A. A. (2004). Theory of change as a tool for strategic planning. Paper presented at the Aspen Institute Roundtable on Community Change in New York, New York. Retrieved from http://theoryofchange.org/pdf/tocII_final4.pdf (accessed September 30, 2010).

Austin, J. E. (2000). *The collaboration challenge: How nonprofits and businesses succeed through strategic alliances.* San Francisco, CA: Jossey-Bass.

Bloom, P. N., & Chatterji, A. K. (2009). Scaling social entrepreneurial impact. *California Management Review, 51*, 114–133.

Bradach, J. L. (2003). Going to scale: The challenge of replicating social programs. *Stanford Social Innovation Review, 1*, 19–25.

Brinkerhoff, P. C. (2000). *Social entrepreneurship: The art of mission-based venture development.* New York: John Wiley.

Brock, D. D., & Ashoka Global Academy for Social Entrepreneurship (2008). *Social Entrepreneurship Teaching Resources Handbook.* Retrieved from http://ssrn.com/abstract=1344412.

Bryson, J. M. (1995). *Strategic planning for public and nonprofit organizations.* San Francisco, CA: Jossey-Bass.

Bryson, J. M. (2004). *Strategic planning for public and nonprofit organizations: A guide to strengthening and sustaining organizational achievement.* San Francisco, CA: Jossey-Bass.

Clark, H., & Anderson, A. (2004). Theories of change and logic models: Telling them apart. Paper presented at the annual meeting of the American Evaluation Association in Atlanta, GA. Retrieved, from http://www.evaluationtoolsforracialequity.org/evaluation/resource/doc/TOCs_ and_Logic_Models_forAEA.ppt (accessed September 30, 2010).

Dees, J. G., Anderson, B. B., & Wei-Skillern, J. (2004). Scaling social impact: Strategies for spreading social innovations. *Stanford Social Innovation Review, 1*(4), 24–32.

Gundry, L. K., & Kickul, J. R. (2007). *Entrepreneurship strategy: Changing patterns in new venture creation, growth, and reinvention.* Thousand Oaks, CA: Sage.

Honig, B. (2004). Entrepreneurship education: Toward a model of contingency-based business planning. *Academy of Management Learning and Education, 3*(3), 258–273.

Magretta, J. (2002). Why business models matter. *Harvard Business Review,* May, pp. 3–8.

Miller, C. C., & Cardinal, L. B. (1994). Strategic planning and firm performance: A synthesis of more than two decades of research. *Academy of Management Journal, 37*(6), 1649–1665.

Paton, R. (2003). *Managing and measuring social enterprises.* Thousand Oaks, CA: Sage.

Rogers, P. R., Miller, A., & Judge, W. Q. (1999). Using information processing theory to understand planning/performance relationships in the context of strategy. *Strategic Management Journal, 20*(6), 567–577.

Seelos, C., & Mair, J. (2005). Social entrepreneurship: Creating new business models to serve the poor. *Business Horizons, 48*(3), 241–246.

Sharir, M., & Lerner, M. (2005). Gauging the success of social ventures initiated by individual social entrepreneurs. *Journal of World Business, 41,* 6–20.

Sherman, A. J. (2007). *Start fast and start right.* New York: Kaplan.

Zahra, S. A., Rawhouser, H., Bhawe, N., Neubaum, D. O., & Hayton, J. C. (2008). Globalization of social entrepreneurship opportunities. *Strategic Entrepreneurship Journal, 2,* 117–131.

Zietlow, J., Hankin, J. A., & Seidner, A. G. (2007). *Financial management for nonprofit organizations: Policies and practices.* Hoboken, NJ: John Wiley.

Organizational Structure

AIM/PURPOSE

The aim of this chapter is to capture the alternatives available to social entrepreneurs as they design and structure their ventures from a legal and organizational perspective. For-profit, nonprofit, and hybrid models are examined and their advantages and limitations discussed.

Once a social entrepreneur has identified an opportunity to pursue and developed a mission, vision, and strategic plan for the venture that will pursue it, deeper thought can be given to the organizational structure of her or his venture. The decision regarding organizational structure is a very serious one that requires careful consideration. It can affect a social venture's financing, accountability, and legitimacy (Lasprogata & Cotten, 2003).

What are the organizational design options available? How should the venture be designed to maximize its effectiveness in achieving its mission and to create significant impact? What are the legal implications of a given organizational structure? How does legal structure affect the venture's ability to acquire resources, particularly financial resources? These are the questions that are addressed in this chapter.

LEARNING OBJECTIVES FOR THIS CHAPTER

1. To appreciate the importance of organizational structure to the financing, accountability, and legitimacy of a social venture.
2. To understand the nature, strengths, and limitations of the pure nonprofit structural form.
3. To understand the nature, strengths, and limitations of the pure for-profit structural form.
4. To understand the multiple manifestations of the hybrid structural form.
5. To master the choice set available to social entrepreneurs when making decisions regarding the organizational structure of their ventures.

GENERAL ORGANIZATIONAL DESIGN OPTIONS

Before entrepreneurship became a major factor in the accomplishment of social goals, the delivery of social services was largely accomplished by entities labeled "charities" or "charitable organizations." These were tax-exempt organizations that the U.S. government gladly relieved of their taxpaying duties because they were undertaking difficult activities that government officials were unwilling or unable to perform in areas such as health, education, and community development (Lasprogata & Cotten, 2003). Furthermore, governments at all levels routinely channeled public grant monies to these entities to help them sustain their efforts. These organizations had a simple nonprofit structure, and because they were clearly engaged in activities that neither the private nor the public sectors had an interest in pursuing, there were rarely conflicts between this sector and the other two.

Things changed substantially in the 1980s, when the Reagan administration introduced its brand of "new federalism." In an effort to reduce the size of the federal government and its budget, responsibilities for many social services were transferred to the local level without federal funding to pay for them. As one consequence, nonprofits were forced to look for other sources of support. The rolling back of federal government responsibility and funding for charitable work had an additional impact: it increased the demand for social services. Thus, nonprofits were hit with increased demand for their services and the loss of a major form of financial support (Lasprogata & Cotten, 2003).

In the Tax Reform Act of 1986 the federal government attempted to redress this problem by expanding tax advantages to individuals and organizations that made donations to nonprofits. While this stimulated private giving to charities, it did not make up for the federal government dollars withdrawn. It also proved not to provide enough additional revenue to support the myriad nonprofits springing up to meet the rising demand for social services (Wei-Skillern, Austin, Leonard, & Stevenson, 2007). Increased competition and a lack of available funding began to force nonprofits to look more comprehensively for financial resources to sustain themselves.

It was this scenario that gave rise to social entrepreneurship as we know it today. Nonprofit charities began looking for ways to legally generate earned income within their nonprofit structures. Some social entrepreneurs decided that the nonprofit model was too limiting and began to create for-profit social ventures. This created nonprofit and for-profit ventures that were enough alike that the latter perceived the former to be waging unfair (subsidized) competition. Still other social entrepreneurs began experimenting with so-called hybrid structures that combined nonprofit and for-profit features.

Into this chaotic scene walks the nascent social entrepreneur. It is clear that this entrepreneur has multiple options from which to choose in structuring her or his venture. It is also clear that organizational structure has a relationship to funding structure. What is *not* always clear is exactly what each of these options entails and

Pure Nonprofit	Hybrids	Pure For-Profit

FIGURE 6.1 The Spectrum of Structural Options in Social Entrepreneurship
Source: Dees, Emerson, & Economy (2001, p. 70).

how each option impacts the ability of the social venture to generate revenue. If these issues could be clarified, presumably social entrepreneurs would be able to make more informed, and less risky, decisions about structuring their ventures.

One way to frame the range of structural options available is as a spectrum, or continuum, with a purely nonprofit form at one end point and a purely for-profit structure at the other. Between these two options lie a host of hybrid structural forms: for-profits with nonprofit subsidiaries, nonprofits with for-profit subsidiaries, nonprofit partnerships, and nonprofit–for-profit partnerships. Figure 6.1 offers a simple depiction of this spectrum.

We will now take each of these major structural forms in order and examine them in some detail.

PURE NONPROFITS

Despite their name, nonprofit organizations are not precluded from generating a profit. They can produce excess revenue (that which exceeds their costs) as long as they observe the "private inurement doctrine." This legal restriction holds that a nonprofit may not distribute its earnings among its investors and owners. These earnings must be plowed back into the organization and its pursuit of its mission. This is the chief distinction between a nonprofit and a for-profit organization (Hopkins, 2001; Lasprogata & Cotten, 2003).

Nonprofits are not necessarily tax exempt, though most are. In the United States, to receive tax-exempt status a nonprofit must apply for same under the Internal Revenue Code. Section 501 of the Internal Revenue Code provides relief from federal income taxes. While there are several types of tax-exempt entities defined in Section 501, the most common are classified in Section 501(c)(3). These are public-serving charities (Hopkins, 2001; Lasprogata & Cotten, 2003). Most nonprofit social ventures carry the 501(c)(3) designation.

Tax-exempt nonprofits originally meet and continue to maintain their status by being in conformance with the requirements of Section 501(c)(3) and the Treasury Regulations. In particular, this means that they must conform to both the "organizational test" and the "operational test." The former requires the nonprofit to clearly state its charitable purpose(s) in its articles of incorporation (most nonprofits are organized as corporations) and also to state that it will engage, in substantial measure, in only those activities that fulfill this charitable purpose(s). The "operational test" opens the nonprofit's operations to examination by the government to determine that they are indeed focused on the organization's expressed purpose(s). Only an insubstantial portion of the nonprofit's activity can be in pursuit of goals outside of its purpose if it is to retain tax-exempt status (Lasprogata & Cotten, 2003). Clearly, this latter rule leaves the door open for substantial subjectivity in its interpretation.

If a nonprofit is found to be engaged in revenue-generating activity that does not meet the operational test, the earnings from that activity are subject to the Unrelated Business Income Tax (UBIT). This tax is levied at the same rate as would apply to a for-profit corporation in the same situation, so as to eliminate unfair competition to for-profits by nonprofits (Lasprogata & Cotten, 2003). This is an especially important consideration when pure nonprofits engage in "social enterprise" by undertaking activities to generate earned income. At this juncture, they are no longer pure nonprofits but have become hybrid organizations that have taken on features of a for-profit company.

Because of the somewhat unclear way in which the operational test has been interpreted by the courts, the fact that the UBIT is seen as onerous by some, and that there are allegations of unfair competition aimed at nonprofits that engage in social enterprise activities, considerable controversy swirls around this issue. Some attorneys and business advisors take a strict constructionist view and advise their nonprofit clients to avoid the UBIT at all costs by engaging in no activities that even hint of being out of perfect alignment with their mission. Others argue that there are worse things than paying taxes and that having to do so merely indicates the nonprofit's success at raising much-needed excess revenue. Still others advise their nonprofit clients to first be innovative in finding ways to generate earned income, and then worry about the legalities, as the latter are still very much in flux.

In order to receive tax-exempt status, a nonprofit organization must file a Form 1023 with the Internal Revenue Service (IRS). If this is done within twenty-seven months of its formation, the IRS's tax-exempt status is retroactive to the day the nonprofit was formed. Once tax-exempt status is received, a nonprofit with more than $25,000 a year in gross receipts is required to file a Form 990, or annual information return. Nonprofits that earn unrelated business income must file a Form 990-T, in addition to their Form 990 (Hopkins, 2001).

One of the chief advantages of adopting the nonprofit structure is the multiple options it affords for generating revenue. Not only does it provide the ability to produce earned income, within the limits discussed, but it makes the social venture eligible to receive philanthropic dollars—both traditional and nontraditional.

There are several types of traditional philanthropy: individual donations, foundation grants, government grants, and corporate giving. Individual donations account for the greater part of philanthropic giving. Although there are fewer foundation grants to be had, they are popular with nonprofit social ventures because they usually provide larger amounts of money (Wei-Skillern et al., 2007). Increasingly, they come with significant strings attached, as foundations are holding their grantees accountable for outputs, outcomes, and impact. Social ventures that pursue foundation grants should be prepared not only to compete vigorously for them but to meet rigorous reporting requirements throughout the granting period as well.

The availability of government grants has generally waned in recent years. However, their accessibility tends to vary with the ideology of the government leadership and with which social issues are in good currency at the time. In general, conservative regimes are less likely to make grants than liberal regimes, but the individual interests of leaders may also be a factor. For example, the Clinton administration was a major proponent of microenterprise development; therefore, substantial support was made available to nonprofit microenterprise programs during that period. The Obama administration has made renewable energy a focus, resulting in grant support for efforts in this arena.

Corporate giving offices have long supported charitable activity in the community or communities where these businesses operate for the purposes of receiving tax write-offs and generating goodwill among customers and prospective customers. These grants are usually relatively small. They are especially attractive to nonprofit social ventures, however, because they are usually given as cash (Wei-Skillern et al., 2007).

The availability of these forms of traditional philanthropic funding is exclusive to nonprofit social ventures. For-profit social entities are not eligible, for two major reasons. First, the tax write-offs that spur individual donations and corporate giving apply only to gifts made to nonprofit organizations. Second, the rules that apply to foundations (and that they impose upon themselves) and governments make it very undesirable to provide grant money to for-profit companies, even when they are pursuing social missions. While private contractors may deliver certain social products or services funded by foundation grants, they typically do so as subcontractors to a nonprofit entity, which is the actual grantee. Government contracting with for-profit companies usually operates under a different set of rules that involve a bidding process. Note that these are contracts and *not* grants.

Traditional philanthropy, as it is usually practiced, presents some challenges to nonprofit social ventures. One such challenge is that grants tend to be short term, typically from one to three years. Yet, as is emphasized in this book, social problems are long term. Thus, nonprofits that receive grants find themselves continuously applying and reapplying for them. This takes time and effort away from pursuing their mission. Another challenge is that grants tend to be highly categorical—that is, funders have very specific activities they want to fund. These activities often constitute only a small portion of the nonprofit's mission. This means that nonprofits must spend considerable time cobbling together funding from multiple sources to cover their various activities. This is highly inefficient (Wei-Skillern et al., 2007).

A third challenge is that many funders only want to fund innovations in their area of giving or to fund high-visibility tangible assets that lend themselves to generating publicity. For example, most foundations seek to fund the launch of new approaches to solving social problems. This allows them to associate themselves with creative thinking and position themselves as champions of social innovation. However, once the new social venture is launched, they are often no longer interested in funding its operations. In fairness, foundations typically warn the grantee of this fact in the application process, as they require a plan for self-sufficiency. However, they do not seem to understand that it is not start-up that is the crucial stage in the life of a venture; it is the first three to five years, when failure often takes place because the entrepreneur lacks the skills to restructure the venture for the next stage in its growth (Lichtenstein & Lyons, 2010). Ironically, the foundation is expending financial resources on starting the venture only to leave it to die of starvation, thereby wasting the initial investment—the equivalent of forcing the hatchling out of the nest too soon.

Governments are guilty of similarly flawed thinking in their granting decisions. As an example, a number of government agencies have made grants to nonprofit ventures in order to develop business incubators to encourage entrepreneurship among economically disadvantaged groups. However, the grants are typically only for the bricks and mortar aspects of the incubator and not for covering the incubator's expenses for developing entrepreneurs and companies. In effect, the government agency is saying that it is more important to successful entrepreneurship to develop and equip a building than it is to develop the skills of the individual entrepreneurs so that they can, in turn, develop their businesses. Just as in the case of the foundations, fledgling ventures are being started but not sustained.

As a result of these challenges and the serious problems they create for social entrepreneurs, several forms of nontraditional philanthropy have emerged in recent years. These include social venture philanthropic organizations, private market investments, e-philanthropy, and longer-term loans by foundations (Wei-Skillern et al., 2007). Social venture philanthropy is epitomized by such organizations as Ashoka, Echoing Green, and the Acumen Fund. These philanthropists have adopted a venture capital model for financing social entrepreneurship. Thus, they have adopted a rigorous vetting process for determining the ventures they will fund. In particular, they are looking for high-impact social ventures—those that will grow significantly, maximizing reach and mission achievement. Like private-sector venture capitalists, social venture philanthropists provide more than merely financing. They supply training, role-modeling, and mentoring to their investees, and they encourage networking among the social ventures in their portfolio (Wei-Skillern et al., 2007). The return on investment they are seeking is social return on investment (SROI). While most of the investment by social venture philanthropists is in nonprofit ventures, organizations like the Acumen Fund and the New Schools Venture Fund do invest in for-profit social ventures as well.

Increasingly, private markets are investing in social ventures. One example is the financial capital made available by private banks to nonprofit microenterprise development programs (MEPs). This money is put into the loan fund maintained by the MEP, from which it lends to very small businesses as a community development and poverty mitigation strategy. The federal Community Reinvestment Act (CRA) incentivizes this type of investment by banks by requiring it in order for them to be able to engage in mergers and acquisitions and to open branches. In addition, some investment funds have begun to offer portfolios that focus on socially and environmentally conscious ventures (Wei-Skillern et al., 2007).

Philanthropy via the Internet has grown rapidly in recent years. This so-called e-philanthropy has not only provided a new way for nonprofits to interact with their donors, but has also spawned several new social ventures with a mission of expanding choice for donors and exposure for small nonprofits—Kiva (www.kiva. org), for example. This type of philanthropy has several advantages (Blackbaud, 2010):

- It allows nonprofits to get money faster.
- It lowers their processing costs.
- It reduces the costs of reaching donors.
- It accesses a greater diversity of donors.
- It yields higher donations, on average.

Some foundations, working with banks, have begun to make longer-term loans to nonprofits as a way to help them with their working capital needs. These loans are made possible through financial instruments called program-related investments (PRIs). PRIs offer flexibility to foundations by equipping them with a tool that lies between traditional grant making and private investment. PRIs can include more than loans. They may also come in the form of loan guarantees, equity investments, and linked deposits, among other types of investment. PRIs permit foundations to generate returns on these investments that are both programmatic and financial (Baxter, 1997; Wei-Skillern et al., 2007). However, the IRS will not permit PRIs that have a "significant purpose" of generating income or property appreciation. Their chief purpose must be to accomplish one or more of the exempt purposes of the foundation (IRS.gov, 2010). The financing of nonprofit social ventures is discussed in more detail in Chapter 7.

The statutes that created PRIs have spawned another form of nonprofit structure called the L3C. This is considered to be a promising structural form because it permits both the pursuit of charitable purposes and the distribution of profits, as long as the former is the primary purpose. This makes engaging in earned income activities easier for nonprofits. If, at some point, profit generation becomes the significant purpose of the L3C, it may convert to for-profit status. An L3C need not be a foundation or associated with one (Tyler & Owens, 2010). L3Cs are still quite new, and legal debate swirls around them. Nevertheless, they represent an interesting variation on the purely nonprofit structural model.

While the purely nonprofit structure offers considerable choice in sources of financing, it is limiting in other ways. It is restricted in the amount of earned income it can generate. It relies heavily on the largesse of others, and, as a result, is beholden to their agendas, objectives, and whims. In most entrepreneurial ventures, entrepreneurs wrestle with the balance between control and access to capital for growth. Social entrepreneurs who operate purely nonprofit ventures have relatively little control, no matter how much financing they receive or from whom. Nonprofits that are tax exempt are, in effect, owned by the public and must strictly adhere to government restrictions and public expectations for impact. For these reasons, many social entrepreneurs are opting for for-profit structures for their ventures.

PURE FOR-PROFITS

The pure for-profit structure for social ventures follows the same conventions as those observed by for-profit commercial ventures. The chief difference is that the former pursue a social mission. They are seeking to do good and to do well at the same time. Because of this, they must hold themselves to high ethical standards. Their ability to sell their products or services, earn a profit, and achieve their social mission is very reliant upon the goodwill they generate with their customers and the general public.

There are several legal structures available to entrepreneurs who choose to structure their venture as a for-profit. The simplest is the sole proprietorship. It is inexpensive and relatively easy (in terms of government requirements) to start. It has a single owner, who pays taxes for the entity through her or his income tax. The biggest drawback to this structure is that the owner is solely liable for debts incurred should the venture fail. That is, the owner bears all the market risk.

Another for-profit structure is the partnership. This is the same as the sole proprietorship in every way, except that the venture has two or more owners. These owners share the tax burden and liability.

A third for-profit structure is the limited liability corporation (LLC). This business form may have a single owner or partners. Despite the fact that it is considered a type of corporation, an LLC cannot sell shares. However, just as in the case of a corporation, the owner is considered separate from her or his business entity; therefore, liability is borne by the LLC, not by its owner(s). Thus, an LLC has the benefit both of being relatively easy and inexpensive to start and of limited liability for the owner.

The final major structure available to for-profit social ventures is the corporation, of which there are two common types: "C" and "S." Both types require that shares be sold in the business and that a board of directors be established. Both forms consider the business to be a separate legal entity and, therefore, liable for debts and taxes. Both are more expensive and more legally complicated to start. The chief difference between these two types of corporation is that the owners of a C corporation can be double-taxed—on the corporation's income and on their individual income—whereas the owners of an S corporation can only be taxed on the earnings of the corporation. The decision about which structure to choose for a for-profit social venture must be determined by the social entrepreneur's goals and priorities, in light of her or his mission.

There is an emerging type of corporation that is not yet widely recognized in a legal sense or known by the general public. It is the "Benefit corporation" ("B corporation"). While C and S corporations are required by law to pursue a profit, B corporations are legally tasked with pursuing both a profit and an articulated public purpose. Performance relative to the company's public purpose is tracked by independent monitors (van den Heuvel, 2010).

B companies are certified and must meet performance standards relative to their impact on their community and the environment and their accountability to employees and consumers (bcorporation.net, 2010). B corporations have been made legal in 25 states and the District of Columbia, at the time of this writing, and are under consideration in Indiana, Kentucky, New Mexico, North Dakota, and Oklahoma (Benefit Corp Information Center, 2015).

Unlike pure nonprofit social ventures, for-profits do not have a widely diverse array of financial resources from which to choose; however, there are several. Among these are FFF (family/friends/founder), gap financing, commercial bank loans, mezzanine capital, angel capital, and venture capital. As was noted in the previous section of this chapter, there are some social venture philanthropists who will invest in for-profit social ventures as well. This discussion is taken up in greater detail in Chapter 7.

While they are not without regulation, for-profit social ventures are not subject to the same level of scrutiny as are nonprofits. If they are privately owned (not publicly traded) they do not need to disclose their financial statements. Also, they can more easily protect their intellectual property. In sum, they have more control over what they do and how they do it. This can be very attractive to many social entrepreneurs, who, like most entrepreneurs, value control very highly. The only time loss of control becomes an issue for for-profits is when angel or venture capitalists insist on having a substantial say in the venture's operations in exchange for their investment. This is the trade-off between control and growth referenced in the previous section.

Social entrepreneurs who choose the purely for-profit structure enjoy greater control over their ventures and the opportunity to generate earnings (profits) that they, as owners, can keep for themselves, while solving a social problem(s) at the same time. However, with a few exceptions they cannot access philanthropic dollars. They must also wrestle with the dilemma of trying to run a business that is attempting to make a profit *and* a business that is pursuing a social mission at the same time. This is much more difficult than it may seem on its surface and sometimes causes for-profit social entrepreneurs to seek out other structural options.

An excellent example of this is the experience of one of the best-known for-profit social ventures in the world: Newman's Own, Inc. Newman's Own is a for-profit food manufacturing and distribution company structured as an S corporation (Wei-Skillern et al., 2007). It gives 100 percent of its after-tax profits to charity. Food is a very competitive industry. Newman's Own has had to work exceptionally hard to establish partnerships with food makers, packagers, and distributors; enhance its product line and its quality; and market its products in order to compete successfully. It has also had to work very hard to identify worthy charities to which to give and to manage the giving process. Ultimately, these two distinct efforts became too much to handle under one structure (Wei-Skillern et al., 2007). That was when Newman's Own, Inc. decided to spin its giving operations off into a nonprofit foundation. Thus, Newman's Own became a form of hybrid organization: a for-profit with a nonprofit subsidiary.

Increasingly, social entrepreneurs who are frustrated by the restrictions of the nonprofit structure and the management vicissitudes of the for-profit structure have chosen to create hybrid structural models. In the next section, we explore the hybrid options available.

HYBRIDS

As the name implies, hybrid structures assumed by social ventures represent various combinations of structural elements from nonprofit, for-profit, and/or government organizations. They are forms of innovation in the vehicles by which social mission can be delivered. The social entrepreneurs who create these structures are generally seeking greater legal and financial flexibility for pursuing their missions.

New hybrid structures are being developed and tested on a regular basis and are limited only by the imagination and the law (or, more accurately, its interpretation). While the ways in which hybrid forms manifest themselves are too numerous to chronicle, it is useful to look at some of the more common structures among them and offer examples of each.

For-Profits with Nonprofit Subsidiaries

Sometimes, social entrepreneurs find it too difficult to pursue their mission through a for-profit structure alone. In some cases it can be detrimental to the success of the profit-making company to attempt to deliver on its social mission at the same time. This was the case with Newman's Own, Inc., discussed earlier in this chapter. As was noted previously, essentially the for-profit Newman's Own, Inc. became a hybrid venture when it created a nonprofit foundation to handle the distribution of its after-tax profits to charities.

In other cases, for-profit social entrepreneurs have decided that they need more than the earned income generated by their ventures to expand their mission achievement. With this in mind, they sometimes create a nonprofit subsidiary that can accept donations and grants that the for-profit could not attract. An example of this is Pura Vida Coffee, which is a for-profit company that sells fair trade and shade-grown coffee in retail stores and via its website, and also operates a Section 501(c)(3) nonprofit, Pura Vida Partners, that manages its many charitable operations in places such as Costa Rica, Ethiopia, Guatemala, and Nicaragua (Pura Vida, 2010). The nonprofit benefits, in part, from earnings on coffee sales, but it also receives donations and grants and is tax exempt. The for-profit can deduct its donations to the nonprofit for tax purposes. This hybrid venture permits maximum mission achievement: Pura Vida Coffee is a values-driven for-profit that benefits its suppliers (coffee farmers) and the environment, while Pura Vida Partners focuses on improving the quality of life of communities in the countries in which its for-profit parent company purchases coffee beans.

It is not always possible to readily create a hybrid solution, however, as the social entrepreneur may be limited by the laws in the context in which she or he is operating. German social entrepreneur Andreas Heinecke, founder of the for-profit social venture Dialogue in the Dark, is an example. Dialogue in the Dark was founded in 1988 with a twofold purpose: (1) to provide corporate human resources offices with training workshops that teach participants about collaboration, emotional intelligence, and dealing with diversity; and (2) to give blind workshop leaders an opportunity to develop skills in communication, leadership, and management. Workshops are held in total darkness. Blind trainers lead these workshops, which are attended by sighted corporate employees. The company also offers dark exhibitions for the general public that are led by blind docents. To date, these workshops and exhibitions have been held in at least thirty countries on four continents. Ultimately, over 6,000 blind individuals have been helped to find employment (Goldsmith, 2009; Dialogue in the Dark, 2010).

Heinecke laments the fact that he does not have a hybrid option. He would like to be able to relieve his tax and regulatory burden, as a for-profit, and he would like access to philanthropic funds. As previously noted, U.S. social entrepreneurs have some options in this regard. In the United Kingdom a designation called the "community interest company" has been created. This is a for-profit structure that allows for putting a larger share of profits toward a social mission and for reduced compliance with government regulations. Heinecke wants to see these hybrid structures spread around the world. For now, Dialogue in the Dark relies on partnerships with large for-profits to maximize mission achievement (Goldsmith, 2009).

Nonprofits with For-Profit Subsidiaries

Sometimes, frustration resulting from the limitations of organizational structure is on the part of entrepreneurs operating nonprofits. They cannot sustain their social ventures on philanthropy alone, and they are troubled by the legal vagaries surrounding the generation of earned income by tax-exempt nonprofit organizations as well as the claims of unfair competition from for-profit ventures (Brinckerhoff, 2000). They may also envision a double benefit to be derived from operating a for-profit venture in conjunction with their nonprofit: not only could the for-profit be an additional source of revenue that is unencumbered by the private inurement doctrine, but it could also engage in values-based activities that further the nonprofit's mission. It should also be noted that debt capital, from either private lending institutions or government loan and loan guarantee programs, is much more readily available to for-profits (Brinckerhoff, 2000).

One example of this form of hybrid structure is Greyston Bakery, located in Yonkers, New York. Simply put, Greyston has a nonprofit parent organization—Greyston Foundation—with a for-profit subsidiary—Greyston Bakery—but it is a true hybrid because these two entities work together seamlessly. To make this relationship clearer, some background is in order.

The bakery itself was founded in 1982 by a former aerospace engineer turned Zen Buddhist priest named Bernard Glassman. Glassman and his meditation group first established the bakery to provide themselves with a livelihood. However, this soon shifted to providing employment to those individuals in the community who are considered "unemployable" (e.g., former drug addicts, prisoners, and recovering alcoholics). It became apparent to Glassman that merely providing these individuals with a job was not enough. They needed affordable housing, social services, and health care as well. This is where creating a Section 501(c)(3) nonprofit foundation came into the picture. The Greyston Foundation could manage the venture's charitable giving, accept donations and earn grants, and coordinate interactions with other nonprofits in the community.

Instead of making the for-profit venture the parent and establishing the nonprofit foundation as its subsidiary, as Pura Vida Coffee did, Glassman chose to do the opposite. This is in keeping with his vision for individual development and subsequent community economic revitalization. The bakery is a viable, profit-making business establishment that teaches people who might not otherwise be given the chance to work in a real-world environment and to understand the world of work, but it is also a source of revenue to the foundation and its mission of developing the infrastructure needed to support the personal growth of the individuals who work at the bakery and others like them throughout the community. Today, the name Greyston Bakery is synonymous with this entire hybrid organization. Its mission reflects this:

Greyston Bakery is a force for personal transformation and community economic renewal. We operate a profitable business, baking high quality gourmet products with a commitment to customer satisfaction.

Greyston Bakery provides a supportive workplace offering employment and opportunity for advancement. Our profits contribute to the community development work of the Greyston Foundation.

As for Greyston Bakery, Inc., it is a B corporation (see the discussion in the section on for-profit business structures earlier in this chapter) that produces baked goods for many of the upscale restaurants in New York City. Since 1988 it has also produced the brownies that are blended into Ben & Jerry's ice cream. In addition, it bakes its own line of "Do-Goodies" brownies. It generates $5 million per year in revenue, operates out of a state-of-the-art baking facility designed by Maya Lin, and provides employment, competitive wages and benefits, and training to sixty-five local residents without regard to their work history (Leung, 2004; Greyston Bakery, 2010). It is a prime example of a successful values-based business.

Brinckerhoff (2000) offers some very practical considerations when exploring the viability of nonprofits with for-profit subsidiaries. A for-profit subsidiary must pay taxes on its profits before donating them to its nonprofit parent. Donations made by the for-profit to the nonprofit parent are not taxable income to the nonprofit. If the nonprofit owns more than 50 percent of the for-profit's stock, the latter will not comply with most funders' arm's-length requirements (Brinckerhoff, 2000, pp. 194–195). A final practical consideration is that most nonprofit parent ventures that establish a for-profit subsidiary own 100 percent of the stock of that subsidiary. For this reason they control the latter's board of directors. This does not mean, however, that both entities can share the same board. Each should have its own distinct board, which can share a few overlapping members but may not have precisely the same members (Lasprogata & Cotten, 2003).

Nonprofits with Nonprofit Subsidiaries

There are instances in which nonprofit social ventures find it beneficial to create their own nonprofit subsidiaries. This form of hybrid social venture might be adopted for several reasons; among them to undertake business activities that are not related to the parent organization's mission but that generate revenue; to increase the prospects of receiving certain grants; to avoid a loss of grant money from funders that reduce their grants if other revenue sources are found by creating a subsidiary nonprofit to retain earnings; to maximize income from property holdings by placing them in an arm's-length nonprofit separate from the parent; or to establish an endowment through the creation of a nonprofit foundation (Brinckerhoff, 2000; Lasprogata & Cotten, 2003; Thompson & Thompson, 2010).

The creation of a nonprofit–nonprofit hybrid by the New York City-based social venture ReServe: Next Steps for Older Adults provides an illustration. ReServe is an organization with the mission of placing retirees in jobs at nonprofit organizations that pay a small stipend and provide an opportunity to use the skills that the retiree has developed over a lifetime to benefit the nonprofit to which they are assigned. Nonprofit agencies that hosted the ReServists were happy to pay the stipend in exchange for the services of a skilled retiree; however, they were not enthused about handling the payroll for the ReServist(s) they hosted (Robert Wood Johnson Foundation, 2007).

The host nonprofits did, however, indicate that they would be willing to pay extra if ReServe would manage the payroll of their ReServists. While payroll management is not an activity that is directly related to ReServe's mission, it does afford the opportunity to generate additional revenue to the organization. With this in mind, ReServe created a nonprofit subsidiary, the chief function of which is to handle ReServists' payroll (Robert Wood Johnson Foundation, 2007).

Nonprofit–Nonprofit Partnerships

Nonprofit–nonprofit partnerships, often referred to as nonprofit consortia, are not the same as the nonprofits with nonprofit subsidiaries described in the previous subsection. A consortium suggests the coming together of two or more nonprofits in a mutually beneficial relationship that allows each member to achieve more than they could alone. By pooling resources in an efficient manner they can maximize mission achievement and community benefit (Lasprogata & Cotten, 2003).

Nonprofit consortia tend to take one of two legal forms: cooperative ventures or strategic mergers or consolidations (Lasprogata & Cotten, 2003). Cooperative ventures, or cooperatives, in the nonprofit arena can have many partners or very few. These partners come together to pursue a joint venture. The partners may have an equal financial stake in the cooperative or they may have varying stakes. No matter the size of each partner's stake, however, they all have equal control over the cooperative's board of directors. This makes cooperative ventures especially attractive to small nonprofits, as they can operate on a level playing field with much larger nonprofits.

An interesting and unusual cooperative venture has been created among nine nonprofits that are fundees of the United Way in Chicago. These are relatively large nonprofits, with a combined budget in excess of $300 million. Their cooperative structure permits them to share back-office operations, resulting in estimated savings of approximately $20 million per year. The savings are achieved through improved economies of scale as they relate to purchasing. These savings can then be plowed into programs that are experiencing high demand but are under-resourced. The Chicago Community Trust made a $400,000 grant to support creation of the cooperative, and members pay an annual fee of 0.13 percent of revenue to participate (Butzen, 2008).

Another example of the cooperative venture approach comes from the journalism industry, which has suffered in recent years because the commercial models of the past are no longer working. The focus on profits ahead of quality news reporting has resulted in newspapers closing, massive layoffs, and declining quality. One response to this crisis has been the exploration of nonprofit or low-profit (L3C) models. One illustration of this is Indymedia, a cooperative newsroom. Indymedia is made up of a global network of volunteer community newsrooms, known as Independent Media Centers (IMCs). Not all of these are financially sustainable, but many regularly and successfully publish local newspapers (Pickard, 2006).

Nonprofit mergers and consolidations create the same result: one organization out of two or more. However, they each accomplish this result in a unique way. Mergers involve the absorption of one nonprofit by another. The nonprofit that does the absorbing (the legal term is "liquidating") acquires the liabilities and assets of the nonprofit that is absorbed. Consolidations involve the coming together of two or more nonprofits into a totally new nonprofit venture. While either merger or consolidation represents a viable structural option for nonprofits (one that brings efficiencies) neither is considered desirable by most nonprofits because one (or more than one) organization loses its identity. For most nonprofits, identity lies in their mission. They are troubled by the idea that the mission, as they envision it, will be lost or altered in an unacceptable way by the reorganization (Lasprogata & Cotten, 2003).

The best way to combat resistance to merger or consolidation is to educate the prospective parties to its benefits: integration of services, expansion of client markets, expansion of resource pools, fuller attainment of mission, and survival (Lasprogata & Cotten, 2003). Perhaps the most powerful message to be delivered is the one that, individually, the parties may not be sustainable, but together in a new organization their chances of survival are greatly enhanced.

The lengthy economic recession that began in the late 2000s has accelerated the nonprofit merger trend, as two examples help to illustrate. In 2009 two major housing-related nonprofits in the Phoenix, Arizona, area elected to merge their operations. UMOM New Day Centers (UMOM) merged the operations of Helping Hands Housing Services (Helping Hands) into its operations. UMOM runs a shelter for homeless and low-income families, while Helping Hands provides affordable housing to low-income households. The merger will allow the two agencies to reach more low-income families in need of housing and to provide seamless support as these families move from a transitional shelter to permanent housing (UMOM, 2009).

One of the keys to the successful merger of UMOM and Helping Hands is their very compatible missions (UMOM, 2009):

- UMOM: "to provide homeless and low-income families with food, shelter and the tools to build a bridge to self-sufficiency."
- Helping Hands: "to break the cycle of poverty for low-income families by providing permanent affordable housing and comprehensive support services."

This is very important. Nonprofits with compatible missions will be less resistant to merger in the first place and will find that merging the cultures of the two organizations is much easier because of their commonalities of purpose.

The second example involves a proposed merger in which Mental Health Care, Inc. of the Tampa Bay area of Florida would take over the assets, operations, and debt of neighboring Achieve Tampa Bay, Inc. Both are nonprofit ventures in the healthcare industry. The proposed merger addresses financial issues, particularly for Achieve Tampa Bay (Manning, 2010).

Achieve dates back to 1953 and is a large organization that grew dramatically in the 1990s. However, it began to experience heavy operating losses between 2004 and 2010, totaling about $1.5 million. This caused cash-flow problems, ultimately resulting in Achieve's inability to meet a demand by the Children's Board of Hillsborough County that it repay a portion of a $6.9 million contract that it had not paid out to nonprofit subcontractors, among them Mental Health Care, Inc. (Manning, 2010).

Under the proposed merger, Mental Health Care, Inc. would pay the nonprofit subcontractors what they are owed, forgive the amount it is owed by Achieve, and pay back over $500,000 owed to the Children's Board. The merger provides Achieve with a preferable option to selling or mortgaging its real property, or closing operations and liquidating assets. Its mission can continue to be pursued and its clients served (Manning, 2010).

While nonprofit mergers continue to face opposition from those who fear job layoffs and mission creep, they appear to be an increasingly popular alternative for stressed organizations. Nevertheless, nonprofits entering into such a structure should carefully weigh the costs and benefits. These should not merely be measured in terms of dollars and cents. Financial issues can be addressed much more easily than can the human issues that arise when incompatible organizations merge. It is this latter set of challenges that receives too little attention when merging or consolidating entities in both the for-profit and nonprofit arenas.

Nonprofit–For-Profit Partnerships

Nonprofit–for-profit partnerships are sometimes referred to as *cross-sector alliances.* They tend to be long term and focused on the partners working together toward a social goal. They are particularly attractive to larger businesses that want to engage in activities that improve the quality of life of the communities in which they do business. In the knowledge economy this can, in turn, come back to benefit the business by making it easier to attract and retain highly skilled workers (Lasprogata & Cotten, 2003). It can also serve to build a larger customer base for the company in the community.

Successful nonprofit–for-profit partnerships tend to have several common characteristics. According to Lasprogata and Cotten (2003), these include:

- a perception by the partners that the partnership is mutually beneficial;
- a complementarity of strategies between the partners; and
- a good fit between the cultures of the partnering organizations.

Activities that benefit both partners are the hallmark of long-lasting partnerships of any kind (Hamlin & Lyons, 1996). A partnership in which only one partner benefits is not a partnership but a case of co-optation, and a partnership that benefits no one is a waste of time and resources. Organizational strategies that complement one another facilitate a smooth partnership. For example, if the product of a commercial business and the mission of a nonprofit venture reinforce one another, this provides the basis of an attractive partnership. Con Edison, the electric utility for New York City, partners with the nonprofit Trees New York by making a $1 donation to the latter's tree-planting fund every time a customer switches from paper to electronic billing. Con Edison enjoys savings and more immediate reimbursement from moving to electronic billing, while Trees New York advances its mission of increasing the number of trees in the city. In addition, an energy utility and a conservation group have complementary missions. Thus, this illustration involves a partnership with mutual benefit *and* a good strategic fit.

A good cultural fit is just as important for nonprofit–for-profit partnerships as it is for nonprofit–nonprofit partnerships (see the previous subsection). This means that either the organizational structures of the partners are a good fit with each other or that one, or both, of the partners is willing to adapt. A business with a top-down management structure may not be a good fit with a nonprofit partner that is more horizontal in its management, unless they are willing to adapt. Prospective partners will need to communicate with and educate each other (Lasprogata & Cotten, 2003).

Many nonprofit–for-profit partnerships have a strong marketing component. This is often referred to as cause-related marketing. A nonprofit with a strong brand (a name and a mission that are highly recognizable and respected) is an attractive partner to commercial businesses because they can benefit from associating themselves with that nonprofit brand. By including the nonprofit brand in their advertising and packaging they can attract customers who have an affinity for the mission of the nonprofit partner. For its part, the nonprofit benefits from the resources it receives from its for-profit partner in exchange for the use of its brand. It should be remembered by nonprofits that their brand has a value, and they are entitled to payment for use of their brand (Wei-Skillern et al., 2007). Furthermore, in many cases opportunities are created for additional donations to the nonprofit when customers buy the for-profit's products.

The Susan G. Komen Foundation, which raises money for breast cancer research, is a good example of a nonprofit with many for-profit partners. These partners benefit from being associated with an organization that fights a disease that affects many people, directly and indirectly. The Komen Foundation receives donations from its for-profit partners and, in some cases, additional donations from the customers of those partners. Yoplait Yogurt had a cause-related marketing campaign jointly with the Komen Foundation, in which Komen's signature pink was the color of the foil tops of the yogurt cartons. If customers kept their pink foil tops and turned them in, a donation was made by Yoplait to the Foundation. The Komen Foundation does a remarkable job of finding for-profit partners. One of the authors of this text recently saw the truck of a private waste hauler rolling down Fifth Avenue in New York City. The truck was painted pink and carried the pink ribbon logo of the Foundation.

CONCLUSION

The social entrepreneur's decision about how she or he will structure the venture is an important one. In particular, it will affect how the venture can be financed, what rules and regulations the venture must adhere to, and how much control the entrepreneur has over the venture. These factors will, in turn, influence the entrepreneur's level of accountability, the amount of mission that the venture can reasonably achieve, and the degree of legitimacy the venture can attain with its stakeholders.

The social entrepreneur has a range of structural options from which to choose. At one end of this spectrum is the purely nonprofit organization, which is constricted in its activities by laws surrounding its tax-exempt status but enjoys a relatively wide array of alternatives for financing those activities. At the other end is the purely for-profit structure, which faces taxation issues and more limited financing options but allows the social entrepreneur more control over the venture and a chance to keep the profits.

The most intriguing aspect of this range of structural options is what lies in the middle of the spectrum: the hybrid structures, which unite features of both nonprofit and for-profit configurations or create combinations of these models taken whole-cloth. While variations on the hybrid theme continue to emerge, the principal forms include for-profits with nonprofit subsidiaries, nonprofits with for-profit subsidiaries, nonprofits with nonprofit subsidiaries, nonprofit–nonprofit partnerships, and nonprofit–for-profit partnerships. Each of these offers its own set of advantages in overcoming specific challenges that social entrepreneurs face.

Such a wide array of structural choices can be overwhelming to the social entre-preneur. However, there is a compass for guiding this decision: the social mission. Simply put, the social entrepreneur should select the organizational structure that maximizes her or his mission achievement.

Case Study 6.1

Jumpstart

Jumpstart is a nonprofit social venture whose mission is to provide low-income preschoolers (four-year-olds) with educational experiences designed to develop their reading, learning, and social skills prior to entering kindergarten. It was founded by two Yale University students in 1993. The basic idea behind Jumpstart was to match these children with college students who have an interest in education and will volunteer time each week to work with them. Jumpstart's first engagement involved students from Yale and fifteen preschoolers in New Haven, CT (Read for the Record, 2010a).

The social problem that Jumpstart's founders were seeking to address is the disadvantage that children from low-income families face in being ready for school, relative to middle- and upper-income children. Research has shown that 35 percent of U.S. children begin their K-12 education unequipped to learn (Fast Company.com, 2005). This burden falls disproportionately on low-income children, who are often as much as two years behind their more economically advantaged peers in terms of reading skills and other measures of academic achievement at the time they start first grade. These problems have an impact on adulthood as well, as 29 percent of all workers in the United States are functionally illiterate. However, research also shows that investing in early learning efforts can help to mitigate this problem (Read for the Record, 2010b).

The Jumpstart model draws upon students who are Americorps members from partner colleges and universities around the country. These college students spend eight to ten hours per week during the academic year. Each week consists of two two-hour sessions at a local preschool. They work in teams, providing each preschooler with one-on-one reading time, group learning time in groups of twelve children, independent learning time, and group creative activity time in a classroom environment (Fast Company.com, 2005). The college student volunteers themselves represent considerable diversity in both their ethnic backgrounds and their college majors. The largest group is White (48 percent), followed by African American (26 percent), Hispanic (15 percent), and Asian (11 percent). While Jumpstart's original idea was to attract education majors, this group makes up only 10 percent of the current volunteers. One-quarter of group members are psychology, social work, sociology, and nursing majors. Another 11 percent are science majors, while 10 percent are business majors (Jumpstart, 2010).

Jumpstart has identified three core program objectives that it pursues: school success, future teachers, and family involvement. Relative to the school success objective, preschoolers enhance their literacy, language, emotional, and social skills. The experiences of the college student volunteers are aimed at preparing them for future positions in education leadership and teaching. Jumpstart involves the preschoolers' families by giving them exercises they can engage in at home with their child that are designed to reinforce classroom learning. Jumpstart also informs families of their preschooler's progress in the program (Jumpstart, 2010).

In 2004, Jumpstart expanded its efforts by engaging a new group of volunteers: senior citizens. This allowed this social venture to expand its learning centers beyond its sixty-two college partners to cover twenty-one cities in sixteen states (Jumpstart, 2010; Read for the Record, 2010c). This action reflects a larger effort to aggressively grow Jumpstart that was begun by one of the social venture's founders and then-CEO, Aaron Lieberman, in about 2000.

Lieberman undertook several initiatives to extend the reach of Jumpstart's mission. He explored the possibility of moving from pairing each college student with one preschooler to pairing them with two children to increase the number of preschoolers assisted. Though this idea was never adopted, it opened the door to pursuing senior citizen volunteers. He also initiated a partnership with the High/Scope Educational Research Foundation of Ypsilanti, Michigan, to establish metrics for measuring impact. This led to the development of a sophisticated impact measurement system that has received considerable acclaim and attracted funding to Jumpstart. Lieberman also realized that Jumpstart was harming its ability to attract college student volunteers by requiring a two-year commitment, so he reduced the commitment to one year, or two semesters. Finally, in 2000 Lieberman and Jumpstart launched a for-profit venture called Schoolsuccess.net, which provides early childhood learning tools for teachers and parents via the Internet. The purpose of Schoolsuccess.net was to spread the mission and provide much-needed earned income revenue to Jumpstart (Jacobson, 2000). Later that same year, Schoolsuccess.net entered into a partnership with Harcourt.com for the purposes of expanding its marketing capacity and tailoring its software for use by gifted children and children with special needs (Education Editors, 2000). Today, Schoolsuccess.net operates under the auspices of Pearson, and the chairman of Pearson Canada sits on Jumpstart's board of directors, as does the president of the Pearson Foundation (Read for the Record, 2010d).

Since its founding, Jumpstart has served over 70,000 preschoolers with millions of hours of volunteer help in developing reading, language, and emotional and social skills (Read for the Record, 2010e). Since 2000, when Aaron Lieberman initiated his scaling strategy, the Jumpstart network has grown at an average rate of almost 30 percent annually, making it one of the leading nonprofit organizations in the education industry (Read for the Record, 2010a).

THOUGHT QUESTIONS

1   What kind of organizational structure does Jumpstart represent?
2   How does Jumpstart's organizational structure reflect its financing needs?
3   On the basis of Jumpstart's story, what would you say is the relationship between organizational structure and growth, or mission expansion?
4   Would you say that the organizational partnerships in the Jumpstart case reflect good fits between partners? Why, or why not?
5   In your opinion, does Jumpstart have the best organizational design for pursuing its mission? Explain your answer.

REFERENCES

Baxter, C. I. (1997). *Program-related investments: A technical manual for foundations*. New York: Wiley.

bcorporation.net (2010). Retrieved from http://www.bcorporation.net (accessed August 11, 2010).

Benefit Corp Information Center (2015). State by state legislative status. www.benefitcorp.net/state-by-state-legislative-status (accessed January 16, 2015).

Blackbaud (2010). White paper: E-philanthropy strategy for nonprofits. Retrieved from http://blackbaud.ca/files/resources/downloads/WhitePaper_ePhilanthropyStrategy.pdf (accessed August 9, 2010).

Brinckerhoff, P. C. (2000). *Social entrepreneurship: The art of mission-based venture development*. New York: Wiley.

Butzen, J. (2008). Nonprofit partnerships: Human service agencies merge back-office functions to save $20M annually. February 13. Retrieved from http://www.missionplusstrategy.com/partnerships/ (accessed August 13, 2010).

Dees, J. G., Emerson, J., & Economy, P. (2001). *Enterprising nonprofits: A toolkit for social entrepreneurs*. New York: Wiley.

Dialogue in the Dark (2010). Retrieved from http://www.dialogue-in-the-dark.com.

Education Editors (2000). Harcourt partners with early childhood site. *Business Wire*, August 28.

Fast Company.com (2005). Jumpstart: winner's statement. Retrieved from http://www.fastcompany.com/social/2005/statements/jumpstart.html (accessed October 18, 2010).

Goldsmith, R. (2009). For-profit or not for-profit? Social enterprises seek a better way. Retrieved from http://knowledge.insead.edu/social-enterprises-seek-a-better-way-090811.cfm.

Greyston Bakery (2010). Retrieved from http://www.greystonbakery.com (accessed August 11, 2010).

Hamlin, R. E., & Lyons, T. S. (1996). *Economy without walls*. Westport, CT: Praeger.

Hopkins, B. (2001). Appendix A: Social entrepreneurs' brief guide to the law. In J. G. Dees, J. Emerson, & P. Economy (Eds.). *Enterprising nonprofits: A toolkit for social entrepreneurs*. New York: Wiley.

IRS.gov (2010). Program-related investments. Retrieved from http://www.irs.gov/charities/foundations/article/0,,id=137793,00.html (accessed August 11, 2010).

Jacobson, L. (2000). College students help jump-start preschoolers' learning. *Education Week*, December 13. Retrieved from http://www.edweek.org/ew/articles/2000/12/13/15jump.h20.html (accessed October 18, 2010).

Jumpstart (2010). Jumpstart's fact sheet. Retrieved from http://www.jstart.org (accessed October 18, 2010).

Lasprogata, G. A., & Cotten, M. N. (2003). Contemplating "enterprise": The business and legal challenges of social entrepreneurship. *American Business Law Journal, 41*(1), 67–113.

Leung, R. (2004). Greyston Bakery: Let 'em eat cake. Bob Simon visits New York bakery that helps those in need. Retrieved from http://www.cbsnews.com/stories/2004/01/09/60minutes/main592 382.shtml (accessed August 11, 2010).

Lichtenstein, G.A., & Lyons, T.S. (2010). *Investing in entrepreneurs: A strategic approach for strengthening your regional and community economy.* Santa Barbara, CA: Praeger/ABC-CLIO.

Manning, M. (2010). Achieve Tampa Bay thrown a lifeline in proposed merger. *Tampa Bay Business Journal,* January 25, 2010. Retrieved from http://www.tampabay.bizjournals.com/tampabay/stories/2010/01/25/story3.html (accessed August 13, 2010).

Owens, M., & Tyler, J. (2009). The L³C: A potentially useful tool for promoting charitable purposes. *CommunityDividend,* November. Retrieved from http://www.minneapolisfed.org/publications_papers/pub_display.cfm?id=4491 (accessed August 11, 2010).

Pickard, V. (2006). Assessing the radical democracy of Indymedia: Discursive, technical and institutional constructions. *Critical Studies in Media Communications, 23*(1), 19–38.

Pura Vida (2010). Retrieved from http://www.puravidacoffee.com (accessed August 11, 2010).

Read for the Record (2010a). Our story. Retrieved from http://www.readfortherecord.org/site/PageServer?pagename=WhoWeAre_OurStory (accessed October 18, 2010).

Read for the Record. (2010b). Our impact. Retrieved from http://www.readfortherecord.org/site/PageServer?pagename=WhoWeAre_OurImpact (accessed October 18, 2010).

Read for the Record (2010c). Our locations. Retrieved from http://www.readfortherecord.org/site/PageServer?pagename=WhoWeAre_OurLocations (accessed October 18, 2010).

Read for the Record (2010d). National board of directors. Retrieved from http://www.readfortherecord.org/site/PageServer?pagename=WhoWeAre_Board (accessed October 18, 2010).

Read for the Record (2010e). Who we are. Retrieved from http://www.readfortherecord.org/site/PageServer?pagename=WhoWeAre_Home (accessed October 18, 2010).

Robert Wood Johnson Foundation (2007). "ReServe" program connects retirees to nonprofit agencies for stipend-paying jobs in New York City. November. Retrieved from http://www.rwjf.org/reports/grr/055774.htm (accessed August 12, 2010).

Thompson & Thompson (2010). Subsidiaries of tax-exempt organizations. Retrieved from http://www.t-tlaw.com/bus-04.htm (accessed August 12, 2010).

Tyler, J. E. III, & Owens, M. (2010). *The L3C: A potentially useful tool for promoting charitable purposes.* Minneapolis, MN: Federal Reserve Bank of Minneapolis.

UMOM (2009). Model program elevates homeless families to permanent housing. Retrieved from http://www.umom.org/docs/UMOM-HelpingHands-Release.pdf (accessed September 6, 2011).

Wei-Skillern, J., Austin, J. E., Leonard, H., & Stevenson, H. (2007). *Entrepreneurship in the social sector.* Thousand Oaks, CA: Sage.

Funding Social Ventures

AIM/PURPOSE

This chapter provides direction for social entrepreneurs in defining the specific capital needs of their ventures with the goal of achieving financial sustainability while balancing social and economic considerations. Investment selection criteria and due diligence processes are presented in detail. The chapter ends with a case study that outlines some challenges to achieving financial sustainability and a set of reflections from a social entrepreneur on the vicissitudes of social venture finance.

LEARNING OBJECTIVES FOR THIS CHAPTER

1. To gain an understanding of the challenges social entrepreneurs encounter when raising capital for their social venture.
2. To examine the questions about the financial drivers of an enterprise that can help direct the social entrepreneur to the appropriate capital sources.
3. To gain an awareness of the intentions of investors across the social capital market.
4. To learn about the role and appreciation of values and mission alignment with investors.
5. To investigate the impact investing market and its categories: commercial and philanthropic.
6. To gain an understanding of "who's who" in investing and funding for social entrepreneurs.
7. To introduce the investment decision and due diligence process of social investors.
8. To learn how to build partnerships with investors in order to create impact.

NAVIGATING THE CHALLENGES OF CAPITAL RAISING

In this chapter, the many funding alternatives available to social entrepreneurs such as philanthropy, earned income, impact investing, and hybrid approaches are considered in light of the previous chapter's discussion of structure. Capital is the fuel that powers a social venture, and success can depend on a social entrepreneur's ability to navigate diverse funding sources. By considering investors as partners in the creation of meaningful impact rather than just funding sources, social entrepreneurs can build more scalable and effective enterprises.

Compared to more traditional capital seekers, social entrepreneurs face an ever-expanding set of funding options but must also address some distinct challenges. Social entrepreneurs have traditionally had two discrete investment sources: grants and fellowships from the public sector or philanthropists and commercial investments and lending from the private sector. Table 7.1 outlines several of these sources and examples that have traditionally been offered, as well as new funding sources from both the public and the private sector.

With an estimated $6 trillion expected to be directed toward social enterprises by 2052, entrepreneurs and investors are experimenting with hybrid forms of social ventures that generate economic, social, and/or environmental benefits (Fulkerson & Thompson, 2008). Simultaneously, both the national and international social capital markets are calling for and demanding higher levels of

Table 7.1
Traditional Sources of Funding for Social Ventures

Sources	Grants	Fellowships	Crowdfunding/ Online Platforms	Angels/ Venture Capitalists	Loan Providers
Examples	Social Innovation Fund, Kaufman Foundation, DoSomething. org, Google Grants	Acumen Fund, Ashoka, Echoing Green, Skoll Foundation, Unreasonable Institute	Kiva, CauseVox, Change.org, Chase Community Giving, Pepsi Refresh Project, Kickstarter	Blue Ridge Foundation, Calvert Group, Good Capital, Gray Ghost Ventures, Investors' Circle, Mission Markets	Calvert Foundation, ShoreBank, Triodos Bank, Partners for the Common Good, Wainwright Bank

transparency and accountability from the social ventures they are funding to demonstrate the impact of such ventures (Rangan, Leonard, & McDonald, 2008).

A new generation of entrepreneurs and investors are increasingly combining the creation of social and environmental impact with the tools of investment (Godeke & Bauer, 2008). This social capital market involves both for-profit and non-profit organizations pursuing financial and social returns while utilizing both philanthropic and financial investment strategies. These blended value investors and social entrepreneurs understand that social or environmental value cannot be neatly separated into financial and societal pieces (Emerson & Spitzer, 2007; Emerson, Fruchterman, & Freundlich, 2007; Godeke & Pomares, 2009). As Jed Emerson (of Blended Value) said,

> There is an idea that values are divided between the financial and the societal, but this is a fundamentally wrong way to view how we create value. Value is whole. The world is not divided into corporate bad guys and social heroes.
>
> (World Economic Forum, 2005)

While this deep gulf between profit-maximizing financial investment and "give-itaway" charity is gradually narrowing, social entrepreneurs still find it difficult to monetize the blended value they create. The reasons for this challenge include (Godeke, 2006; Godeke & Bauer, 2008; Godeke & Pomares, 2009) the following:

- Social enterprises tend to use transformative and disruptive forces to create impacts which may accrue to a segment of society or society at large rather than a discrete set of customers. In other words, the recipients or beneficiaries of a social enterprise's service or product may not pay for it directly. This can lead to an externality that hinders the social enterprise from optimizing its business model.
- In this social capital market, the demand typically comes from social entrepreneurs who need capital to move beyond the start-up phase of their businesses. This is a significant funding gap for social enterprises, be they nonprofit or for-profit ventures.
- Raising capital for collaborative activities is difficult because the benefits cannot be completely captured by the social enterprise. For example, highly cost-effective programs that reduce societal costs may not be captured by the public budgeting process.
- Although social entrepreneurs may provide innovative solutions, funders of existing programs may not have the risk appetite to support new projects in lieu of existing programs.
- The time horizon needed to address social and environmental issues may not be aligned with the time frames of the potential funders. Social enterprises are

typically designed to maximize value in the long term, while investors tend to have shorter time horizons. While social entrepreneurs may find favorable donor funding, these public-sector and philanthropic sources can be unpredictable over time.

■ Traditional early-stage investors expect to receive an appropriate risk-adjusted return on their investments to compensate for the risk of start-up ventures. Given that mission-related impact is the goal of a social entrepreneur rather than wealth creation, these return expectations can be misaligned with the income generation ability of the social enterprise.

■ Hybrid structures can raise issues of subsidies among the public, philanthropic donors, and private-sector players. Philanthropic donors cannot just mitigate the risk of commercial investors, but need to advance their charitable goals. This sharing of the blended value may raise issues of public subsidy being captured by private investors, thus impeding the flow of capital.

■ Finally, social entrepreneurs cannot rely solely on market signals and pricing to indicate to potential investors how successful they have been in achieving mission-related impact.

ESTABLISHING THE CAPITAL NEEDS OF THE SOCIAL ENTERPRISE

Based on the business plan, a social entrepreneur will have a clear sense of the revenues and expenses from her or his enterprise and should be able to clearly define expected funding needs. Before approaching potential investors, it is essential to have a clear understanding of the nature of the enterprise's financial drivers in order to determine the appropriate investors and to understand the reasons a particular type of capital (grant, debt, equity) makes the most sense, given the business plan.

The following questions about the financial drivers of an enterprise can direct the social entrepreneur to the appropriate capital sources (Godeke, 2006; Godeke & Bauer, 2008; Godeke & Pomares, 2009):

■ What combination of financial, social, and environmental value (the triple bottom line) is being created in the enterprise? What opportunities and challenges exist to monetize this value?

■ Is financial sustainability a viable goal given the social or environmental mission of the enterprise? Does the enterprise require a specific amount of start-up capital to build operational capacity before it becomes financially self-sustaining?

■ What are the earned income opportunities for the enterprise? How do they relate to the overall revenues and expenses of the enterprise?

■ Can revenues from one type of service or tiered pricing model be used to provide service to further the social or environmental mission of the enterprise?

- What are the operating efficiencies to the business plan that can generate additional revenue or decrease expenses?
- Does the enterprise generate sufficient excess earned income streams to repay debt?
- What assets does the enterprise own or control which could be used as collateral to support debt?
- Does the enterprise require ongoing grant subsidy because it is creating value for the community or public that cannot be readily monetized?
- What are the working capital needs of the enterprise? Does the enterprise require bridge funding in order to operate until payments are received for the services or products it provides?
- Does the enterprise project sufficient profitability to attract market-rate debt or equity?
- Is equity an option for the enterprise, given the mission and legal structure?

On the basis of a clear understanding of these financial and mission drivers, a social entrepreneur can approach the correct investors (Godeke & Bauer, 2008; Monitor Institute, 2009). Social entrepreneurs seeking finance must understand how investors will assess both their business and its social impact. In general, sectors with hard assets can be more readily financed, while other, non-asset-based sectors, such as human services, may need to demonstrate predictable revenues from fees if they are to be "bankable." Capital tends to flow to larger, better-capitalized organizations, while other highly effective social enterprises may not operate at a financially efficient scale (Godeke, 2006).

UNDERSTANDING THE INTENTIONS OF INVESTORS

Investors who seek to make investments that generate social and environmental value as well as financial returns (Monitor Institute, 2009) are not a homogeneous group. Different types of investors coexist: institutional, philanthropic, or high-networth individuals. Institutional investors include public and private pension funds, insurance companies, or banks. Under the label "philanthropic," one can find foundations and nonprofit organizations that decide to make impact investments.

RISK, RETURN, AND IMPACT

In a well-functioning capital market, risk is inversely related to return. A major goal of designing and managing an investment portfolio is to maximize total return while keeping overall risk at an acceptable level. With the introduction of the additional dimension of impact, investors' perceptions and considerations of

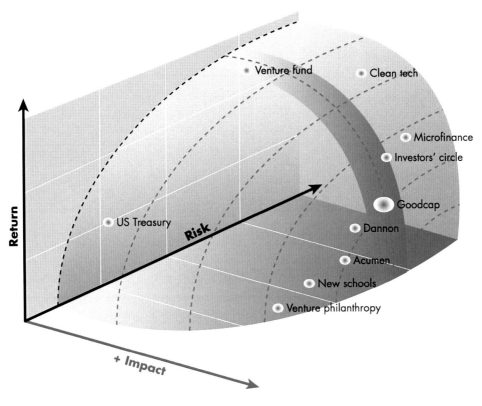

FIGURE 7.1 Risk, Return, and Impact

Source: From the report Impact Assets Issue Brief no. 2, *Risk, Return and Impact: Understanding Diversification and Performance Within an Impact Investing Portfolio.*

the risk and return relationship will be altered. Social entrepreneurs must find alignment with their investors' social or environmental impact goals as well. Successful investors in social enterprises seek to continually tighten the link between their investment decision making and generation of impact. The social entrepreneur must understand how a potential investor's values and mission, theory of change, and impact themes align with her or his own (see Figure 7.1).

VALUES AND MISSION ALIGNMENT WITH INVESTORS' INTENTIONS

For a social venture, both the values and the mission should be aligned with the intentions of the possible investors. Outlined below are several concerns when a social entrepreneur is trying to find the right match between the venture and investors' goals.

- Motivation: Understanding investor intent is key to raising capital. Investors can have very distinct motivations in seeking financial returns. While philanthropists may have personal connections to a particular mission, large institutions such as pension funds or foundations may be targeting specific policy objectives.

- Issues: Investors typically establish clear program and sector guidelines to prioritize investment opportunities. Do the social enterprise's issues meet these guidelines? Is the enterprise focused on widespread global problems such as poverty, disease, or climate change, or specific or domestic issues like literacy, local education, or affordable housing? Geographic choices must also be made, as well as decisions about how a social enterprise can best effect change—through leaders, institutions, or both?

- Evaluation: Investors establish benchmarks to compare their investment and assess performance. What is the investor's time horizon and level of engagement? What is their tolerance for risk?

- Approaches: Is the social enterprise's strategy to create impact (its theory of change) in alignment with the investors'? What problem is it trying to solve? Does the investor want to support philanthropic efforts or attract commercial capital? A social enterprise should understand how its own activities line up with the impact themes of particular investors. Some of the more common themes around which investors organize their activities include Climate Change; Energy; Water; Community Development; Social Enterprises; Health and Wellness; Sustainable Development; and Education (Godeke & Pomares, 2009).

The next section elaborates on the investment decision-making process, the impact of which investors use when considering social enterprise investment opportunities. On the basis of the financial and impact drivers of a social enterprise, a social entrepreneur can determine which forms of investment are the best fit. While the most significant factor is where the investment lies on a continuum ranging from charitable grants to commercial, risk-adjusted capital, another dimension is the involvement level of the investor in the social venture. Some investors in social enterprise practice venture philanthropy, which applies the high involvement of venture capital to grant making.

MISSION-RELATED INVESTMENT CONTINUUM

The F. B. Heron Foundation pioneered the integration of mission-related investment across its entire asset allocation. It created a mission-related investment continuum to provide a framework within the Foundation's overall asset allocation to use as a tool to evaluate mission-related investment opportunities. By

Mission-Related Investment Continuum

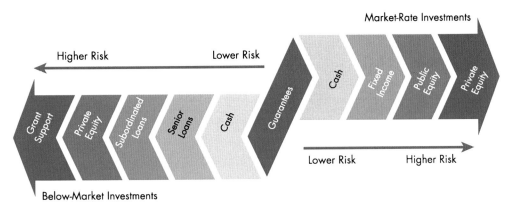

FIGURE 7.2 Mission-Related Investment Continuum
Source: Godeke & Bauer (2008).

viewing grants as part of a broader range of philanthropic tools available to foundations to create impact, F. B. Heron has been able to seek out the best agents for achieving impact in a program area, whether through a nonprofit or for-profit opportunity. F. B. Heron has systematically built out its mission-related investment portfolio across a range of asset classes and program areas while increasing the total share of mission-related investments in its endowment. This expansion followed a clear investment discipline and conformed to the Foundation's overall asset allocation policy, performance benchmarks, and prudent underwriting practices (see Figure 7.2).

GRANT FUNDING

A number of foundations, including Ashoka and the Skoll Foundation, provide seed-stage and growth-stage grants to social ventures. The Draper Richards Foundation for Social Entrepreneurship, for example, provides early-stage grants of $300,000 over three years to social entrepreneurs. Additionally, some investment funds are aimed at specific disadvantaged regions or populations. For example, the Acumen Fund, a nonprofit global venture fund based in New York, focuses on locations in India, Pakistan, and East Africa. Yasmina Zaidman, a spokeswoman at Acumen, says that the fund's social investors or donors are not interested in reaping financial rewards. Instead, she says, "they are looking to invest in philanthropic ventures; the return they're looking for is the social impact."

THE IMPACT INVESTING MARKET[1]

Impact investing can be defined as "investments intended to create positive impact beyond financial return" (JP Morgan Global Research, 2010). The difference with philanthropy lies in the fact that philanthropy has traditionally focused on gifts made by individuals and organizations to benefit society and the environment, whereas impact investing requires a minimum of return of principal.

Altruism, externalities (e.g., climate change), and information asymmetries all create opportunities for impact investors to make a difference. The opportunities for the field include a growing interest among capital providers who seek diversification and a new approach to money management that enables them to also "make a difference"; a greater recognition of the need for effective solutions to social and environmental challenges (e.g., new investment opportunities) and early successes in the fields of microfinance, community development, and clean tech.

IMPACT INVESTOR CATEGORIES: COMMERCIAL AND PHILANTHROPIC

Impact investors approach the question of financial return and impact very differently. Traditionally, impact investors such as US-based public pension funds have been restricted to making only market-rate investments because of their understanding of their fiduciary responsibilities. Similarly, a foundation's charitable status may drive it to make below-market impact investments. High-net-worth individuals and families may use multiple avenues to pursue their impact investment objectives. The authors of an impact investing report by the Monitor Institute (2009) coined the terms "financial-first" and "impact-first" investment to describe this distinction:

1 Financial-first investors seek to optimize financial returns with a floor for social or environmental impact. This group tends to consist of commercial investors who search for subsectors that offer market-rate returns while yielding some social or environmental good. These investors may be driven by fiduciary requirements, as in the case of pension plans.
2 Impact-first investors seek to optimize social or environmental returns with a financial floor. This group uses social or environmental good as a primary objective and may accept a range of returns, from principal to market rate. This group is able to take a lower than market rate of return in order to seed new investment funds that may be perceived as higher risk or to reach tougher

---

1 Emerson talks of the "Social Capital Market."

social or environmental goals that cannot be achieved in combination with market rates of return.

When one looks across the universe of impact investors, it is important to keep this distinction in mind in order to understand the investment opportunities specific impact investors will pursue. However, investors may also make both financial-first and impact-first investments. This clear separation between financial returns and impact may be less appropriate for investors who use a broader, more integrated approach, including both financial and nonfinancial factors, when evaluating their investment opportunities (see Figure 7.3).

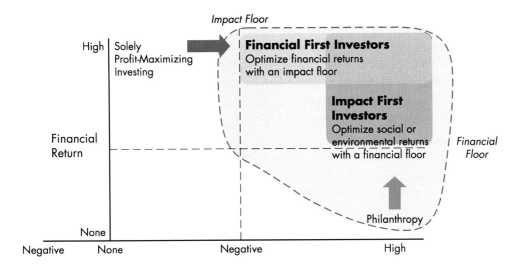

FIGURE 7.3 Impact Investor Categories

Source: Jessica Freireich and Katherine Fulton, *Investing for Social and Environmental Impact*, Monitor Institute (2009) (http://www.monitorinstitute.com/impactinvesting/documents/InvestingforSocialand EnvImpact_FullReport_005.pdf).

HYBRID TRANSACTIONS, PUBLIC–PRIVATE PARTNERSHIPS

In some cases, investors with diverse goals can co-invest in hybrid transactions. These hybrid structures enable social entrepreneurs to customize their capital structures while also reflecting the preferences of specific investors regarding risk, return, and impact. For example, development finance banks such as the IFC (International Finance Corporation) may co-invest with private investors and philanthropists. Such structures can even attract agnostic, commercial capital into impact investment opportunities. The negotiations among these parties can slow deal closings and increase costs. Nevertheless, it is through these risk-sharing mechanisms that hybrid structures can create additional value for social entrepreneurs by improving the terms and increasing the amount of available capital.

FINDING THE RIGHT FORM OF INVESTMENT

On the supply side of the impact investing market are the investment opportunities that social entrepreneurs offer to potential investors. As is stressed by Emerson, Freundlich, and Berenbach (2007, p. 5), "the current landscape of capital for social enterprise is somewhat ill-formed": there is very little focus on the risk-taking expansion capital needed by social enterprises, whether nonprofits or for-profits. These authors review in detail the instruments currently available in the nonprofit capital market and the challenges linked to their use by social enterprises. For instance, social enterprises using private equity might put their mission at risk because most equity investors remain profit seekers. Social ventures' capital funds are quite restrictive in that they target conventional market rates of return and focus on industries with inherent social benefits, such as environmental technologies or microfinance. Foundations can invest their endowments, or nonprofit organizations (e.g., the Acumen Fund) can invest their fund balances in social enterprises through program-related investments (PRIs) when prioritizing a social purpose and only secondarily expecting financial returns. When it comes to debt—money loaned at a stated interest rate for a fixed term of years—different types of debt financing are available to social entrepreneurs. Among them, traditional banking institutions provide (1) business loans (more readily accessed by for-profit social enterprises), and (2) loans that qualify for CRA (Community Reinvestment Act)[2] credits (nonprofit social enterprises may access these low or zero-interest loans); equity-like capital (for nonprofits) takes the form of a subordinated long-term loan, and investors are more focused on social value creation versus financial value creation. Finally, grants from governments, foundations, and corporations have the advantage of requiring no financial repayment (Godeke, 2006; Godeke & Bauer, 2008; Godeke & Pomares, 2009).

Many different ways have been used to represent the different investment vehicles that could suit social enterprises. Continuum models have been used with different variables, such as the percentage of social vs. financial returns—thereby falsely suggesting that one needs to be sacrificed for the other, the risk-adjusted rate of return compared to the market rate, or the level of financial risk. Others have mapped the investment vehicles along two axes, such as commercial to

---

2 The Community Reinvestment Act of 1977 requires commercial banks and other deposit-taking institutions to address the financial needs of underserved communities in their service areas. The law arose to address discriminatory lending practices of banks in low-income communities.

charitable and high to low involvement (Westlund & Bolton, 2003), or commercial to social enterprise and the stages of enterprise development (Emerson, 2000; Emerson & Spitzer, 2007).

Besides these rather traditional financing vehicles, diverse impact investment opportunities are emerging across multiple asset classes that provide investors with market-rate investments, or substantial social impact, while still generating positive financial returns (Bridges Ventures and the Parthenon Group, 2009). The expansion into new asset classes is helping to broaden the reach of impact investment, while allowing investors to diversify across multiple asset classes. Moreover, the perception that impact investment necessitates accepting sub-market-rate returns is eroding as impact-first funds demonstrated that they could also generate market-rate returns. This evolution could be explained by behavioral finance principles.

Behavioral finance tells us that both investors and social entrepreneurs deal with the real-world complexity of financial markets by relying on heuristics versus traditional finance that uses models in which people are self-interested and rational. Evidence from psychology, economics, and finance indicates that both assumptions are unrealistic and that people can instead be altruistic and less than totally rational. As a consequence, investors and social entrepreneurs are subject to behavioral biases that can cause irrational financial decisions. Unrealistic conditions and the presence of externalities, public goods, and imperfect information can lead to market failures.

While the bulk of non-grant investment into social enterprises will be in the form of impact-first and financial-first structures, there are a range of tools, as discussed below, that investors can use to generate impact across their publicly traded as well as private market investments (Godeke & Pomares, 2009).

PUBLICLY TRADED AND PRIVATE MARKET INVESTMENTS

Active Ownership Strategies

As a long-term owner and fiduciary of holdings in publicly traded securities, an investor has the ability to influence corporate behavior and further her or his desired impact through proxy voting, shareholder resolutions, and informal shareholder engagement with the corporate management of the companies held in a portfolio. Many companies have changed their policies and practices on a host of issues important to impact investors, not only because of market forces but also because their shareholders demanded change.

Screening

Screening is the practice of buying and selling publicly traded securities based on the evaluation of impact criteria that reflect personal or institutional values. An investment decision may be to avoid certain companies (negative screening) or to support particular companies (positive or best-in-class screening).The ultimate goal of screening is for the portfolio to reflect the investor's values and mission, mitigate risks, and use investment capital to encourage or discourage specific corporate behaviors.

Impact-First Investments

Impact-first investments can be made by foundations as well as public-sector and high-net-worth impact investors. Some impact investments made by U.S. foundation impact investors are categorized as program-related investments (PRIs).

Financial-First Investments

Financial-first investments create a risk-adjusted rate of return in addition to creating specific desired outcomes. For example, public and private pension funds, along with insurance companies and other institutional investors, are increasingly seeking to attract capital to underserved urban markets and build assets in low-income communities. These programs target financial-first returns against established financial benchmarks in addition to generating social and environmental benefits.

Guarantees

Guarantees are another important tool impact investors use to mitigate the credit risk created by an organization when it receives a loan from a bank or other lending institution. Investors can use their assets as collateral to provide security (guarantee) to an organization based on this collateral. Unlike other impact investments, a guarantee may not require upfront deployment of cash by the impact investor. Through guarantees, an investor can create more impact by leveraging her or his guarantee with additional capital from other investors.

These tools and tactics, as displayed in Figure 7.4, can be used across a range of investment asset classes and impact themes. This figure outlines some of the investment opportunities available to impact investors.

Illustrative Landscape of Impact Themes with Asset Class Exposures

Asset Classes

Social, Environmental or Blended Impact Themes	Liquidity — Cash/Cash Alternatives	Income and Wealth Preservation — Notes/Other Debt Obligations	Income and Wealth Preservation — Bonds	Income and Wealth Preservation — Absolute Return/Low Equity Correlated	Capital Appreciation and Wealth Growth — Public Equity	Capital Appreciation and Wealth Growth — Equity Long/Short	Capital Appreciation and Wealth Growth — Private Equity	Inflation Protection — Real Estate	Inflation Protection — Commodities, Timber and other Real Assets
Climate Change	Green Bank Deposit		Tax-exempt green bonds	CO$_2$ Trading	Positive and Negative Screening		Clean Tech Venture Capital	Green REITs	
Energy			Screened Corporate Bonds	Alternative Energy Project Finance	Exchange Traded Funds (ETFs)	Renewable Energy	Energy Efficiency Venture Capital		Sustainable Feedstocks
Water			Corporate Infrastructure Bonds	Water Treatment Project Finance	Unit Investment Trust, Closed End Funds	Water Funds	Water Technology Venture Capital		Water Rights
Community Development	Community Bank CDs	Foreclosure Repair		Microfinance Institutions Debt	Shareholder Proxy Voting		Community Development Venture Capital	Transportation — Smart Development Funds	
Social Enterprises		Social Enterprise Credit			Micro-Cap Listed Social Companies		Small and Medium Enterprise	Conservation/ Ecotourism	
Health and Wellness				Structured Public Note			Consumer Product Venture Capital	Organic Farming	
Sustainable Development	Trade Finance Guarantee/ Deposit		Smart Growth Municipal Bonds	Blended Debt Equity Hybrid Structures	Thematic Screening			Ranch Land, Agriculture	Sustainable Timber
Education	Linked Deposit/ Guarantee		Charter School Bonds				Education Private Equity	University Green Building	

FIGURE 7.4 Investment Opportunities Available to Impact Investors

Source: Godeke & Pomares (2009).

WHO'S WHO IN INVESTING AND FUNDING

Financial Institutions

Banks can provide commercial as well as low-interest rate loans to social enterprises. Because of the regulatory requirements of the Community Reinvestment Act, commercial banks in the United States are required to lend into low-income communities. Sectors of particular interest to banks are community development, health care, and education. Many community development financial institutions such as the Nonprofit Finance Fund pool together various sources of funding, such as donations from wealthy individuals, foundations, financial institutions, and corporations. These funds differ from regular investment funds as they generally anticipate lower than market-rate returns. Their larger motive tends to be advancing social causes (Godeke & Pomares, 2009).

Angels and Venture Capitalists

For-profit social enterprises can seek out cash infusions from angel investors or venture capitalists (VCs) that have a social bent. These investors typically want market-rate returns in exchange for their financial support. They are partial to entrepreneurs with plans to do good in the world—and they are usually willing to wait a little longer than traditional angels or VCs to reap returns. For example, the Investors' Circle, a network of angel investors and VCs, says it invests "patient" capital in companies that address social and environmental issues.

Of course, any entrepreneur who works with an angel or a VC gets more than money. Angels and VCs work closely with entrepreneurs to shape the company, sometimes taking board seats or management positions. A social angel or VC isn't any different, but will work within the social enterprise's mission to eke out market-rate returns, says David Berge, founder and managing member of Underdog Ventures, a social venture capital firm in Island Pond, Vermont. "A social VC is going to be predisposed to like what you're doing," he adds.

Corporate Social Responsibility and Corporate Citizenship

Corporations can be good partners for a social enterprise if the impact goals are aligned. Corporations support social entrepreneurs through grants from their corporate foundations or through their operating divisions, which may see a social enterprise as an opportunity to innovate or to reach a new market. For example,

Muhammad Yunus of the Grameen microfinance bank entered into a partnership with Groupe Danone, the French food giant, to produce healthier yogurt in Bangladesh. The business was structured as a social business in which Grameen and Danone agreed to reinvest all of the profits back into the yogurt operations after their initial investment was repaid (Yunus, 2007).

DIRECT VERSUS FUNDS STRATEGY

The decision to make direct investments and/or to utilize funds and other types of intermediaries is a critical step in the execution of an impact investing strategy. The decision to utilize a direct and/or fund-driven approach may be a function of impact themes and desired level of engagement in the investment process. For example, in the impact themes of affordable housing and microfinance there is a wide range of funds through which an investor could invest. In other sectors, investors may have to work to create and seed such funds or look to investment opportunities with secondary or tertiary effects related to a primary impact theme (e.g., the impact on health through a microfinance investment). The due diligence process will differ between direct investment and funds as well.

Focusing on initiatives at the bottom of the pyramid, the Monitor Institute's report (2009) argues that overcoming the barriers to scale includes efforts beyond the actors directly implementing market-based solutions, namely commercial investors, impact investors, traditional philanthropists, and large corporations (p. 115). Actions to increase the odds of success of smaller social enterprises precisely include making capital available in "smaller, more patient, and flexible chunks" (p. 116), pointing to the key role of impact investors.

STRUCTURAL CHALLENGES FOR IMPACT INVESTING

Launching and investing in social ventures creates unique challenges for both the social entrepreneur and the investor. Inefficiencies in raising capital due to a lack of commonly defined performance metrics measuring the capital and social return on investment along with inadequate information flows between the investor and the entrepreneur are often cited as key challenges (Emerson & Bonini, 2003). As the executive director of one global social venture investment fund observed,

> [S]ome social investors assume they are seeking competitive financial returns, and believe that screening investments into publicly traded

stocks and bonds is sufficient . . . others are willing to put their principal at risk, seeing some return as being a net positive over straight philanthropy.

(Berenbach, in Emerson & Bonini, 2003)

Indeed, Emerson et al. (2007) highlight the different sources of capital available for social investing, including market-rate capital (socially screened funds), near-market-rate capital (social and community development venture capital), and capital that does not yield a return (strategic philanthropy). The impact investing industry still suffers from inefficiencies that limit its impact. The challenges it faces include the lack of efficient intermediation, which implies high search and transaction costs, fragmented demand and supply, complex deals, and underdeveloped networks.

PATIENT AND GROWTH CAPITAL

Moving beyond seed funding is difficult since "the core of social enterprise activity falls outside the conventional definition of market-rate, risk-adjusted returns" (Emerson et al., 2007, p. 5). Therefore, new forms of growth or expansion capital are needed such as equity or equity-like capital forms, besides traditional nonprofit (grants, fund-raising, and limited use of debt) and for-profit (market-rate private equity and debt) financing. Indeed, the former is available to cover start-up requirements but not subsequent organizational expansion, whereas the latter seeks a full, conventional market rate on ROI that social enterprises are not able to offer. As a consequence, the dearth of growth capital and risk-taking capital makes it as competitive and scarce as early private equity is for for-profit ventures (Emerson et al., 2007).

As a consequence, the type of capital demanded by these social entrepreneurs must be long term and risk-tolerant. Overholser (2006) stresses the need for growth capital so that, once it is scaled, the enterprise can be sustained, and for expansion capital in cases where the enterprise needs to replicate the program across cities and regions. By definition, "growth capital is used to build the means of production," and as an initial catalyst it "covers the deficits a firm incurs en route to sustainability." When focusing on nonprofit social enterprises only, Overholser explains the failure of the market for "nonprofit growth capital" by the missing distinction between building an enterprise and buying from an enterprise. His main argument is that the commingling of investments and revenues in standard nonprofit accounting makes it very difficult to determine whether takeoff has been achieved. As a consequence, investors are left blind to the outcomes of their investments.

Similarly, the notion of patient capital refers to "money that pays the bills while an organization learns to fend for itself" (Overholser, 2006). This role is comparable to the role filled by equity investors in the for-profit sector. As is stressed by Emerson et al. (2007), social investment opportunities need a new kind of capital, which must be patient but also bear risk: there is often "a premium for doing good" that philanthropically minded stakeholders will accept more readily than more conventional investors might do. Overholser concludes by arguing that raising the money during the journey and not before is one of the main reasons that nonprofits rarely reach their potential.

THE INVESTMENT DECISION PROCESS

When it comes to the investment decision process, one size does not fit all. In a survey aiming at realizing the potential of the impact investing market, it was shown that there exist six segments of investors who have different priorities and motivations (Hope Consulting, 2010). Those in the first group consider safety as a primary decision criterion so that financial return on investment predominates over social benefits. Second, the "socially focused" first support the causes that are important to them. Those in the third group of investors attach a lot of importance to the quality of the organization, meaning a strong business model and a good track record. The last three groups consist of the "hassle-free," who do not want to get overly involved; the investors who personally belong to the social entrepreneur's social network; and, finally, "skeptic" investors are not interested in blending social and financial value creation and prefer keeping their charitable giving and financial investment separate. According to the study results, these first three segments control more than three-quarters of the current and future impact investment market. And despite their differences, each segment (except the skeptics) prioritizes the same five barriers, which all relate to the immaturity of the market (these are: Lack of track record; Don't know where to find; Don't see advisors recommending; Limited advice available; and Insufficient ratings/benchmarks), not the social or financial qualities of the investment opportunities.

THE DUE DILIGENCE PROCESS

After an initial review the impact investor will complete a full review of the financial statements of the social enterprise and other relevant organizational materials as well as project-specific documentation such as projections and business plans (Godeke & Pomares, 2009). A clear assessment of the quality of the management team is a key element of the due diligence. The due diligence process for impact investments also needs to consider potential "impact risks" and their mitigation. Careful consideration of the mission alignment of the management will be crucial.

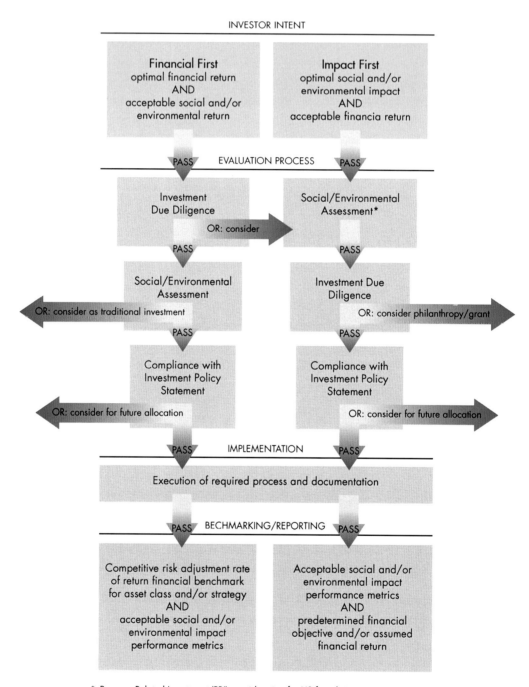

INVESTOR INTENT

Financial First
optimal financial return
AND
acceptable social and/or
environmental return

Impact First
optimal social and/or
environmental impact
AND
acceptable financia return

PASS   EVALUATION PROCESS   PASS

Investment
Due Diligence

OR: consider

Social/Environmental
Assessment*

PASS   PASS

Social/Environmental
Assessment

OR: consider as traditional investment

Investment Due
Diligence

OR: consider philanthropy/grant

PASS   PASS

Compliance with
Investment Policy
Statement

OR: consider for future allocation

Compliance with
Investment Policy
Statement

OR: consider for future allocation

PASS   IMPLEMENTATION   PASS

Execution of required process and documentation

PASS   BECHMARKING/REPORTING   PASS

Competitive risk adjustment rate
of return financial benchmark
for asset class and/or strategy
AND
acceptable social and/or
environmental impact
performance metrics

Acceptable social and/or
environmental impact
performance metrics
AND
predetermined financial
objective and/or assumed
financial return

* Program-Related Investment (PRI) consideration for US foundations
** Noted to Investment Policy Statement if PRI for US foundation

FIGURE 7.5 Due Diligence Processes

Source: Godeke & Pomares (2009).

The following are some due diligence questions to be asked in relation to impact investments:

- What is the impact investment thesis for this opportunity and how does it further specific impact goals?
- Is this a financial-first or an impact-first investment?
- Who are the principals involved in the investment?
- Does the transaction leverage other sources of capital?
- What are the impact and financial risks and how are they distributed?
- Will this investment enable a project to happen that otherwise would not?
- Are there behavioral finance aspects to consider?
- Does the investment raise reputation or policy issues?
- Where would this transaction fit in an overall asset allocation?

Impact investors such as the KL Felicitas Foundation (see Figure 7.5) have developed due diligence processes through which they jointly assess the investment returns and social or environmental impacts to determine whether a particular opportunity meets the Foundation's investment policy statement requirements and impact and financial performance benchmarks.

BUILDING PARTNERSHIPS TO CREATE IMPACT

Successful impact investing is based on moving beyond a false assumption that social entrepreneurs and investors must choose between social and environmental impact *or* financial return. Specifically, both entrepreneurs and investors can benefit from:

- optimizing for environmental and social impact *and* applying the rigor of investment management tools;
- embracing new business models *and* adhering to recognized financial theory; and
- expanding the scope and scale of philanthropic capital *and* maintaining adherence to fiduciary responsibilities.

By considering investors as partners in the creation of meaningful impact rather than just funding sources, social entrepreneurs can build more scalable and effective enterprises. When raising capital, social entrepreneurs need to find appropriate investors who are not just providing funds but can bring a range of resources to the enterprise. By understanding the financial and impact drivers of her or his enterprise, a social entrepreneur can seek out the right partners.

QUESTIONS FOR "CONNECTING THE DOTS"

1 What are the two types of capital that social entrepreneurs have traditionally used to fund their enterprises? How are these sources evolving?
2 What are some of the barriers social entrepreneurs face when raising capital which traditional entrepreneurs do not have?
3 What drivers of a social entrepreneur's business plan would lead to grant funding? Debt? Equity?
4 How can impact be integrated into a risk/return framework?
5 What is impact investing? What are the two most important impact investing categories?
6 What distinct roles can financial institutions, corporations, and angel investors play in raising capital for social enterprises?
7 What new investment forms are needed for social enterprises?
8 What is due diligence and how is it done?

VOICES FROM THE FIELD

A New Approach to Microfinance

Since the pioneering origins of Grameen Bank over three decades ago, microfinance has grown into a formidable industry. While the sector has been showered with praise for its contribution to ending the cycle of poverty, it has also been attracting its share of controversy. Muhammad Yunus's vision of microfinance was to break the cycle of poverty by lending to the poor for small businesses that were not serviced by the existing banking infrastructure. In his experience, because of their lack of any other option, the poor were being exploited by loan sharks that charged up to 10 percent interest per day. Grameen would change all that by offering micro-loans at a tiny fraction of that interest rate. In order to scale the model, Grameen offered one simple loan product, which required equal weekly repayments over fifty-two weeks. This way, loan officers could physically collect all payments from a village with one weekly visit. Grameen dealt with collateral by requiring loans to be "guaranteed" by four other residents of the village.

This was called the joint liability model, which essentially relied on peer pressure to ensure high repayment rates. Indeed, the model scaled well, and by 2008 there were more than 3,000 microfinance institutions with over 150 million customers and an estimated $30 billion in outstanding loans. Most of these institutions have simply applied the Grameen model to their respective markets. However, with its success and high returns has also come much criticism. Some claim that microfinance is creating a debt trap for the poor. Others believe the interest rates being charged are still too high (typically over 20 percent per annum). In addition, with all the fever behind the industry, it has attracted its share of unscrupulous players, some of which are simply cheating poor borrowers.

As with any kind of lending, there is no question that microfinance can be effective and has uplifted societies in all parts of the world. The problem, as with any financial product, is when it is used in excess. It is not uncommon these days to find households with micro-loans from multiple institutions, using one loan to pay off another. It is also important to recognize that the Grameen model has its limitations. For one, there is no real way to assess the viability of businesses that it funds. As an example, it would not be unusual to find a multitude of cigarette shops in a small village, all funded through microfinance. In addition, with a weekly repayment cycle the model entirely ignores the agricultural sector, where the timing of repayment must match the harvest cycle. In countries like India, this means ignoring 60 percent of the population.

Recognizing the need for a modified approach, BASIX was set up in Hyderabad in 1996 by the social entrepreneur and visionary Vijay Mahajan. BASIX is a livelihood promotion institution with three essential legs to its business: financial services, agricultural/business development services, and institutional development services. Unlike most of its peers, BASIX wraps micro-lending with an array of services to enhance the sustainability of the businesses that it funds. BASIX also offers a variety of loan products in order to cover the agricultural sector as well. Services that BASIX offers include advisory for agricultural yield enhancement, value chain growth, improving access to suppliers and customers, formation of federations and cooperatives, and accounting and management systems. Such a variety of offerings does call into question the ability for an organization to scale. However, after fourteen years BASIX has over 1.5 million customers in sixteen states in India. This makes it the fourth-largest microfinance institution in India and among the top ten in the world.

BASIX's involvement with cotton farmers in the Adilabad district of Andhra Pradesh provides a unique insight into what makes it stand apart. Starting in 1996, BASIX began extending micro-loans to groups of cotton farmers in the district. Simultaneously, it began an extensive study of the cotton sector in the region. The study uncovered a number of issues. Farmers were overusing pesticides, causing significant soil depletion and yield loss. They were also being taken advantage of by commission agents. These agents would extend credit to farmers for pesticides and fertilizers, but under the condition that farmers sell their crop to them at lower than market prices. BASIX began by establishing a collaboration with the Andhra Pradesh Agricultural University to apply new integrated pest management (IPM) techniques on several farms. This brought down the cost of pesticides from Rs. 750 per month per acre to just Rs. 75, immediately removing the shackles that the agents had on the farmers. Having built trust with the farming community, BASIX then embarked on helping them organize into cooperatives to improve their buying and selling power. Today, the district has over twenty cotton cooperatives, and operating margins on individual farms have improved by up to 10 percent. One cooperative, Koutla-B, has eighty-three members and generates Rs. 120 million in revenues and about Rs. 1 million in net profits annually. With its accumulated returns, the cooperative has since installed a price display terminal in the village and recently inaugurated a Rs. 1.1 million ginning factory to convert raw cotton to tradable bales. In 2005 the president of the cooperative was awarded the Fellowship Award for Rural Prosperity by India's president, Dr. A. P. J. Kalam.

Over the years, BASIX has developed vertical knowledge in cotton, groundnuts, dairy, soybean, pulses, and vegetables, and has applied similar models to enhance livelihood in these sectors. While its approach takes longer to realize returns, the BASIX model fosters the creation of high-margin, high-growth businesses with exceptional loyalty—the kinds of customers any institution would yearn for. The effort involved is high, but it is certainly a powerful new approach to microfinance where everyone can win.

Source: Hans Taparia, on March 16, 2010 (used with permission)

VOICES FROM THE FIELD

Funding Social Ventures: Approaches, Sources, and Latest Perspectives

Founded in 2002, Bridges Ventures is an innovative UK investment company that delivers both financial returns and social and environmental benefits. It currently has four funds: Ventures Fund I and II, the Social Entrepreneurs Fund, and a Sustainable Property Fund. The company has grown over the past eight years from the first £40 million fund to approximately £150 million under management. The following is an interview with Antony Ross, executive director of Bridges Ventures.

Q: Could you please give a bit of background about the Social Entrepreneurs Fund? The Social Entrepreneurs Fund was launched in November 2008 by Bridges Ventures to address the funding gap often faced by fast-growing social enterprises looking to scale. The fund has so far raised £9 million for investment and focuses on scalable social enterprises that deliver high social impact whilst operating with a sustainable business model. Investors include foundations from the financial sector, private donors, the National Endowment for Science, Technology and the Arts (NESTA), and the Office for Civil Society. Additionally, the social enterprises that we invest in have the opportunity to benefit from consulting advice from Monitor Group to help them reach scale. Bridges Ventures also works closely with UnLtd, the Foundation for Social Entrepreneurs, to help social entrepreneurs seeking funding to become investment-ready.

Q: What was the inspiration behind the Social Entrepreneurs Fund?

The idea behind the fund was to bridge the funding gap that social entrepreneurs face as they look to scale and match them with those in the investment community that recognize a broader agenda exists than just maximizing shareholder returns. There are a sufficient number of investors who want to focus on maximizing social impact, even though their return would not be as high as [is offered by] traditional equity investments. As experienced fund managers, we aimed to match the opportunities investors look for with social enterprises that need cash. We identify and structure deals for investors and provide capital and hands-on support to the enterprises with funding.

Q: What are the criteria for selection?

The Bridges Social Entrepreneurs Fund invests in social enterprises based in England that have:

- a clear social mission;
- a robust business plan that ideally follows strong historical revenue growth;
- the ability to grow to scale and increase their social impact;
- a financially sustainable model;
- the ability to generate surpluses to repay financing;
- a strong management team with considerable experience in the business and ideally a passion for social enterprise.

Q: Could you describe the investment process the Social Entrepreneurs Fund employs? How does the process differ for the Social Entrepreneurs Fund? In other words, how does funding a social venture differ from funding a regular venture?

We are similar to any VC in that when analyzing the business, we look at its model of sustainability. Our investment process is very similar to the ventures funds' process. The general process is to examine business plans as they come into our office and review the financial model if available. We look to see if the business model is sustainable and if social impact is made. We then make the decision whether to take it forward and meet the team. If deciding after meeting with the team that we would like to progress, we will develop a proposal to take to our first investment committee to gain their approval, and begin due diligence. After due diligence has satisfied any outstanding questions we may have and we would like to invest, we take the deal to our second investment committee to get final approval before confirming the deal with the entrepreneur or business.

Our model is slightly different compared to our ventures fund, which looks first to see if [a proposal] meets its location or sector criteria and then looks to maximize returns in that business. Rather, we look to see if the business model is a fit and how social impact can be maximized. The question we ask is: As the business grows, will its social impact grow? Is it truly a social enterprise? For example, asking an entrepreneur about how they plan to exit often highlights the difference between a profit-maximizing business and a social enterprise. If the choice of buyer is between someone who offers a lower price but intends to continue the mission versus a corporation that pays a much higher price but is unlikely to grow the business, the decision to sell varies depending on the objectives of the business.

Additionally, part of our objectives for the fund was to share learnings in this space. We have advisory meetings three times a year to share learnings and hope to see more funds like these set up in the future so that social investment can become its own asset class.

Q: What is the size of the investment and how is it structured?

Each investment made by the fund will be up to £1.5 million, structured as a flexible and tailored investment, usually in the form of quasi-equity, and repayable, with an appropriate return, through the social enterprise's trading activities. We invest in both early-stage and development capital.

We tailor each investment to ensure that it fits the needs of each particular social enterprise, while also allowing the Social Entrepreneurs Fund to make a reasonable financial return to demonstrate a sustainable funding source for social enterprises. We work closely with the social entrepreneurs we support to help them realize their ambitions and maximize their social impact.

Recipients of the fund benefit from the equity-like structure, which differs from loans schemes or a pure equity structure where a social venture may suffer loss of control and mission drift if goals are different. The Social Entrepreneurs Fund offers flexible structures, such as subordinated debt with royalty payments that rise with revenue.

Q: What is the most significant challenge you have faced as a fund?

The size of our fund is £9 million, which will allow us to make a couple of deals a year for the fund. The challenge is finding enough sustainable social enterprises to invest in. Many have a valuable social mission, but few have a solid business model. The capital exists in this space, but more social enterprises need dynamic leadership with a sound, sustainable financial model. The investor appetite exists, but the sector needs more dynamic leaders and role-models. Many of the social enterprises we see want to remain focused on the local community and lack the visionary leadership necessary to grow the business. As the fund grows and the social enterprise sector evolves, the fund could potentially start backing incubator businesses that are looking to fill a need, often in the healthcare or education space, and that address a local requirement, rather than businesses that have sprung up organically.

Q: Can you give an example of one of your investments?

HCT is a community transport business that employs close to 500 employees and reinvests its profits to fund local transport services for the mobility-impaired, and provides training programs for its employees and others interested in a career in the bus industry. What makes HCT unique as a transport company in London is that it aims to reinvest 30 percent of the prior year's profits into community transport and education projects in the local areas in which it operates, primarily in east London. The surpluses also fund the delivery of relevant training programs for the unemployed or those with low or no formal qualifications, over and above requisite training for HCT's own staff. In addition, HCT delivers a social impact intrinsic to its business model, including saving car journeys through the use of buses and of community group transport, and paying a high proportion of the wage bill to employees in disadvantaged areas due to the location of its depots.

Q: What are some of the challenges you see social enterprises facing in this current climate?

Currently, there is a gray zone as to where social enterprises fit. They are neither a strictly commercial venture nor a charity. The sector is still very much in its incubator stage, but for the sector to evolve, social enterprises need to be recognized as [having] a different status by the government, thus allowing them to benefit from tax reductions.

The sector also needs to properly brand itself so investors, employees, and customers know that this space represents a massive opportunity. Similar to how the Fairtrade logo exists, in the future there's potential for a recognized Social Enterprise mark.

In addition, the sector needs to grow sufficiently to gain critical mass. If you look at all successful entrepreneurial areas, for example Silicon Valley, or the area around MIT or Cambridge, there is a supportive ecosystem in place where risk is encouraged and opportunities exist should one venture fail. These "clusters" both provide support and an infrastructure, and alleviate risk by providing other companies to work at if a venture is unsuccessful.

Social enterprises will also need to attract and pay for talent. The sector is benefiting from professionals who have established themselves in their chosen field and have decided to make a switch to the social sector.

Q: What is your vision for the Social Entrepreneurs Fund and the social enterprise sector?

Ideally, I would like to see the overall social enterprise sector grow so that we as a fund can back the best social enterprises and be a key contributor in growing the social enterprise space. We want to pick the best business in each space, so they become role-models in each of the spaces and encourage further growth. One of our objectives is to back enough successful social enterprises so that people recognize the social enterprise model as real and material. We have the potential to make a contribution to growing this new corporate model, operating with a broader stakeholder agenda than to purely maximize profit.

We also have an opportunity as a fund to make a contribution to growth of this market. As this market grows, more funds will spring up, thus funding further social enterprises. I wouldn't be surprised if in the long run our fund became a European fund rather than a UK fund.

About Antony Ross

Antony has over twenty years of private equity investment experience in a wide range of businesses from early-stage development opportunities to later-stage management buyouts. He is responsible for the Bridges Social Entrepreneurs Fund. Antony studied mechanical engineering at Bristol University and has an MBA from London Business School. He is a Teaching Fellow in Entrepreneurship at London Business School.

Case Study 7.1

PODER (Project on Organizing, Development, Education, and Research)[3]

Ben Cokelet, founder and executive director of PODER, was both ecstatic and overwhelmed at what had happened in the past twenty-four hours. His social venture team had just won the 2009 Stewart Satter award in New York University's prestigious social business plan competition. The $100,000 in cash plus pro bono support in legal and marketing services would be most welcome despite the fact that PODER had already established financial viability in its first year by selling corporate accountability services to

3 This case was written by Mark D. Griffiths for the purposes of classroom discussion. The case is not intended to serve as an endorsement, as sources of primary data, or as an illustration of effective or ineffective management.

five large nongovernmental U.S. organizations. Ben knew he had to develop a much more detailed financial plan focusing specifically on the total amount of funds needed to get the venture started and the total amount needed to ensure viability for the first three years. And, he had to do it soon as he was meeting with interested financial backers in the next week.

Background

PODER (Project on Organizing, Development, Education, and Research) is a corporate accountability firm whose mission is to strengthen democracy and development in Latin America. While most companies in the region operate responsibly, an intransigent few do not, and these few foster corruption and spoil the marketplace for investment. They resist transparency and the rule of law, and their actions impact negatively on workers, communities, and the environment. Although civil society groups such as trade unions and other nongovernmental organizations attempt to hold these companies accountable, too often their efforts fall short because they lack the tools to succeed. PODER provides these tools. By empowering groups with high-quality information and strategic solutions to eliminate corporate malfeasance, PODER shines a light in the dark corners of the global economy. The company offers three principal services: (1) business intelligence and analysis on companies in Latin America; (2) strategic engagements with companies to incentivize compliance; and (3) operational strengthening and capacity building for civil society groups. PODER is a blended value firm that generates economic, social, and environmental value. It provides the first two services for fees, intending to make a profit, and donates the third service to local organizations on a pro bono basis.

How PODER Works

The client, in consultation with PODER, determines the project's target, objectives, and deliverables. PODER establishes an information discovery plan that guides its researcher on topics including methodology, timeline, contact list, threat assessment, and security. The researcher compiles and organizes relevant open-source intelligence from a variety of sources, including books, news sources, academic journals, legal cases, Internet resources, government publications, and innovative technological methods. The researcher then expands the preliminary contact list to include anyone who could potentially assist in the information-discovery process. The researcher then develops a strategy to contact individuals in government, business, the legal profession, the media, nongovernmental organizations, etc. Espionage and other information technologies are critical inputs. Analysis of the open-source and human intelligence follows, and a report is prepared for the client.

In addition to paying clients, PODER also partners with workers, communities, and civil society organizations to provide pro bono services such as operational strengthening, strategic planning, research, organizing, campaigning, and negotiation training, so that they can intercede effectively with companies to ensure corporate accountability. PODER supports these organizations to strengthen their capacities for collective action and to overcome Latin American silence and impunity regarding human rights violations and corruption.

How Does PODER Benefit Companies? How Does PODER Benefit Grassroots Groups in Latin America?

Business intelligence and political risk information: pro bono services
Supply chain transparency: training and capacity building
Ethical and legal compliance: operational strengthening
Mitigated investment risks: strategic planning
Increased financial sustainability: campaign coordination
Avoidance of corruption, graft, and bribery: local and international coalition building
Certification of operations and suppliers: organizing for collective action
Corporate social responsibility: research
Multi-stakeholder partnerships with civil society organizations: multi-stakeholder partnerships

Crucial Needs and Risks

PODER's success depends on its ability to impress each client with its knowledge in any given field and its expertise in synthesizing and communicating this knowledge in a friendly, timely, and strategically useful way. PODER must recruit and retain top talent, and ultimately set the industry standard for corporate accountability services. For its proof-of-concept phase, PODER recruited a discreet, diverse, and talented management team with backgrounds in relevant fields who are well versed in Latin America and are multilingual and multicultural. In addition to the management staff, the firm also hired five experienced field staff located in Mexico City.

The strength of PODER's team is the train-the-trainer model implemented by the executive director, who trains each staff member to successfully perform corporate accountability services. PODER must hire a strong operational director with business experience if it wishes to expand this business model.

PODER stated that it would not hire any management and administrative staff until September 2010, so as to delay significant overhead costs to coincide with the organization's initial scale. However, sales revenue should be sufficient to pay the salaries of research consultants starting in Q1-09.

In 2008, PODER's highest-paid consultant earned approximately US$4,000 per month, without benefits. The lowest-paid consultant earned approximately US$650 per month, without benefits. The average employee earned US$1,000 per month, without benefits. For comparison purposes, a typical NGO in Mexico pays US$600–US$1,200 per month, not including benefits. In 2008 the executive director earned an average of US$5,500 per month, without benefits; however, he only billed for six months of the year. Starting in 2009, Ben anticipated needing to draw approximately $4,000 per month from May 2009 through August 2010.

During its proof-of-concept phase, PODER obtained two rent-free office spaces in Mexico City. When not in the field, its research consultants performed information-gathering duties from one of these offices or their homes. However, PODER stated that in Q3-10 it would establish a headquarters in Mexico City to ensure the safety of its personnel, the integrity of its information, and professionalism for its clients. PODER will open offices in Q3-11 and Q3-12 in strategic locations in Mexico to achieve operational synergies between its clients and their corporate accountability objectives.

PODER deals in sensitive information in a risky environment. Thus, the overriding concern is the safety of its personnel. PODER only provides services if the potential threats resulting from a project are limited to being followed, put under surveillance, or being harassed. Anything beyond this is unacceptable. PODER will also purchase substantial insurance to cover the firm should an incident occur, as well as catastrophic death and dismemberment insurance for its personnel and their families.

PODER takes many precautions, including protecting the identity of personnel and collaborators, insuring assets and personnel, maintaining communication protocols, using security equipment, storing sensitive information offsite, and practicing counterintelligence to reduce risks. Should a security problem arise, PODER relies on independent security consultants, legal help, and a rapid-action network to ensure the quickest, most effective response possible.

Financial Projections

In 2008, PODER was almost completely financially sustainable, capturing sales revenue of $49,200 and $10,000 from an angel donor. Total expenses (including SG&A—selling, general, and administrative expenses) came to $60,000. From 2009 until initial scale (Q3-10), PODER conservatively estimated that it would capture $280,000 in accumulated revenue from the sale of five Discovery Projects and three Strategic Engagements, while COGS (cost of goods sold) was expected to amount to approximately $30,000.

However, significant one-time start-up costs of approximately $50,000 to establish a headquarters in Mexico City and a field office elsewhere in Mexico were anticipated in both Q3-10 and Q3-11. To scale effectively, both sales and non-sales revenue must increase, including philanthropic donations and the Stewart Satter Social Venture Competition Award. PODER estimated that an infusion of $70,000 in foundation grants between Q1-09 and Q4-11, as well as the $100,000 Satter Award, would enable it to overcome its net income loss after start-up expenses, to scale in affected communities, and to invest in the human and technological resources necessary. Additionally, PODER has developed a separate philanthropic fund-raising plan for 2009–2013. As a new social venture, PODER currently finds itself between the conceptual and the start-up phases. Though it established a proof of concept in 2008, PODER has yet to integrate all facets of the business model into its day-to-day operations.

The potential new investors in PODER expect projections to be made monthly for years 1 and 2 and quarterly for years 3 to 5. Some key assumptions are as follows:

1. PODER is to be financed by philanthropy from years 1 to 5 and no debt will be considered.
2. Units of sales are defined as three month-long projects—Discovery Projects (DPs) and Strategic Engagements (SEs). PODER was to receive a 25 percent down payment upon engagement and will receive the balance upon completion, estimated to be the end of the second month following the engagement.
3. DPs and SEs are priced at $36,000 and $33,750 respectively. See Table 6.2 for the estimated timing of the DPs and SEs.
4. Accounting and legal expenses were estimated to be $5,000 per month until September 2009, at which time they were expected to increase to $7,500 per month.
5. Salaries were expected to be $41,100 per month, advertising to be $7,500 per month, telephone expenses to be $3,000 per month, insurance to be $8,250 per month, and rent is estimated at $6,000 monthly, all starting in September 2009.
6. Depreciation is estimated at $878 per month until the end of Q2-11, when it will increase to $1,757 per month before increasing again to $2,635 in Q4-12.
7. PODER was expected to incorporate legally by September 2010, when salaries and other expenses initially incur.
8. PODER will make important capital expenditures of $32,498 in September 2010, $1,757 in Q1-11, and $34,255 in both Q3-11 and Q4-12.
9. Ben Cokelet committed to funding the first four months of operations. He estimated that he would need to contribute $7,500 on the first day, $2,875 by the end of the first month, $2,894 in the second month followed by $2,913 and $2,934 respectively over the next two months.
10. PODER estimated that it would perform pro bono work of $2,000 in September 2010, Q1-11, Q1-12, and $3,000 per quarter commencing Q1-13.

Cost of goods sold is variable, linked to the number of projects that it performs. PODER expects these will be constant and maintained at 60 percent of revenue, and estimates that it will be able to maintain constant operating margins of 40 percent. Since the firm operates primarily in the business intelligence, analysis, and accountability industries, it expects working capital to be small or even negligible. PODER will not provide its clients with term payments, incur debt with suppliers, or maintain inventories. However, it will need cash to operate, at a level that was expected to start at $5,000 in 2009. A minimum monthly level of cash of $3,000 was expected to be needed until September 2010, after which it should be approximately 7 percent of total revenues.

Primarily retained earnings and philanthropic donations will finance PODER; however, some venture capital will also be necessary. Ben hopes to use the Satter Award funds due to be received at a later date to cover initial costs, and by the end of year 5 the company will be financed mainly by donations (73 percent) and profits. PODER does not expect to incur debt.

Table 7.2
Anticipated Sales and Philanthropic Gifts, January 2009 through Q4-13

	Discovery Project @ $36,000	Strategic Engagements @ $33,750	Philanthropic Gifts
May-09	1	0	
Sept-09	1	1	
Jan-10	1	1	$20,000
May-10	1	1	
Jun-10	1	0	
Sep-10	1	1	$50,000
Oct-10	1	1	
Q1-11	2	2	
Q2-11	2	3	
Q3-11	3	3	$50,000
Q4-11	3	3	$50,000
Q1-12	3	3	
Q2-12	5	3	
Q3-12	5	3	
Q4-12	5	5	$50,000
Q1-13	5	5	$50,000
Q2-13	5	5	$200,000
Q3-13	5	5	$300,000
Q4-13	6	6	

PODER was expected to legally incorporate by Q3-10. Since its initial costs are variable and low, allowing for a profit margin of 35 percent, PODER will only need $20,000 from venture capital to begin operations. As of Q3-10, however, PODER's fixed costs were expected to increase considerably. PODER aimed to have collected $70,000 from philanthropic donors by that time. It expected that these donations will have increased to $550,000 by Q4-13. A good part of these funds will be allocated for new offices that PODER will open (one in Q3-11 and another in Q3-12). PODER does not plan to give donors an equity stake.

PODER's success will be driven by its ability to sell services, build relationships with clients, and continue generating new revenue, which is why the sensitivity analysis is needed and should be linked to the quantity and pricing of sales. Ben knew that the best method for performing sensitivity analysis was to assume that revenues are incurred later than anticipated and that expenses occur sooner than anticipated. However, he was also concerned about the validity of some of his assumptions and how to estimate their impact if his projections were a little off.

QUESTIONS FOR "CONNECTING THE DOTS"

1 In relation to the PODER case study, how much additional funding should Ben Cokelet need for 2009 and 2010? How confident are you of these estimates?

2 How much total funding does Ben Cokelet need by Q4-13? How confident are you of this estimate?

3 Discuss the operational risks Ben faces in implementing PODER.

4 What factors or costs has Ben failed to take into account?

5 What do you see as the most crucial assumption made? How would you analyze the impact of this assumption?

REFERENCES

Bridges Ventures and the Parthenon Group (2009). *Investing for Impact: Case Studies across Asset Classes.* Retrieved from http://www.bridgesventures.com/sites/bridgesventures.com/files/Investing%20 for%20Impact%20Report.pdf.

Emerson, J. (2000). The nature of returns: A social capital markets inquiry into elements of investment and the blended value proposition. Working Paper, Division of Research, Harvard Business School, Boston, MA.

Emerson, J., & Bonini, S. (2003). Blended value map. Retrieved from http://www.blendedvalue.org (accessed December 20, 2010).

Emerson, J., Freundlich, T., & Berenbach, S. (2007). *The investor's toolkit: Generating multiple returns through a unified investment strategy.* Retrieved from http://www.blendedvalue.org/media/pdf-investors-toolkit.pdf (accessed November 20, 2010).

Emerson, J., Fruchterman, J., & Freundlich, T. (2007). *Nothing ventured, nothing gained: Addressing the critical gaps in risk-taking capital for social enterprise.* Retrieved from http://www.benetech.org/about/downloads/NothingVenturedFINAL.pdf (accessed January 25, 2011).

Emerson, J., & Spitzer, J. (2007). *From fragmentation to function.* Oxford: Saïd Business School, University of Oxford.

Freireich, J., & Fulton, K. (2009). *Investing for social & environmental impact* (Monitor Institute). Retrieved from http://www.monitorinstitute.com/impactinvesting/documents/InvestingforSocial andEnvImpact_FullReport_005.pdf (accessed January 9, 2011).

Fulkerson, G., & Thompson, G. (2008). Fifteen years of social capital: Definitional analysis of journal articles 1988–2003. *Sociological Inquiry, 78,* 536–557.

Godeke, S. (2006). Hybrid transactions in the US social capital market. *Alliance Magazine, 11*(3), 49–51.

Godeke, S., & Bauer, D. (2008). *Philanthropy's new passing gear: Mission-related investing.* New York: Rockefeller Philanthropy Advisors. Retrieved from http://www.rockpa.org/document.doc?id=16 (accessed January 9, 2011).

Godeke, S., & Pomares, R., with A. V. Bruno, P. Guerra, C. Kleissner, & H. Shefrin (2009). *Solutions for impact investors: From strategy to implementation.* New York: Rockefeller Philanthropy Advisors. Retrieved from http://www.rockpa.org/document.doc?id=15 (accessed January 9, 2011).

Hope Consulting (2010). *The goal and structure of the Money for Good project*. Retrieved from http://www.hopeconsulting.us/pdf/Money%20for%20Good_Final.pdf (accessed December 13, 2010).

JP Morgan Global Research (2010). *Impact investments: An emerging asset class*. Retrieved from http://www.jpmorgan.com/cm/cs?pagename=JPM/DirectDoc&urlname=impact_investments_nov2010.pdf (accessed December 20, 2010).

Overholser, G. (2006). Patient capital: The next step forward? Nonprofit Finance Fund. Retrieved from http://nonprofitfinancefund.org/files/docs/2010/2-0-2006PatientCapitalFinal.pdf (accessed January 12, 2011).

Rangan, V. K., Leonard, H. B., & McDonald, S. (2008). The future of social enterprise. Harvard Business School Working Paper 08-103. Retrieved from http://www.hbs.edu/research/pdf/08-103.pdf (accessed December 12, 2010).

Westlund, H., & Bolton, R. (2003). Local social capital and entrepreneurship. *Small Business Economics*, *21*(2), 77–113.

World Economic Forum (2005). *Blended value investing: Capital opportunities for social and environmental impact*. Geneva: World Economic Forum.

Yunus, M. (2007). *Creating a world without poverty*. New York: PublicAffairs.

Measuring Social Impact

AIM/PURPOSE

This chapter discusses how the ability to measure and communicate the impact of a venture's efforts still remains a significant challenge for most social firms. The importance of this activity is reviewed and an assessment methodology that can ultimately be used to maximize organizational effectiveness and market a social venture's value to its key stakeholders is examined.

LEARNING OBJECTIVES FOR THIS CHAPTER

1. To gain an understanding of the value of measuring a venture's social impact.
2. To understand the multiple benefits of learning how to measure social impact.
3. To examine the steps involved in measuring, quantifying, and monetizing impact for a venture's stakeholders (investors, management team, employees, etc.).
4. To look at examples of how to measure and quantify a new venture's social impact.

Social entrepreneurs often have difficulty coming up with a precise and measurable indicator that can accurately represent the amount of social return generated by their ventures (Saul, 2004; Trelstad, 2008). Increasingly, organizations are feeling pressure from funders to account for their social returns (Clark, Rosenzweig, Long, & Olsen, 2004).

One of the most challenging and potentially frustrating aspects of a social entrepreneur's work can be measuring and also communicating the positive social impact of his/her organization (Porter & Kramer, 1999; Kramer, 2005; Kramer, Graves, Hirschhorn, & Fiske, 2007). For example, how should we measure the "return on investment" of better health, cleaner air and water, families having nourishing food on their tables, or children receiving education they would not have had access to otherwise? As expressed by Stannard-Stockton (2007),

> [C]alculating the "good" done is tough. First because knowing what "good" means is hard, secondly because relating "good" to dollars is like translating a symphony into organic chemistry, and third because identifying cause and effect is tough (did your grant create more jobs, or did the economy just happen to get better?).

Moreover, the diversity and overlapping nature of the domains encompassed by many social enterprises bring an additional layer of difficulty to this endeavor (Clark et al., 2004; Chambers, Karlan, Ravallion, & Rogers, 2009).

As is highlighted in Chapter 7, the social impact investing industry is growing rapidly, with $50 billion in committed funds already available for impact investing, rising to $500 billion in ten years. Within this rapidly expanding marketplace, funders, investors, and other stakeholders want to know the kinds of returns they can expect to get and are getting for their investments and donations (Saul, 2004; Merchant & Van der Stede, 2007). Yet, often, organizations are powerless to give them more than moving stories and anecdotes (Saul, 2004). It is observed that current approaches to measuring social impact have not yet reached maturity primarily because of two factors (Scholten, Nicholls, Olsen, & Galimidi, 2006):

1   The general lack of maturity in social program evaluation. The field of social program evaluation—the process of collecting social impact and social outcome data—and the methods of calculating the costs of social program delivery are not very well developed. Many important benefits that occur as a result of social programs are not monetized and the dollar values of outcomes do not consistently capture the full range of societal benefits or costs, thus resulting in a variety of errors in the final answers. Therefore, comparing the social value of various programs is not similar to comparing the financial returns on investment (ROIs). The infrastructure that makes financial comparisons and ratios possible took years to develop. In comparison, the social sector has only been measuring value creation in recent years. More resources need to be allocated to developing an infrastructure for such calculations in the social sector.

2   The variety of purposes that organizations have for conducting these analyses. At present, there is a lack of consensus about how one should use cost-related impact data to make certain investment decisions. While some leading practitioners feel that it is appropriate to use cost and impact data to make funding allocation decisions *across* program areas, others feel that it should be used to only compare similar programs. There is an ongoing debate with regard to the

manner in which these cost-based approaches can be used, thus resulting in the lack of maturity that is currently observed in the field.

THE BENEFITS OF LEARNING HOW TO MEASURE SOCIAL IMPACT

One of the main benefits of learning how to calculate a firm's social impact is a clear picture of the measurable results of the organization's work (Saul, 2004; Merchant & Van der Stede, 2007). Social entrepreneurs can become more aware of which of their programs are working and which are not (Kramer, 2005; Tuan, 2008). This will allow them to allocate resources where they are having the greatest impact. Another benefit lies in being able to make a stronger case to your stakeholders that your organization is achieving its mission. Social entrepreneurs no longer need to rely considerably on the same stories and anecdotes or a fuzzy "sense" that things are moving in the right direction; they can support the case for the organization's success in hard data. It is another tool in their toolbox for showing that the social firm and its work are on track and worthy of investment.

Finally, when they learn how to measure their firm's social impact, they can identify themselves and the organization with the cutting edge of the industry. Clearly, the trend in the world of social enterprise is toward (emphasizing) more objective reporting and accurate accounting for social impact (Scholten et al., 2006; London Business School, 2009). Part of measuring your impact relates directly back to your theory of change and how you relate your value proposition and activities to the outcomes and impact that you would like to achieve.

STEPS TO MEASURING SOCIAL IMPACT

1. Define Your Social Value Proposition (SVP)

The firm's SVP is a brief description of the social venture's organization, the value it provides, and the impact it can have on individuals and society. It should also articulate why your customers and those that benefit from your offering will want to buy the firm's product or service offering(s) over alternative or substitute offerings from other organizations (including the government). This first step involves beginning a conversation with the social venture's stakeholders. Stakeholders will differ by type of organization, but here are the most common ones:

- constituents or beneficiaries of your work;
- board members;

- key leadership of your organization;
- key partners;
- affiliates or chapter leaders;
- government officials;
- individual donors;
- institutional funders.

With all of these various stakeholders, the types of questions the social entrepreneur will want to ask include:

- How would you define success for the work we do?
- What outcomes do you value most about our work?
- Do you think we were successful last year? If so, why? Or if not, why not?
- What's the ultimate impact that you value from our work? For example, in five years' time, how will the world look different if we are successful?
- What do you think the project needs to accomplish over the next one to three years to achieve this longer-term impact?
- What data or evidence would you need to see that would convince you that our work has been successful?

Many of these questions will not only assist the social entrepreneur in determining the venture's SVP but also assist in crafting the organization's theory of change (as discussed in Chapter 5) and logic model.

2. Quantify Your Social Value

After having a discussion with stakeholders, the social entrepreneur should identify social indicators that are mentioned most frequently across all types of stakeholders. These indicators should be further parsed by which can actually be measured. The social entrepreneur can then choose the top three or four measurable social indicators that are aligned with the conversation and interests of the stakeholder. Once named, these indicators can then be tracked over time. For example, a solar panel retailer might believe that deriving energy from solar power is cleaner and less harmful for the environment and thus might define its social indicators as:

- number of solar panels installed per fiscal year;
- percentage of panels installed that replace other forms of energy; and
- savings in air emissions (in dollars, or in particulates per 1,000?) related to non-solar power energy generation per sale.

VOICES FROM THE FIELD

In 1991, Martin Fisher and Nick Moon founded ApproTEC, which in 2005 became KickStart. Their model was based on a five-step process to develop, launch, and promote simple money-making tools that poor entrepreneurs could use to create their own profitable businesses.

KickStart's early efforts focused on building and food-processing technologies. But in Africa, 80 percent of the poor are small-scale farmers. They depend on unreliable rain to grow their crops and have, at most, two harvests per year. KickStart realized that irrigation would allow people to move from subsistence farming to commercial agriculture provided they had two valuable assets: a small plot of land and basic farming skills.

In 1998, KickStart developed a line of manually operated Money-Maker Irrigation Pumps that allow farmers to easily pull water from a river, pond, or shallow well (up to 25 feet deep), pressurize it through a hosepipe (even up a hill), and irrigate up to 2 acres of land. The pumps are easy to transport and install, and retail at between $35 and $95. They are easy to operate and, because they are pressurized, they allow farmers to direct water where it is needed. It is a very efficient use of water, and, unlike flood irrigation, does not lead to the buildup of salts in the soil.

With irrigation, farmers can grow crops year-round. They can grow higher value crops like fruits and vegetables, get higher yields, and, most importantly, they can produce crops in the dry seasons when food supplies dwindle and the market prices are high. Because of the long dry seasons and growing population, there is potential for many thousands of farmers to start irrigating without flooding the market. There are local, urban, and even export markets for the new crops.

KickStart continued to expand across Kenya, proving that their model was scalable. In 2000, KickStart expanded into Tanzania, and in 2004 into Mali. Other organizations have distributed their pumps across Africa and today, thousands are in use in Uganda, Malawi, Zambia, Sudan, and Rwanda.

Measure and Move Along

KickStart's model is based on the "diffusion of innovation" theory. When a new product is first introduced into any new market, sales are few and the costs per sale are high. In fact, as the market is building, items are sold at a loss until the market reaches a "tipping point." Right now it costs KickStart $300 to get a family out of poverty, but once this tipping point is reached, the cost per family helped out of poverty drops to zero.

The more radically new the product is, the more expensive it is to make these early sales. In the private sector, these early losses are subsidized by investors. KickStart uses donor funds the same way a for-profit would use venture capital.

A Permanent Solution

By using donor funds as smart subsidies, KickStart is building a permanent solution to poverty. It has set three measures of success for itself:

1   Do the people whom it has helped out of poverty, stay out of poverty?
2   Can more people avail themselves of the solution, without additional investment from KickStart?
3   Is KickStart becoming more self-sufficient as an organization?

KickStart's Total Impact to Date

The following data are taken from an impact report as of January 1, 2011:

Pumps sold: 166,500

■   Kenya: 60,500
■   Tanzania: 40,900
■   Mali: 8,200

Enterprises created: 106,700

■   Kenya: 49,200
■   Tanzania: 33,500
■   Mali: 6,900

People moved out of poverty: 533,700

■   Kenya: 246,200
■   Tanzania: 167,600
■   Mali: 34,700

New profits and wages generated annually: $107 million
Bang for buck ratio (dollars earned by farmers for each donor dollar spent): 1:15
Cost to KickStart to get one family out of poverty forever: $300
Cost per person moved out of poverty: $60

KickStart says:

> We could base our claims of success on the number of pumps we've sold to date. But this tells us nothing about whether we are meeting our mission—helping people get out of poverty. To know this we have to measure how much more money the buyers of our technologies earn as a result of owning them. KickStart has developed a systematic, replicable method to measure our impacts. Every product comes with a one-year guarantee and every buyer fills out a guarantee form when they buy the product. The guarantee reduces the perceived risk of buying the product, and the forms give KickStart a database of all pump owners. From this database, we select a statistically valid sample of recent purchasers. These customers are visited within a month of purchasing the products, before any impacts have been realized, then again at eighteen months, and again three years after purchase.
>
> Source: http://www.kickstart.org/about-us/history/, http://www.kickstart.org/what-we-do/process/step-05.php

3. Monetize Your Social Value

The last step in measuring social impact is monetizing the social value of the social indicators chosen in Step 2. The reason for monetizing is that it not only increases the credibility of the social venture and its mission, but also establishes metrics that can be used to evaluate a venture's effectiveness in achieving the desired social impact (Scholten et al., 2006; London Business School, 2009). Moreover, it attracts a broader range of investors to the firm in facilitating planning and communication with socially minded investors and stimulating short-term and long-term capital flow. The next section concentrates on approaches that can be used to monetize a social venture's social impact.

APPROACHES TO ESTIMATING SOCIAL IMPACT

Currently a great deal of research is being carried out. There is a lot of interest among nonprofit and charitable organizations in regard to the application of certain business principles and methods to monetize social impact. Melinda T. Tuan (2008) has provided insight into eight integrated approaches that offer some fresh possibilities in how to monetize a firm's social value. It is pertinent to highlight that there is no perfect methodology, but rather a variety of methods that provide different lenses for viewing social value creation. The following are profiles of Tuan's eight integrated approaches for measuring social impact.

1. Cost-Effectiveness Analysis

Cost-effectiveness analysis (CEA) involves the calculation of a ratio of cost to a non-monetary benefit or outcome (e.g., cost per child cured of malaria). It is used when monetizing the impact or benefits of a program is not possible or not desirable. The benefit of using this method is that it is relatively straightforward, given that it does not require the conversion of the impact or outcome of the given program into monetary units. However, a drawback of the method is that it can account for only one area of program impact at any given time. Given that program impacts are measured in natural units (life-years saved, child graduating from school), unless those units are common across all areas of impact, it is not possible to aggregate across them.

2. Cost–Benefit Analysis

Cost–benefit analysis monetizes the benefits or outcomes of a program along with its costs in order to compare them and observe which are greater. It is one of the most challenging approaches, since it requires the ability to place a dollar value on the impact of a particular program. As a result of this, it tends to provide in accounting terms the net benefits to society as a whole that occur as a result of the initiative. CBA answers the question of whether or not it is worthwhile to undertake a program by providing the net benefits to key stakeholders and society (benefits less costs). It also provides the decision maker with the ability to compare different initiatives and see which one has the greatest merit (i.e., which has the largest net benefit). It is widely used across the public, private, and nonprofit sectors to evaluate a series of investment decisions (Zerbe, Bauman, & Finkle, 2006; Zerbe & Bellas, 2006).

Case Study 8.1

Cost–Benefit Analysis Example

Let us take as an example of a cost–benefit analysis a hypothetical organization called Give Back Get Back (GBGB). This social venture promotes and facilitates volunteerism among New York City's youth population with the goals of:

- supplying volunteer services for New York's pressing community needs;
- reducing the number of "at-risk" youth by providing meaningful opportunities for civic development;
- growing "volunteers for life."

The Social Business Venture Opportunity

GBGB's business is to deliver youth volunteer resources to a wide variety of social ventures that rely on volunteer labor and contributions to provide returns to the community. By pooling and matching volunteers with the right program, and empowering them to give back to their community, GBGB will increase the number of volunteers and increase the amount of volunteering in the youth population overall in New York City. Essentially, GBGB will act as the "matchmaker" between volunteers and social or communal organizations and provide incentives to its volunteers (members) to encourage consistent, habitual service.

Through partnerships with key stakeholders within the local community—specifically, philanthropically focused local businesses, large corporations with philanthropic divisions or interests, and existing community charities and humanitarian organizations—GBGB will increase the throughput to and from these organizations of volunteer manpower and physical resources.

Business Model

Although GBGB will be a nonprofit organization, several revenue streams and secondary and tertiary income streams will be established to support the fiscal requirements of the organization. Advertising revenues on the GBGB.org website and in-kind donations from partner organizations will be a major source of financial support for GBGB in the short run. Government (federal and local) grants and foundation donations will be secondary financial support outlets, mainly in the early seed stages of GBGB. Membership fees imposed on specific corporate sponsors, payable either monetarily or through providing key resources needed by a large number of community-based activities (e.g., lumber and hardware to be distributed for a Habitat for Humanity® housing build effort), will allow GBGB to shift from initial monetary support plans to a more sustainable earned income revenue model.

Lastly, GBGB will strive to keep its costs at a bare minimum through a variety of innovative methods. Office space will be employed to have a physical presence in low-income areas that subsidize real estate expenses for nonprofit organizations. Marketing and advertising will rely on in-kind donations from local business partners. Computer and phone hardware and software will be gathered through charity drives and donation solicitations. All operational and logistical functions will rely on virtual communication and participation, mainly over the internet or via phone calls, to reduce travel and logistical expenses (fleets of cars, gasoline costs, etc.). By keeping GBGB small and focused, costs will be minimized, allowing GBGB to efficiently give back to the community. Figure 8.1 profiles GBGB's social impact indicators and logic model.

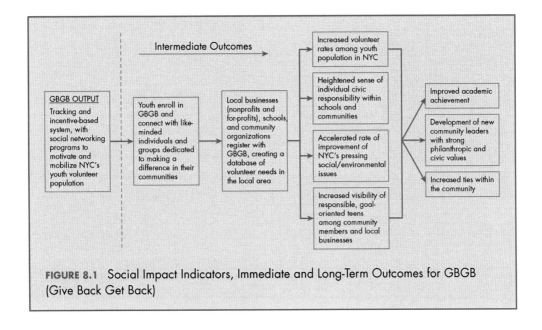

FIGURE 8.1 Social Impact Indicators, Immediate and Long-Term Outcomes for GBGB (Give Back Get Back)

While GBGB's cost–benefit analysis (Figure 8.2) provides useful and comprehensive methods for assessing impact, REDF's social return on investment (SROI) model measures environmental and social value in a different way.

3. REDF's Social Return on Investment (SROI)

REDF is a nonprofit venture in San Francisco that supports employment for low-income and formerly homeless individuals by making grants to several nonprofit enterprises (see www.redf.org). It developed its SROI framework in the late 1990s, which resulted in the publication of SROI reports and methodologies.

SROI is a method for measuring environmental and social value not currently reflected in financial statements, in comparison to funds invested. This measurement includes the qualitative and quantitative impact of making a social investment. It is used to judge the impact of an investment on stakeholders and to ascertain ways in which performance can be improved. The SROI methodology continues to be refined and now includes elements of cost-effectiveness analysis, which allows for an integrated cost-based approach to social value creation (Scholten et al., 2006; London Business School, 2009).

Cost–Benefit Analysis   **Max number of years = 3**

GBGB promotes and facilitates volunteerism among NYC's youth population with the goals of: (1) supplying volunteer services for community needs; (2) reducing the number of "at risk" youth by providing opportunities for civic development and (3) growing "volunteers for life."

Parameter	Value
Discount rate	4%
Number of years	4
Number of volunteers per week	10
Hours volunteered per week	10
Hours volunteered per year	520
NYC Minimum wage	$ 7.25
Cost of supervision per year	$ 30,000.00
Other program costs per year	$ 10,000.00
Initial setup costs	$ 10,000.00

Intangible Benefits	
Number of prosecutions averted	10
Average prosecution cost	$ 570.09
Average public defender cost	$ 322.02
Number of incarcerations averted	3
Average annual juvenile incarceration (3 yrs) and probation (1 yr)	$ 5,482.88

	0	1	2	2
Benefits per year (C10*C12) – cost savings to orgs		$ 37,700	$ 37,700	$ 37,700
Benefit of Court costs averted (G9*(G10+G11)) – cost savings to society		$ 8,921	$ 8,921	$ 8,921
Benefit of Cost of incarceration averted (G13*G15) – cost savings to society		$ 16,449	$ 16,449	$ 16,449
Costs per year C17; C15+C16	$ (10,000.00)	$ (40,000.00)	$ (40,000.00)	$ (40,000.00)
Net per year (benefits – costs)	$ (10,000.00)	$ 23,069.74	$ 23,069.74	$ 23,069.74
Discounted benefits		$ 60,644	$ 58,312	$ 56,069
Discounted costs		$ (38,462)	$ (36,982)	$ (35,560)

Benefit–Cost ratio = $ 1.48 [Discounted savings/costs]

NPV = $70,904.56

IRR = 229%

FIGURE 8.2 Cost–Benefit Analysis for GBGB

4. The Robin Hood Foundation's Benefit–Cost Ratio

The Robin Hood Foundation targets poverty in New York City by finding and funding the best and most effective programs and partnering with them to maximize results. Robin Hood's benefit–cost ratio captures the best estimate of the collective benefit to poor individuals that Robin Hood grants create per dollar cost to the organization (Weinstein & Lamy, 2009). This ratio serves to translate the outcomes of diverse programs into a single, monetized value that measures poverty alleviation on a continued basis. However, the benefit–cost ratio is used by Robin Hood only to make decisions regarding individual grants rather than allocation decisions among portfolios. This ratio serves to highlight which programs Robin Hood should fund and how much it should invest in such initiatives.

5. The Acumen Fund's Best Available Charitable Option (BACO) Ratio

The Acumen Fund's goal is to fight poverty through the investment of patient capital to identify, strengthen, and scale business models that effectively serve the poor. It champions this approach as a complement to both charity and market approaches (www.acumenfund.org/about-us/about-us.html).

The Best Available Charitable Option (BACO) ratio serves to ascertain the prospective merit of an individual investment opportunity when compared to making a charitable grant (Brest & Harvey, 2007). The ratio is reassessed on an annual basis after investment. A simple example to illustrate the logic of BACO: By making an investment into "X," it would cost Acumen less than $0.02 to protect one individual from malaria for one year, in comparison to $0.84 through a BACO. Hence, it is seen that Acumen's investment in the fight against malaria is more cost-effective than the BACO.

6. The William and Flora Hewlett Foundation's Expected Return (ER)

The William and Flora Hewlett Foundation sets out its goals as follows:

> The Foundation's programs have ambitious goals that include: helping to reduce global poverty, limiting the risk of climate change, improving education for students in California and elsewhere, improving reproductive health and rights worldwide, supporting vibrant performing arts in our community, advancing the field of philanthropy, and supporting disadvantaged communities in the San Francisco Bay Area.
>
> (www.hewlett.org/about)

The Foundation uses a formula for its decision making as follows:

Expected Return = (Outcome * Probability of Outcome * Philanthropic Contribution)/Cost

This formula forces program officers to test their assumptions and logic models against the expected return (ER) value, quantify high-level trade-offs between investments within an investment portfolio, and ideally make better funding decisions. The ER of various investments is considered before funds are actually allocated.

7. The Center for High Impact Philanthropy's (CHIP) Cost per Impact

The Center for High Impact Philanthropy (CHIP) provides independent analysis and decision-making tools to make sure that philanthropic funds are achieving the greatest impact (see www.impact.upenn.edu). Its "cost per impact" measure is promoted as a measure critical to high-impact giving. It was developed by alumni of the Wharton School at the University of Pennsylvania who wanted to compare desirable social change to the costs of organizing programs intended to bring about such change. Reports published by CHIP outline the ways in which individual philanthropists can have an impact, and also provide estimates of cost.

8. The Foundation Investment Bubble Chart

Finally, certain nonprofits use a bubble chart to display comparative information regarding multiple organizations or programs. The purpose of the bubble chart (similar to such displays used by investment managers in the for-profit world) is to illustrate a set of reporting metrics at the organizational or program level that are common across the programs of a nonprofit or a segment of a foundation portfolio (e.g., number of people reached with bed nets vs. percentage of bed nets utilized).

Concluding Thoughts on the Above Methods

While the eight above-mentioned methods have certain similarities, their differences lie in the following (Tuan, 2008):

■ the manner in which outcomes or benefits are estimated;
■ the manner in which costs are calculated;

- the manner in which uncertainty and probability of success are taken into account;
- the manner in which outcomes are translated into natural units (shadow prices, etc.).

While all the methods provide meaningful insight into estimating social value creation, none of them can be declared the "perfect" cost-based approach for making decisions (Trelstad, 2008; Tuan, 2008). Rather, employing a single consistent approach to funding decisions and considering the external environment would lead to the best possible outcome for a social venture.

ADDITIONAL RESOURCES FOR MEASURING IMPACT

Tools and Resources for Assessing Social Impact (TRASI)

TRASI is an interactive online database that provides tools and resources for measuring social value creation. The user-friendly website provides approaches to assessing social impact, strategies for creating and conducting an assessment, and ready-to-use tools for measuring social change (see http://trasi.foundationcenter. org). The database is managed by the Foundation Center, which works in partnership with McKinsey & Company to address the growing interest in the field of measuring social value creation.

The database consists of more than 180 distinct evaluation approaches from a range of organizations such as social investors, foundations, NGOs, and microfinance organizations. Before an evaluation technique is uploaded on the database, it is reviewed by a team of experts who use a four-step process to assess its appropriateness. In order to do so, they determine the scope of the tool or resource and determine the staff and stakeholder involvement that would be required for its use. It is therefore observable that the tools available through TRASI have been put through an evaluation system, thus increasing their reliability.

The TRASI website also has a "Terms Defined" section in which it defines in detail each of the terms it employs that may be unfamiliar to users. It has a series of videos that include discussions on social impact assessment by thought leaders in the field which serve to provide the user with a broader idea of social value creation and measurement before getting into the specifics of the database. New tools and assessment methodologies are continuously added and such updates are sent out to the TRASI community through a variety of methods such as email and the social media.

VOICES FROM THE FIELD

D.light

While India's economy doubles in size roughly every nine years, it is a shame that over half the population—600 million people—are not yet on the electric grid. The country's highly regulated energy sector continues to be mired in corruption and bureaucracy, curbing its growth. Over 130 years after the invention of the light bulb, 1.6 billion people worldwide still have no access to electricity, mostly for similar reasons. On top of that, most households with access to the grid get limited power. The village of Bhandgaon, in the relatively prosperous industrial state of Maharashtra, gets just twelve hours of power a day, alternating between day and night each week. As a result, most households still use dangerous kerosene lamps every day to read, to cook, or simply to walk around.

In 2007, Stanford MBA graduates Sam Goldman and Ned Tozun embarked on a journey to change all that. As part of a class at Stanford's Institute of Design, they designed a low-cost solar-powered LED lamp prototype. They decided to commercialize the project with the launch of D.light Design, and in less than three years have sold to over 1 million consumers in thirty countries. D.light launched in India with a product called Nova. The Nova provides up to twelve hours of bright light on a day's charge, and doubles up as a mobile phone charger. It is eight to ten times brighter than a kerosene lamp, 30–50 percent more efficient than a fluorescent light, and costs about $30. Today, D.light has three products, including the Solata and the Kiran. The Kiran provides eight hours of light on a day's charge and is four times brighter than a kerosene lamp. Launched in October 2009, the Kiran is dubbed the "kerosene killer." It costs just $10, making it the most affordable quality solar lantern in the world. It provides 360-degree illumination, which is good for cooking, working, studying, or traveling.

D.light is unique among companies in its space in that its products are designed with tremendous consumer focus and it uses the world's best design principles. For example, the Kiran is portable: it can be hung from a wall or ceiling, or placed on any surface. The Nova was designed to be water resistant and protect from dust and large insects. With eighty people, and offices in India, China, and Africa, the company has also built a deep sales and distribution infrastructure. The company is backed by major venture capital firms including the Acumen Fund, Nexus Venture Partners, and Draper Fisher Jurvetson, giving it the financial muscle to move quickly. D.light aims to reach 100 million consumers by 2020.

D.light's social impact is far-reaching. First, its products completely eliminate the need for kerosene lamps. Low-income households spend 5–30 percent of their income on kerosene, so D.light products pay for themselves in as little as six months.

Second, bright light supports income-generating activities such as agriculture and retail. The United Nations Development Programme estimates that families with improved lighting have up to a 30 percent increase in income due to improved productivity at night. Next, D.light customers report that children's study time increases by a factor of two to four times after the purchasing of a solar lantern, resulting in greater learning and higher test scores.

By removing the need for kerosene lamps, D.light products also solve the problem of indoor air pollution. The UN Millennium Development Goals Report estimates that indoor air pollution from kerosene lamps claims the lives of 1.5 million people each year through suffocation, burns, and fires. Finally, every kerosene lamp removed from a household removes 1 ton of carbon dioxide emissions into the atmosphere over five years. Kerosene lamps are currently responsible for 100 million tons of carbon dioxide emissions into the atmosphere, making them one of the largest sources of greenhouse gases in developing nations. Planet Earth will certainly not miss them! To learn more about D.light, visit www.dlight design.com.

Hans Taparia, on June 16, 2010 (used with permission)

QUESTIONS FOR "CONNECTING THE DOTS"

1   What are the main benefits of measuring a venture's social impact? Why is measuring social impact so important in comparison to traditional entrepreneurial start-ups?

2   How can measuring a firm's social impact have an influence on making sure the venture is effective in staying true to its mission?

3   Given an already established social venture that you are aware of, what recommendations would you make as the social entrepreneur concerned begins to measure her or his impact?

4   With the social venture identified in question 3 in mind, consider the three or four key outcomes that they should be measuring over time. What method would you recommend to the social entrepreneur to quantify and monetize her or his impact?

5   What suggestions would you make to a nascent social entrepreneur to make her or him more effective in marketing and communicating social impact across various stakeholders?

Case Study 8.2

Indego Africa

Overview

Model

Indego Africa (IA) is a Section 501(c)(3) nonprofit social enterprise that attacks systemic poverty by delivering access to export markets and job skills to African women. The components of this model include:

- Fair trade partnerships. IA partners with cooperatives (co-ops) of world-class artisans in Rwanda—all women, many of them survivors of the 1994 genocide—and pays them a fair trade price, including 50 percent in advance of production, for their contemporary accessories and home décor products.
- Export market access. IA sells its partners' products through high-end retailers—like Ralph Lauren, Anthopologie, and Nicole Miller—across the United States, and through its online store (http://shop.indegoafrica.org).
- One hundred percent of profits devoted to education. IA invests all of its profits from sales, and all donations, in culturally tailored training programs for its co-op partners in financial management, entrepreneurship, literacy, and computers—all taught by Rwanda's top university students.

Mission

IA strives to empower thousands of independent African businesswomen to lift themselves out of poverty. Within five years of partnering with IA, each artisan cooperative should include the following:

- Women generating income. Women consistently earn more than $2 per day through their own initiative and oversee households that are entirely free of hunger, inadequate housing, and school absenteeism.
- Women leveraging valuable long-term skills. Women deploy new high-value skills to earn supplemental income in their own community—whether at a cooperative, another employer, or their own business.
- Women running profitable export businesses. Women manage cooperatives that are fiscally responsible, effective in product design and delivery, and dynamic contributors to the community—all while engaging the global export market on their own terms.
- Women feeling hopeful and confident. Women translate their experiences of financial success and increased productivity into a lasting sense of self-worth and pride, knowing that anything can be accomplished by working together with others and relying on their own strength.

History

Founded in 2006 by Matt Mitro with assistance from his father, Tom Mitro, Indego Africa was born through deep experience with the continent. American by birth, Matt spent his childhood in Nigeria, where Tom worked as an oil executive. By the time Matt graduated from American University's Washington College of Law in 2003 and started as a global finance attorney at a law firm in Washington, DC, he had been to over twenty African countries. Rwanda, a country with unusually clear legal frameworks for doing business, was selected out of several options only after Matt and Tom developed the IA business model.

Benjamin Stone brought IA in as his pro bono client at Orrick, Herrington & Sutcliffe LLP (Orrick) in 2007, where he was a complex commercial litigation attorney. Ben then initiated an unusual corporate responsibility partnership with Orrick that allowed him to move to IA full time in 2008. Orrick also provides IA with office space in New York City and has set up two computer centers at IA's partner co-ops.

IA made its first product orders with its Rwandan co-op partners in November 2007 and launched its training programs in June 2008.

The Need

Indego currently partners with five artisan co-ops of women in Rwanda, located in Kigali, Kicukiro District, Bugesera District, and Kayonza District. The co-ops are independent, for-profit businesses that consist of more than 250 remarkable women, many of whom cope with HIV/AIDS; suffer from psychological trauma; have little formal education; care for several children, including orphans from the 1994 genocide; and are the sole provider in their household.

Before partnering with Indego, 93 percent of the women earned less than RwF 550 (US$1.00) per day, typically by carrying water on an unreliable basis (meaning that they were paid to carry water from its source to another location but that the work was sporadic). This paucity of income had devastating effects. Roughly 60 percent were under-nourished, 50 percent could not read, and only 68 percent of their children were attending school regularly. The problem was not work ethic or ambition; it was a simple issue of opportunity and access.

Guiding Strategy

The IA mission is achieved by fusing business best practices with principles borrowed from the social sector: collaboration and transparency. This strategy includes:

- A business-minded approach. With infrastructure and systems rivaling those of companies ten times its size, IA is poised to scale its model throughout Africa. This approach includes short- and long-term strategic planning; a highly scalable supply chain and distribution system, directly accessed by artisans; documenting and institutionalizing policies and procedures across all business units; adhering to best practices in accounting and maintaining strict financial controls; deploying cutting-edge communication, information sharing, and social media tools; and formalizing training methodologies for academic review and third-party replication.

■ Competency through collaboration. IA builds on its institutional expertise by partnering with a wide variety of NGOs, corporations, government entities, and academic institutions.

■ Transparency and ethics. IA employs unrivaled standards of transparency and ethical conduct in its operations, including sharing all pricing and market data with its artisan partners and posting all corporate documents online.

Retail Strategy

The IA retail strategy combines high-quality design, advanced supply chain logistics, and fair trade practices to (1) generate sustainable income for artisans, and (2) scale IA's operations. This strategy includes:

■ High-quality products for large retailers and online customers. IA offers high-end retailers and online shoppers contemporary accessories and home décor products that are custom designed or from a popular IA line.

■ Scalable supply chain. IA has fully outsourced its order fulfillment, warehousing, and online sales to Fulfillment by Amazon, which expedites the rollout and distribution of its product lines. IA's artisan partners—who learn and apply product codes—are integrated into the global distribution and e-commerce process.

■ Personalized, socially responsible sourcing. In addition to sourcing its products on a strict fair trade basis, IA includes the name and signature of each artisan on its hangtags and then directs customers to that artisan's photo and biography online.

Development Strategy

The IA development strategy features training in competencies that improve and diversify its partners' income-generating skills. This succeeds by:

■ Linking market access with ground-breaking training. Because training is tied to income-generating activities and involves skills that can be applied to their own businesses, artisans immediately grasp its real-world benefits and are more likely to remain active and highly motivated participants.

■ Harnessing local talent. IA has hired fourteen students through Generation Rwanda—an NGO that awards highly competitive university scholarships to socially vulnerable Rwandan students—to teach its training programs. These young leaders receive formal mentoring, evaluation, and job opportunities from IA, expanding the program's impact on the community.

- Mutual respect and artisan input. IA does not impose top-down solutions to development challenges. Instead, IA has created programs by combining the input of its artisan partners with the business acumen and experience of its management team.
- Measuring social impact. Rather than speaking only selectively and anecdotally about its impact, IA conducts a comprehensive annual social impact assessment that (1) compiles developmental information for each artisan, and (2) measures how well IA programs are achieving their intended objectives. See below for more information.

Sustainability from Three Perspectives

The path to economic independence and sustainability follows a series of developmental stages at both the individual level (artisan women) and the organizational level (partner co-ops and IA itself):

- Individual women artisans. The IA program starts by (1) providing basic income and financial skills, and then adds (2) new job skills and (3) micro-enterprise education and opportunities. Once the stages are completed, each artisan will be an independent businesswoman capable of supporting herself *without IA's assistance.*
- Partner cooperatives. The cooperative must first become an enterprise that (1) the women trust to operate ethically, and (2) experiences profitability in the export market through IA. Eventually the cooperative should also (3) reach the local market on its own, and (4) engage the export market *without IA's assistance.*
- Indego Africa. Two stages of IA's mission have been completed: (1) proving and standardizing the model in Rwanda, and (2) beginning to scale the model in Rwanda. The final stages of establishing IA as a sustainable enterprise—(3) expanding to new countries and (4) achieving long-term financial stability—require the immediate *commitment of large retail partners and impact donors.*

Measuring Social Impact

Methodology

In February 2008, IA instituted a baseline assessment focused on four categories: Personal Security, Education, IT Skills, and Fair Trade. Sixteen women from IA partner co-op Cocoki and twenty-eight women from IA partner co-op Covanya participated. The survey included a questionnaire with thirty-one multiple-choice questions and two open-ended questions. In March 2009, IA conducted a follow-up assessment. IA is currently instituting a third assessment. How are the data from the surveys analyzed? Can anything IA does relative to measuring social impact be tied to the methodologies presented in this chapter, or is there a very simple approach of surveys or descriptive statistics?

Social Impact Results

Since launching its operations, IA has stimulated more than $50,000 in product sales revenue for more than 200 Rwandan women and their approximately 800 dependants, and conducted hundreds of hours of long-term skills training programs. To verify its impact more specifically, however, IA also measures the developmental progress of its partners using quantitative metrics and other qualitative tools. Key results from IA's 2009 Social Impact Report (the full report is available at www.indegoafrica.org/ socialimpact) include:

- enhanced quality of life: a ca. 585 percent increase in the number of women who are satisfied or very satisfied with their quality of life;
- increased income: a ca. 336 percent increase in the number of women earning more than $1 per day;
- greater food security: a ca. 96 percent increase in households eating at least twice a day;
- higher child education rate: a ca. 17 percent increase in the number of women reporting that some or all of their children attend school;
- better housing conditions: a ca. 42 percent reduction in the number of women with no permanent residence and a 26 percent increase in the number of households with beds for all residents;
- more bank accounts: a ca. 153 percent increase in bank account ownership;
- better access to communication: a ca. 138 percent increase in the number of households with a telephone.

More than Income: Confidence

IA's artisan partners are also now graduating from IA's training programs and pursuing higher level education opportunities. Emelienne Nyiramana, aged 33, Treasurer and Master Seamstress at IA partner co-op Cocoki, gained admission in July 2010 to the Goldman Sachs 10,000 Women Initiative Entrepreneurship Certificate Program at the School of Finance and Banking in Kigali. She is now the first program participant to blog about her experience (see http://socialenterprising.indegoafrica.org).

Staffing

IA operates with an extremely lean paid staff and a large unpaid staff of full-time and part-time volunteers and interns in both the United States and Rwanda. The team in the United States is as follows:

- Founder and CEO, *Matt Mitro*: went without pay from November 2006 through June 2008 and now receives an extremely modest salary from IA. Full time.

- Senior Vice President and General Counsel, *Benjamin Stone*: paid by Orrick from September 2008 through September 2011. Full time.
- Chief Financial Officer, *Conor French*: a high-performing transactional attorney; joined IA full time in July 2010 for one year without pay. Full time.
- Deputy General Counsel, *Deirdre McGuidan*: recent law school graduate on ten-week paid fellowship from Brooklyn Law School. Full time.
- VP of Sales & Marketing, *Manica Piputbundit*: completing her MBA part time at Stern, originally (spring 2010) Sales & Marketing Intern; stayed on with elevated responsibilities. Unpaid, part time.
- VP of Development, *Sierra Visher*: student at NYU Wagner, originally (spring 2010) Fundraising & Development Intern; stayed on with elevated responsibilities. Unpaid, part time.
- Sales & Marketing Manager (originally, summer 2010, Sales & Marking Intern), Sales & Marketing Intern, Communications Coordinator, VP of Technology (originally, summer 2010, Technology Intern), Legal Intern. All unpaid, part time.
- Board of directors: Consisting of six members, including Matt and Tom Mitro, five of whom joined at IA's founding in 2006. Besides Matt, Tom, and one new member, the board is not involved in significant governance or fund-raising initiatives.
- Board of advisors: Launched in September 2010 and made up of eight visionary leaders from a wide range of industries. Main responsibilities include facilitating strategic introductions and providing high-level advice and counsel.
- Regional boards: Consisting of more than 150 IA supporters in New York City, Washington, DC, Chicago, Los Angeles, Milwaukee, and San Francisco, IA regional boards draw from a spectrum of ages and professions to plan events and promote the IA mission.

The staffing in Rwanda is as follows:

- Rwanda Programs Director, *Sarah Dunigan*: MBA graduate with extensive business and development experience; started as unpaid full-time volunteer in July 2009, commenced paid position with IA in July 2010.
- Rwanda Operations Manager, *Jean de Dieu Niyomugabo*: Rwandan law school graduate; joined IA in 2008 as paid full-time employee.
- Senior Designer & English Literacy Director, *Ellie Kates*: originally (spring 2010) Rwanda Intern, elevated to full-time paid position in July 2010.
- Senior Development Officer, *Alex Kennedy*: an investment banker at Goldman Sachs in London with an MA in African Economics and Politics. Joined IA in August 2010 for next year without pay (was expected to take over from Sarah in December 2010).
- Generation Rwanda Trainers: At just $60 per month for one intern's expenses, fourteen of Rwanda's top university students teach Indego Africa's training programs.

Financials

IA generates revenue from two primary sources: product sales and donations (which include individual contributions, foundation grants, corporate giving, and events). IA's gross revenues for 2009 were $126,071, which included $26,453 (21 percent) in product sales and $99,751 (79 percent) in donations. During 2008 and 2009, product sales and donations averaged 25 percent and 75 percent, respectively, of IA's revenue stream. In 2009 a decrease in product sales due to the economic downturn and reduced consumer spending was offset by an increase in donations primarily attributable to the enhanced fund-raising performance by IA's regional boards.

IA's expenses for 2009 were $73,263, comprising $58,764 (80.2 percent) in in-country program costs, $8,515 (11.6 percent) in fundraising event costs, and $5,984 (8.2 percent) in management and administrative costs. In addition, in 2009 IA's costs of purchasing, storing, and transporting products were $20,146.

Going forward, IA anticipates earning between 36 percent and 48 percent of its revenues from product sales. For 2010, IA projected $54,828 in product sales and $120,150 in donations, against $90,218 in expenses and $56,921 in costs of purchasing, storing, and transporting products, resulting in an annual surplus of $28,670. At the time of writing, IA expected that it would exceed its 2010 projections.

Challenges

Staffing

IA has recruited highly accomplished and talented volunteers, but turnover remains high as internships end, graduate students return to school, and executives making longer-term contributions for free must eventually find paid employment. In addition, Matt and Ben make very little money and Ben is entering his third and most likely last year of sponsored leave from Orrick. How does IA sustain and scale its operations with such an unusual staffing framework?

Scaling

In principle, IA should only scale its training programs to the extent that each additional co-op partner is able to run a profitable business, which requires a corresponding scale in market demand. If IA scales the training programs faster than IA's ability to deliver sufficient product orders to its new artisan partners (because of great fund-raising), the artisans might be idle and discouraged. How does IA scale its social enterprise model?

Measuring Social Impact

Challenges include:

- Comfort with questioner. In a country where genocide survivors were betrayed by their own families and closest friends, accurate social impact data can be collected only when the interviewee trusts the person who is asking the very personal questions.
- Education and context. The women in IA's partner co-ops have varying education levels and, accordingly, survey questions must be vetted for comprehension and cross-cultural translation.
- Balancing organizational priorities. IA is a complex organization with competing strategic priorities. When a given hour of staff time could be spent on new sales or income opportunities or new training programs, it can be challenging to dedicate sufficient time to measurement, and many stakeholders still emphasize financial performance over social impact.
- Costs and effects on competitiveness. IA has many competitors, both for-profit and nonprofit, who supply handmade African products to high-end clientele. While IA has a strong commitment to verifiable social impact, the costs of implementing a robust program (staffing, survey development, mathematical analysis, opportunity cost) directly affect IA's financial bottom line. Many of IA's competitors have no similar social impact assessment program and have a theoretical cost advantage.

THOUGHT QUESTIONS

1 Evaluate the multiple components of IA's model. What key stakeholders would you consider engaging at the beginning in helping them define their social impact?

2 On the basis of IA's mission, what suggested outcomes that can be tracked over time would you offer to its management team?

3 Evaluate IA's baseline assessment approach, which focused on four categories: Personal Security, Education, IT Skills, and Fair Trade. What are the strengths and weaknesses of this approach?

4 Given the number of challenges IA has in measuring social impact, what recommendations would you make to the management team in overcoming some of these challenges?

REFERENCES

Brest, P., & Harvey, H. (2007). Assessing investment opportunities in international development: The Acumen Fund's BACO analysis (unpublished).

Chambers, R., Karlan, D., Ravallion, M., & Rogers, P. (2009). *Designing impact evaluations: Different perspectives*. New Delhi: International Initiative for Impact Evaluation.

Clark, C., Rosenzweig, W., Long, D., & Olsen, S. (2004). *Double bottom line project report: Assessing social impact in double bottom line ventures*. Retrieved from http://www.community-wealth.org/articles/ social.html.

Kramer, M. (2005). *Measuring innovation: Evaluation in the field of social entrepreneurship*. Skoll Foundation and FSG Social Impact Advisors.

Kramer, M., Graves, R., Hirschhorn, J., & Fiske, L. (2007). *From insight to action: New directions in foundation evaluation*. FSG Social Impact Advisors.

London Business School (2009). *SROI primer*. Retrieved from http://sroi.london.edu (accessed January 30, 2011).

Merchant, K., & Van der Stede, W. A. (2007). *Management control systems: Performance measurement, evaluation and incentives*. Upper Saddle River, NJ: Prentice Hall.

Porter, M. E., & Kramer, M. R. (1999). Philanthropy's new agenda: Creating value. *Harvard Business Review*, November–December, pp. 121–130.

Saul, J. (2004). *Benchmarking for nonprofits: How to measure, manage, and improve performance*. St. Paul, MN: Fieldstone Alliance.

Scholten, P., Nicholls, J., Olsen, S., & Galimidi, B. (2006). *Social return on investment: A guide to SROI analysis*. Amstelveen, the Netherlands: Lenthe.

Stannard-Stockton, S. (2007). *Social return on investment*. [Weblog Tactical Philanthropy: Chronicling the Second Great Wave of Philanthropy.] Retrieved from http://tacticalphilanthropy.com/2007/07/social-return-on-investment (accessed January 30, 2011).

Trelstad, B. (2008). Simple measures for social enterprise. *Innovations*, 3(3), 105–118.

Tuan, M. (2008). *Measuring and/or estimating social value creation: Insights into eight integrated cost approaches*. Seattle: Bill & Melinda Gates Foundation. December.

Weinstein, M. M., & Lamy, C. (2009). *Measuring success: How Robin Hood estimates the impact of grants*. New York: Robin Hood Foundation.

Zerbe, R., & Bellas, A. (2006). *A primer for benefit–cost analysis*. Cheltenham, UK: Edward Elgar.

Zerbe, R., Bauman, Y., & Finkle, A. (2006). An aggregate measure for benefit–cost analysis. *Ecological Economics*, 58, 449–461.

Scaling the Social Venture

AIM/PURPOSE

This chapter examines both the advantages and challenges of scaling social ventures and how to leverage the advantages and meet the challenges effectively. A particular focus is placed on tactics and strategies for the expansion of mission achievement. In Chapter 2, we noted that a goal of growth is an important characteristic of a true entrepreneur. This distinguishes them from a small business owner or someone who is self-employed. Similarly, true social entrepreneurs have a goal of growth for their social venture. Their passion for their mission drives them to seek to maximize its achievement; to extend the venture's reach.

There are many examples of small nonprofits pursuing a social mission. They tend to serve a geographic area the size of a small rural community or an urban neighborhood. This is often the place where these nonprofits were first formed. As Wei-Skillern, Austin, Leonard, and Stevenson (2007, p. 260) report, the "mom and pop" nonprofit is not an unusual phenomenon. Less than 1 percent of new nonprofits formed in the past thirty years ever grow to the point of having a budget that reaches or exceeds $20 million. In fact, 80 percent of the over 1.3 million nonprofits in the United States have very small budgets of under $100,000.

The managers of these nonprofits are content to keep their organizations small, serving a small market niche—a neighborhood soup kitchen, a local homeless shelter, or a community program to assist abused women and children. There is absolutely nothing wrong with this. These organizations play an important role in their communities. However, they are not social ventures in the purest sense of that term.

In the business entrepreneurship world, growth is referred to as "scaling" or "scaling up." The purpose for scaling is to maximize profit by capturing additional market share or reaching new markets. Scaling is pursued for a variety of reasons and in a variety of ways; however, the ultimate goal is increased financial return on investment. While the spread of mission accomplishment is the focus of scaling in social entrepreneurship, it, too, goes about this for varying reasons and in varying ways. In this chapter, we talk about why social entrepreneurs pursue growth, what challenges they face in doing so, and the growth strategy options available to them.

LEARNING OBJECTIVES FOR THIS CHAPTER

1. To understand the salient reasons for scaling a social venture.
2. To appreciate and address the obstacles to scaling.
3. To identify the organizational capacities essential to a scaling effort.
4. To master the strategies available to social entrepreneurs for scaling their ventures and the strengths and limitations of each of those strategies.

WHY GROWTH?

Growth is what is expected of social entrepreneurs. Social venture philanthropists, such as Ashoka, Echoing Green, and the Acumen Fund among others, use venture capital models to assist high-impact social ventures. Their strategies demand that the ventures in which they invest maximize their social return on investment (SROI). Foundations want their grant dollars to achieve as much social mission as possible. A surging movement is underway that advocates the double bottom line (profits + social impact) or the triple bottom line (profits + social impact + positive environmental impact) among for-profit ventures. The emerging paradigm for social ventures, be they nonprofit, for-profit, or hybrid, is that they will strive to expand.

This does not mean that all social ventures must, can, or even should become gazelles (David Birch's term for high-growth, high-impact ventures), but it does suggest that they ought to be actively seeking opportunities to extend the reach of their missions—locally, regionally, nationally, and, in some cases, globally. If we accept this assertion, then the question becomes: How best to proceed? However, before we undertake to answer this question, it is helpful to understand the challenges to growth faced by social ventures.

CHALLENGES TO GROWTH

Why begin an exploration of scaling in social entrepreneurship with a discussion of those things that stand in the way of growth? On its surface this may seem defeatist; however, by first highlighting challenges, we are better positioned to think strategically about those factors that will overcome these obstacles and facilitate successful growth. Challenges to growth might be thought of as being of two major types: internal to the social venture and external to it. Brooks (2009), citing Betty Henderson Wingfield, discusses six internal challenges that social ventures experience during the scaling process:

1   Staff and board members of the social venture may not share the lead entrepreneur's vision for growth. Growth involves change. While social entrepreneurs are change agents, the rest of the organization may fear change or see it as only being necessary in a crisis.
2   More specifically, in some organizations, particularly those organized as nonprofits, market-based growth may not be comfortable. It may, in fact, fly in the face of organizational culture. It may be viewed by some as detracting from the social mission, rather than building capacity to expand mission achievement.
3   Nonprofit social ventures, unlike most for-profits, are legally controlled by their boards of directors. When the lead entrepreneur's vision for growth is not in sync with that of the board, the latter can block growth. The authors are aware of several instances in which the board ousted the founding entrepreneur of a nonprofit social venture with whom they did not agree.
4   Social entrepreneurship takes place on a very public stage, unlike commercial entrepreneurship. Social ventures have multiple stakeholders, including the community. If the community in which a social venture is operating concludes that the venture is using public resources in a way that is wasteful or lacking in integrity, it may not hesitate to withdraw its support, making growth very difficult, if not impossible.
5   As discussed in Chapter 8, social ventures are held to a very high standard of accountability. If they cannot clearly demonstrate that they are achieving their missions in a measurable way, they will have trouble sustaining themselves at present levels, let alone attracting the investment required for scaling. Social outcomes and impact are exceptionally difficult to measure.
6   Successful growth requires adequate and appropriate human resources. The necessary skill sets must be put in place, through either hiring new employees or replacing those who are not capable. Again, organizational culture can get in the way of this. As an example, there are numerous large, established nonprofit organizations that offer a pleasant, accepting work environment. No one is ever fired and very few leave of their own volition. This means that unproductive employees are not replaced, outmoded skill sets are often not updated, and there is no career succession pathway. This tends to create an organization that not only lacks the capability to grow but is hostile to growth and change as well.

Dees (2001) offers a slightly different perspective by identifying two general types of resistance to innovation, or change—threat based and inertia based—that may be either internal or external to the social venture and reflect some of Brooks' typology at a more general level. As the name implies, *threat-based resistance* comes when people see the change as a personal threat to them. This threat may emanate from a perception that the change may require that they develop new competencies from the ones they currently possess (see Brooks' sixth internal challenge, above). It may also come from a concern that the change challenges the core values of the individual or venture (Brooks' second internal challenge). However, the market being served by the social venture may also perceive a risk in the change if it threatens to disrupt the status quo. This would be an example of an external threat that could spawn resistance. As an illustration, a social venture that seeks to expand from a purely local service area to a national one may experience threat-based resistance from social ventures in other markets that provide essentially the same service.

Inertia-based resistance is much more likely to be internal to the venture than external. It manifests itself when, on balance, it is easier to continue with the status quo than to make the change. Sometimes this happens when people within the venture do not know about or understand the reason for growth and change. Brooks' challenge involving the staff, board, and/or other stakeholders not subscribing to the lead social entrepreneur's vision might be an example. If the lead entrepreneur does not make his vision for growth understandable and compelling, there may be resistance to its implementation. If the prospect of growth creates uncertainty or a perception of risk within the venture, this may also lead to inertia-based resistance. Finally, a perception that the change is inconvenient and, therefore, not worth pursuing could cause both internal and external resistance. For example, if the staff sees growth as entailing more work than it is worth, they are likely to resist the growth initiative. It may also be that customers (target beneficiaries) outside the venture perceive that switching to a new process or service is not worth the effort, and they will resist participating (Dees, 2001).

It should also be noted that the fact that social ventures have two sets of customers—target beneficiaries and investors—can be an additional obstacle to growth. Not only can the pursuit of financing distract social entrepreneurs from scaling mission achievement, but the requirements and expectations that come with financial support when it is obtained can be at odds with the growth plans of the social venture as well.

None of this is to suggest that growth and change are impossible. However, social entrepreneurs must understand that when they seek to scale their ventures they are likely to encounter some form of resistance; therefore, they must plan and act accordingly. Simply put, they must try to anticipate the resistance and build their growth strategies in such a way that the resistance will be minimized or precluded.

GROWTH STRATEGIES

Capacity Building

As LaFrance et al. (2006, p. 2) have noted: "The primary purpose of scaling is to grow social impact to better match the magnitude of the need or problem a social entrepreneurship seeks to address." Before this growth can be successfully achieved, however, it is important to prepare the social venture in question by ensuring that it has the proper capacity to implement and sustain the growth. In their compelling report *Scaling capacities: Supports for growing impact*, LaFrance et al. (2006) identify and examine seven capacities necessary for scaling in social entrepreneurship: mission, structure, model, culture, data, resources, and leadership and governance. Attention to building these capacities can help mitigate the internal resistance to growth and change discussed in this chapter.

As is emphasized throughout this book, mission is the driver of all social ventures. It clearly states the venture's purpose for being in existence, reflecting its values and the needs of the stakeholders it serves. It gives the venture its focus and acts as its compass as it navigates the treacherous currents of change. Without a clear mission a social venture can easily drift, losing its direction, diminishing its impact, and hastening its demise.

Growth, or scaling, of a social venture involves considerable change. In preparation for growth, a venture should revisit its mission to ensure that it is up to date, clear, and understandable to all stakeholders. Then, the venture should use its mission to guide it in making growth decisions. Growth should support the mission, not detract from it, causing mission drift.

Structure is another important capacity consideration when scaling a social venture. The organizational structure of the venture, and the way in which it is managed, will play a role in how, and how successfully, it will grow. At issue here is often the trade-off between flexibility and control (LaFrance et al., 2006). On the one hand, the social entrepreneur wants to be flexible enough to give her or his organization and its staff the leeway to take advantage of windows of opportunity and the power to innovate in the field. On the other, she or he wants to ensure the consistency and quality of the service(s) provided. LaFrance et al. (2006) use the approach to growth called "branching" (we discuss branching in greater detail later in this chapter) as a prime example of a situation that spawns this tension. The headquarters wants to be able to control the quality and the impacts of its branch offices. Yet, this kind of long-distance management can be expensive and difficult. It can also stifle the entrepreneurial effectiveness of the branches and their ability to adapt to their local context. LaFrance and colleagues recommend pursuing a balance between control and flexibility through good management skills, effective communication, building and maintaining a robust technology infrastructure, and holding branch offices accountable for outcomes as opposed to rigid performance standards (LaFrance et al., 2006, p. 8).

First, modeling what works in one's social venture can be an important prelude to scaling. This involves documenting how the venture works—its opportunity, its business model, its operations—in a clear and systematic way. Not only should the keys to success be codified, but the order in which they must take place should be documented. Doing the right things in the wrong order can be deadly to a venture. Once a model is established it can more readily be replicated, not just by the founder and core management team but by outsiders as well (LaFrance et al., 2006).

This presents an opportunity to address the importance of having a clear business model to the scaling of social ventures. For-profit social ventures have a distinct advantage over nonprofits in this regard, for two reasons. First, for-profits generally have only one set of customers. When they improve these customers' lives through their work, they have integrated their social mission achievement with their source of revenue: earned income. Nonprofits, as noted earlier in this chapter, have two sets of customers: beneficiaries and funders. They must add value for both of these customer groups, making the alignment of social mission and financing more difficult (Foster, Kim, & Christiansen, 2009). Second, there are numerous clearly established, tried-and-true business models for for-profit ventures; this is less true for nonprofits (Foster, Kim, & Christiansen, 2009).

A sound business model is essential to the sustainability and growth of any venture. If a reliable stream of cash flow cannot be maintained, the venture will not survive, and if excess revenue (over costs) cannot be generated, there are no resources for growth. Too often, nonprofits pursue revenue (funding) anywhere they can get it. However, this is not a sustainable practice. Research has shown that as a nonprofit grows, its sources of funding are fewer and more fixed in their motivations and in the protocols for accessing them (Foster, Kim, & Christiansen, 2009). Because of this, a more systematic, well-articulated plan for reaching them is essential—a business model.

Foster, Kim, and Christiansen (2009), in an article in the *Stanford Social Innovation Review*, offer ten business models (or *funding models*, as they call them) for nonprofits. It is beyond the scope of this book to examine all ten in detail. However, the models can be grouped by the type of funding source they are pursuing. There are models that focus on funding from many individual donors. Other models are government funded. One model focuses on funding from corporations, while another pursues funding from one, or a very few, foundations or individuals. Finally, two models rely on a mix of sources. The most important point here is that these are clear, well-considered approaches to generating funds that reflect the realities of the funding markets. They help the nonprofit social venture to achieve the kind of match between mission and revenue that for-profits do.

Another important capacity of a social venture that is poised for successful growth is an organizational culture that supports the social mission. This is a culture that shares common values, assumptions, norms and behaviors. This unified culture underlies all aspects of the venture's work and is supported by rituals designed to further cement the bond among the members of the organization (LaFrance et al., 2006). When the culture is strong and unified behind the social mission, the venture is more likely to be able to scale successfully without damaging the mission or the organization.

A good system for gathering and analyzing data is an essential capacity for growth. Data may be used in four major ways (LaFrance et al., 2006):

1   to identify and document new needs on the part of target beneficiaries that may require expansion into new geographical or program areas;
2   to document the success of the social venture, justifying the scaling of its impact;
3   to be used for purposes of marketing the social venture to attract material and political support and pave the way for growth; and
4   to ascertain weaknesses in the venture's programs or services that can be addressed or aspects of delivery that can be improved upon, thereby better preparing the venture for successful scaling.

Essential to this capacity is an organizational culture that supports assessment and evaluation. Also crucial is the technology infrastructure for maintaining and analyzing the data and reporting the results of the analyses (LaFrance et al., 2006).

An absolutely essential capacity for scaling is having the necessary resources. There are numerous costs associated with growth, but most fall into two categories: costs of expansion and costs of professionalization (LaFrance et al., 2006). The costs of expansion include those for the acquisition of additional space and equipment as well as additional personnel. The costs of professionalization derive from the need to pay for more highly skilled human resources. Depending on organizational structure (see Chapter 6), a growing social venture may seek to generate financing from a variety of sources, using a variety of strategies. Ultimately, though, LaFrance et al. (2006) argue that the most sustainable approach to scaling is to strive to integrate program development with resource development. This most often means engaging external partners and supporters (including businesses and governments) through the venture's mission. An increasingly popular tactic among social ventures for reaching out to these partners and supporters is the use of celebrity spokespeople (LaFrance et al., 2006). Many celebrities seek to actively champion social causes, whether it is because they truly believe in the cause or merely see it as good for their careers. Either way, their influence can bring the attention and support necessary to allow a social venture to scale successfully.

The final important scaling capacity has to do with the social venture's leadership capability and governance apparatus. Strong leadership from the venture's founder and management team, in tandem with a strong board of directors, makes appropriate growth that is right for the venture at a particular point in time possible. Effective leaders and boards help the venture to determine whether to grow and how best to grow, and then to assist them in getting the resources they need. Leadership need not be solely top-down. The late Jeff Timmons of Babson College, a long-time entrepreneurship educator, used to like to say that successful entrepreneurs "make heroes" out of others in their organizations. The more widespread leadership is in the organization, the better positioned that organization is for growth (LaFrance et al., 2006).

The preceding are the capabilities that should be in place as a social entrepreneur begins to scale her or his enterprise. Once the decision has been made to grow, the next question should be: "How do we grow?" There are multiple options available.

Dissemination

The simplest and fastest way to scale a social venture is via dissemination. This strategy involves making a social venture's services and intellectual property (e.g., tools, processes, and frameworks) widely available to people and organizations around the world who want to use them. This hand-off of information and knowledge often takes place through face-to-face training workshops, webinars, teleconferences, demonstration sites, how-to manuals and handbooks, procedural templates, and models. The focus is on expanding the reach or impact of the venture virtually, in light of the fact that there is no actual physical expansion out from the headquarters.

This approach is also relatively inexpensive because it does not necessarily involve acquiring additional facilities, equipment, and human capital. As the use of the Internet and new telecommunications technologies becomes more sophisticated and widespread, social ventures that use dissemination as their growth strategy will be able to further reduce costs by replacing face-to-face training and consultation with long-distance electronic forms of interaction. The Center for Rural Entrepreneurship (CRE), a nonprofit social venture with a mission aimed at helping local rural communities enhance their economies by fostering entrepreneurship, spent its first ten years scaling its impact by sending its small staff into the field to conduct multi-day workshops, training programs, and consultations. This became unsustainably expensive and was stretching the staff very thinly. Recently, CRE changed its dissemination strategy to make greater use of the Web. While it still does the occasional face-to-face activity to build and maintain relationships with its clients, CRE now offers training webinars and disseminates its publications, training materials, case studies, and other tools through its website.

Another example of a social venture that has grown largely through dissemination is KaBOOM! This nonprofit organization facilitates the construction of playgrounds for children living in economically and socially disadvantaged neighborhoods. It does this by organizing the community to find and deliver volunteer labor and supervisory skills and donated supplies, and then KaBOOM! coordinates the use of these resources in building a playground. The KaBOOM! model involves partnerships between private corporations, governments, other nonprofit entities, and private residents (Wei-Skillern et al., 2007).

KaBOOM! generates over 90 percent of its cost of operations from earned income derived through dissemination activities—educating communities in how to initiate and manage a playground-building project, providing handbooks, offering demonstrations, spreading awareness of the importance of playgrounds to the health and well-being of children, etc.—for which it charges fees for service, licensing fees, product costs, or cause-related marketing fees (Wei-Skillern et al., 2007, p. 250). Thus, KaBOOM! is growing its mission achievement capability across the United States while covering most of its costs at the same time. For KaBOOM! it is clearly more important to rapidly spread the building of playgrounds than it is to control every aspect of how they are built.

Dissemination is not the scaling strategy of choice for every social venture. However, for those concerned about cost, speed of adoption, maximizing mission accomplishment, and/or fostering relationships with social sector players, it can be a very efficient and effective way of doing business. The downside is clearly the lack of control over the quality of the product or service that this strategy yields. If a social entrepreneur does not trust others to execute the work well or to take pride in it, or does not trust her or his ability to train others to do the work or to instill appropriate pride, that entrepreneur will likely not choose dissemination as a mechanism for achieving growth.

Another impediment to the use of this strategy is when the social entrepreneur is in possession of intellectual property (IP) that she or he is especially concerned about protecting. The social entrepreneur may worry that licensing and nondisclosure agreements are not enough to keep others from widely disseminating her or his IP and destroying the venture's competitive advantage, particularly if it is a for-profit social venture. As more for-profits populate the social entrepreneurship scene, this is likely to become an increasingly common problem. It raises an interesting question. In social entrepreneurship involving a for-profit entity, which should take precedence—the venture's IP and the private value it affords, or the maximization of the spread of the social mission? Can these two things be harmoniously integrated?

Dees (1998) tells us that social value trumps private value every time in social entrepreneurship. However, much of Dees' early work was focused on nonprofits and how to make them more entrepreneurial. Is it "wrong" for a for-profit venture to try to balance doing good and doing well? The fact is that the social sector, by its orientation, is not very sensitive to issues of IP. It is commonly assumed that *everything* is in the public domain. So-called "borrowing"—where IP is routinely used without compensation or attribution—is commonplace. Government agencies, foundations, and other social sector actors have been known to either freely share IP without the owner's permission or to try to claim that any IP used in a project that they fund belongs to them. Unless and until these attitudes change, talented for-profit social entrepreneurs are likely to avoid working with these social sector entities, particularly through dissemination arrangements, and to seek other strategies that may well make the services they provide more expensive.

Branching

One such scaling strategy that tends to be more expensive is branching. This approach achieves growth by creating multiple offices in locations other than the headquarters. These offices are owned, staffed, and controlled by the headquarters. The branching strategy is attractive to some social entrepreneurs because it maximizes control. Thus, entrepreneurs worried about consistent quality of service and/ or protection of IP will find it particularly appealing.

The trade-off is that branching is the most expensive form of social venture growth. It requires buying or leasing additional facilities, buying or leasing office equipment, hiring and training additional staff, and managing from a distance. It is not a particularly efficient approach to growth (Wei-Skillern et al., 2007).

While long-distance management costs have been mitigated somewhat by new communications technologies, such as tele- and videoconferencing, and more horizontal management structures, the remaining costs of branching are not as easily lessened. In addition, the more far-flung the branches, the more difficult it is to coordinate staff schedules.

A seldom considered "cost" of branching lies in the message it sometimes sends to local people, institutions, and partners in the venues where branches are located. In essence, it says, "We don't trust you to do our work in your community well." It is the antithesis of the dissemination strategy, which implies trust and openness. Another alternative, the affiliation strategy (described next), permits substantially more local autonomy than branching. While branching brings control and its benefits to the home office, it can engender a negative atmosphere that interferes with local social capital building that helps to achieve mission. Most local people are uncomfortable with ceding control to outsiders. Employing locals to staff and manage a branch can help with this problem, but it does not alter the fact that ultimate control resides elsewhere.

Affiliation

Affiliation shares common characteristics with branching: there is typically a "home office" and several (sometimes many) outlying offices scattered across the country and/or around the world. All of these offices share a mission and a brand (Wei-Skillern et al., 2007). However, the connection between the home office and the affiliates is usually more relaxed. The affiliates are locally managed and staffed and are typically financially self-supporting. In some organizations (Habitat for Humanity is a good example), affiliates make regular donations to the home office (Wei-Skillern et al., 2007).

This approach to scaling is substantially less expensive to implement because the self-sufficiency of local affiliates precludes the need for major facility, resource, and staffing investments by the home office or headquarters (Wei-Skillern et al., 2007). In the struggle between control and cost, affiliation represents a compromise between dissemination and branching. Through affiliation, a social venture can grow while keeping costs down and maintaining a modicum of control. Affiliation is less threatening to local communities than branching because the degree of outside control is reduced

Nevertheless, it is important to note that among affiliate models there is a fair degree of variability relative to the level of control by the home office. An example of a very loose affiliation arrangement is that of Social Venture Partners (SVP). SVP makes matches between individual philanthropists and local nonprofits, providing the latter with funding and business management advice. Founded in Seattle, SVP grew through affiliation to other cities around the United States. The affiliates enjoy considerable autonomy, with the home office playing the role of information and knowledge broker, and using licensing agreements to protect its mission and brand (Dees, Anderson, & Wei-Skillern, 2004). Dress for Success represents another variation on affiliation that emphasizes greater control by the home office. The mission of Dress for Success is to provide women who cannot afford to buy a suit to wear to job interviews or to a job itself with a donated suit. Since launching in New York City in 1996, Dress for Success has expanded to cities around the world by affiliation. Affiliates are independent nonprofits, but they are required to have uniform facilities and programs that emanate from the headquarters (Dees, Anderson, & Wei-Skillern, 2004). Despite this variation in level of control among affiliation models, it remains true that affiliates are considerably more autonomous than branches.

Social Franchising

We have seen that in social entrepreneurship there are hybrid legal structures and hybrid financing approaches; therefore it should come as no surprise that there is a hybrid scaling strategy as well. Social franchising, an increasingly popular vehicle for growth, has been described by some as a hybrid of branching and affiliation (Wei-Skillern et al., 2007).

Like commercial franchising, social franchising involves a parent venture, the franchisor, and affiliated ventures, the franchisees. While the franchises are independently owned and operated, franchisees must pay a franchising fee and royalties to the franchisor. In return, the franchisees receive a brand, product, or service specifications, and operating assistance and support (Wei-Skillern et al., 2007). This approach to franchising is called "package franchising" and was developed by Howard Johnson in the 1930s (Cohen, 2010).

In social franchising the fees and royalties tend to be lower than for commercial franchises. In many social franchising models, royalties are not required at all (Cohen, 2010). One major challenge in this regard is establishing the value of what the franchisor brings to the relationship. Because social return on investment (SROI) is more difficult to measure than financial return on investment (ROI), placing a dollar figure on the value of a franchise can be difficult. There are emerging methodologies for calculating the value of a social brand, which may be a good place to start. For now, however, social franchises are likely undervalued. As a result, social franchisors tend to adopt the position that expanding mission achievement and having good relationships with their franchisees are the primary goals of their efforts.

A major part of the attraction of the social franchising model is the fact that it permits scaling at a faster rate and a lower cost than does branching, and it still allows for a measure of control over quality and the brand (Wei-Skillern et al., 2007). This is a compromise that many social entrepreneurs are quite happy to live with. Social franchisors also enjoy the fact that this is a relatively risk-free mechanism for scaling (Tracey & Jarvis, 2007). For their part, franchisees get a tested business model and a relationship that mitigates their own risk (Tracey & Jarvis, 2007).

Before a social venture decides to pursue social franchising, it should consider the following (Dees et al., 2004; Tracey & Jarvis, 2007; Cohen, 2010):

- Does the venture have an easily described and readily understandable business model for which quality can be clearly measured? If not, there may be nothing to franchise. This business model must involve a robust brand, competitive products and services, and the commitment and capacity of the franchisor to provide assistance that is consistently effective over time. These are the same business concept elements that make commercial franchises successful.
- Does the franchise model being considered fit the mission of and the major challenges faced by the would-be franchisor?
- Is there flexibility in the model to permit feedback from franchisees and adjustments based on that feedback?

A study by Tracey and Jarvis (2007) found that successful social franchising efforts have a strong business model, franchisees who have previous experience operating ventures (business or social), incentive structures that bring the missions of the franchisor and franchisee into alignment, and clear separation between the social and business aspects of their double bottom line. These findings imply that care should be taken when selecting franchisees to ensure that they have the skill set to effectively manage their ventures. They also imply that, while control on the part of the franchisor may be a goal, franchisees need some freedom as a means to guarantee mission alignment. Finally, for some social franchisors, attempting to balance the successful operation of the venture and the achievement of social mission within the same organization may prove burdensome. This is often a key reason why hybrid organizational structures are chosen—a for-profit to chase revenue and a nonprofit to pursue social mission. A social franchising arrangement can play the same role, allowing the franchisor to concern itself with economic outcomes, while franchisees focus on social outcomes (Tracey & Jarvis, 2007).

An example of a successful social franchising effort is Green Star Services Delivery Network in Pakistan. Green Star was created by Population Services International and Social Marketing Pakistan to provide family planning services and contraceptive products to low-income women in urban areas. Green Star acts as the franchisor that has linked together thousands of privately owned pharmacies and clinics in cities across Pakistan under the Green Star brand (McBride & Ahmed, 2001). Another example is celebrity chef Jamie Oliver's Fifteen restaurants, which hire unemployed youth as apprentices and teach them kitchen skills. The first Fifteen opened in London and the concept has been spread by social franchising to Cornwall, UK, Amsterdam, and Melbourne, Australia.

As noted, for each of these major scaling strategies an issue is the balance of cost and control. Figure 9.1 compares relative cost and control levels for each strategy.

Scaling Strategy	Cost	Control
Dissemination	Low	Low
Affiliation	Moderate	Moderate
Branching	High	High
Hybrid (Social Franchising)	Moderate	High

FIGURE 9.1 Relative Cost and Control Levels by Scaling Strategy

SCALING ENHANCERS

While they cannot technically be considered scaling strategies, there are two important sets of activities that, when employed strategically, can enhance growth. These are marketing and networking.

Marketing

While marketing is automatically considered a major factor in any commercial venture's scaling efforts, it is less commonly thought of as a growth technique in social entrepreneurship, and when it is, the emphasis of marketing efforts is on attracting more philanthropic dollars to nonprofit ventures. This is rather surprising given the realities. For for-profit social ventures, growth in markets, and profits, are closely tied to the ability to accomplish social mission—the double bottom line. Nonprofit social ventures must also concern themselves with marketing, especially in light of the fact that more than 50 percent of the cash income of NGOs worldwide is derived from earned income activities (Wei-Skillern et al., 2007). Marketing is a way of heightening awareness of the social venture and its mission, and of driving customers/beneficiaries to its door.

Marketing 101 tells us that every social venture, no matter its legal or financing structure, should include a marketing plan in its business plan. That marketing plan should consist of a market analysis, a competitive analysis, and a marketing strategy. The market analysis should identify who the customers of the venture are—their demographics, behavior patterns, and lifestyle characteristics. It is often useful to break down that mass market into a more refined set of market segments. For example, if a social venture's mission is to find housing for the homeless, then, rather than thinking of the homeless as a monolithic group—an undifferentiated or mass market—it might be more useful to think about subgroups of the homeless: individuals vs. families; those who are homeless due to mental health problems vs. alcoholism/drug abuse vs. economic distress; men vs. women vs. children; etc. This would permit the housing solutions offered to be better targeted to the affected subgroup, making them more efficient and effective.

Social entrepreneurship guru Jerr Boschee takes the use of market analysis a step further. He urges that it be used as a form of triage by social ventures, particularly nonprofits that attempt to offer too many services. He asserts that "the first rule of entrepreneurship is contraction" (Boschee, 2006, p. 2). This reflects a piece of common wisdom that management specialists offer to entrepreneurs operating new enterprises, which is to start out by sticking to what you do best, rather than moving away from your core business. Once an entrepreneur has mastered her or his core business, she or he can then begin to contemplate pursuing additional lines of business, as long as these do not venture too far away from the company's core capacity and capabilities. Boschee (2006) states that the balance between social need and profit potential must be assessed, and those services that do not make significant contributions to both should be ended. This can only be done by knowing the venture's market and its segments. Boschee (2006, p. 2) goes on to assert that this approach will actually allow the venture to grow:

> Social entrepreneurs have discovered that reducing their number of products, services and target markets has actually enabled them to serve more people and to serve them better, because they've had the time and resources to expand their most effective and needed lines of business and to carefully introduce new products and services.

The second phase of the marketing plan is the competitive analysis. Here, the social venture identifies its competition and how it is unique relative to them. This distinguishing feature of the product or service of the venture is the social value proposition (discussed in Chapter 3). Information from the market and competitive analyses is then used to prepare a marketing strategy for the social venture. This strategy lays out a plan for featuring the SVP and for the appropriate pricing, promotion, and distribution of the product/service. This must be done for each identified market segment.

An increasingly important aspect of marketing is *branding*. In business entrepreneurship, branding involves making the company unique from its competitors in a way that will stick in customers' minds. This might be accomplished through the creation of a distinctive logo, requiring employees to wear uniforms, the development of a catchy tag line, and so forth. However, in essence, a brand is an effective reflection of the unique value proposition of the business's product or service. That is, what ultimately gives a company a brand is the way in which customers think about its product or service and the latter's value to them.

The same is generally true in social entrepreneurship; however, the connection between the customer, and all stakeholders, and the social venture is often more emotional (Wei-Skillern et al., 2007). For example, Memorial Sloan-Kettering Cancer Center (MSKCC) is a nonprofit cancer hospital and research center in New York City. It has a strong reputation as being one of the best in the world at what it does. Nevertheless, its true brand and, subsequently, its ability to attract exceptional resources to the accomplishment of its mission and to the growth of the organization is the emotional dimension of cancer. Virtually everyone has been touched by cancer in some way. Furthermore, MSKCC has helped many people and their families to fight this deadly and debilitating disease in a sensitive and caring way. This has yielded incredible goodwill toward MSKCC over the years.

Professor Jennifer Aaker of the Stanford University Graduate School of Business has stated that "A brand is a promise to a customer" (Pimentel, 2007). For a social venture, that promise is one of changing something for the better. When a social venture consistently delivers on this promise and can demonstrate that, its brand is established.

The emergence of branding in social entrepreneurship has brought with it another phenomenon: cause-related marketing. Cause-related marketing involves a private for-profit company seeking to associate itself with a social venture with a strong brand for marketing purposes. Marketing research has shown that people like to buy products and services that are associated with a social or environmental cause. This situation is enhanced when the social venture involved has a strong reputation; that is, it is widely recognizable and has a mission that creates an emotional attachment for customers.

While the benefits to the for-profit, commercial business are apparent, the advantages to the social venture may be less so. Cause-related marketing can be a very effective way for a social venture, particularly one with a nonprofit structure, to raise money for expanding its reach. The (RED)™ campaign, which raises money for the Global Fund for HIV/AIDS, Tuberculosis and Malaria prevention, is a highly successful example of this. (RED)™ has entered into numerous cause-related marketing agreements with commercial businesses, among them Apple Computers, Belvedere Vodka, Converse, Hallmark, Nike, and The Gap. Under a licensing agreement with (RED)™ each company makes a product that features the color red—a label, a T-shirt, a laptop computer, and so forth. When the products are sold, a portion of the proceeds goes to the Global Fund. The commercial businesses are trading on the "good name" of the (RED)™ campaign and people's emotional reaction to its mission. The campaign, for its part, is getting access to a wider donor base and the scaling opportunities that this affords (Fritz, 2011).

All of this suggests that the commercial business and the social venture are negotiating these marketing arrangements on a level playing field. Yet that may not always be the case. Clearly, the social venture's brand has value to the commercial enterprise or the latter would not pursue the relationship. If the social venture does not know what that value is—cannot put a dollar value on its brand—then it is at a disadvantage. However, if the social venture comes to the negotiation with a clear idea of the value of its brand, then it will be able to bargain for a fair return on the use of that brand (Wei-Skillern et al., 2007). In addition, this knowledge puts the social venture in the position of being the initiator of such partnerships should it choose to actively pursue them.

This latter discussion raises another issue relative to marketing by social ventures. Not all social entrepreneurs know how to market effectively, particularly many nonprofit social entrepreneurs. This has given rise to a cadre of for-profit consultants and advisors in this arena, but it has also spawned some additional social entrepreneurship in the form of social ventures whose mission it is to provide marketing expertise to other social ventures that need it. One such organization is the Taproot Foundation.

Taproot was founded by Aaron Hurst in 2001. Hurst, who has experience in both the nonprofit world and in commercial marketing, recognized that many nonprofits do not have adequate money or expertise to launch a successful marketing effort. Yet marketing is essential to their fund-raising, earned income, and scaling activities. Hurst's idea was to find professional marketing people who were willing to donate their time as volunteers, sort them into teams, and assign each team to a nonprofit client. Each team is supported in its efforts by a Taproot grant that covers the costs of materials and production. These grants are non-cash grants to the nonprofit, which gives them the freedom to do what needs to be done without outside scrutiny. In essence, the grants are grants of professional expertise (Orr, 2005).

Taproot maintains offices on both US coasts—one in New York City and one in San Francisco. On average, it serves between 100 and 200 client nonprofits per year (Orr, 2005, p. 1).

Sometimes marketing help for social entrepreneurs does not focus on branding or getting the social venture's message out more effectively. Sometimes it is simply getting the social venture's product to a wider market. The latter is the kind of help afforded by Roozt.com. The clients of Roozt.com are typically for-profit social ventures that are pursuing the triple bottom line: economic, social, and environmental value (Kaplan, 2010).

Roozt.com offers them a Web platform for selling their products, with a twist. A given product from a single social venture is featured for one day only and is the only product featured that day. In addition, an exclusive discount is offered on that product. The idea is both to support social ventures and to change the mindset of consumers. Brent Freeman, the founder of Roozt.com, likes to point out that not only is his company helping social entrepreneurs to sell their products, but he and his colleagues are also compiling best practices and other knowledge to share with these ventures, and for the latter to share with each other. Furthermore, Roozt.com is giving consumers the opportunity to move from buying solely out of self-interest to buying products that further the work of social entrepreneurs and contribute to the well-being of society. If this is not enough, each purchase on Roozt.com also supports the work of charities other than the social venture whose product was purchased. On average, between one and two consumers sign on to Roozt.com every two minutes (Kaplan, 2010).

Networking

While, arguably, the strategies for scaling discussed earlier in this chapter—dissemination, branching, affiliation, and social franchising—all involve some level of networking, networking in general is not always thought of as a formal path to growth in social entrepreneurship. Yet networking, or social capital building, is an excellent way to expand the reach of a social venture and to marshal the resources required for future growth.

When considering networking as a scaling tactic, a social entrepreneur should take into account three important concerns:

1   With whom should I build alliances?
2   Why is networking necessary and beneficial under the circumstances?
3   How should I approach successful alliance building?

With Whom Should I Build Alliances?

A useful framework for thinking about potential networking, or alliance building, and who might be a part of your social venture's network, is the Value Net (see Figure 9.2), created by Brandenburger and Nalebuff (1996) and noted earlier in this book. In the Value Net model, these researchers use game theory to think about the market ecosystem in which any venture operates. The market ecosystem is home to the activities of several major market players, which Brandenburger and Nalebuff call customers, suppliers, substitutors, and complementors.

Customers and suppliers are self-explanatory labels, and the relationships between the venture in question and these two groups of market players are relatively obvious. However, substitutors and complementors may be less obvious. "Substitutors" is another label for competitors. These are the ventures in the market ecosystem that offer products or services that customers may seek to buy instead of the products or services of the venture in question. Complementors are those ventures in the ecosystem whose products or services are necessary to using the

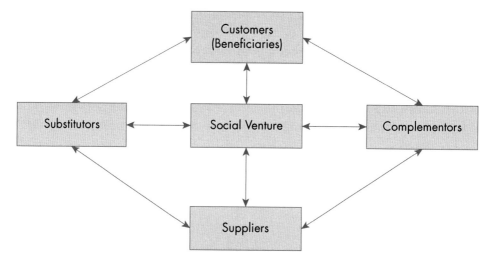

FIGURE 9.2   The Value Net for Social Entrepreneurship

Source: Brandenburger & Nalebuff (1996).

products or services of the venture in question. For example, if the latter venture makes computer software, then its complementors might make computer hardware. If the venture in question were a social venture that fights childhood obesity by teaching children to cook using healthy, low-fat ingredients, then its complementors might include farmers who raise free-range livestock or organic produce.

Brandenburger and Nalebuff (1996) urge us to think of these relationships as being in constant motion, with players shifting roles. Today's supplier may be tomorrow's customer. Complementors could, theoretically, become substitutors, and substitutors could be complementors at some point in time. With this insight and understanding, we as entrepreneurs can become proactive in our relationship building, seeking to manipulate the ecosystem in our favor, much as a player in a game attempts to manipulate other players to her or his advantage.

Relationship building need not be quite so Machiavellian, however, and this is where this model has applicability to social entrepreneurship and the scaling of social ventures through networking. Social ventures need to see their market ecosystems as being "in play" and ripe for making friendships that increase the number of customers they reach, expand the resources available, lower the costs of inputs, and turn competitors into collaborators (the concept of co-opetition noted in Chapter 1). As has been discussed elsewhere in this book, competition in social entrepreneurship is typically over resources. If competitors share a similar mission with the social entrepreneur's venture, it is likely that they will be able to recognize the advantage in sharing resources. If suppliers can be sold on the social venture's mission, they may well go beyond the traditional supplier role to accommodate the venture's success. The packers and distributors that work with Newman's Own, Inc. believe so strongly in the latter's mission that they routinely go over and above what would normally be expected of them, and they make generous donations to the company's nonprofit foundation as well (Wei-Skillern et al., 2007).

There are often opportunities for competitors to be persuaded that they are actually the social venture's complementors. Rather than competing, providers of affordable housing to low-income households could organize themselves to provide complementary services in the process. Viewing one's market ecosystem in this way opens up almost limitless opportunities to build new alliances that will better serve one's social venture and its ability to scale its reach.

Why is Networking Necessary and Beneficial?

Our discussion of the "who" in networking has helped answer this question to a limited extent. Social entrepreneurs network to gain advantages in the market. However, this explanation does not get at the root causes of the growing need to network. Wei-Skillern et al. (2007) identify four reasons to network: resource scarcity, growing competition for resources, a growing societal appetite for greater efficiency, and increasing demand for documented performance.

By and large, social entrepreneurs compete for limited resources, not customers. This assertion contains two important considerations. First is the fact that resources are limited. This has always been the case. Whether it is financial, physical, human, or social capital, the supply is finite. This has only been exacerbated during the recent Great Recession. As the economy constricts, nonprofit, for-profit, and hybrid social ventures are often starved of resources. Second, the number of social ventures continues to grow. Between 1997 and 2007 the number of nonprofits alone increased by 64 percent (Wei-Skillern et al., 2007, p. 192). With the resource supply dwindling and resource competition increasing, social entrepreneurs are being squeezed.

While this is a dire set of circumstances in one sense, it is a major opportunity in another for those willing to act on it. Networking with resource competitors to share resources and maximize mission achievement, networking with complementors to increase compatibility and share resources, networking with suppliers to reduce the cost of inputs, and networking with customers to streamline service delivery and reduce resource requirements are all viable ways to deal with resource scarcity and competition, and position the social venture for future growth.

Because resources are scarce, it is not surprising that there is a greater demand by society for increased efficiency in the way in which resources are allocated and used. For for-profit social ventures that have the benefit of market discipline in their favor, this may be less of an issue. Greater efficiency yields greater profits. However, the fact that nonprofits are not disciplined by the market makes them more vulnerable to inefficient behavior. Investors in nonprofit social ventures are now insisting on greater accountability relative to the efficient use of the resources the investors provide. This translates to greater scrutiny of nonprofit operations. However, herein lies an opportunity. Because there are fewer resources, particularly philanthropic support, for nonprofits, more social ventures that are structured in this way are moving to engage in social enterprise (finding ways to generate earned income). If this earned income is to be maximized, greater efficiency in the way in which it is produced is essential; thus, market discipline is introduced into the nonprofit sector. Increased revenue makes scaling possible. Networking can aid this process by helping to cut the cost of producing goods or services for sale.

A final reason as to why networking is necessary and beneficial is that there is a growing demand for performance accountability. No matter what their structure, investors are calling upon social ventures to prove their social impact. This means that from their inception, social ventures must have a theory of social impact or theory of change. They must be able to show the connection between their activities and the impact they seek to make.

Chapter 8 discussed social impact measurement at length; however, a brief example here may help to illustrate the chain of argument in a theory of change. One of the authors' former students started a social venture, the mission of which is to help economically disadvantaged, inner-city youth gain access to a high-level college education. This venture offers each student help with tailoring their high school class schedule to best prepare them for college; assistance in preparing for college entrance examinations; arranging college visits; and other college preparatory services that their families could not afford. These activities can first be connected to a set of outputs: total number of students being served, number of students who take the entrance exam preparation course, etc. As students move through the program, these outputs can be linked to a set of outcomes: the number of students scoring above 1,100 on the SAT, the percentage of students admitted to college, the percentage of the program's students who graduate from college, and so forth. As time goes on and program alumni pursue their lives and careers, it is hoped that these outcomes may be linked to a change in the standard of living of participants and their families, to participants coming back to their communities to give back, and to a greater number of college-educated residents of the community—true social impacts. Thus a clear path from intervention to impact is created, and investors can feel comfortable that their investments make a genuine difference.

In order to make its theory of change implementable, this social venture has built strong networks with the knowledgeable professionals who serve on its board, with college admissions offices, with entrance examination preparation providers, and with the public school system, among others. Not only has the social venture made these players in the college admissions world more visible, accessible, and affordable to disadvantaged urban youth, it has also pulled them together into a team that has the capacity and capability to achieve true social impact and to grow that impact.

How Are Effective Networks for Social Entrepreneurship Built?

Ultimately, networks involve the coming together of distinct individuals and organizations. Successful networks are therefore about successful relationships. Such relationships require that attention be paid to several factors.

As is the case with virtually every aspect of social entrepreneurship, mission is a key to successful networks. Sharing similar missions makes it substantially easier for social ventures to work together effectively. Competitors for resources that share a common mission quickly realize that competing is not productive in the sense that it diminishes both organizations' capacity to achieve that mission. Collaboration is the rational approach.

Embedded within the mission of every social venture is that venture's *values*. These are the things that the venture and its founding entrepreneur(s) hold dear. Values may include making a profit, creating social value, both of these things together (a double bottom line), maintaining a quality working environment for employees, protecting the natural environment, and so on. Much like a successful marriage between two people, a successful partnership between organizations involves shared values. Understanding a venture's own values is the first step toward recognizing those values in prospective partners.

Successful networks also have partners that share a common vision or common goals (Hamlin & Lyons, 1996; Wei-Skillern et al., 2007). If the organizations in a network are not heading in the same general direction, it is very difficult to sustain the relationship. Organizations contemplating entering into a partnership should each articulate their own vision or goals and share these with each other. These can then be negotiated into a set of goals for the network that complements each member's ability to meet its goals.

On every successful team there are specified roles that need to be played and a member designated to play each role (Hamlin & Lyons, 1996; Wei-Skillern et al., 2007). A basketball team is a partnership made up of five members. Each member has a role to play—the point guard, the shooting guard, the power forward, and so forth. When each member of the team plays his role effectively and in harmony with all other team members in their roles, the team flourishes. This is made possible because the roles are clearly defined and each member understands his role relative to that of his teammates. However, when roles are unclear, individual members fail to understand their role in the larger scheme, or members seek to play roles other than their own, chaos ensues and the team (the partnership) disintegrates.

Successful networks, or partnerships, also need effective leadership (Hamlin & Lyons, 1996). Too often, it is assumed that assembling the network is enough, as though, once the parties are brought together, the new entity will automatically be capable of running itself. This is a dangerous assumption with potentially damaging consequences. Someone, or some people, must lead. The leader might be one of the organizations in the network. It might be a governing body made up of representation from each of the parties to the network. It could be a leader elected democratically by the member organizations. However leadership is chosen, it is essential to moving the network forward.

Finally, it is important to recognize that the number and types of networks required by a social venture vary with the latter's stage in its life cycle. The pre-venture and start-up stages are the periods when the most networking takes place (Greve & Salaff, 2003). This is very understandable when one thinks about growth as being a series of new start-ups by an existing venture. The management challenge involves attempting to manage both an existing venture and a start-up at the same time (Wei-Skillern et al., 2007).

CONCLUSION

True social entrepreneurs scale their ventures in order to maximize the reach of their mission. This is expected by those who invest in them. There are challenges to growth that must be faced; however, there are also acquired capabilities that can help social entrepreneurs to overcome these challenges.

The challenges to scaling include those that are internal and those that are external to the social venture. Among the internal challenges are internal stakeholders (board of directors, staff) who do not see the need for growth, an antithetical organizational culture and/or mission, boards that are openly hostile toward the founding entrepreneur, the withdrawal of community support, the inability to demonstrate impact, and a stagnant internal human resource pool. External challenges may include resistance from competitors in new markets being penetrated or a perception by prospective target beneficiaries that the costs of switching from the current way of doing things are too high.

There are a variety of strategies for clearing these hurdles and pursuing growth. The first of these is to ensure that the necessary organizational capacities are in place to enable successful scaling. These include a clear mission, appropriate structure, ability to model or codify what works, a supportive culture, good and germane data, ample resources, capable leadership, and an adequate governance apparatus. The second strategy involves choosing the most appropriate structural growth option(s) from among the major options of dissemination, branching, affiliation, and social franchising. Third is to employ the process, tools, and techniques of marketing as growth-enhancing strategies. Finally, networking or alliance building can be a powerful strategic approach to accomplishing the scaling of a social venture.

None of this is intended to suggest that small nonprofit organizations with no expectations of growth are not important to the social sector. They clearly have a role to play in addressing social problems. However, if we accept the definition of entrepreneurship articulated in Chapter 2, true entrepreneurs have a goal of growth for their ventures. It follows, then, that true social entrepreneurs strive to scale their ventures.

Case Study 9.1

FareStart® and Catalyst Kitchens® (formerly Kitchens With Mission)

Catalyst Kitchens® is a nonprofit social venture launched in 2005 by another social enterprise, FareStart®, to provide technical assistance to other organizations that want to emulate the success enjoyed by FareStart® in serving the homeless and other disadvantaged populations. Its story offers an interesting and unique perspective on scaling in social entrepreneurship.

The story begins with FareStart®. This is a large nonprofit venture in Seattle which addresses two needs of that city's homeless and disadvantaged population: (1) the need for the provision of regular meals, and (2) the need to move these individuals toward independence through employment. FareStart® meets these needs by employing homeless and disadvantaged people in its commercial kitchens, which, in turn, serve meals to the larger homeless and disadvantaged population. In this process, these individuals are trained to work in the food industry.

FareStart® began its work twenty years ago. It provides four major services: culinary training for homeless and unemployed adults, contract meal provision to low-income childcare programs and homeless shelters, a barista training program for homeless youth, and housing and social services for its clients. This social venture has served more than 3.25 million meals over its history and continues to serve 3,000 meals per day. Each year, FareStart® trains more than 250 individuals and provides housing and social services to over 400 people. Its culinary training program places 88 percent of its trainees in jobs. Its youth barista training program has a 60 percent placement rate (Kitchens With Mission, 2010a).

Culinary training program trainees receive over sixteen weeks of both classroom and kitchen training. The on-the-job-training takes place in FareStart®'s contract kitchen and its retail kitchens, which create meals for four operations: FareStart® Café, FareStart® Catering, FareStart® Restaurant, and Guest Chef Events. These latter operations generate earned income that finances over 60 percent of its budget. The FareStart® Café also serves as the training ground for the youth baristas (Kitchens With Mission, 2010a).

The dual facts that FareStart® successfully trains and places unemployed individuals in the food-service industry and generates substantial earned income in the process has made its model of great interest to other organizations around the United States that are pursuing a similar mission. This presented FareStart® with an opportunity. It could spread its mission by working with these organizations to help them achieve comparable success in their own efforts. However, FareStart® feared that if it became directly involved in consulting, using its own staff, it would dilute its capacity to achieve its mission in Seattle. With this in mind, FareStart® created a nonprofit division called Kitchens With Mission, later changing the name to Catalyst Kitchens®.

Catalyst Kitchens® began as a three-year pilot program. Its founder and director is David H. Carleton, who was formerly FareStart®'s head of Communications and Business Development. Carleton holds a BA from McGill University and a Masters of Communications from Northwestern University. He has experience in the media, publishing, and Internet industries (Kitchens With Mission, 2010b).

Like its parent organization, Catalyst Kitchens® pursues a mission of helping those who are considered by society to be "unemployable" to learn skills in the food-service industry and to get a job in that industry. Unlike FareStart®, however, Catalyst Kitchens® does not accomplish this by creating its own kitchens and culinary training processes in other locations but by helping other communities to create their own. Thus, Catalyst Kitchens® is helping FareStart® to scale its reach across the country.

The way in which Catalyst Kitchens® accomplishes this is complex and layered, which can make its approach confusing to observers. While Catalyst Kitchens®'s model is not branching out, it does pursue long-term relationships in the communities where it works. Its approach is not purely affiliation or dissemination, either. Some have suggested that what they do is a form of social franchising; however, Catalyst Kitchens®'s leadership does not believe this is true because its partners in each of the communities in which it works maintain total ownership (Cohen, 2010).

So, what *is* Catalyst Kitchens®'s model for scaling the work of FareStart®? In essence, Catalyst Kitchens® creates a partnership with a local nonprofit in each community into which it is invited. It then links these nonprofits into a national network (the Catalyst Kitchens® Network) which shares information, knowledge, best practices, and group access to corporate sponsorships that likely could not be obtained individually. As the Network grows in size and strength, its value to its members increases. This is the lever that Catalyst Kitchens® uses to keep its partners in line and pursuing quality and performance. If they do not, they can be dropped from the Network (Cohen, 2010). This is the broad framework of the model, but the complexity lies within each partnership arrangement.

While no two Catalyst Kitchens® partnerships are exactly the same, there is a staged process that Catalyst Kitchens® follows in all cases. This process consists of five stages: exploratory, planning and development, implementation and launch, program development, and catalyst kitchen (see Figure 8.3). In the exploratory stage, Catalyst Kitchens® researches how the partner nonprofit currently handles its food-service operations, provides a tour of FareStart® and begins to think about things such as the business model, performance outcomes, and client eligibility criteria with the partner. In the planning and development stage, strategic planning is undertaken and a business plan begins to take shape (Kitchens With Mission, 2010c).

Implementation and launch, as the name suggests, is the stage in which the new program gets underway. It includes the first year of operations. During this time, the

FIGURE 9.3 Stages of Development of Kitchen With Mission (KWM) Partnerships

Source: Catalyst Kitchens® Website (www.catalystkitchens.org).

program staff is hired, the training process is outlined and train-the-trainer efforts for the program staff are conducted, and local partners to assist with referral and job placement are identified. Catalyst Kitchens® provides direct staff and operational support to the partner during the launch (Kitchens With Mission, 2010c). At this point, the Catalyst Kitchens®-based food-service program is in place and ready for further refinement.

Catalyst Kitchens® calls stage 4 "program development." In this stage, the classroom and on-the-job training program becomes more refined. Any adjustments that need to be made to the program staff and to the organizational culture are made. Students are transitioned from the classroom into the production process. The social enterprise elements of the overall program are put in place. In the final stage, catalyst kitchen, the new program achieves several important milestones: it now clearly tracks outcomes; it has a staff retention rate of over 80 percent; its social enterprise activities cover close to 100 percent of operating expenses; its kitchen is ServSafe compliant and over 70 percent of the food it serves is fresh, and its job placement rate is over 70 percent (Kitchens With Mission, 2010c). This is, of course, an ideal state that will vary from partner to partner as to how long it takes to achieve.

Clearly, the value that Catalyst Kitchens® offers each of its partners lies in the time and money saved by not having to reinvent the concepts, processes, and protocols that FareStart® has already developed and proved. In addition, Catalyst Kitchens® can help its partners adapt the model to local conditions while maintaining standards (Kitchens With Mission, 2010c). The more partnerships Catalyst Kitchens® builds, the more valuable this latter form of assistance becomes.

Catalyst Kitchens® maintains a 40/60 balance between earned income (fees for service) and philanthropy in its sustainability model. Its fee structure relative to activities in the five-stage process is as follows (Kitchens With Mission, 2010c):

Workshop and tour of FareStart®	$550
Strategic planning workshop	$1,000–$3,000
Program development	$2,250–$5,000
Program launch	$950–$1,900
Partner program site visit/assessment	$3,000–$5,000
Train the trainer	$1,900 (on-site)
	$650 (at FareStart®)

A recent survey of partners reveals several of Catalyst Kitchens®'s outputs and outcomes to date. The twenty (of twenty-nine) Catalyst Kitchens® partners who responded have served a total of over 269,140 individuals. They have produced over 4 million meals, and have enrolled 1,175 trainees. The partners graduated 720 trainees, 542 (about 75 percent) of whom were placed in full- or part-time jobs and 60 (approximately 8 percent) of whom went on to obtain an advanced education (Kitchens With Mission, 2010d).

In late 2008 the board of FareStart® voted to extend Catalyst Kitchens®'s mission for another five years to 2013.

THOUGHT QUESTIONS

1 Do you agree with Catalyst Kitchens®'s leaders that it is not a social franchise? Why, or why not?

2 What are your thoughts on FareStart®'s approach to scaling? What are its advantages? Its limitations?

3 In your opinion, would the FareStart® model work as effectively in an industry other than food service? Why might food service lend itself particularly well?

4 Catalyst Kitchens® relies on Network membership to give it control with its partners. Is this a sustainable strategy? Explain.

5 Catalyst Kitchens® conducted a survey of its twenty-nine partners to gauge impact, to which it received twenty responses. Thus, about one-third of the partners did not respond. If you were David Carleton, how would you manage this situation?

6 How does Catalyst Kitchens®'s approach reflect organizational capacity building as discussed in this chapter?

VOICES FROM THE FIELD

Stephen Rynn, Director, Mission of the Immaculate Virgin

When Steve Rynn talks about his social venture, the nonprofit Mission of the Immaculate Virgin (MIV) on Staten Island in New York, he starts with the organization's venerable history. It was founded in 1871 by Father John Drumgoole on the Lower East Side of Manhattan. It was originally a domicile for homeless orphans who had come to the United States as victims of the Potato Famine in Ireland. These children were routinely sent to the Midwest to work on farms. Father John sought to keep them in New York by providing them with a home in the city. However, the city posed too many challenges to these children, and Father John eventually moved his operation to a 550-acre working farm on Staten Island, which he called Mount Loretto.

Over time, MIV's mission has evolved. It became a place where the City of New York could send orphans who, because of mental disabilities, could not be placed in the foster care system. Later, MIV became more community based in its focus, providing services to Staten Island residents. Finally, it began to specialize in developing vocational training programs for autistic children and young adults.

As part of this latter effort, MIV created a full-service screen printing shop called "Possibili-Tees" which specializes in making T-shirts. The purpose of

Possibili-Tees was to provide these mentally challenged individuals with *both* clinical help with their disability *and* vocational training that would make them more attractive to prospective employers.

Rynn explains that autism is a very complex condition that presents itself in a variety of ways. One manifestation is obsessive-compulsive disorder (OCD). Another is impulse control disorder, and there are many more. Each disorder affects the individual challenged by it in different ways. However, each disorder also brings with it an aptitude that can be useful in the workplace if the proper match is made between the individual and the specific job to be performed. As an example, some people who have OCD perform very well in those aspects of screen printing that require patience and attention to detail. Rynn provides another example. People with impulse control disorder tend to suddenly break from a task in order to do something else (e.g., reciting lines from movies). They do this to soothe themselves when they become stressed. This prevents them from engaging in the team-oriented work required for those activities related to the printing itself. However, they prove to be very effective T-shirt folders, a more individual activity. Thus the key to successfully employing autistic individuals is to diagnose their condition accurately and then match them to a work function that fits the condition. This has become MIV's new social value proposition.

Rynn believes it is important to operate this program as a social venture which generates earned income that can sustain it over time. His reasoning is based on two factors. First, there are very few philanthropic dollars available for this kind of work. An earned income strategy is the only way to sustain the clinical aspects of treating autism. Second, this approach affords a compelling way to show employers that autistic people can be good employees. Possibili-Tees has become a demonstration of how an enterprise can thrive with a workforce made up entirely of autistic individuals.

This earned income approach also provides a mechanism for growth. As Possibili-Tees passes the break-even point and generates profits, it has the financial resources to expand the reach of its mission by employing more autistic individuals. Its success with Possibili-Tees has caused MIV to explore still other options for growth. One of these opportunities is to create another social venture, this time in the food preparation industry, which, like screen printing, involves tasks that lend themselves to employing autistic persons. Specifically, MIV is looking at starting a catering business. An added advantage of this type of business is that it leverages the excess capacity the organization has in its kitchen facility. A catering business is also a good fit with MIV's existing mission and model.

MIV's success with Possibili-Tees has opened up yet another opportunity for scaling. Other nonprofits with similar missions approach MIV on a regular basis wanting consultation on how they can replicate the Possibili-Tees model. Steve Rynn notes that this phenomenon has taught him two important lessons. First, he is struck by how impactful being able to successfully employ people deemed "unemployable" is, particularly in an economy like that of the Great Recession. This drives him as a social entrepreneur to want to spread MIV's mission as widely as possible. Second, he has seen at first-hand how having a regular job changes people's lives in other ways. For example, people whose autism caused them not to speak start talking because they must do so routinely in their work. Similarly, those who were not social become better at interacting with other people. Work is literally therapeutic.

With these lessons in mind, Rynn actively shares the Possibili-Tees model with other organizations in the hope that more autistic people will be reached in a very effective manner. This is a good example of scaling by dissemination.

Rynn readily admits that originally MIV was not well positioned to grow in these ways. It did not have the necessary management expertise. In order to gain this expertise it retained the National Executive Service Corps (NESC), a nonprofit organization that utilizes volunteers from the private sector to help other nonprofits develop earned income strategies. NESC helped MIV to establish benchmarks for its work and to create a business plan to guide growth. This has paved the way for MIV's active pursuit of its growth initiatives.

QUESTIONS FOR "CONNECTING THE DOTS"

1 In your opinion, is it possible for a social venture to grow too large? If not, why not? If so, under what circumstances might this be the case?

2 What is the difference between growth and development? How can and should they be related?

3 A nonprofit social venture with a mission to help autistic people to better assimilate into their larger community wants to expand its operations by locating a home for autistic adults in a neighborhood in an adjacent community. The neighborhood residents stage a rally against the home, at which protesters carry placards reading "Not in our Backyard." What type of challenge to scaling is this, and how might it be overcome?

4 Does a social entrepreneur have a moral obligation to grow her or his venture? Why, or why not?

REFERENCES

Boschee, J. (2006). Strategic marketing for social entrepreneurs. Retrieved from http://www. socialent. org/pdfs/StrategicMarketing.pdf (accessed September 28, 2010).

Brandenburger, A. M., & Nalebuff, B. J. (1996). *Co-Opetition*. New York: Broadway Business.

Brooks, A. C. (2009). *Social entrepreneurship: A modern approach to social value creation*. Upper Saddle River, NJ: Prentice Hall.

Cohen, K. C. (2010). Scaling social impact through social franchising. *Social Enterprise Reporter*, May 20. Retrieved from http://www.sereporter.com/?q=node/320 (accessed September 16, 2010).

Dees, J. G. (1998). The meaning of social entrepreneurship. Unpublished paper. Retrieved from http://www.caseat duke.org/documents/deps_sedef.pdf (accessed June 22, 2010).

Dees, J. G. (2001). Mastering the art of innovation. In J. G. Dees, J. Emerson, & P. Economy (Eds.). *Enterprising nonprofits: A toolkit for social entrepreneurs*. New York: Wiley.

Dees, J. G., Anderson, B. B., & Wei-Skillern, J. (2004). Scaling social impact: Strategies for spreading social innovations. *Stanford Social Innovation Review*, Spring, pp. 24–32.

Foster, W. L., Kim, P., & Christiansen, B. (2009). Ten nonprofit funding models. *Stanford Social Innovation Review*, Spring, 32–39.

Fritz, J. (2011). Cause-related marketing: What you need to know. Retrieved from http:// nonprofit. about.com/od/fundraising/a/causemarketing.htm (accessed March 25, 2011).

Greve, A., & Salaff, J. W. (2003). Social networks and entrepreneurship. *Entrepreneurship Theory and Practice*, *28* (1), 1–22.

Hamlin, R. E., & Lyons, T. S. (1996). *Economy without walls: Managing local development in a restructuring world*. Westport, CT: Praeger.

Kaplan, A. (2010). The social enterprise movement's next big deal. July 1. #*Socent Conversations, SocEnt LA*. Retrieved from http://socentex.com (accessed September 29, 2010).

Kitchens With Mission (2010a). The example. Retrieved from ttp.//www.kitchenswith mission.org/theexample.html (accessed October 7, 2010).

Kitchens With Mission. (2010b). Team. Retrieved from http://www.kitchenswith mission.org/ team. html (accessed October 7, 2010).

Kitchens With Mission (2010c). Who we are. Retrieved from http://www.kitchenswith mission.org/whoweare.html (accessed October 7, 2010).

Kitchens With Mission (2010d). Measuring impact. Retrieved from http://www.kitchenswith mission. org/impact/nationaloutcomes.html (accessed October 7, 2010).

LaFrance, S., Lee, M., Green, R., Kvaternik, J., Robinson, A., & Alarcon, I. (2006). *Scaling capacities: Supports for growing impact*. LaFrance Associates, LLC, July.

McBride, J., & Ahmed, R. (2001). *Social franchising as a strategy for expanding access to reproductive health services*. Bethesda, MD: Commercial Markets Strategies Project.

Orr, A. (2005). Attracting attention: The Taproot Foundation provides organized volunteers who deliver marketing expertise. *Stanford Social Innovation Review*, Spring. Retrieved from http://ssir. org/articles/entry/attracting_attention. Accessed January 6, 2016.

Pimentel, B. (2007). A brand is a promise to a customer. *Stanford GSB News*. Stanford Graduate Business School, September. Retrieved from http://www.gsb.stanford.edu/news/headlines/2007 aakerbrandpromise.html (accessed September 29, 2010).

Tracey, P., & Jarvis, O. (2007). Toward a theory of social venture franchising. *Entrepreneurship Theory and Practice*, *31* (5), 667–685.

Wei-Skillern, J., Austin, J. E., Leonard, H., & Stevenson, H. (2007). *Entrepreneurship in the social sector*. Thousand Oaks, CA: Sage.

www.jamieoliver.com. Accessed March 25, 2011.

Social Intrapreneurship

AIM/PURPOSE

This chapter is aimed at describing and examining the phenomenon of social entrepreneurship that takes place within an existing organization. The focus is on intrapreneurship within large for-profit corporations (corporate social entrepreneurship) and how it is distinct from traditional corporate social responsibility. Additionally, the chapter also explores entrepreneurship within nonprofits pursuing an earned income strategy.

LEARNING OBJECTIVES FOR THIS CHAPTER

1. To understand the nature of social intrapreneurship.
2. To be able to distinguish between corporate social entrepreneurship and corporate social responsibility.
3. To understand the concept of "shared value."
4. To recognize the skills required for successful social intrapreneurship.
5. To understand the role of organizational environment, or context, in fostering social intrapreneurship.

It has been observed in the business entrepreneurship field that, while we tend to equate entrepreneurship with business start-up, entrepreneurship and innovation can, and should, take place at every stage in the business life cycle (Lester, 2004; Lichtenstein & Lyons, 2010; Molian, 2012). This suggests that individuals within larger firms can think and act like entrepreneurs. These entrepreneurs are often referred to as "intrapreneurs," a term attributed to Gifford Pinchot (Macrae, 1982).

Intrapreneurs must possess the same basic skill set required of successful entrepreneurs, but they also must be able to carry out their work within the often more bureaucratic structure of a large organization.

The equivalent players in social entrepreneurship are the *social entrepreneur* and the *social intrapreneur* (Brenneke & Spitzeck, 2009). The social entrepreneur is typically the founder of a new social venture that he/she grows and sustains. The social intrapreneur commonly operates within a large for-profit business or corporation as a *corporate social entrepreneur* (although this could be a nonprofit, as we discuss later in this chapter). Michelini and Fiorentino (2012) further distinguish between these two forms of social enterprising by noting that they have different business models. While social entrepreneurs focus on creating social value and view the creation of economic value as a means to achieving sustainability for their social ventures, social intrapreneurs work through their core business (whatever that may be) to create *shared value*—both economic and social value—that benefits the corporation and its community (Austin et al., 2005; Elkington & Hartigan, 2007; Porter & Kramer, 2011).

THE CONCEPT OF "SHARED VALUE"

Underlying most discussions of corporate social entrepreneurship or social intrapreneurship is the concept of *shared value* (Elkington & Hartigan, 2007; Michelini & Fiorentino, 2012; Pavlovich & Corner, 2014). This concept as it applies to corporations is widely attributed to Porter and Kramer (2006), who first articulated it in an article in the *Harvard Business Review* and later expanded upon it in the same outlet (Porter & Kramer, 2011).

Porter and Kramer are talking about value creation in for-profit corporations. They lament the fact that corporations in recent years have become focused on short-term profits and shareholder value at the expense of the needs of society. They observe that this has prompted policy decisions by governments that, with the best of intentions, only make things worse. They believe that the remedy for this situation is for corporations to put the emphasis on shared value.

Shared value permits a broader definition of capitalism that includes using markets to solve social problems as well as economic challenges (Porter & Kramer, 2011). Corporations must pursue economic and social value in tandem, with one reinforcing the other. To pursue economic value alone leaves corporations and society vulnerable. Creating social value fosters the equity and stability necessary to permit economies to continue to develop (see the discussion in Chapter 1 in the section "Social Entrepreneurship's Unique Qualifications"). It is, therefore, good for businesses and for communities to create social value.

Porter & Kramer (2011) acknowledge that the shift to a corporate focus on shared value will not be easy. Merely giving lip service to the concept will not be enough. Engaging in charitable activities and/or environmentally friendly operations solely for the purpose of enhancing the corporation's image or attracting a particular market segment will not be sufficient. A greater commitment must be made. Part of this commitment must be to developing corporate leadership with a stronger understanding of and sensitivity to societal problems; to acquiring the skills to foster partnerships between the private, public and nonprofit sectors; and to embracing the role of social value in making corporations truly productive (Porter & Kramer, 2011). Crucial also is an understanding by government officials of business and how economic value is created. As Hamlin and Lyons (1996, p. 167) assert, we need more "public entrepreneurs and private statesmen." This brings us back to corporate social entrepreneurship.

CORPORATE SOCIAL ENTREPRENEURSHIP VS. CORPORATE SOCIAL RESPONSIBILITY

Students of social entrepreneurship are often very interested in corporate social responsibility (CSR) because of the latter's social orientation and its apparent commitment to sustainable business practices. As a result, there is often confusion about the relationship between the two. This is not surprising, given that scholars often define CSR in terms that make it appear that it is essentially social entrepreneurship within a corporate organization.

Hockerts (2007) argues that CSR fundamentally embodies shared value creation (as described above) through its concern with the pursuit of both profits for shareholders and social good. Carroll (1991) and Kotler and Lee (2005) emphasize that through CSR corporations build social responsibility into their economic decisions. Several scholars highlight the corporate–community partnerships that CSR pursues (Austin, 2000; Austin et al., 2004; Tracey et al., 2007).

While all of this is true, it does not tell the complete story. CSR involves a very broad spectrum of activities that may include philanthropy, cause-related marketing, environmental sustainability and energy conservation, among others. All of these activities are laudable and can be beneficial to society; however, they are driven by the economic goals of the corporation, not by a social mission. As Crisan and Borza (2012) found in their study of social entrepreneurship and CSR in Romania, when forced to choose between their CSR activities and their economic goals most companies will opt for the latter. In fact, very often CSR is more about corporate image building, bending to societal pressure, cost saving to enhance profits, and capturing new markets, than it is about mission-based commitment to pursuing social good. It involves the pursuit of economic value, with social value as a by-product that can be sacrificed, if necessary (Crisan & Borza, 2012).

According to the definition of "social entrepreneurship" adopted in this book, CSR is not social entrepreneurship. Perhaps more importantly, given the subject of this chapter, it is not corporate social entrepreneurship or social intrapreneurship. If we subscribe to Michelini and Fiorentino's (2012) definition of social intrapreneurship noted earlier in this chapter, then social intrapreneurs create truly shared value—a genuine blending of economic and social values. Austin et al. (2006, p. 170) contend that corporate social entrepreneurship is "the process of extending the firm's domain of competence and corresponding opportunity set through innovative leveraging of resources, both within and outside its direct control, aimed at simultaneous creation of economic and social value."

According to Porter and Kramer (2011), creating shared value must go beyond traditional CSR to thinking and acting on the part of the corporation that reflects a deeper understanding of how economic well-being and social well-being are inextricably linked to one another in a mutualistic relationship that sustains both. An example might be the so-called "inclusive businesses" that pursue their economic goal of increasing their market and enhancing their brand by including low-income individuals and groups in their value chains as a way to address the social problem of poverty (SEKN, 2011).

WHAT IT TAKES TO FOSTER SOCIAL INTRAPRENEURSHIP

The successful encouragement of social intrapreneurship requires that attention be paid to both agency and context—to the individual intrapreneur and to the corporate environment in which that intrapreneur must operate. As is the case with all entrepreneurs, social intrapreneurs must be properly motivated to undertake the difficult work they do; they must develop the skills required to do this work; and they need a context that is supportive of their efforts.

Skills

While there is research on the motivation of social entrepreneurs (see pp. 22–23 in Chapter 2) and about the role conscious awareness (Pavlovich & Corner, 2014) plays, which arguably apply to social intrapreneurs, very little has been written about the skills required for success in this arena. Most of the discussions among entrepreneurship scholars are about whether or not skill in entrepreneurship can be built through education and training (Fayolle et al., 2005; Henry & Treanor, 2010; Putta, 2014). Lichtenstein and Lyons (2001) have attempted to identify four types of skill necessary for successful entrepreneurship: technical, managerial, entrepreneurial, and personal maturity, and they have argued that these must be developed through practice and coaching. They later expanded this thinking to social entrepreneurship (Lyons & Lichtenstein, 2010).

The work done in the skills arena in the social entrepreneurship literature has largely focused on competencies (Thompson, 2002; Weerawardena & Mort, 2006) or on combinations of principles, resources, and behaviors (Boschee, 2001; Brinckerhoff, 2001; Lock, 2001; Sharir & Lerner, 2006). Urban (2008) attempted to develop a set of skills for social entrepreneurship and test them. While his work is essentially developmental, Urban argues that social entrepreneurs need basic business management skills but that there are also essential skills that are unique to social entrepreneurship. He found core skills for social entrepreneurship to include leadership, fund-raising, and project administration.

The research to date provides us with only very rudimentary guidance as to the skills necessary for successful social intrapreneurship. However, it is not unreasonable to deduce that social intrapreneurs must have the skills that are specific to the social "industry" in which they are working. For example, if such an intrapreneur is helping her multi-national corporation (MNC) build low-income individuals and their businesses into the MNC's value chain in the developing countries in which it operates, she must have the skills peculiar to that work (e.g., language skills, cultural skills, skills in coordinating wealth-creating value chains). It also would be safe to say that social intrapreneurs need the basic skills of business management—accounting, finance, marketing, strategy, etc.—necessary to their corporation's pursuit of economic value (Lyons & Lichtenstein, 2010). They will need the opportunity recognition and creation skills of entrepreneurs (Drucker, 1985; Sarasvathy, 2007; Lyons & Lichtenstein, 2010). They will also need the skills necessary to effecting deep change or transformation required of social entrepreneurs, such as social capital building skills and the skills necessary to change mindsets (Praszkier & Nowak, 2011). Finally, it stands to reason that successful social intrapreneurs need the ability to think and act systemically in order to seamlessly link all of the behaviors that reflect these skills together into a system of truly blended value within their corporate environment.

Environment

This brings us to a discussion of the corporate environment within which social intrapreneurs work. As is true of most large organizations, corporations can be top-down in structure, inflexible in operations, intolerant of failure, slow to change, intolerant of creative or "maverick" behavior and rewarding of conformity, isolating and siloed, and focused on the organization at the expense of the individual (Kenney & Mujtaba, 2007; Feyzbakhsh et al., 2008; Kuratko, 2009). While this is not the rule for all corporations and tremendous strides in organization development have been made in recent years, these characteristics continue to define many corporate environments around the world and certainly stand as obstacles to entrepreneurial behavior within these organizations' walls.

This situation has spawned a considerable literature on how to improve the corporate environment in support of entrepreneurship, with both scholars and practitioners ringing in. These prescriptions reflect a growing recognition that intrapreneurship does not merely happen through the heroic efforts of a few determined individuals. It also requires intentional intervention by the corporation to create an environment that is conducive, without neglecting the fact that the individuals who take on this entrepreneurial work must be properly skilled (Seshadri & Tripathy, 2006; Menzel et al., 2007; Gomez-Haro et al., 2011). Hass (2011) has described this as balancing independence and integration.

Menzel et al. (2007) caution that intrapreneurship cannot be successful in environments that do not work to remove obstacles to it or when there are too few individuals behaving entrepreneurially. The latter situation may be, in part, an issue of proper mindset. As Seshadri & Tripathy (2006, p. 17) observe, intrapreneurship must involve a "basic transformation of perspective from 'employee' to 'psychological owner' or intrapreneur." However, there are numerous other factors that are deemed essential for effective intrapreneurship.

Among the many factors that have been identified are:

1   Having a vision for entrepreneurship within the organization—corporations must build intrapreneurial activity into their goals (Kuratko, 2009);
2   Sharing creative ideas within the organization in a learning environment—a context must be created in which people can communicate and engage each other across functional silos (Seshadri & Tripathy, 2006; Gomez-Haro et al., 2011);
3   Support, even advocacy, from upper-level management (Seshadri & Tripathy, 2006; Menzel et al., 2007; Kuratko, 2009);
4   Building trust within the corporation on multiple levels, as trust makes a sharing and learning culture possible and gives individuals the courage to innovate (Stull & Aram, 2010);
5   Properly skilled personnel, including market knowledge (Menzel et al., 2007; Balasundaram & Uddin, 2009) and entrepreneurial behavior training (Gomez-Haro et al., 2011);
6   Tolerance for failure within the corporation—the acceptance of failure as part of the learning process and not as a reason for stigmatization (Seshadri & Tripathy, 2006; Kuratko, 2009);
7   Reduced bureaucracy and thought given to appropriate organizational structure (Menzel et al., 2007; Balasundaram & Uddin, 2009);
8   Physical space, time and other resources expressly dedicated to intrapreneurial activities (Menzel et al., 2007; Kuratko, 2009);
9   Rewards for the good work of intrapreneurs (Kuratko, 2009); and a team approach (Seshadri & Tripathy, 2006; Kuratko, 2009).

While this is not an exhaustive list, it delineates the major elements of a context that fosters intrapreneurship in an efficacious manner.

It has even been suggested that there is an order to developing such an intrapreneurial environment. Badal (2012) has developed a simple four-point process:

1 Break down the existing silos and recognize that people from across the corporation can contribute to intrapreneurial efforts.
2 Find people with the appropriate knowledge and skills and supply them with the financial, human, physical and social capital to help them be successful.
3 Create a supportive context, with elements like those enumerated above.
4 Monitor and measure progress toward achieving the organization's intrapreneurial goals.

With only minor modification, the preceding discussion on the commercial intrapreneurship environment can be applied to social intrapreneurship. The chief differentiator is the mission-driven aspect of the latter. Social intrapreneurs are passionate about solving social problems and thereby igniting social change. This tends to place the onus on the social intrapreneur to be her/his own advocate within the corporation. The social intrapreneur must make the business case for their social mission and find the best way for using corporate resources to create economic and social value (Simms, 2008).

Whereas commercial intrapreneurship tends to emphasize creating a supportive infrastructure and finding and developing the intrapreneurs to take innovation forward, social intrapreneurship focuses more on intrapreneurs who self-identify and then find the right fit for their endeavors within the corporate structure. This is because experience shows that social intrapreneurs are not readily identified by corporate leadership and can emerge from any part of the corporation, nor is their path predictable (Simms, 2008). Thus, social intrapreneurship is more likely to be emergent than intentional; whereas, commercial intrapreneurship could be either (Mintzberg, 1978).

Successful social intrapreneurs must look for ways to use their company's products or services to generate social change. They must then "sell" their ideas to corporate leadership using the language of business, not that of the social sector. They may need to seek resources both inside and outside the corporation. Simms (2008) tells of one social intrapreneur who realized that he would not get the start-up funding needed to launch his social venture from his corporation, so he sought financial capital from external social investors. Social intrapreneurs often have to identify where in the corporate structure their social ventures can thrive. Counter-intuitively this may not be the CSR unit or the corporate foundation. It may be that a social venture is best embedded in operations or in the marketing department (Simms, 2008).

Apropos of the last observation, Hindustan Unilever's Shakti program is an example of a social intrapreneurship initiative located in the corporation's sales department, permitting its full integration into the business model (Allianz et al., 2008). From the social value creation perspective, Shakti addresses the problems of poverty in rural areas in India, a lack of product choices for the rural poor due to a virtually nonexistent retail distribution infrastructure and poor transportation, and a lack of empowerment among low-income women (Allianz et al., 2008). Relative to economic value, Hindustan Unilever wanted to expand the market for its products to low-income, under-populated areas of India, which have been identified as potentially very lucrative based on bottom-of-the-pyramid (BoP) thinking (Prahalad, 2006).

The Shakti program blends these two types of value by training women in these rural areas in sales, bookkeeping, and general business knowledge. The idea is to prepare them to become Hindustan Unilever distributors; although, some choose to start their own businesses. Whichever path they choose, the women become models for others and catalytic leaders in their communities (Allianz et al., 2008). Community development is fostered and the corporation expands its market and builds strong relationships with that new market, which creates brand loyalty and enhances reputation (Allianz et al., 2008).

SOCIAL INTRAPRENEURSHIP IN NONPROFITS

So far, we have been treating social intrapreneurship as though it only takes place within for-profit corporations. However, it can arguably occur within large and small nonprofit organizations as well, particularly nonprofits that pursue earned income strategies as opposed to relying exclusively on philanthropy. Such organizations are sometimes referred to as "social enterprises" (Lyons et al., 2010).

In their study of smaller nonprofit social enterprises in Australia and New Zealand, Verreynne & Harris (2009) explore the nature of social intrapreneurship. They found that social intrapreneurship in such organizations is spawned by need. As management and staff encounter challenges, they engage in innovation that adds value for their clients. Several of their findings directly support the prescriptions for successful commercial social intrapreneurship noted above: an entrepreneurial culture within the organization is optimal, the support of the organization's management is essential, and social intrapreneurship should be explicitly part of the organization's mission. They also discovered that intrapreneurial thinking and acting can take place at any, and every, level of the organization. Finally, they observed that social intrapreneurs tended to build networks in order to acquire needed resources for pursuing their mission.

In their case study of Stiftung Liebenau in Germany, Schmitz and Scheuerle (2012) found several similar elements of social intrapreneurship in nonprofit organizations. Stiftung Liebenau is a large nonprofit that provides education, employment, housing, and healthcare assistance to the mentally challenged, the elderly, and youth needing special education. The organization is regularly challenged by the need to match the way its services are legally structured to its clients' needs to ensure effective delivery and adequate funding. As a result, the nonprofit must engage in perpetual innovation (Schmitz and Scheuerle, 2012).

In order to support and perpetuate this required innovation, Stiftung Liebenau maintains an environment that allows for the independence of managers, as they generate and test new ideas for service delivery. In the spirit of "lean start-up" (see Chapter 4), failure is tolerated and viewed as a way to learn what works and what does not and to keep the organization flexible and responsive to its clients' needs. Stiftung Liebenau is careful to try to hire qualified people and to provide them with adequate training and coaching. Another important aspect of this organization's intrapreneurial culture is its regular use of networking with other providers to deliver services, which necessitates creativity in designing the organizational structures that make these networks perform well (Schmitz and Scheuerle, 2012).

Thus, social intrapreneurship efforts in corporations and in nonprofits share many common characteristics. The chief difference is that nonprofits are expressly social mission-driven: they are inherently focused on creating social value. Arguably, they need not concern themselves with shared value because generating economic value is not part of that vision. However, even this difference may not be as great as it initially appears. Because these nonprofit organizations are pursuing earned income as a means of achieving financial sustainability, they are, in effect, pursuing a form of economic value (although not a profit), which suggests that a slightly modified type of shared value is in fact being pursued.

Case Study 10.1

CEMEX's Patrimonio Hoy Initiative

Among low-income families in Mexico, it is everyone's dream to be able to build their own house. While many try, they face serious obstacles to success. First, they can only afford to buy small quantities of building materials at a time, making for piecemeal construction that can take years and leading to degradation of building materials, due to a lack of proper storage facilities. In addition, very few materials suppliers are willing to undertake the expense of delivering small loads to the remote places where these low-income homebuilders reside. Finally, the would-be homebuilders typically lack the architectural and engineering skills required to design and construct modern houses (*Business Today*, 2011).

Enter Mexico-based CEMEX, one of the largest construction materials companies in the world, with over $15 billion in annual sales, over 40,000 employees, and cement production capacity of 94 million tons (CEMEX, 2014). During an economic down cycle in Mexico in the mid-1990s, the company was losing sales overall but recognized that its low-income market was relatively stable. Further analysis showed that this was a $500 million a year market that could be expanded. Pursuing it more aggressively would help to stabilize market fluctuation and diversify the customer base (Business Today, 2011).

With this in mind, CEMEX engaged in what some have termed an "ethnographic approach" to modifying its business model to meet the needs of its low-income market by embedding some of its managers in low-income neighborhoods in Guadalajara (Allianz et al., 2008). The information gathered through this effort resulted in the creation of the social enterprise Patrimonio Hoy within CEMEX, which officially began operations in 2000. Patrimonio Hoy can be interpreted literally as "Patrimony Today," or as "Property Now," "Personal Property Now" or "Wealth Now" (Allianz et al., 2008; *Business Today*, 2011; Shared Value Initiative, 2013).

Credit for developing Patrimonio Hoy is given to Luis Sota, who was the full-time consultant to CEMEX for the project (Allianz, et al., 2008). He recognized that there was a clear business argument for CEMEX's pursuit of the low-income home-building market, which included the following benefits to the company (Business in the Community, 2010; CEMEX, 2014; *Business Today*, 2011):

1   A sustainable source of revenue from a large market—Patrimonio Hoy achieved breakeven in 2004 and has been operating at a profit since;
2   Brand loyalty from low-income households—Customers are highly satisfied and actively engage in word-of-mouth advertising;
3   Reputation as a socially responsible company—Patrimonio Hoy has been the recipient of several awards, including the World Business Award (International Chamber of Commerce, United Nations Development Program and Prince of Wales International Business Leader's Forum) in 2006 for its work in support of the UN's Millennium Development Goals; the 2007 Corporate Citizen of the Americas Award from the Trust for the Americas; and the 2009 United Nations HABITAT Business Award;
4   A gateway to additional related markets—Patrimonio Hoy programs have been established in Colombia, Costa Rica, the Dominican Republic and Nicaragua. The success of Patrimonio Hoy has also led to the creation of additional social enterprises within CEMEX that address such issues as rebuilding after hurricane and typhoon damage, building and renovating public institutions, and engaging communities in paving unpaved streets and sidewalks through microloans, among others.

Soto also recognized the social value that could be created. Through its work, Patrimonio Hoy addresses two of the UN's Millennium Development Goals: Goal #1 to eliminate severe poverty; and Goal #3 to promote equality and empowerment for women. It does this by making housing affordable and by engaging women in promoting the program in their neighborhoods and paying them a commission for customers they engage.

The design of the program reflects the economic and social value to be created. Patrimonio Hoy is a membership organization, charging its clients a small weekly fee of about $10 to $15 for their participation (Shared Value Initiative, 2013, p. 2). Drawing upon the traditional Mexican lending system called *tanda*, the program creates borrowing groups of three members. The membership fee is charged to the group, which commits to a 70-week membership period. The fee serves as a loan toward 80 percent (after a 20 percent discount) of the cost of building materials that will be delivered in seven installments over the 70-week period, with the exception of a small portion that goes to CEMEX to cover the cost of the "package" of services provided. Included is an annual interest on the loan of 15 percent. In this way, Patrimonio Hoy has created a micro-finance system for low-income homebuilders. The "package" that is provided to each member group includes building materials, the delivery of those materials, one year of storage for those materials in case of building delays, access to an architect and an engineer to help oversee the home-building project, a fixed price for the building materials over the 70-week membership period, and infrastructural improvements to local public schools (Business in the Community, 2010; Shared Value Initiative, 2013).

The full Patrimonio Hoy market has been divided into 100,000-person regions. Each region is managed by a team of between one and four staff members, including the architect and the engineer. Promoters, who recruit members to the program, are hired in each region. These promoters are typically women from the low-income neighborhoods that work with public schools and neighborhood retailers. Both the regional managers and the promoters are paid based on the rate of loan repayment and the length of time member groups remain committed to the program within the region (Business in the Community, 2010; *Business Today*, 2011; Shared Value Initiative, 2013).

Patrimonio Hoy has grown to over 100 centers and has assisted over 350,000 families in building and owning their own home (CEMEX, 2014), an asset that contributes to wealth creation. To date, the program has lent over $135 million. It has increased the market value of the houses it finances by about 20 percent because of the quality of construction ensured by the participation of professional architects and engineers in each project. Homes can be built three times faster and at one-third of the cost of the average Mexican house. Patrimonio Hoy creates jobs for masons and for promoters. The great majority of promoters are women (95 percent), and more than 50 percent of them have no formal work experience. Nearly one-third of the programs create home-based businesses (CEMEX, 2014).

CEMEX reports that its customer satisfaction rate is, on average, over 80 percent. This further enhances brand loyalty by low-income households and the company's reputation for social responsibility. The loan repayment rate has been found to be about 99 percent. This not only indicates that the program design works, but it is also good news for regional managers and promoters of Patrimonio Hoy, as it means greater compensation for their efforts. Luis Soto, Patrimonio Hoy's designer, has observed that he believes that the program's success is due to the trust that was built when CEMEX listened to its low-income customers and added value for them by meeting their needs (Allianz, et al., 2008).

CEMEX is looking to improve upon Patrimonio Hoy in several ways. They are exploring ways to improve upon the business model that will permit further scaling of the program. In conjunction with this, they are conducting feasibility studies regarding entering additional developing countries. They have also launched a pilot program that raises awareness of climate change by offering energy-efficient appliances (CEMEX, 2014).

THOUGHT QUESTIONS

1 Is Patrimonio Hoy a true example of social intrapreneurship, based on the discussion in this chapter? Explain your response.
2 What shared value, if any, is created in this case?
3 Luis Soto was an external consultant to CEMEX when he developed Patrimonio Hoy. Do you think this was an advantage or a disadvantage as he pursued this opportunity? Why?
4 What kinds of contextual challenges might CEMEX face as it continues to roll out Patrimonio Hoy in developing countries around the globe?
5 Can you think of other ways to add value for customers to Patrimonio Hoy's package of services?

QUESTIONS FOR "CONNECTING THE DOTS"

1 How do the environments of for-profit and nonprofit organizations differ from each other? What are the advantages and disadvantages of each as they relate to fostering social intrapreneurship? Do you think one type of organization is inherently more conducive to social intrapreneurship than the other? Explain your response to this latter question.
2 According to some observers, the lines between corporate social entrepreneurship and CSR are becoming increasingly blurred. Do you agree? Why or why not?
3 Which do you find personally more attractive, social entrepreneurship or social intrapreneurship? Explain your answer.
4 What are your thoughts on shared value? Is it the best explanation for social intrapreneurship? Is it sustainable? Explain.

REFERENCES

Allianz, IDEO, Skoll Foundation, & SustainAbility (2008). *The social intrapreneur: A field guide for corporate changemakers*. London: SustainAbility Ltd.

Austin, J. (2000). *The collaboration challenge: How nonprofits and businesses succeed through strategic alliances*. London: Peter Drucker Foundation.

Austin, J., Wei-Skillern, J., & Lefort, A. (2004). Starbucks and Conservation International. Teaching Note, 304-100. Boston: Harvard Business School, Division of Research.

Austin, J., Leonard, H., Reficco, E., & Wei-Skillern, J. (2005). Social entrepreneurship: It's for corporations. In Nicholls, A. (Ed.), *Social entrepreneurship: New paradigms of sustainable social change*. Oxford: Oxford University Press, 169–181.

Badal, S. (2012). Building corporate entrepreneurship is hard work. *Gallup Business Journal*, September 25, 2012. http://businessjournal.gallup.com/content/157604/building-corporate-entrepreneurship-hard. Accessed August 15, 2014.

Balasundaram, N., & Uddin, M. S. (2009). Determinants of key favorable environment for intrapreneurship development: An empirical study of some selected companies in Chittagong, Bangladesh. *Buletinul, LXI* (2), 29–35.

Boschee, J. (2001). Eight basic principles for non-profit entrepreneurs. *Nonprofit World, 19* (4), 15–18.

Brenneke, M., & Spitzeck, H. (2009). Social intrapreneurship. Paper presented at the 22nd EBEN Annual Conference, Athens. Retrieved from www.eben.gr/site/Papers/Spitzeck%20Heiko%20Social%20Intrapreneurship.pdf (Accessed July 25, 2014).

Brinckerhoff, P. (2001). Why you need to be more entrepreneurial – and how to get started. *Nonprofit World*, 9 (6), 12–15.

Business in the Community. (2010). CEMEX – Patrimonio Hoy: Coffey award supported by the Department of International Development. www.bitc.org.uk/print/our-resources/case-studies/cemex-patrimonio-hoy. Accessed August 18, 2014.

Business Today. (2011). Cemex grew its profits by helping the poor to help themselves. November 22. http://businesstoday.intoday.in/story/innovation-cemex/1/20184.html. Accessed August 18, 2014.

Carroll, A. B. (1991). The pyramid of corporate social responsibility: Toward the moral management of organizational stakeholders. *Business Horizons*, July–August, 39–48.

CEMEX (2014). Company profile. www.cemex.com/AboutUs/CompanyProfile.aspx.

Crisan, C. M., & Borza, A. (2012). Social entrepreneurship and corporate social responsibilities. *International Business Research*, 5(2), 106–113.

Drucker, P. F. (1985). *Entrepreneurship and innovation*. New York: Harper Business.

Elkington, J., & Hartigan, P. (2007). *The power of unreasonable people: How social entrepreneurs create markets that change the world*. Boston, MA: Harvard Business School Press.

Fayolle, A., Gailly, B., Kickul, J., & Lassas-Clerc, N. (2005). Capturing variations in attitudes and intentions: A longitudinal study to assess the pedagogical effectiveness of entrepreneurship teaching programs. Cahiers de Recherche No. 2002/11. Lyon, France: EMLYON.

Feyzbakhsh, S. A., Sadeghi, R., & Shoraka, S. (2008). A case study of intrapreneurship obstacles: The RAJA Passenger Train Company. *Journal of Small Business and Entrepreneurship*, 21 (2), 171–180, 251.

Gomez-Haro, S., Aragon-Correa, J., & Cordon-Pozo, E. (2011). Differentiating the effects of the institutional environment on corporate entrepreneurship. *Management Decision, 49* (10), 1677–1693.

Hamlin, R. E., & Lyons, T. S. (1996). *Economy without walls: Managing local development in a restructuring world*. Westport, CT: Praeger.

Hass, B. H. (2011). Intrapreneurship and corporate venturing in the media business: A theoretical framework and examples from the German publishing industry. *Journal of Media Business Studies, 8* (1), 47–68.

Henry, C., & Treanor, L. (2010). Entrepreneurship education and veterinary medicine: Enhancing employable skills. *Education & Training, 52* (8/9), 607–623.

Hockerts, K. (2007). Managerial perceptions of the business case of corporate social responsibility, CSR & Business in Society, Copenhagen Business School Working Paper Series No. 03-2007. Copenhagen: Copenhagen Business School Center for Corporate Social Responsibility.

Kenney, M., & Mujtaba, B. G. (2007). Understanding corporate entrepreneurship and development: A practitioner view of organizational intrapreneurship. *Journal of Applied Management and Entrepreneurship, 12* (3), 73–88.

Kotler, P., & Lee, N. (2005). *Corporate social responsibility: Doing the most good for your company and cause*. New York: Wiley.

Kuratko, D. F. (2009). The entrepreneurial imperative of the 21st century. *Business Horizons, 52,* 421–428.

Lester, D. L. (2004). An American entrepreneur manages across the life cycle. *Journal of Business and Entrepreneurship, 16* (1), 104–118.

Lichtenstein, G. A., & Lyons, T. S. (2001). The entrepreneurial development system: Transforming business talent and community economies. *Economic Development Quarterly, 15* (1), 3–20.

Lichtenstein, G. A., & Lyons, T. S. (2010). *Investing in entrepreneurs: A strategic approach for strengthening your regional and community economy*. Santa Barbara, CA: Praeger/ABC-CLIO.

Lock, I. C. (2001). Summary report of proceedings: Strategic alliance: Seeking common ground. Edmonton, Alberta: Canadian Centre for Social Entrepreneurship, University of Alberta. Retrieved from http://www.bus.ualberta.ca/ccse. Accessed August 18, 2014.

Lyons, T. S., Townsend, J., Sullivan, A. M., Drago, T. (2010). *Social enterprise's expanding position in the nonprofit landscape*. New York: National Executive Service Corps.

Lyons, T. S., & Lichtenstein, G. A. (2010). A community-wide framework for encouraging social entrepreneurship using the pipeline of entrepreneurs and enterprises model. In Fayolle, A., & Matlay, H. (Eds.). *Handbook of Research on Social Entrepreneurship*. Cheltenham, UK: Edward Elgar.

Macrae, N. (1982). Intrapreneurial now. *The Economist*, April 17.

Menzel, H. C., Aaltio, I., & Ulijn, J. M. (2007). On the way to creativity: Engineers as intrapreneurs in organizations. *Technovation, 27,* 732–743.

Michelini, L., & Fiorentino, D. (2012). New business models for creating shared value. *Social Responsibility Journal, 8* (4), 561–577.

Mintzberg, H. (1978). Patterns in strategy formation. *Management Science, 24* (9), 934–948.

Molian, D. (2012). Entrepreneurial value creation: Are business schools doing their full part? *Journal of Strategic Management Education, 8* (4), 233–252.

Pavlovich, K., & Corner, P. D. (2014). Conscious enterprise emergence: Shared value creation through expanded conscious awareness. *Journal of Business Ethics, 121,* 341–351.

Porter, M. E., & Kramer, M. R. (2006). Strategy and society: The link between competitive advantage and corporate social entrepreneurship. *Harvard Business Review, 84* (12), 78–92.

Porter, M. E., & Kramer, M. R. (2011). Creating shared value. *Harvard Business Review, 89* (1/2), 62–77.

Prahalad, C. K. (2006). *The Fortune at the Bottom of the Pyramid*. Upper Saddle River, NJ: Wharton School Publishing.

Praszkier, R., & Nowak, A. (2011). *Social entrepreneurship: Theory and practice*. Cambridge, UK: Cambridge University Press.

Putta, S. S. (2014). Improving entrepreneurs' management skills through entrepreneurship training. *Journal of Commerce and Management, 5* (3), 459–474.

Schmitz, B., & Scheuerle, T. (2012). Founding or transforming? Social intrapreneurship in three German Christian-based NPOs. *ACRN Journal of Entrepreneurship Perspectives, 1* (1), 13–36.

SEKN (Social Enterprise Knowledge Network). (2011). Inclusive business: Engaging the poor through market initiatives in Iberoamerica. Cambridge, MA: David Rockefeller Center for Latin American Studies, Harvard University Press.

Seshadri, D. V. R., & Tripathy, A. (2006). Innovation through intrapreneurship: The road less traveled. *Vikalpa, 31* (1), 17–29.

Shared Value Initiative. (2013). Patrimonio Hoy: Access to housing and finance. Retrieved from http://sharedvalue.org/sites/default/files/resource-files/SharedValueinAction_Cemex_12-2013.pdf. Accessed August 18, 2014.

Sharir, M., & Lerner, M. (2006). Gauging the success of social ventures initiated by individual social entrepreneurs. *Journal of World Business, 41*, 6–20.

Simms, J. (2008). Innovation's new frontier. *Director, 62* (3), 48–49, 51–53.

Stull, M., & Aram, J. D. (2010). Exploring trust as an influencing mechanism of Intrapreneurship. *International Journal of Management and Marketing Research, 3* (3), 17–38.

Thompson, J. L. (2002). The world of the social entrepreneur. *The International Journal of Public Sector Management, 15* (5), 412–431.

Tracey, P., Phillips, N., & Haugh, H. (2007). Beyond philanthropy: Community enterprise as a basis for corporate citizenship. *Journal of Business Ethics, 58* (4), 327–344.

Urban, B. (2008). Social entrepreneurship in South Africa: Delineating the construct with associated skills. *International Journal of Entrepreneurial Behaviour & Research, 14* (5), 346–364.

Verreyne, M., & Harris, C. (2009). Social intrapreneurship: The case of small nonprofit firms in Australia and NZ. *Proceedings of the 2009 ICSB World Conference, Seoul, Korea*. London: International Council for Small Business.

Weerawardena, J., & Mort, G.S. (2006). Investigating social entrepreneurship: A multidimensional model. *Journal of World Business, 41*, 21–35.

Social Entrepreneurship and Environmental Sustainability

AIM/PURPOSE

This chapter provides an overview of the environmental aspects of social entrepreneurship. It explores the challenges and opportunities for the social entrepreneur to create and build an environmentally sustainable organization. It also provides a framework (sSWOT) that can be used to develop an environmental sustainability strategy for new and existing firms.

LEARNING OBJECTIVES OF THIS CHAPTER

1. To gain an understanding of the environmental aspects of social entrepreneurship.
2. To understand the variety of challenges and obstacles in the environmental sustainability field.
3. To learn about the variety of green opportunities for social entrepreneurs across a variety of industries.
4. To construct a strategic framework (sSWOT) that can be used as a guide in developing a sustainability strategy for a social enterprise firm.
5. To provide a case in which students have the opportunity to identify and address the inherent difficulties a fledgling environmental firm has in commercializing its technologies.

Over the past several years, there has been an increase in entrepreneurs who are focused on the environmental aspects of social entrepreneurship—alternative energy, clean technology, environmental protection, sustainability in our food systems, etc. While it is hard to quantify how many of those entrepreneurs are

72% of American consumers think it is important to buy from green companies *(2011 Green Brands Survey)*.

Consumers are most willing to buy green products in the grocery aisle *(2011 Green Brand Survey)*.

29% of smartphone users utilize apps to reduce environmental impact and 18–33% of users cite social media as a source of sustainability information.

"Shareholder resolutions focusing on social and environmental issues made up the largest portion of all shareholder proposals in 2010 and 2011" *(2012 State of Green Business Report)*.

Increasingly companies are engaging in "shadow pricing" (putting price tags on environmental costs) *(2014 State of Green Business Report)*.

FIGURE 11.1   Challenges and Obstacles in the Field—The Tragedy of the Commons

Source: Author-generated

classified as "green" entrepreneurs, some say it is as high as 11 million alone in the United States and data from The Green Market says the sector will double from $1.37 trillion a year in 2010 to $2.74 trillion by 2020. Figure 11.1 displays some of the latest trends and consumer perspectives in the environmental sustainability field.

As discussed in previous chapters, the domain of social entrepreneurship is replete with possibilities and innovations to effectively address and potentially solve some of society's most intractable problems. In this section, we highlight the role of "Tragedy of the Commons" and examine how it represents both opportunities and obstacles for the social entrepreneur.

The Tragedy of the Commons refers to the depletion of a shared resource by individuals acting independently and rationally, according to one's self-interest, despite knowing that abusing the common resource is contrary to those individuals' long-term, best interests. The first use of the term is attributed to Garrett Hardin's 1968 *Science* article (first outlined in an 1833 pamphlet by W. F. Lloyd) describing European farmers sharing common land on which they could graze their cattle. It is in each herder's interest to put every cow he acquires on the land, even if the quality of the commons is damaged for all through overgrazing. The individual receives all of the benefits from any additional cow, but damage to the commons is shared by the group.

The Tragedy is often applied to a discussion of environmental issues and is a model for a great variety of society's current resource-based problems, including over-irrigation, habitat destruction, over-fishing, and traffic congestion. It is especially applicable to this chapter, namely in terms of air pollution, where strong economic forces are encouraging the use of the atmosphere as a free-for-all dumping ground for greenhouse gases. Any solution to this problem will clearly be a social good of mammoth proportions. But the fact is that any one of the seven billion people on Earth has an incentive to avoid the cost of controlling polluting emissions, even though this in turn creates the problem of the "Free Rider," i.e., an individual who benefits from another's work without paying for it.

MODERN APPROACHES AND SOLUTIONS

Generally speaking, there are two practical ways to try to overcome any Free Rider problem: (1) compulsory participation (taxation)—a form of regulation, and (2) linking the public good to a desirable private good (getting people to pay voluntarily). In the case of air pollution, the most common solutions to date have been centered on compulsory participation through a carbon tax or emissions trading ("cap-and-trade"). In recent years, more attention has been spent on ways to "privatize" the commons. That is, convert the common good into private property giving the new owners an incentive to enforce its sustainability. Clearly, this may be possible as a solution to traffic congestion, for example, through the use of toll roads. However, it is unlikely to be successful in the case of air pollution.

A carbon tax as a potential solution to the air pollution problem works this way. A tax is levied on the carbon content of fuels that are used, offering a potentially cost-effective means of reducing greenhouse gas emissions. This Pigouvian tax (i.e., a levy on activities that generate negative social costs) penalizes producers of greenhouse gases who do not pay the full social costs of their actions. Simply put, the tax on emitting pollution is based on the carbon content of the fuel used in the manufacturing process.

The other major approach is emissions trading (cap-and-trade), a market-based approach that provides economic incentives for reducing the emissions of pollutants. A central authority (governmental body) sets a limit (cap) on the amount of pollutant that may be emitted. The cap is then allocated or sold as permits, which represent the right to discharge a specified volume of the pollutant. Firms are required to hold permits equivalent to their emissions (so, for example, one emissions permit may be considered equivalent to one metric ton of carbon dioxide emissions). Because the total number of permits cannot exceed the cap, total emissions are limited to that level. After a cap has been set, individual companies are then free to choose how or if they will reduce their emissions. Failure to report emissions and/or surrender emission permits is generally punishable through a government oversight mechanism that imposes fines that in turn increase the cost of production. Ideally, firms will choose the least expensive means of complying with the pollution regulation. In many cap-and-trade systems, organizations that do not pollute (and therefore have no obligations) can also participate in trading; environmental groups, for example, can purchase and retire emission permits, thereby driving up the price of the remaining permits.

Both of these methods are highly controversial and easily politicized, with opposition to environmental regulation centering on the increased costs of doing business through taxation, relocation of businesses, higher unemployment, and outright denial of any linkage between carbon emissions and greenhouse gases. In fact, such "top-down," bureaucratic approaches provide the social entrepreneur with the opportunity to address the problem with a more practical "bottom-up" approach. In particular, entrepreneurial innovation employing public–private partnerships are often successful.

ENTER THE SOCIAL ENTREPRENEUR

In essence, social entrepreneurs resolve the Free Rider problem by using innovative methods to bring the solution to the Tragedy (be it a product or service) to market *and* have the consumer pay for the any social costs. Thus, the Tragedy itself provides the opportunities for social entrepreneurs to perform a necessary and socially/ environmentally beneficial service at appropriate prices.

VOICES FROM THE FIELD

Social Entrepreneurship Cases in the Clean Technology Sector

Rentricity

Rentricity, one of the original start-up companies in the NYC ACRE cleantech support system, has been named a "Later Stage Global Top 10 greentech company"—chosen from a field of 4,000. The award by the Global Cleantech Cluster Association (GCCA) also named Rentricity as the winner of the "Best of Water" category for 2011 (AlaskaDispatch.com, 2011).

The firm recovers energy from excess water pressure in pipes to produce clean, renewable electricity. It targets water, wastewater, and industrial infrastructure to produce electricity that is then sold into the electric grid or used behind-the-meter. Rentricity Inc. is a renewable energy company using unique energy recovery configurations to transform the untapped energy in various man-made processes into electricity. Rentricity Flow-to-Wire (SM) systems have no environmental impact and represent a new class of clean, renewable hydrokinetic energy.

Established in 2003, the company is based in New York City with offices in New Jersey, Connecticut, and Pennsylvania.

GCCA recognized Rentricity for winning access to sources of growth capital and management guidance. The Association also cited Rentricity for significant success in growing the cleantech industry in New York City and for its support of regional green job growth. Rentricity became a commercial venture in 2008 and joined NYC ACRE the following year. Founder and President Frank Zammataro kept the young company self-financed and last year it generated $500,000 in revenue. Rentricity has completed two commercial projects and has four other projects in development. Among them is a project funded by the New York State Energy and Research Development Authority (NYSERDA) to develop wastewater solutions for New York City. As Zammataro notes:

> This international recognition gives us inspiration, and we hope to use it as a springboard to find our first project outside of North America . . . NYC ACRE's nomination of Rentricity for the GCCA award has now expanded its support for us beyond New York City and the State of New York to the global cleantech community.
>
> (AlaskaDispatch.com, 2011)

ThinkEco

Founded in 2008, ThinkEco, Inc. is a New York City-based company developing easy-to-use energy efficient technologies for the consumer market. The company is R&D driven, and has developed patent-pending technologies that make electricity conservation simple and easy. The company's product is the modlet— i.e., the modern outlet—a best-in-class device for monitoring and managing electricity at the plug-load level. The modlet has an average payback period of six months, saving users approximately 10 percent on their electricity bill with no behavior change required. The product addresses the fact that power is consumed by appliances and electronic equipment even when not in use. Studies have shown this standby power use is responsible for up to 26 percent of the average electric bill, and is steadily rising annually as more appliances and gadgets are purchased for the home.

The modlet is a patent-pending electricity conservation solution for homes and offices that eliminates wasteful energy use by automatically turning off power to your appliances when not needed. Appliances are plugged into the modlet which in turn is plugged into an existing electrical outlet. The modlet creates a schedule of "on" and "off" times, shutting off power at the plug and thus eliminating wasteful electricity use. These money-saving schedules can be viewed and modified through a computer's web browser. The firm recently announced that the Association of Energy Service Professionals (AESP) has recognized the coolNYC program with two energy awards: 1) Outstanding Achievement in Residential Program Design and Implementation; and 2) Outstanding Achievement in Pricing and Demand Response.

HEVO, Inc.

HEVO, Inc. (Hybrid & Electric Vehicle Optimization) is a Service Disabled Veteran Owned Small Business (SDVOSB) headquartered at the NYC ACRE. Founder and U.S. Army veteran, Jeremy McCool, launched HEVO in November 2011, while finishing his graduate degree at Columbia University. Built on the vision of creating the global standard for wireless charging, the mission of HEVO is to accelerate the adoption of electric vehicles through the deployment of a wireless charging network. By offering a wireless charging option for electric vehicles (EVs), HEVO will provide a safe, fast, and cost affordable charging method that eliminates the hazards and inconveniences associated with plug-in charging. To this end, HEVO Power and a team of engineers from NYU Poly have developed a wireless charging solution for commercial fleets to overcome such problems as driver error in remembering to plug in their vehicle, faulty connections between cords and vehicle charging terminals, cluttered sidewalks, and tangled loading bays. HEVO is unique because the proprietary wireless charging technology provides customers with faster charging rates while being comparable to plug-in stations in price and efficiency. HEVO has also created a telematics platform that integrates mobile devices with the wireless units—broadcasting charging station locations, availability, directional guiding support, and centralized billing for its customers and is preparing for commercialization of its first generation line which includes: a wireless charging station, wireless vehicle receiver, and an advanced mobile application.

HEVO initiated its Pathfinder Launch Program for EV manufacturers, fleets and municipalities to pilot its products over a 90-day period. They have successfully received multiple Letters of Commitment from select partners to participate in a pilot program that will allow its products to be sold through the partners' customer network and thus meet its 2014 sales projections (SeedInvest.com: accessed 2013).

Sollega, Inc.

Launched in 2009, Sollega, Inc.'s technology is based on its Solar PV Racking System. Their value proposition is three-fold: 1) simpler, faster assembly of solar arrays based on a different and better designed mounting system; 2) lower cost through reduced labor costs; and 3) lower risk for customers through an industry leading roof protecting design.

Sollega simplifies and accelerates the adoption of solar energy technologies by reducing the mounting and installation costs associated with solar arrays. The current growth in the solar market is decreasing the cost of solar modules (panels). Even if the modules were free, the total installation cost from current racking hardware and labor would still be too high to make solar power competitive with coal. Sollega partners include NYU-Poly, Industrial and Technology Assistance Corporation (ITAC), and NASA/Space Alliance Technology Outreach Program (SATOP).

Specifically, the product holds solar panels to roofs. Sollega manufactures the simplest solar mounting systems on the market, saving labor time and cutting overall project costs thereby decreasing the cost of solar energy and increasing the project return on investment (ROI). The system reduces labor costs by up to 50 percent; a significant portion of the total installation cost is labor. It uses off the shelf hardware, stacks for easy shipping and job site staging, and minimizes or eliminates roof penetrations. The product is made in the USA using recycled materials and is itself completely recyclable. The product is fully developed and production is being scaled to meet initial demand.

Sollega's competitive advantage is not only that their product is simpler, cheaper and easier to use, but also that the manufacturing process has both a low overhead and an inherently quick iteration cycle leading to the ability to innovate quickly. They also have strong ties to the solar industry through their partner company (Sustainable Energy Partners) allowing for the flexibility to adjust to changing market conditions. Finally, their target market and go-to-market strategy is unique. The domestic market for flat roof mounting systems is estimated at approximately $500 million. They are going after the market penetration on three distinct fronts: 1) direct to solar installers; 2) working with solar equipment distributors; and 3) working with other trades, especially roofing and electrical contractors.

DEVELOPING AN ENVIRONMENTAL SUSTAINABILITY STRATEGY FOR NEW AND EXISTING FIRMS: INTRODUCING THE sSWOT

A sustainability SWOT (or sSWOT) provides a new twist on the familiar strategic analysis framework. It can be used by a social enterprise to push the boundaries for their organization and how they can build a sustainability mindset and new products/services, processes, and ways to create additional value for the firm (beyond its social value and impact).

Specially, here are the following steps and questions you may want to consider in a sSWOT analysis:

1   What or who do you want to inform? This goes back to your core values, social value proposition, and theory of change discussed in earlier chapters. Having a

clear vision of what you would like to see happen and change from an environmental perspective will help drive your future decisions and exploit opportunities others have yet to confront.

2   What do you and others see changing? This is related to the first step but narrows down the specific environmental challenge you are addressing. It may be on innovations that reduce greenhouse gas emissions, water availability and quality, food availability and its impact on production, etc.

3   What are the environmental challenges that are impacting how you are operating and creating value for others? Examine the threats to your new firm across the value chain (consider how you may source your raw materials to production, distribution to final consumption). Investigate trends that may result in costs and customer preferences that can have an influence on how you finally produce and sell your product or service.

4   Beyond threats, what are the opportunities where there is a growing gap in which you and others can create new solutions for challenges within the environment? Examine new possibilities that have not previously existed and the types of changes that can re-invent business models and products/services to confront environmental change.

5   What are the unexpected ways you can use your core strengths to meet environmental challenges? Consider the talent of your team, your social value proposition, environmental credentials, supply chain relationships, and community and public partnerships that will allow you to use your strengths to address environmental challenges.

6   What are your weaknesses, vulnerabilities, obstacles, and risks that may make it difficult to address the environmental challenges? Consider a wide range of partners who may face similar risks within and outside your industry and how you can partner with them to overcome these risks.

7   Given your investigation of the opportunities, threats, strengths and weaknesses, what insights can influence your team, customers, and funders in investing in your business? These may be the insights that are clearly aligned with the environmental challenges identified and your social value proposition and key performance indicators. For example, you may present a new environmental idea, process, or product/service that creates opportunities for revenue growth, decreasing rising costs, attracting new customers and new markets, and increasing overall operational efficiency for your new firm.

8   What can we do to implement our new environmental idea, product/service, process in the near-term, mid-term, and long-term? What type of funding and changes in our current operations are necessary in the near-term? What partnerships, suppliers, and customers can be engage so that we can scale our environmental innovation to other locations and markets in the mid-term and long-term?

VOICES FROM THE FIELD

The World's First Solar Road Is Producing More Energy than Expected (used with permission)

In its first six months of existence, the world's first solar road is performing even better than developers thought. The road, which opened in the Netherlands in November of last year, has produced more than 3,000 kilowatt-hours of energy—enough to power a single small household for one year, according to Al-Jazeera America.

"If we translate this to an annual yield, we expect more than the 70kwh per square meter per year," Sten de Wit, a spokesman for the project—dubbed SolaRoad—told Al Jazeera America. "We predicted [this] as an upper limit in the laboratory stage. We can therefore conclude that it was a successful first half year."

De Wit said in a statement that he didn't "expect a yield as high as this so quickly".

The 230-foot stretch of road, which is embedded with solar cells that are protected by two layers of safety glass, is built for bike traffic, a use that reflects the road's environmentally friendly message and the cycling-heavy culture of the Netherlands. However, the road could withstand heavier traffic if needed, according to one of the project's developers.

So far, about 150,000 cyclists have ridden over the road. Arian de Bondt, director of Ooms Civiel, one of the companies working on the project, said that the developers were working on developing solar panels that could withstand large buses and vehicles.

The SolaRoad, which connects the Amsterdam suburbs of Krommenie and Wormerveer, has been seen as a test by its creators—a stretch of bike lane that, if successful, could be used as a model for more roads and bike lanes. The researchers plan to conduct tests of the road over the next approximately two and a half years, to determine how much energy the road produces and how it stands up to bikers. By 2016, the road could be extended to 328 feet.

Though the Netherlands' solar road seems to be going as planned, solar roads overall typically aren't as effective at producing energy as solar arrays on a house or in a field. That's because the panels in solar roads can't be tilted to face the sun, so they don't get as much direct sunlight as panels that are able to be tilted. However, solar roads don't take up vast tracts of land, like some major solar arrays do, and they can be installed in heavily populated areas.

One couple is set on making solar roads a reality in the United States. Scott and Julie Brusaw created an Indiegogo campaign last year to help fund their Solar Roadways project, and the campaign raised more than $2.2 million. The United States might have to wait a while to see solar roads installed, however. As Vox pointed out last year, cost could be a major barrier for solar road construction in the

United States. And according to a Greentech Media article from last year, one of the biggest things that officials still aren't sure about with the roads is safety. They want to be sure the roads can stand up to heavy traffic, and that the glass protecting the solar panels won't break. "We can't say that it would be safe for roadway vehicular traffic," Eric Weaver, a research engineer at the Federal Highway Administration's research and technology department, told Greentech Media. "Further field-traffic evaluation is needed to determine safety and durability performance."

QUESTIONS FOR "CONNECTING THE DOTS"

1 What do you think are some of the greatest environmental challenges facing our world today? Those facing your own community?
2 What is the "Tragedy of the Commons"? How is it present today? (Provide examples.)
3 Choose a green opportunity from the ones listed in the chapter. How would you go about launching this opportunity?
4 Discuss the importance of conducting a sSWOT analysis. Apply the guide to your own green opportunity identified in #3.
5 What advice and recommendations would you give the entrepreneurs who founded Solar Roadways? Do you think it is feasible? What do they need beyond funding to get their idea off the ground?

Case Study 11.1

Verdant Power: A Case of Ethical Leadership

It is the passion and the desire to empower people with electricity and clean water and the power to make decisions that keeps me up at night.
Trey Taylor, President & Head of Market Development

"It just isn't getting any easier even after almost 10 years!" mused Trey Taylor, President and Head of Market Development for Verdant Power (VP) in early January 2010. Once again, he and co-founder Ron Smith were faced with the need to approach US-based institutional investors for additional funding to continue managing their $34 million firm from the start-up phase through the next growth phase starting in mid-2010. And, the amounts involved were not trivial. VP estimated it needed $20 million in additional equity capital, as well as up to $50 million in project financing to complete its demonstration projects, license the world's first tidal energy and river projects, improve its technologies, build corporate capabilities and relationships as well as develop a portfolio of commercial projects. The problem as always was the different orientation of the investors from the vision and motivation of the company's management and founders.

What the investors never seemed to understand was the internally well-accepted dual mission of Verdant Power. Ron Smith, the firm's Chairman and Chief Executive Officer expressed the opinion shared by many VP employees and management:

> My motivations are a combination of business and social aspirations. My career orientation has never really been focused on getting extremely wealthy but more in the work and the creation of something unique.

VP had started with a vision to create renewable electricity generation using underwater turbines for small communities. While VP management was unanimous in adhering to this vision, its main focus for economic viability reasons had to be on the business challenges involved in commercializing marine renewable technology and generating a revenue stream to become a sustainable operation. Thus, the company was almost constantly in the process of funding, building and testing different technologies.

The company needed to raise money and attract investors. When presenting to institutional funders, VP, as a for-profit company, faced potential investors with very little interest in the firm's social aspect. Lenders wanted to hear that the sole objective is making money for them. Hence, Taylor and Smith constantly had to address the tension created between how an organization like VP communicated with the investment community and the firm's motivation, direction and objectives. If the investors thought management was not focused on making money, they could well choose not to invest. Making matters worse was the nemesis of any growth company—cash flow. VP has had to rely extensively on the founders' savings and government research grants to operate without having a revenue stream. The lack of profits has also made it hard for VP to approach private equity investors. Further, most government funds require matching funds which means that, even with government funding, VP has had to find private investors. Due to the uncertain financial returns based on the risks involved, most investors do not seem to want to invest in unproven technology; but they do invest in projects, which (importantly) implies that a reliable technology exists. Currently, almost all of VP's funding comes from grants that are dedicated to commercializing specific components and sub-components of its technology.

By commercializing its technology, the company hopes to have its systems used in communities worldwide and to empower citizens by providing a reliable and clean source of electricity. VP's management believes that access to local, reliable electricity will help developing countries grow, stimulating economic development and wealth creation. For example, access to affordable local reliable electricity would enable countries to set up cell phone towers, put computers in schools, and use satellite-accelerated Internet for distance learning and telemedicine. As Trey Taylor puts it:

> I think about Central Asian and African young girls. The reason they are not in school is because they spend a lot of time during the day gathering water and firewood. If instead, our systems could help pump clean water and electrify schools then these young girls could be in schools too.

Further, VP executives believe that not only are they developing multiple technologies and deploying them in arduous conditions, but that they and their competitors also may be paving a path to regulatory reform. The firm believes that the U.S. Congress and the Department of Energy must act to break a regulatory policy stranglehold on development and commercialization of clean technologies and that the Federal Energy Regulatory Commission (FERC) should grant a license to any such operation that plans to connect to the national electrical grid. However, many wave and tidal developers complain that the licensing process is tailored to much larger-scale energy projects, and provides unnecessary hurdles for experimental ventures such as VP.

Company Overview

The firm, founded in 2000 and headquartered in New York City, has positioned itself as a site and project developer that specializes in the design and application of marine renewable energy using proprietary kinetic hydropower technologies. VP's technology focuses on developing underwater turbines to generate and bring to market reliable energy from the natural water currents of rivers, tides and man-made channels. The company's Kinetic Hydropower Systems have been undergoing rigorous testing in New York City's East River since 2002. The project has progressed from an initial demonstration array of six turbines to a full field of turbines that produces more than 77MWh (megawatt hours) of grid-connected power—enough to supply electricity to approximately 175 homes. If operated continuously, the field has the potential to generate enough power for nearly 8,000 homes.[1]

In three phases, this project seeks to develop and deliver electricity using VP's Free Flow System. The electricity has been used to power facilities on Roosevelt Island at no charge as part of a community partnership and to optimize turbine spacing and power production. During the two-year (2006–2008) second phase, VP operated six full-scale turbines to demonstrate the Free Flow System as an efficient source of renewable energy. In 2010, a Pilot Commercial License was secured from the Federal Energy Regulatory Commission (FERC) to build-out the third phase to a 1 MW, 30-turbine array. This last phase must occur in consultation with both the State and City of New York and other federal agencies to provide clean, renewable power to the City. With FERC licensing, this is destined to become the world's first multi-unit commercial tidal energy facility.

VP is currently the only company demonstrating renewable energy production in a major population center. Once commercialized, the technology will be applicable for deployment in other sites around the world and in dense population centers. Other technology developers in the marine renewable industry are focused on utility scale (traditional industrial-sized), large ocean energy systems, which cannot be deployed at most population centers.

---

1 VP's East River community-based project is associated with the Roosevelt Island Tidal Energy (RITE) Project where the objective is to generate 10 megawatts of electricity from changing tidal flows using 300 underwater turbines. Despite its name, the East River is not a river but rather a tidal strait connecting Upper New York Bay on the south end with the Long Island Sound on the north end.

Technologies

VP's technologies for generating and distributing electricity can be situated wherever energy demand is high and flowing water is available. The systems can also be scaled up for use in deep-sea offshore locations where the strongest currents exist. VP's core technologies involve two kinetic hydropower systems—the *Free Flow System* and the *Rapid Flow System*.

Free Flow System (for Natural Waterways)

Resembling wind turbines, Free Flow System turbines are rotated by the currents of tides and rivers. In tidal settings, the turbines are designed to pivot 180 degrees to generate power on both the ebb and flood tides. In river settings, the turbines are stationary and generate continuous power from the unidirectional flow of the river. Installed underwater, the systems are invisible from shore and operate silently without the need for dams or other major civil works, and do not redirect the natural flow of the waterway.

The turbine rotors are designed to rotate at a slow and fixed speed over a wide range of water velocities making the system safe for fish passage and delivering steady, efficient electricity to the grid. The effect of the turbines on the river's aquatic life, particularly fish, and the regulations associated with environmental protection have been a major challenge for VP to address. The East River alone is home to an estimated 54 different fish species. Conventional hydro turbines, which turn at 600 to 700 rpm, are known to entrap and kill fish. VP claims that their slower turning turbines (32 rpm) allow fish plenty of time to avoid the system's moving parts.

The company had initially budgeted about $750,000 for fish studies but that number now runs into the millions of dollars. Unfortunately, very little direct research of tidal stream systems exists and most direct observations consist of releasing tagged fish upstream of the device(s) and direct observation of mortality or impact on the fish. A key aspect of the project's second phase was to identify any effects of the turbine array on the local environment and safe fish passage. VP's strategy has been to take a slow, multi-phase approach and collaborate with state and federal regulatory agencies as well as research institutions.

During this two-year demonstration period, VP conducted unprecedented monitoring activities and asked a local environmental group to participate and monitor alongside of them to corroborate the results. Although the results of these activities showed no evidence of increased fish mortality or injury, there are several interested parties questioning the practices and seeking further research and results. There are also concerns being expressed by several agencies about untested technology being implemented in the city's waters.

Rapid Flow System (for Constructed Waterways)

VP's Rapid Flow System is designed to generate electricity from flowing waters found in constructed waterways, including irrigation canals, aqueducts, wastewater facilities, and industrial plant channels. While the water in these man-made channels contains natural kinetic energy from continuously flowing water, it generally moves too slowly to generate power in a cost-effective manner. To compensate, VP's Rapid Flow System accelerates the velocity of the water just before it passes through a vertical-axis turbine.

The Rapid Flow System also allows for easy integration with water purification units. Thus, the Rapid Flow System can generate both clean energy and potable water from the same flow. After two years of extensive lab testing, VP is planning to launch a field demonstration project of this integrated water and clean energy system in a canal at Dow Chemical Company's Freeport, Texas facility.[2]

Projects

As of January 2010, VP had deployed seventeen tidal and river turbines in three locations in the United States and Canada. In addition, listed below are other key international operational milestones that the company has achieved:

1   Brazil—Working with both the Todo Trading Company and Future Trends global reports, VP has identified more than 1,000 diesel-powered generators in Amazon Basin villages.
2   China—American Sino Renewable Energy Development Program, on behalf of VP, has initiated favorable discussions with the Guangdong Electric Power Development Company for the development of projects in Guangdong and Hong Kong.
3   India—Through the International Clean Energy Alliance and Globally Managed Services India, an organization that specializes in customer relationship and advisory services, VP has developed interest from Indian states such as Gujarat and West Bengal for project development.
4   South Korea—With support from the Gyeongbuk Provincial Government, VP has a Memorandum of Understanding with the Institute of Renewable Energy and Environment for developing integrated offshore wind and tidal power systems to create the world's largest renewable energy industrial park.
5   New Zealand—New Zealand Trade and Enterprise is working with the company to help meet the country's goal of 90 percent of electricity production from renewable resources by the year 2025.
6   United Kingdom—UK Trade & Investment is working with VP and linking their collaborative efforts with the Department of Business Enterprise and Regulatory Reform as well as Scottish Development International, an organization that promotes international trade and encourages overseas companies to invest, to help the UK triple its renewable energy production within the next ten years.
7   Turkey—The Company has a Letter of Understanding (LOU) with the Society Development Corporation and its affiliate Havasu Enerji Sistemleri to develop projects in Turkey.
8   Malaysia—The Company has an LOU with GTS Power Ltd. for projects in Cambodia.

In North America, VP is working on three demonstration projects as a first phase toward deploying commercial projects which are set to begin in 2011. These projects and their main details are displayed in Exhibit 11.1.

2   Intellectual Property coverage for these technologies includes eight filed U.S. patent applications; international applications in Europe, Canada, and Japan; three disclosures in development; and twelve technical concepts in patent development.

Project Name	Location	Source, Capacity	Key Characteristics
RITE/ NAVY	East River; New York, NY and Puget Sound; Seattle, WA	Tidal Power, Projected 5MW Capacity	World's first grid-connected field of tidal turbines 80 MWh+ energy delivered to customers (first in world) 9,000+ operational hours (world leader) Partnerships with New York State, New York City, U.S. Department of Energy and U.S. Navy
CORE	St. Lawrence River; Cornwall, ON	River Power, Projected 15MW Capacity	Would demonstrate Free Flow System in river setting Commenced Verdant Power international operations Would demonstrate capacity factors more than double those of wind and solar (80–90%) Partnerships with Canadian Federal and Provincial Governments
ACE	Dow Chemical Plant Canal; Freeport, TX	Canal Power, Field (Beta) Test	Would demonstrate Rapid Flow System in field setting Would demonstrate highest capacity factors; triple those of wind and solar (90–100%) Partnership with Dow Chemical Company

EXHIBIT 11.1   Projects (North America)

Source: author-generated, based on the various interviews at VP.

Market Potential

VP plans to locate its projects near electrical load centers, i.e., major urban/industrial areas at suitable sites close to grid connections, generally in water depths of less than 35 meters. The firm has concentrated its development at ten sites with the greatest long-term potential in terms of sustained energy generation, first in North America and then in the UK. The ten projects are forecasted to have an installed capacity of 1 GW by 2018. The systems can also be used as base power for integrated and hybrid renewable energy systems when combined with wind and/or solar power and are scalable which greatly simplifies infrastructure, financial, and system planning, and leads to lower unit costs.

Coal, because of its abundant supply in the United States, has been largely relied upon to satisfy growing electricity demands. However, it is also the leading contributor of carbon dioxide and has been linked to climate change. To control the emissions from coal-fired power generation, carbon dioxide emission is likely to be charged a significant economic price in the foreseeable future. If the price is high, as some economic models suggest (from $50 to $100 or more per ton emitted), and if a liquid secondary market emerges for trading emission allowances, this could raise average energy prices by 30–60 percent or more. See Exhibit 11.2 for a comparison of fuel costs.

Recently, shale gas has emerged in the United States as a cheap new energy source with roughly half the carbon dioxide emissions of coal, which could significantly affect the electricity generation landscape. It may have the potential to drive the average energy prices much lower than the renewable energy companies project and could seriously impact the market for emissions allowance.

However, recent studies[3] have also revealed that shale gas, the product of a highly controversial extraction method called hydraulic fracturing ("fracking") brings with it a greater greenhouse gas impact potential than conventional oil, gas, and coal over a twenty-year period. It has also been suggested that fracking has led to minor earthquakes and tremors in and around the drilling sites.[4]

Considerable infrastructure is also required not only to extract the gas but also to transport it via pipeline to refineries. The construction of new pipelines in the United States is being hotly contested with opposition protestors taking the position that "all pipelines leak."[5] Overall, there appears to be considerable and on-going debate on the environmental and human health dangers of shale gas. Until it is resolved, it is anticipated that governments will continue to support the transition to safe, sustainable non-carbon fuel sources.

In 2009, the World Bank forecasted that, within the next forty years, there would be a $5 trillion global industry in renewable energy technology. Policies such as the Kyoto Protocol and aggressive renewable energy requirements have made sustainability a global imperative although in some cases governments, where the money for technology development is, have not acted accordingly. To support growth in the sector, public economic incentives have been adopted worldwide including Production Tax Credits, Investment Tax Credits, and grants seeking to advance sustainable technologies.

Total Addressable Market

The total addressable market for kinetic hydropower is estimated by the U.S. Department of Energy to be 250 GW. This figure comprises an estimated 63 GW from tidal, 137.5 GW from river, and approximately 50 GW from constructed waterways resources. Approximately 20 percent of this market is to be found in developed countries, VP's initial primary target market. The total North American market easily exceeds 25,000 MW and according to the New York State Energy Research and Development Authority, there is more than 1,000 MW of kinetic hydropower potential just within the state of New York.

A National Research Council Canada study concluded that: "a vast resource of energy exists in [Canada's] flowing waters. If [free-flow] devices currently under development prove sufficiently economical to place in the general areas identified by this study, then the impact on Canada's future energy demand could be very significant." This analysis

3 Howarth, R. et al., Methane and the greenhouse-gas footprint of natural gas from shale formations, Climatic Change Letters, in press.

4 See, for example, "Fracking Earthquakes: Injection Practice Linked to Scores of Tremors," Charles Choi, 8/6/12 accessible at http://www.livescience.com/22151-fracking-earthquakes-fluid-injection.html.

5 See, for example, "Keystone XL pipeline brings out the protest in locals," Molly Hennessy-Fiske, *Los Angeles Times*, 10/19/2012 accessible at http://www.wask.com/waskfm/news/nationworld/la-na-texas-pipeline-20121020,0,3186103.story?page=2.

		Supply Outlook (2005)	2005 Cost/kW Installed	Cost/kW (U.S. Cents) (2005)	Supply Outlook (2008)	2008 Cost/kW Installed	Cost/kW (U.S. Cents) (2008)
Coal	Fuel costs have risen by 30–50% over the past 2 years. Coal plant construction has doubled in 4 years. Financing of facilities impaired in the U.S. via major bank redlining, suspension of some U.S. Government loan guarantee programs, and environmental pressures at the State level	Plentiful	$1,500	4–6	Tightening	$3,000–$3,200	5–8
Natural Gas	Increasingly imported from more distant sources, at greater costs, including added transport, storage, processing facilities, and supply chain vulnerabilities. U.S. fuel prices hit a 2-year high in March 2008 at $10+, and kept increasing, while some competing LNG importing countries are signing new purchase contracts at $14–18.	Costs Escalating	$1,800–$2,000	5–7	Costs Escalating	$2,000–$2,200	7–11
Wind	Component scarcity seems the main immediate problem increasing system costs. Turbine costs are up $400/kW since 2001, resulting in higher delivered system costs. 85% of U.S. market now controlled by four firms. Listed prices do not reflect required additional transmission system upgrades (ranging up to an additional 50% of capital costs) to bring the wind energy from generation areas to ultimate users.	Sustainable	$1,400–$2,000	4.5–14	Sustainable	$1,800–$2,400	5.5–14
Solar	Increases in efficiencies have not resulted in meaningful reduced costs as global pricing competition pulls much of world production into selected high tariff areas. Shortages of materials have sustained high prices, while longer-term constraint is lack of adequate storage capacity.	Sustainable	$8,000–$8,750	20–38	Sustainable	$8,000–$8,750	20–38
Marine—current costs	Industry is at early stage with limited production volume and installation experience. The relatively current production costs are offset by various government mandates and incentives directed at renewables in general and marine renewables specifically, which reduce the effective costs to early adaptors to competitive levels.	Sustainable	$5,000–$7,000	15–26	Sustainable	$5,000–$7,000	15–26
Marine—future costs	Costs should decline 15–18% each time production volume doubles. Manufacturing consultants' "should cost" studies support these analyses.	Sustainable	$1,500–$4,000	5–11	Sustainable	$1,500–$4,000	5–11

EXHIBIT 11.2 Comparison of Fuel Sources

Source: The chart compares 2005 cost information as reported by the Energy Information Agency Annual Energy Outlook 2005) to Spring 2008 reports from industry and government sources.

continues: "for just three main river reaches in which consecutive cross-sections may be exploited, and for only thirteen tidal current cross sections, over 110 TWh/year (tetrawatt hours per year) of kinetic energy have been identified."[6] At an 80 percent capacity factor, this translates into more than 15,000 MW of potential installed capacity.

The potential for tidal power around the world may be even greater. The UK has allocated more than the equivalent of $100 million for the accelerated development of tidal power technologies, including construction of the European Marine Energy Center (EMEC) testing facility. The Carbon Trust estimates in its 2006 Future Marine Energy report that: "tidal stream energy could become competitive with current base costs of electricity within the economic installed capacity estimated for the UK, 2.8 GW." VP has identified more than 120 North American potential tidal locations, each with multiple development sites suitable for the company's systems.

Competition

VP is positioned between upstream conventional hydropower facilities (dam and run-of-river systems), and downstream kinetic hydropower (ocean energy technologies), including offshore tidal power and wave energy systems.

The majority of the ocean energy technologies are large, weighing in the tens of tons and measuring up to 30 meters in height at full scale. They also have much larger single unit capacities than VP's units, with several developers claiming that their single units will generate between 300 kW and 1–2 MW. However, to attain this output, they are designed to operate in depths of 35–45 meters, typically far offshore and/or in remote regions, thus requiring long transmission lines and highly specialized installation equipment and supporting infrastructure found only in more developed regions of the world. There appear to be five direct competitors to VP (see Exhibits 11.3 and 11.4). These competitors are all targeting tidal sites generally in water depths of more than 35 meters and at remote locations.

Three of VP's key competitors are based in the UK and benefit from both EU and UK governmental financial and technical support. In 2005, the UK government invested £50 million in a program to nurture wave and tidal projects through a combination of direct grant subsidies to developers, funding of a specialized test facility to accommodate field demonstrations of pre-commercial units, and regional and national resource assessment mapping and surveying. This financial advantage is complemented by a collaborative relationship with environmental regulators, which seems to have resulted in minimal environmental conflicts during the initial pre-commercial testing phase of the UK-based operating units. The combined financial, technical, and environmental assistance is an extraordinary advantage when compared to U.S. regulatory standards and, as a consequence, VP estimates its UK competitors have much lower development costs.

---

6 *An Evaluation of the Kinetic Energy of Canadian Rivers & Estuaries* was prepared for the National Research Council Canada, Hydraulics Laboratory, Ottawa, Ontario, Canada—March 1980.

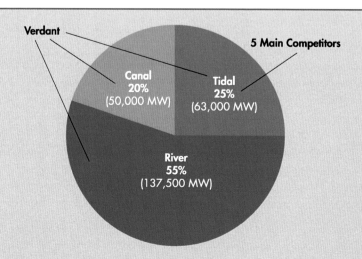

EXHIBIT 11.3   Total Addressable Market (Verdant Power vs. 5 Competitors)

Source: derived from U.S. Department of Energy, Ocean Energy Council (tidal), World Energy Council (river), and an estimate based on existing and planned constructed waterways (canal).

Competitor Name	Location
Marine Current Turbines (MCT)	United Kingdom
OpenHydro Group	Ireland
Clean Current Power	Canada
Lunar Energy	United Kingdom
Hammerfest UK	United Kingdom (formerly Norway)

EXHIBIT 11.4   Key Competitors

Organization

As of January 2010, the company employed twenty full-time employees and consultants with several vendors also dedicating additional full-time equivalents to company operations. The key personnel are listed in Exhibit 11.5. Once the technology has been commercialized, VP's management hopes to staff a position titled "Chief Social Officer." This person's primary responsibility will be to address the electricity needs of developing countries and communities and to work with the local communities worldwide to deploy VP systems.

   VP's organization is anchored around two main teams, an in-house Resource Assessment (RA) team and the Project Development (PD) team. Both teams help VP's efforts in expanding its capacity to identify and develop potential projects, to obtain needed equipment, and to secure government support for the Free Flow System and Rapid Flow System technologies. The RA team is tasked with identifying potential sites and guiding the selection of those locations that are the most promising. The PD team is charged with identifying and securing commitments for potential commercial build-outs.

Verdant Power is led by a seasoned management team comprising the following individuals:

Ron Smith: Co-founder, Chairman and Chief Executive Officer, leads both management and operations. He is also responsible for Verdant Power's internal regulatory compliance and permitting initiatives. He has led the development of successful start-ups and has held positions with Booz-Allen management consultants and Bendix Aerospace Group. He holds an MBA from Harvard Business School and an M.S. in Systems Management from USC.

William H. "Trey" Taylor: Co-founder, President and Head of Market Development, leads marketing and business development efforts. He was founder and President of the Interactive Marketing Institute and consulted with BGE (Baltimore Gas & Electric) and Price Waterhouse World Utilities Group, and has held senior marketing positions at Edison Electric Institute, ITT Corporation., British Telecom, Ogilvy & Mather, and Procter & Gamble. His graduate studies are in Urban Education at the University of Minnesota. He holds a B.S. in Political Science & History from Portland State University.

Kevin Lynch, CPA: Co-founder, Chief Financial Officer, manages finance, accounting, and purchasing activities. He also shares in direct project management oversight responsibilities. He has over twenty-five years' of experience in financial consulting with fast-growing companies.

Dan Costin, Ph.D., PE: Chief Engineer, formerly with Northern Power Systems, has twenty years' experience in design and analysis of mechanical systems; nineteen patents awarded for rotating equipment and wind turbine design; and has extensive project and functional management experience.

Dean Corren: Director of Marine Current Technology leads the development of kinetic hydropower systems. He has consulted on energy and technology and performed research on a wide range of energy technologies as a Research Scientist at New York University.

Mary Ann Adonizio, PE: Director of Resource Assessment, has more than thirty years' experience in power generation and transmission project engineering, development, and management for the electric utility industry and renewable energy projects. She has an extensive history in resource assessment and environmental analysis in the hydropower industry.

EXHIBIT 11.5 Principal Management Team and Governance

Source: based on information by VP's management.

Proposed Business Models and Projects

VP's management envisions 330 MW of operating projects by the end of 2016 and more than 1,000 MW by the end of 2018, all utilizing its proprietary technologies. Projects are developed with experienced owner/operators, who provide VP with significant cash flows to fund further project development and growth. The company's revenue model includes a continuation of grant funding from governments in the short term to offset a significant portion of demonstration project costs. VP forecasts that, as of 2012, net revenues from river and tidal projects as well as from licensing will begin to materialize. VP's time horizon and priorities analysis is presented in Exhibit 11.6.

VP plans to generate commercial revenue and profit from the development of river and tidal projects generating renewable electricity in North America and the UK as well as other international jurisdictions. It will license its proprietary technologies and know-how to power producers in selected international markets. When opportunities arise, it will sell its interest in completed projects and redeploy the proceeds towards additional project development.

Verdant Power Priorities, Plans, and Programs

Horizon 1: Extending and defending the core businesses—where most resources are focused.

Horizon 2: Building emerging businesses—where qualification, relationship building, and prototyping are typically used to prove out and refine (or reject) an initiative before it is absorbed into core operations.

Horizon 3: Creating viable options for the future—where other promising options are evaluated as possibilities for future development.

Within this framework, Verdant Power's current plan might be summarized as follows:

Horizon 1	Horizon 2	Horizon 3
Complete current round financing—$20 million equity; $50 million project	Qualify and initiate additional U.S. and Canadian Free Flow System Projects	Institutionalize project development and partnering for international commercial projects
Validate Free Flow Deployment/ Retrieval System (CORE Project —St. Lawrence River)	Establish UK corporate and project presence	Roll out Free Flow System River and Tidal Projects in selected country markets
Validate Submarine Cabling/ Anchoring System (Puget Sound)	Commercialize Navy Project	Roll out Rapid Flow System projects in selected country markets
Reduce Free Flow System costs via Generation 5 demonstration	Qualify additional country markets and Free Flow System Projects (Turkey, Brazil, India, China, etc.)	
Commercialize projects RITE Project CORE Project (2011) UK Project (2012)	Establish Rapid Flow System market strategy and supply chain	
Identify and develop strategic partnership for commercial projects	Establish supply chain and logistics for multiple international projects	
Analyze and develop supply chain	Prototype Rapid Flow System (ACE) at Dow Chemical	
Further assess North American sites plus UK market, resources and sites		
Target Time Lines 6–24 Months	*Target Time Lines 18–36 Months*	*Target Time Lines 24–60 Months*

EXHIBIT 11.6   Horizon-Priorities Analysis

Source: based on review of VP corporate documents.

Project Economics

VP's profitability is a function of its ability to assess, select, and permit attractive projects and build them in partnership with established project developers/owners. Exhibit 11.7 illustrates what a typical owner could expect in the near term, and over the next few years as technological improvements already in the company's development pipeline are introduced into the field.

	Current Status 2012–3 Niagara # 1	4–5 Years Out 2014 CORE Build-Out	6–7 Years Out 2017 Great Lake # 4
Gross Revenue (Ontario Standard Offer) in 3rd Production Year	$4,563.000	$18,250,000	$27,375,000
Project Size in MW	5	20	30
Capacity (in kW)	110	110	110
Capital Cost Required	$20,473,000	$56,081,000	$74,219,000
Cost per MW	$4,094,000	$2,804,050	$2,473,967
O&M/G&A Expense	$2,223,000	$6,465,000	$8,840,000
EBITDA in 3rd Production Year	$2,340,000	$11,785,000	$18,704,000
IRR: Assuming 50% Pre-Tax	5.9%	18.4%	21.8%

EXHIBIT 11.7 Cost and Revenue Projections of Current and Future Projects

Source: this information was provided by Ron Smith.

Cost Reduction Drivers

Current cost parameters are based on the company's experience in fabricating and installing a small number of handcrafted units in relatively shallow tidal areas. Key components of the overall capital cost structure include: (1) costs of manufacturing the turbine system, (2) costs to deploy and purchase cabling, (3) regulatory costs to obtain required permits and licenses, and (4) the actual net production of the systems. This last factor is influenced by the velocity of the underlying water resource, its depth (which may allow for larger turbine rotor sizes), and the duration of its flows.

Management has identified the following significant cost reduction drivers, which are the focus of current RD&D activities:

1   Economies of Scale—Cost reductions due to economies of scale are generally predicted to be 15–18% each time that volume doubles. Commencing in 2010, volumes are projected to more than double in each succeeding year.
2   Installation and Retrieval—The Company's design efforts are positioned to simplify and reduce the expense of initial deployment and subsequent maintenance.

3   Regulatory Costs—Regulatory costs associated with innovation are often burdensome, particularly in the United States. To address these issues, the company has been working with key regulatory agencies at both the federal and state levels that have resulted in a number of precedent-setting rulings and structural licensing improvements. In addition, greater emphasis has been placed on establishing projects in more advanced hydropower jurisdictions (e.g., Canada and the UK), while simultaneously continuing to develop hydro systems that operate in less regulated man-made waterways. The company has been mobilizing a larger coalition of industry supporters to fund more of the expense of longer-term reform efforts.

At the time of VP's investment round in August 2006, the company's valuation was approximately $33.8 million. The ownership of the company's fully diluted common shares/equivalents as of January 2010 is provided in Exhibit 11.8.

Share Holder	Number of Common Shares/Equivalents	Percentage of Share Held	Price Range
Management	16,610,232	40%	$.00–$1.25
Business Angels/Friends & Family	10,595,365	26%	$.15–$1.25
Tudor Investment Corp	8,822,606	21%	$.85
Employees/Consultants	5,366,076	13%	$.00–$1.25

EXHIBIT 11.8   Capitalization (as of January 2010)
Source: this information was provided by Ron Smith.

In Exhibit 11.9, VP's financial projections are presented. Net revenues represent contributions to overhead from various demonstration and commercial projects plus licensing. Only modest increases to overhead expenses are anticipated because a significant amount of the company's costs will be absorbed by the special purpose structures (investment companies) established for project development. These projections do not take into account other incentives available in many jurisdictions and advantageous to investors and project developers. These possible complementary revenue streams are described in Exhibit 11.10.

Future Developments

VP intends to apply the lessons it learned from the New York project and other field tests and incorporate them into the development of next-generation Free Flow Systems. The advancement to the next generation (Generation 5) focuses on overall parts reduction to facilitate commercial manufacturing and reduce maintenance costs. VP is also in the process of developing enhanced blade designs for its Free Flow System turbine in partnership with the U.S. Department of Energy, the U.S. National Renewable Energy Laboratory, and Sandia National Laboratories. The purpose of the redesign is to enhance structural strength and streamline manufacturing, as well as to scale up turbine rotors to 11 meters or more for use in deeper, faster waters.

Income Statements (Annual)

	2010	2011	2012	2013	2014	2015	2016
Project Contributions							
Net Revenues from Projects							
Demonstration Projects	-1,080,625	-251,520	240,000	360,000	360,000	360,000	360,000
Licensing, Royalties, Equip Sales & Cnsltg	—	—	7,865,600	8,225,600	6,622,800	6,962,800	7,362,800
River Projects	-625,000	645,000	1,020,000	142,108	5,996,776	4,759,477	9,537,213
Tidal Projects	-1,125,000	-562,500	2,040,000	402,341	5,666,364	12,589,702	30,169,338
Total Net Revenues from Projects	-2,830,625	-169,020	11,165,600	9,130,049	18,645,940	24,671,979	47,429,351
Overhead Expenses							
Research and Project Development							
Staffing	970,000	1,152,600	1,175,652	1,199,165	1,223,148	1,247,611	1,272,564
Travel, etc.	38,500	40,425	48,510	58,212	69,854	83,825	100,590
Computers, Software, Materials	30,600	31,212	37,454	44,945	53,934	64,721	77,665
Contingencies @ 15% of costs net of staffing	13,820	14,327	17,193	20,631	24,758	29,709	35,651
Total Research and Project Development	1,052,920	1,238,564	1,278,809	1,322,953	1,371,694	1,425,866	1,486,470
Marketing and Sales							
Staffing	476,500	567,630	578,983	641,500	654,330	667,417	680,765
Travel, etc.	33,000	34,650	41,580	49,896	59,875	71,850	86,220
Association Membership	20,400	20,808	24,970	29,964	35,956	43,147	51,777
Conferences, Trade Shows, etc.	45,900	46,818	56,182	67,418	80,902	97,082	116,498
Other	20,400	20,808	24,970	29,964	35,956	43,147	51,777
Contingencies @ 15% of costs net of staffing	22,943	24,617	29,540	35,448	42,538	51,045	61,254
Total Marketing and Sales	619,143	715,331	756,225	854,190	909,557	973,688	1,048,291

Operations

Staffing	1,192,500	1,460,250	1,503,500	1,533,570	1,564,242	1,595,527	1,627,437
Travel, etc.	58,200	61,710	74,052	88,862	106,635	127,962	153,554
Premises	171,324	174,750	209,701	251,641	301,969	362,363	434,835
Website & Communications	71,340	72,767	87,320	104,784	125,741	150,889	181,067
Computers, Software, Supplies, Equipment Rentals	80,896	87,410	102,013	122,416	146,899	176,279	211,534
Intellectual Property Maintenance	163,200	166,464	199,757	239,708	287,650	345,180	414,216
Consultants—Regulatory, Lobbying, Compliance	247,600	510,400	612,480	734,976	881,971	1,058,365	1,270,039
Legal	124,200	143,010	171,612	205,934	247,121	296,546	355,855
Accounting	44,800	47,040	56,448	67,738	81,285	97,542	117,051
Insurance	55,000	57,750	69,300	83,160	99,792	119,750	143,700
Fees—Capital Accounts	1,200,000	—	—	—	—	—	—
Contingencies @ 15% of costs net of staffing	194,841	264,260	316,537	379,844	455,813	546,975	656,370
Total Operations	3,603,901	3,045,811	3,402,720	3,812,633	4,299,118	4,877,378	5,565,658
Total Overhead Expenses	5,275,964	4,999,706	5,437,754	5,989,776	6,580,369	7,276,932	8,100,419
EBITDA	-8,106,589	-5,168,726	5,727,846	3,140,273	12,065,571	17,395,047	39,328,932
Depreciation	516692	465023	418521	376669	339002	305102	274591
EBIT	-8,623,281	-5,633,749	5,309,325	2,763,604	11,726,569	17,089,945	39,054,341
Interest Expense	164612	164612	164612	164612	164612	164612	164612
EBT (Earnings Before Taxes)	-8,787,893	-5,798,361	5,144,713	2,598,992	11,561,957	16,925,333	38,889,729
Taxes (30% after loss carry fwds)	0	0	0	0	0	966404	11666918.7
Net Earnings	-8,787,893	-5,798,361	5,144,713	2,598,992	11,561,957	15,958,929	27,222,810

Balance Sheets (Annual)

	2010	2011	2012	2013	2014	2015	2016
ASSETS							
Current Assets							
Cash	10,169,088	4,700,393	9,564,526	12,750,637	23,912,463	39,732,798	65,421,643
A/R	367,058	270,212	917,721	750,415	1,532,543	2,027,834	3,898,303
Prepaid Expenses	–	–	–	–	–	–	–
Inventory	–	–	–	–	–	–	–
Other currents assets	446269	446269	446269	446269	446269	446269	446269
Total Current Assets	10,982,415	5,416,874	10,928,516	13,947,321	25,891,275	42,206,901	69,766,215
Plant and Equipment (Net)	49,967	44,970	40,473	36,426	32,783	29,505	26,555
Other LT assets	5,116,956	4,605,260	4,144,734	3,730,261	3,357,235	3,021,511	2,719,360
Goodwill (Net)	–	–	–	–	–	–	–
Total Assets	16,149,338	10,067,105	15,113,724	17,714,008	29,281,293	45,257,917	72,512,130
LIABILITIES							
Current Liabilities							
Accounts Payable	672,613	440,410	388,818	431,962	474,957	526,552	588,465
Credit Card Accounts	32,559	32,559	32,559	32,559	32,559	32,559	32,559
Other Current Liab	896,876	896,876	896,876	896,876	896,876	896,876	896,876
Total Current Liabilities	1,602,048	1,369,845	1,318,253	1,361,397	1,404,392	1,455,987	1,517,900
LT Note	1,646,117	1,646,117	1,646,117	1,646,117	1,646,117	1,646,117	1,646,117
Total Liabilities	3,248,165	3,015,962	2,964,370	3,007,514	3,050,509	3,102,104	3,164,017
EQUITY							
Equity Capital	32,640,534	32,640,534	32,640,534	32,640,534	32,640,534	32,640,534	32,640,534
Retained Earnings*	-19,739,361	-25,589,391	-20,491,180	-17,934,040	-6,409,750	9,515,280	36,707,579
Total Equity	12,901,173	7,051,143	12,149,354	14,706,494	26,230,784	42,155,814	69,348,113
TOTAL LIABILITIES AND EQUITY	16,149,338	10,067,105	15,113,724	17,714,008	29,281,293	45,257,918	72,512,130

* includes other write-offs not documented in case

Cash Flow Statements (Annual)

	2010	2011	2012	2013	2014	2015	2016
Operating Activities							
Net Earnings	-8,787,893	-5,798,361	5,144,713	2,598,992	11,561,957	15,958,929	27,222,810
Depreciation	516,692	465,023	418,521	376,669	339,002	305,102	274,591
Working Capital Changes							
(Increase)/Decrease Accounts Receivable	-91,750	96,846	-647,509	167,306	-782,128	-495,291	-1,870,469
(Increase)/Decrease Inventories	—	—	—	—	—	—	—
(Increase)/Decrease Accounts Other Current Assets	—	—	—	—	—	—	—
Increase/(Decrease) Accounts Payable	-1,989,645	-232,203	-51,592	43,144	42,995	51,595	61,913
Increase/(Decrease) Other Current Liabilities	—	—	—	—	—	—	—
Net Cash Provided/(Used) by Operating Activities	-10,352,596	-5,468,695	4,864,133	3,186,111	11,161,826	15,820,335	25,688,845
Investing Activities							
(Increase)/Decrease Plant	—	—	—	—	—	—	—
(Increase)/Decrease Equipment	—	—	—	—	—	—	—
Net Cash Used in Investing Activities	—	—	—	—	—	—	—
Finance Activities							
Increase/(Decrease) Common Stock	20,400,000	—	—	—	—	—	—
Net Cash Provided/(Used) by Financing	20,400,000	0	0	0	0	0	0
INCREASE/(DECREASE) IN CASH	10,047,404	-5,468,695	4,864,133	3,186,111	11,161,826	15,820,335	25,688,845
CASH AT BEGINNING OF YEAR	121,684	10,169,088	4,700,393	9,564,526	12,750,637	23,912,463	39,732,798
CASH AT END OF YEAR	10,169,083	4,700,393	9,564,526	12,750,637	23,912,463	39,732,798	65,421,643

EXHIBIT 11.9 Financial Projections (2010–2016)

System Installations, Sales and Leasing

Verdant Power produces systems that generate renewable energy from tides, rivers, and manmade channels. The Company expects that total project construction revenues from the installation of these systems will exceed $1B U.S. through 2016 based on the installation of systems capable of producing 330 MW.

Electric Power Production

Verdant Power's technology and facilities produce renewable electricity—green power. The demand for green power has accelerated due to state and federal policies and the growth of voluntary green power purchase markets, along with the generally improving economics of renewable energy development.

Intellectual Property

Verdant Power presently has 12 patents pending, 6 additional patent disclosures, and 12 additional patentable concepts under consideration.

Renewable Portfolio Standards

These standards require local utilities to purchase renewable energy from producers like Verdant Power, at prices higher than otherwise, sometimes at a multiple of the wholesale market price for non-renewable energy.

Renewable Energy Credits

Renewable Energy Certificates are tradable environmental commodities in the U.S. that represent proof that 1 megawatt-hour (MWh) of electricity was generated from an eligible renewable energy resource. In states that have an REC program, Verdant Power is credited with one REC for every 1,000 kWh or 1 MWh of electricity it produces.

Revenue Support/Feed-in Tariffs

A Revenue support/feed-in tariff is an incentive structure that encourages the adoption of renewable energy through government legislation.

Federal and State Income Tax Credits

Federal and State income tax credits have been a significant stimulus to renewable energy investment in the U.S. for over 30 years. State credits, although sometimes limited because of more restricted investment pools, can also provide instant refunds of up to 33% of total project capital costs.

Carbon Emissions Trading

Carbon (CO_2) makes up 77% of the Green House Gasses thought to be responsible for global climate change. Thus, carbon finance is emerging as a vast global marketplace providing incentives and mandates for pollution reduction and direct boons for new renewable energy technologies.

Capacity Payments/Capital Cost Buy-Downs

Capacity payments/Capital Cost Buy-Downs are available in many jurisdictions under varying parameters, ranging up to approximately 25% or more of the initial capital costs of the installed system, depending on project size, location, and technology.

Subsidized R&D Support

Subsidized Research and Development Support is another area of growing significance in North America. The net effect reduces technology development costs to the private sector, generally with no permanent reciprocal obligation to the funder.

EXHIBIT 11.10 Complementary Revenue Streams Summary

Source: based on data provided by VP Management.

During the next five years, VP plans to build two demonstration and ten multiple-phase commercial projects with the goal to further refine its technology and project development capabilities for commercial operations. Exhibit 11.11 provides a summary of the VP's plan to realize its initial goal of 330 MW of installed capacity in North America and the UK. This project pipeline reflects the company's plan for scale up, production design, and manufacturing of the Free Flow System. (The Rapid Flow System is sidelined to beta tests.)

	2011	2012	2013	2014	2015	2016	Total
Tidal	0	5	10	50	30	155	250
River	3	2	5	5	35	30	80
Canal	0	0	0	0	0	0	0
Total	3	7	15	55	35	185	330

EXHIBIT 11.11 2011–16 Project Pipeline (in MW)

Source: this information was provided by Ron Smith.

Future Challenges

One of the remaining barriers to the marine renewable industry, in addition to technology troubles and high capital requirements, is the cumbersome regulatory process. The FERC is yet to approve VP's invitation to create a three-to-five-year study license for new technology. There is a significant danger that the marine renewable energy industry will not be successful in the United States due to adversarial and exceedingly risk-averse regulatory policies. VP has spent more money on environmental studies and assessments than it has on building products or developing technology.

For example, as part of obtaining a demonstration permit, VP had to conduct numerous studies, including: benthic habitat characterization; a water quality assessment; an East River hydrodynamic survey; a mobile hydro-acoustic survey; a fixed hydro-acoustic survey; an assessment of impacts on any rare, threatened, or endangered fish species; a biological survey of the East River; a recreational resources assessment; a navigational and security assessment; and a historical resources assessment. VP was required to complete these studies before even approaching the FERC with an application for a license to build and operate a commercial scale project in the East River.

In contrast, countries such as Canada and the UK have established what seem to be considerably more favorable policies. VP and its competitors also claim to be able to obtain funding from Canada much faster and more easily than from the United States.

THOUGHT QUESTIONS

Both Trey Taylor and Ron Smith believe they have ensured that VP possesses an explicit, multidimensional, and well-documented strategy for revenue generation and growth. They understand that to achieve VP's social goals and bring its ideas to fruition, it is important to be commercially successful and to generate revenue. Its operations must be effective and it must invest for further growth.

Trey knew that he and Ron had to come up with a convincing pitch on why U.S.-based institutional investors would want to trust them with as much as $70 million. In their view, the key to the argument had to lie not only in addressing the fact that VP had a proven technology implying that there was demand for their product, but also that the environmental sustainability resulting from VP's commercialization of renewable energy would lead to increasing demand and thus profits in the future. That is, they had to convince potential investors that VP's competitive advantage lay in having an economically viable, scalable technology that was also environmentally friendly.

Trey and Ron also anticipated the problem of having to address whether or not to continue operating in the rigidly regulated U.S. market. Would the investors in the short run and VP's long-term social goals be better served by moving operations to a friendlier operating environment such as Canada or the UK? For that matter, should the firm more aggressively pursue its social goals by approaching governments in the developing world or international institutions such as the World Bank directly? Finally, given the internally well-accepted dual mission of VP, did Trey and Ron have an ethical duty as leaders of the VP to prioritize the firm's operating goals? Were the social objectives really more important and immediate than their fiduciary responsibility towards shareholder wealth maximization? Do the social objectives and their fiduciary responsibilities really compete?

REFERENCES

AlaskaDispatch.com (2011). http://www.adn.com/article/global-cleantech-cluster-association-names-new-york-city-startup-rentricity-global-top-10-list Accessed October 23, 2014.

Green Brands Survey (2011). http://www.cohnwolfe.com/en/ideas-insights/white-papers/green-brands-survey-2011 Accessed October 23, 2014.

State of Green Business Report (2012). https://www.greenbiz.com/research/report/2012/01/state-green-business-report-2012 Accessed October 23, 2014.

State of Green Business Report (2014). https://www.greenbiz.com/research/report/2014/01/19/state-green-business-report-2014 Accessed October 23, 2014.

The Social Entrepreneurship Support Ecosystem

AIM/PURPOSE

The purpose of this chapter is to introduce the concept of the support ecosystem for social entrepreneurship. The origin and nature of such support ecosystems is discussed. The types of entrepreneurship support organizations that constitute an ecosystem are explored. Moreover, a strategy for being intentional and systemic in assembling an ecosystem is presented.

LEARNING OBJECTIVES FOR THIS CHAPTER

1. To understand the value and importance of social entrepreneurship support ecosystems.
2. To grasp the conceptual underpinnings of support ecosystems and the issues they are meant to address.
3. To recognize the types of organizations that are part of an ecosystem.
4. To understand the importance of systemic linkages between support organizations and how to foster those linkages.

We begin this chapter with a story intended to illustrate the importance of support for entrepreneurs from the context, or community, of which they are a part. This is a story about a professor of entrepreneurship who was invited to a university in the United States to talk with various units across campus about entrepreneurship and how it might benefit them.

The professor started his day in the College of Fine Arts. The students and faculty he talked with were very enthusiastic about both the possibility of creating businesses around their art and the creativity and innovation that entrepreneurial thinking engenders. They were brimming with ideas for arts-based enterprises. The students of the School of Nursing, though a bit more reserved, were equally enthusiastic about what entrepreneurship could do for their professional and personal ambitions. The professor was met with a similar reception in the School of Engineering, and this carried on throughout the day until he made his final visit.

The last conversation of the day was with twenty-five–thirty students in the School of Business, specifically in the Entrepreneurship Program. The students were subdued. The professor, thinking that this might be due to the late-afternoon timing of the meeting, quickly tried to engage them. He asked them what he thought was a benign question: "How many of you are planning to start a business?" Only two hands went up. The professor was surprised and asked those who had not raised their hands why this was so. Repeatedly, the answer was that these students of entrepreneurship were afraid that if they started a business, they would have to do it alone, without any support. With growing sadness, the professor tried to assure them that, in fact, there are many forms of support for entrepreneurship and that successful entrepreneurs never pursue their goals alone, but he couldn't help but feel that the cause was already lost. How was it that students of entrepreneurship, the people within the university who should know the field best, were the least enthusiastic and optimistic about its application?

On the flight home, the professor reflected on his experience. He thought about how, too often, entrepreneurship education is about agency—the opportunity recognition process of the individual, the preparation of a business model or business plan for the enterprise, the daunting pursuit of financing—as though entrepreneurs operate in isolation from their context. Is it any wonder that many entrepreneurship students feel disconnected and alone? The professor vowed that upon returning to his home university, he would advocate for and develop the inclusion of coursework that would inform entrepreneurship students of all of the assistance that their community provides them with, how to find it and use it effectively, and how to be successful at building the networks that are essential to efficacious entrepreneurship. Because, the fact is that entrepreneurs need never work alone. There is always a "community of support," if you know where to look.[1]

This is no less true for social entrepreneurs. In fact, because social entrepreneurs serve stakeholders that include the community and compete for resources (not customers), which tends to foster cooperation with their peers and others, they are arguably even more attached to their context. In Chapter 2 of this text, we discussed Mair and Noboa's (2006) model of intention formation, in which they observe that in order for social entrepreneurs to perceive that they can successfully

---

1 This is a fictional story, but is representative of the authors' composite experiences relative to the dearth of coverage of community support for entrepreneurs in entrepreneurship education.

pursue their mission they need to believe they have social support. So, in this spirit, we offer this chapter on the support ecosystem of social entrepreneurship.

SUPPORT ECOSYSTEMS

In recent years, there has been a growing interest in *entrepreneurial ecosystems*. The term comes, of course, from the field of ecology and refers to the "habitat" of which entrepreneurs are a part. This habitat has been defined in different ways. Arguably, the work of Porter (1985) and others on "industry clusters" was an early way of thinking about the business ecosystem, with its focus on the geographic coalescence of suppliers, manufacturers, and distributors. In the mid-1990s, Feldman (1994) introduced the concept of an "innovative infrastructure," with both hard (e.g., utilities, transportation, and broadband) and soft (organizations that support entrepreneurs, accommodating government, and colleges/universities that produce ideas and a skilled workforce) elements that supported entrepreneurial activity. Richard Florida's 2002 book *The Rise of the Creative Class* suggested that successful innovative communities were diverse, attractive, welcoming, and supportive of educated individuals who drive the knowledge economy.

The concept of the "entrepreneurial community," another perspective on the entrepreneurial ecosystem, came into good currency about this time. The Edward Lowe Foundation (2002) identified five characteristics of entrepreneurial communities:

1   a culture of support in the community—the community is diverse, open to new ideas, and freely shares information;
2   a beneficial infrastructure—in the spirit of Feldman's (1994) "innovative infrastructure," this includes such features as a college/university, Internet access, and an effective transportation system;
3   a supportive government—a local government that is flexible and supportive of business activity;
4   extensive networking—networks between entrepreneurs and between entrepreneurs and resource providers; and
5   a variety of financial capital sources—multiple sources of both debt and equity capital.

The W.K. Kellogg Foundation included these and the introduction of entrepreneurship into the school system in their definition of an entrepreneurial community (Dabson et al., 2003).

Lichtenstein, et al. (2004, pp. 6–7) define "entrepreneurial communities" as engaging in specific behaviors that can be categorized as follows: (1) a "critical mass" of entrepreneurs engaged in market-producing or renewing activities; (2) a distinct "community" of entrepreneurs within this critical mass of activity that is identifiable to the larger community or region; and (3) entrepreneurial thinking and acting by all members of the community—nonprofit, private, and public—that fosters creativity and innovation. These authors further argue that entrepreneurial communities are best built by creating a *system* of support, tailoring the system created to the specific culture and needs of the community, placing the focus of the system on the development of entrepreneurs as opposed to businesses, developing new roles and tools that assist with the community-wide incubation of entrepreneurs, and operating the system as an enterprise, the product of which is the economic transformation of the community.

In very recent years, the Ewing Marion Kauffman Foundation of Kansas City, Missouri, with a mission of promoting entrepreneurship, has popularized the term "entrepreneurial ecosystem." They have undertaken a major effort to identify cities around the world that are successfully fostering entrepreneurship and the factors that are contributing to that success. These factors often include helpful government policies, entrepreneurship support initiatives (e.g., business incubators, co-working sites, competitions, and so forth), and entrepreneur networks, among others. The Foundation has even created a multi-media channel, called ID8 Nation, on its website (entrepreneurship.org) that documents these ecosystems (Kauffman Foundation, 2014).

Whether they are called "entrepreneurial communities" or "entrepreneurial eco-systems," it is clear that these communities of support for entrepreneurship share several common characteristics. They are systemic, placing the focus on the entire environment in which entrepreneurs operate. As such, they emphasize networking among the key players in the environment, including and especially the entrepreneurs. They require that everyone in the system—businesses, government, and NGOs—is thinking and acting in support of entrepreneurship. They involve an infrastructure that provides financial, human, physical, and social capital to the context's entrepreneurs. Perhaps most importantly, these systems give form to the importance of context, and not merely agency, to successful entrepreneurship.

APPLYING THE ECOSYSTEM CONCEPT TO SOCIAL ENTREPRENEURSHIP

In his seminal book *How to Change the World*, David Bornstein (2007, p. 3) observed, "One of the most important things that can be done to improve the state of the world is to build a framework of social and economic supports to multiply the number and the effectiveness of the world's social entrepreneurs." Interestingly, Bornstein makes this assertion immediately following a discussion of the heroic agency of these individuals. His point is that society should be supporting these remarkable people, but in making this statement, he is also acknowledging that social entrepreneurs' agency is not sufficient if the world is serious about scaling social good. We need to create support ecosystems for social entrepreneurs.

However, what should such ecosystems look like? Are the needs of social entrepreneurs distinct enough that they require their own ecosystem, or can the same ecosystems that support business entrepreneurs support them? These are not simple questions to answer, nor should they be treated as such. As was noted in Chapter 2, there are unique aspects to social entrepreneurship including its mission focus, high level of accountability to a broad group of stakeholders, and requirement that it mediate at the crossroads of the business and social sectors. Yet, successful social entrepreneurs must also possess business skills. These waters are being further muddied by the rise of for-profit social enterprises, discussed in Chapter 6.

Perhaps answering these questions is not clear-cut and requires hybrid thinking. It could be that success lies in using business entrepreneurship ecosystem approaches, modified to reflect the unique needs of social entrepreneurs. This immediately raises the question, "What are the needs of social entrepreneurs?"

Lichtenstein and Lyons (1996) attempt to answer this question by developing an assessment tool for diagnosing the needs of business entrepreneurs (see Figure 12.1). They argue that entrepreneurs' needs can be defined by the intersection of two variables: the resources required for success and obstacles to getting and/or using those resources. They place these required resources into four broad categories: (1) business concept—a viable idea around which a profitable business can be built; (2) physical resources—physical, human and financial forms of capital; (3) core competencies/skills—the broad range of skills necessary to successfully operate a business (think: the skills one learns in business school); and (4) market—all aspects of a market including customers, customer relationship, distribution channels, and so forth.

Lichtenstein and Lyons (1996) identify nine categories of obstacles that can either obstruct an entrepreneur's ability to acquire these resources or impede her/his use of them once they are acquired. These include: (1) a lack of availability—the resource does not exist in the entrepreneur's context; (2) a lack of visibility—the resource exists, but the entrepreneur doesn't know of its existence; (3) a lack of affordability—the resource is unaffordable to the entrepreneur; (4) transaction barriers—these are nonfinancial obstacles such as government licenses, and regulations, cultural differences, gender issues, and the like; (5) a lack of self-awareness—the entrepreneur doesn't know what he/she doesn't know; (6) lack of accountability—either not being willing to take a high level of responsibility or not knowing how to do so; (7) emotional obstacles—false pride, self-doubt, and many more; (8) a lack of capability—not being able to effectively use and manage a resource once it is acquired; and (9) a lack of creativity—the inability to identify new ideas/opportunities or develop solutions to challenges.

When these two variables are brought together, as they are in Figure 12.1, they permit the entrepreneur, or a support provider, to assess specific obstacles to

Required resource	Obstacles								
	1 Availability	2 Visibility	3 Affordability	4 Transaction Barriers	5 Self-awareness	6 Accountability	7 Emotions	8 Capability	9 Creativity
1. Business concept: Idea for product or service									
2. Physical resources: Supplies/raw materials, space, equipment/plant, money/capital									
3. Core competencies/skills: Managerial, technical/operational, financial, legal, administrative									
4. Market: Product or service, customers, distribution channels, Transportation									

FIGURE 12.1 Entrepreneurial-needs Diagnostic Matrix

Source: Adapted from Gregg A. Lichtenstein and Thomas S. Lyons, *Incubating new enterprises: a guide to successful practice* (Washington, D.C.: Aspen Institute, 1996). Copyright © ICMA 2010. Used by permission.

specific resource requirements. This enables a more precise intervention(s) for addressing the need.

Arguably, this tool could be readily applied to assessing the needs of social entrepreneurs as well. The business concept is the solution to the social problem the social entrepreneur is addressing through her/his mission. Physical resources are very similar. The differences are not so much in the required resources themselves, but in the interventions. There may be a few specialized core competencies/ skills that are required of social entrepreneurs, such as grant-writing skills, non-profit budgeting skills, and the like. Market resources are also similar. Customers may be called "clients" or "beneficiaries," but social entrepreneurs still need people to serve, information on those people, mechanisms for maintaining relationships with them, and channels through which they can deliver their products/services to this market. Lichtenstein and Lyons's (1996) obstacles appear to be universal to all entrepreneurs.

Once a tool like this one is used to identify the needs of the community's entrepreneurs, existing support assets can be allocated efficiently and effectively. Gaps in assistance can also be readily identified. Support assets can be "mapped" by the obstacles to getting and using required resources that they best address. This, in turn, permits the community to think systemically about its support ecosystem.

POTENTIAL ASSETS IN A SUPPORT ECOSYSTEM

Business entrepreneurship support ecosystems typically include nonprofit, private and public entrepreneurship support organizations (ESOs). Among these are accounting firms, angel capital investors, banks, business coaching practices, business consultancies, business incubators, business plan/pitch competitions, co-working facilities, entrepreneur networks, law offices, mentoring programs, micro-lenders, micro-enterprise developers, one-stop business centers, and venture capital investors, among others. In general, these ESOs provide technical (business development) assistance and/or financial (debt and equity capital) assistance.

While such support ecosystems for social entrepreneurship are still evolving and not yet as complete as those for commercial entrepreneurship, they do exist, particularly in more urban communities. In some cases, social entrepreneurs can avail themselves of the assistance provided by ESOs that traditionally help business entrepreneurs. For example, the Baruch College Small Business Development Center (SBDC) in New York City offers free business counseling to social entrepreneurs and evening seminars tailored to their needs. In other instances, new programs and organizations have been created specifically in support of social entrepreneurship.

Sometimes, these support activities are broad-based and provided by municipal government. In a study of U.S. cities with populations over 50,000, Korosec and

Berman (2006) found that almost 75 percent of these communities provided help to social entrepreneurs by heightening public awareness of the social problems they were trying to solve, assisting them with the implementation of their programs, offering aid in locating resources, and connecting them with other organizations that could help in the pursuit of their mission. However, most support for social entrepreneurs is much more narrowly focused.

SOCIAL ENTREPRENEURSHIP INCUBATORS/ ACCELERATORS

One of the most popular forms of support for social entrepreneurs is the incubator for start-up social enterprises. This concept comes from the local economic development world, where it is used as a tactic in a strategy to foster community economic development through nurturing the creation and growth of small for-profit businesses. As the term "incubator" implies, these facilities support fledgling businesses until they are strong enough to operate on their own. Typically, this is a period of about three years (Koven & Lyons, 2010).

True business incubators tend to offer a range of services to their client entrepreneurs. These have been called "full-service incubators." Their package of services commonly includes: (1) space for business operations that can be expanded or reduced based on need, making it appropriately affordable; (2) business services (reception, access to the Internet, photocopying, etc.) that can be shared by all of the businesses in the incubator, thereby reducing costs; (3) business development services that can include access to information, counseling, training, and coaching; (4) assistance in finding financing; and (5) the opportunity to network among entrepreneurs operating within the incubator facility (Koven & Lyons, 2010). At some incubators, the networking opportunity has evolved into the provision of "co-working space," which allows entrepreneurs to gather to share ideas, experiences, information, and mutual support. More is said about co-working later in this chapter.

Another variation on the business incubator model is the business accelerator. In the commercial entrepreneurship environment, an accelerator is an incubator that attempts to speed up a start-up's development process by intensively infusing resources, such as venture capital. The time of incubation is greatly reduced. This tactic is used mostly with high technology businesses that require substantial early investment to support research and development. It also tends to be more successful when the entrepreneurs involved are highly experienced and the company has great potential for rapid scaling.

These basic incubation and acceleration models have been applied to fostering social ventures as well (see Table 12.1). An example is the Propeller Incubator in New Orleans. Propeller provides nonprofit and for-profit social entrepreneurs and

Table 12.1
Selected Social Entrepreneurship Accelerator and Incubator Programs World-wide

Program	Location
Agora Accelerator	Managua, Nicaragua
Artemesia	São Paulo, Brazil
Benetech Labs	Palo Alto, CA, USA
Bethnal Green Ventures	London, UK
Beyond Business	London, UK
Blue Ridge Foundation	New York, NY, USA
Canadian Cleantech Accelerator	San Jose, CA, USA
Catalyzer Startup Accelerator	Hyderabad, India
Centre for Innovation, Incubation and Entrepreneurship	Ahmedabad, India
Centre for Social Innovation	Toronto, Canada, and New York, NY
Change Accelerator	Newport and Providence, RI, USA
Dasra Social-Impact	Mumbai, India
Emerge Venture Lab	London, UK
Fledge, the "conscious company" Accelerator	London, UK
GoodCompany Ventures	Philadelphia, PA, USA
Greenstart Accelerator	San Francisco, CA, USA
GSBI Accelerator	Santa Clara, CA, USA
Hub Ventures	San Francisco, CA, USA
Hult Price	Boston, MA, USA
Imagine H2O Prize Competition and Accelerator	San Francisco, CA, USA
Impact Engine	Chicago, IL, USA
Investment Accelerator Fund	Ontario, Canada
Kick, "our" Incubator	Multiple locations
Matter Media Entrepreneurship Accelerator	San Francisco, CA, USA
NYC Acre	New York, NY, USA
Ogunte Make a Wave Pre-Incubator Program	London, UK
Panzanzee	Chicago, IL, USA
Pipa	Rio de Janeiro, Brazil
Praxis Accelerator Program	Chicago, IL, USA
Propeller	New Orleans, LA, USA
Rock Health	San Francisco, CA, UK
Rural Technology Business Incubator	Chennai, India
Sidekick School	London, UK
Social Impact Lab	Berlin, Germany
Social Entrepreneurs of New Orleans (SENO)	New Orleans, LA, USA
Social Innovation Camp	Multiple locations

Program	Location
Startl Accelerator	New York, NY, USA
StartX Accelerator	Palo Alto, CA, USA
The Unreasonable Institute	Boulder, CO, USA
Tummi Urban Ventures Accelerator	San Francisco, CA, USA
Unltd India	Mumbai, India
Venture Greenhouse	San Rafael, CA, USA
Villgro	Chennai, India
Village Capital	Atlanta, GA, USA
Young Foundation Accerator	London, UK

Sources: www.innov8social.com/2011/10/start-up-accelerator-and-incubator.html and http://quora. com/Are-there-any-social-entrepreneurship-incubators-or-accelerator-programs.

foundations with shared workspace and meeting facilities, which it rents (Propeller, 2014). Panzanzee in Chicago is a social enterprise incubator that provides workspace, help with developing business concepts and strategies, funding, and business model development. It also sponsors peer group meetings and other networking events. It regularly hosts an event called "Raise the Barn," at which a selected entrepreneur is asked to pose a challenge and invited entrepreneurs, business people and investors try to brainstorm a solution that blends economic value and social mission (Panzanzee, 2014).

The nonprofit reSET, the Social Enterprise Trust, is located in Hartford, Connecticut and is dedicated to promoting and supporting social enterprise. It does so using several approaches including offering co-working space, operating a social enterprise accelerator, hosting an entrepreneur-in-residence, holding an annual pitch competition, and housing a design lab (Social Enterprise Trust, 2014).

The Social Enterprise Accelerator in the reSET program offers a useful example of the accelerator model. It aims to help social entrepreneurs develop innovative models to create economic and social value, test their business assumptions, and build a strong business model. It uses Lean Start-up principles and methodology (see Chapter 4), focusing on customer engagement as the most effective way to build a business. The Accelerator consists of a fifteen-week program that offers the following (Social Enterprise Trust, 2014):

1 four months of co-working membership;
2 participation in reSET's network;
3 collaborators to help with meeting financial and social impact goals;
4 access to professional staff and advisers at reSET; and
5 opportunity to learn from outside speakers, including successful entrepreneurs, in peer-group sessions.

In an effort to qualify applicants for admission to the Accelerator, reSET emphasizes a high level of commitment to their social business and pursuing its mission, a strong business concept, and commitment to full participation in the accelerator program. It charges participants a $1,025 program fee and makes scholarships available (Social Enterprise Trust, 2014).

Case Study 12.1

Centre for Social Innovation, New York City

An example of the business incubation concept as applied to social entrepreneurship is the Centre for Social Innovation (CSI) located on the west side of Manhattan Borough in New York City, in the Chelsea neighborhood. It is a branch of the original Centre for Social Innovation founded in Toronto, Ontario, Canada in 2004. In fact, CSI, New York City is the third branch of the original and the first located outside of Toronto.

CSI, New York City opened in May 2013, in a 24,000 square feet space in the historic Starrett-Lehigh Building. It follows the classic business incubation model of fostering resource and risk pooling for small, start-up enterprises by providing affordable space, shared basic business services, access to technical/business development assistance, help with obtaining financial resources, and an environment that fosters networking (Koven & Lyons, 2010). As such, CSI facilitates collaboration among mission-driven enterprises and their leaders (entrepreneurs) in order to lower their overhead costs and enhance their ability to launch successfully.

Affordable Space

The CSI facility is divided into open-concept desk space and enclosed offices for client social entrepreneurs. Space is variably priced by its type. A place at a shared desk (called a "hot desk") ranges from $125 per month to $400 per month. Hot desk space varies by the hours per month the space may be used and the hours of meeting room time permitted. For example, a Hot Desk 25 package gives the social entrepreneur 25 hours per month during which to utilize the desk space and two hours of meeting room access; whereas, a Hot Desk Unlimited package lets the entrepreneur use the shared desk as often as he or she likes during the month and gives them five hours of meeting room access. A private desk (open space, not shared) is the social entrepreneur's to use for the entire month, along with seven hours of meeting room access, for $450/month. CSI offers an open space concept option for teams as well. The "Team Cluster" package is a dedicated table for up to six team members and seven hours of meeting room access. This type of space starts at $1,050 per month. A private office package starts at $1,200 per month. It is enclosed and dedicated space and includes eight hours of meeting room access (nyc.socialinnovation.org).

These rates are reasonable when compared to office space on the wider New York City market; however, for those social entrepreneurs for whom these prices may pose a challenge, CSI permits substituting volunteer time at the Centre for rent. CSI also puts on a competition, called "Agents of Change," that provides free use of space for 20 winners (Cunniffe, 2013). Similar to many other business incubators, CSI has an option for those social innovators who either do not need space or who do not want it. These clients are called "members" and receive discounted meeting room space, access to CSI's online network, and invitations to special events held at the Centre. Membership costs $30 per month. In business incubation parlance these members are known as "affiliates"—client entrepreneurs who work outside the facility but can enjoy the other benefits provided by the incubator. All of these packages afford the client social entrepreneur 24/7 access to the facility (nyc.socialinnovation.org).

Shared Business Services

Shared business services are basic amenities that support business activity. Because they are shared among CSI's many clients, they can be provided at a lower cost than the same services purchased by an individual enterprise on the open market. This is an example of the chief advantage of resource pooling.

CSI offers access to copiers and printers, audio-visual equipment, and the Internet. In addition, clients may use the facility's kitchen and other common areas. All of these shared services are built into the space rental packages. Clients can also rent additional meeting room access at member rates (nyc.socialinnovation.org).

While rental/shared business service fees do not cover all of CSI's costs, they are an important source of earned income. This helps to supplement CSI's budget and allows it to sustain itself.

Technical/Business Development Assistance

This type of assistance focuses on helping the client social entrepreneurs to get the knowledge and develop the skills necessary to start, grow and sustain their social ventures. At CSI, the responsibility for coordinating this activity belongs to the "Community Animator." This individual determines the needs of clients and makes the necessary connections to help both inside and outside the Centre (Stiles, 2013). This help may come from mentors in the community or from the 20 to 30 workshops put on by the Centre each month. The workshops cover such topics as social impact measurement, labor laws affecting social entrepreneurs, and collaborative governance, among others (Stiles, 2013). A review of workshop events listed on the CSI website in 2014 and 2015 yielded the following subjects:

1   Be Social Change Class: The Power of Purpose & Your Personal Mission
2   Return on Change Workshop Series: Session 2: Developing a Business Plan
3   Six Degrees of Social Innovation
4   Return on Change Workshop Series 3: Business Budgeting
5   Return on Change Workshop Series 4: How to Raise Capital
6   Return on Change Workshop Series 5: Learning the Terms Sheet
7   Return on Change Workshop Series 6: How to Put Together Financial Models

8   Return on Change Workshop Series 7: How to Pitch Investors
9   Building Partnerships with Impact
10 Use Narrative to Communicate, Inspire & Activate Your Community
11 Success DNA

All workshops are made available to the public.

Help with Obtaining Financial Resources

At CSI, this service is provided through the efforts of the Community Animator, who makes the necessary connections in the community. Also, some of the workshops address financing, as noted above.

Fostering Networking

At the heart of everything that CSI does is the spirit of networking: networking among member social entrepreneurs and networking between those entrepreneurs and partners in the community that can assist them in pursuing their missions. The Community Animator personifies this spirit, and the facility, itself, is designed to foster interaction.

The Director of Design, Matthew Cohen, has created a space that encourages people to engage with one another. The walls are glass, and many of them roll up (garage door style), in order to perpetuate the feeling of openness and facilitate the ability of the whole space to accommodate a large gathering of up to 200 people. The private desks and "hot desks" are all situated in the middle of the space in an open concept. At the heart of the facility is the kitchen, which serves as a gathering place. A diagonal walkway bisects the space, connecting everything in much the same way that Manhattan's famed avenue, Broadway, does (Bromberg, 2014). A casual observer is immediately struck by the buzz of conversation in this hive of activity.

Membership

CSI calls its clients "members." All prospective members must complete an application form designed to ascertain whether or not they are pursuing a social mission and that they are a good fit with CSI's mission. Members range from individuals to organizations and from start-ups to more established entities. There are even impact investors who participate. Altogether, CSI hosts approximately 150 member organizations, including both those with nonprofit and those with for-profit legal structures (Duran, 2014).

Social venture philanthropists Ashoka and Echoing Green are among CSI's "big name" members (Duran, 2014). Other members include (American Entrepreneurship Today NY, 2014):

1   Cool Culture—a nonprofit that arranges access to New York City's cultural institutions for low-income families;
2   The Opportunity Lab—this organization helps double bottom line businesses with growth strategies;

3   The Water Trust—a nonprofit that helps to improve the quality of water, hygiene and sanitation in East Africa;

4   Drive Change—a food truck business that employs youth released from jail; and

5   American Prison Data Systems—a platform that allows prisoners to learn English, get a GED, and engage in a variety of other educational activities.

Sustainable Environs

Even CSI's internal physical space reflects its social mission. As designer Matthew Cohen puts it, "Social innovation can't be divorced from responsible building practices" (Bromberg, 2014). Most of the items in the facility—doors, desks, kitchen cabinets, etc.—are repurposed. New wood surfaces have been made by a nonprofit enterprise called Brooklyn Woods, which employs the underemployed and "unemployable." Accent pieces throughout the incubator, such as sculpture and vintage globes, were purchased from Furnish Green, which supports the Nature Conservancy with 50 percent of its profits (Furnish Green, 2014).

The CSI is a good example of a full service business incubator in the social sector; a viable social entrepreneurship support organization. In some respects, it functions as a traditional incubator, but in many others, it is just as innovative as its client social enterprises, as a good ESO should be.

Note

The authors would like to thank Esther Saka of Baruch College for her help in gathering information for preparing this case.

THOUGHT QUESTIONS

1   How does CSI's ability to "incubate" social enterprises go beyond the walls of the facility itself?

2   Can you think of other types of partnership that CSI might pursue in its endeavors to support social entrepreneurs in New York City?

3   How does CSI address the needs of its client entrepreneurs using the diagnostic framework developed by Lichtenstein and Lyons and presented earlier in this chapter?

4   CSI places considerable emphasis on the value of the design of its facility. How important is a social innovation incubator's design to its effectiveness? Why?

CO-WORKING SPACES

Incubators and co-working spaces share much in common, and, in fact, many incubators also offer co-working spaces, as is the case with the examples provided above. However, there are a large number of freestanding co-working spaces as well. The concept behind co-working is very simple: entrepreneurs benefit from face-to-face interaction with other entrepreneurs. They can learn from each other, share information, explore ideas, derive emotional support, and get feedback, among other advantages. Above all else, co-working is about human collaboration.

Some co-working spaces are quite modest. In the Field Center for Entrepreneurship at Baruch College, co-working is a weekly session held on Friday afternoons in the Center's training room. It involves student start-up entrepreneurs, entrepreneurship faculty, and occasionally investors and entrepreneurs from the larger community. It focuses on providing feedback to the student entrepreneurs relative to their business models or specific problems they are facing. Commercial entrepreneurs and social entrepreneurs both participate in these sessions.

Some co-working spaces are more sophisticated. Washington, DC's Affinity Lab is an example of one of the earliest co-working spaces to serve social entrepreneurs. It was founded in 2001 in the District's U Street neighborhood. Like Baruch College's space, it serves both commercial (typically in the technology and creative industries) and social entrepreneurs together. Unlike the College's co-working model, Affinity Lab can accommodate up to sixty-five businesses in 5,000 square feet of space. Some of this space is dedicated to desks reserved for members. Some of it is for desks that are made available on a first-come, first-served basis. There are also couches and meeting rooms all arranged in a very open floor plan. The idea is to facilitate organic collaboration in an unstructured way (Rominiecki, 2012).

Other examples of co-working in the social enterprise space are SocEnt Baltimore, Forge Portland, and mission*social. SocEnt Baltimore occupies two floors in a rowhouse. On the first floor there is a shared kitchen, an outdoor patio and a conference room. The second floor currently includes desks in approximately 1,200 square feet of floor space, which is expected to grow as more space on that floor is acquired. The co-working facility sells memberships at $225 per month. As of this writing, SocEnt had eight member social entrepreneurs and was generating revenue just above breakeven, making it sustainable (Zaleski, 2014).

Forge Portland is a brand new co-working facility in Portland, Oregon that caters to nonprofits, social enterprises, and freelancers. According to its founder, Robert Bart, Forge Portland aims to provide its members with workspace, community, and access to free resources (Impact Entrepreneurs, 2014). The co-working space occupies 6,000 square feet in the downtown, and it also serves as a meeting and event area in the evenings. The free services offered by Forge Portland include mentoring, intern placement, business development, referral to legal services, and the use of accounting and web templates. Members can rent the work desks provided for $50 per month for access once per week, $225 per month for full-time access, and $325 per month for private access. Forge Portland hopes to create its own internal support ecosystem by both encouraging collaboration among its members and supporting those who support social entrepreneurs. In this way, members have ready access to reliable sources of assistance (Impact Entrepreneurs, 2014).

In San Francisco, mission*social is a co-working space that makes it very clear that it serves *only* entrepreneurs with a passion for making a difference in the world. The space is located on the top floor of its building and has an open floor plan. It permits clients to rent furnished desks for open space which they can furnish as they see fit. The space also includes conference rooms with Skype capability, a shared kitchen, a pool table, Wi-Fi and wired Internet access, and private booths for telephone and Internet calls (mission*social, 2014).

SOCIAL ENTREPRENEUR NETWORKS

Sometimes social entrepreneurs do not need dedicated space in which to collaborate. They can build their own virtual communities, using in-person meetings at varying locations and on the Internet. There are numerous advantages to the social entrepreneur in joining such networks. Like co-working spaces, they bring like-minded people together to support one another by fostering longer-term personal and professional relationships, providing a forum for the joint creation and/or sharing of ideas, facilitating the sharing of resources, and giving a greater voice to social entrepreneurship actions.

There are many of these networks worldwide. In the UK, alone, the following social entrepreneur networks flourish, among others (Impact Hub, 2014):

1   The Guardian Social Enterprise Network—https://register.theguardian.com/social-enterprise
2   The Social Entrepreneurship Meetup Group—http://social-entrepreneurs.meetup.com
3   Impact Hub Westminster Yammer Community—http://westminster.impacthub.net/membership-2
4   The RSA Fellowship Social Entrepreneurs Network—http://rsafellowship.com/group/socialentrepreneursnetwork
5   Social Innovation Exchange (SIX)—http://www.socialinnovationexchange.org/home
6   The Global Social Entrepreneurship Network—http://gsen.unltd.org.uk/plan.php
7   The Social Entrepreneur Empowerment Network—http://www.facebook.com/SEEnetwork

In the United States, the Social Venture Network (SVN) has been in existence since 1987 and has incubated such well-known organizations as SVN Europe, the American Sustainable Business Council, Net Impact, Business for Social Responsibility, and the Alliance for Local Living Economics. SVN includes in its theory of change its contribution to the social entrepreneurship ecosystem (Social Venture Network, 2014).

Some social entrepreneur networks can be found within universities. An example is University of Pretoria Gordon Institute of Business Science's Network for Social Entrepreneurs (NSE). NSE is broadly inclusive and aims to help its members to both think creatively and innovatively and to develop the skills they need to be successful entrepreneurs. They do this by staging informational forums, inspirational events, breakfasts, and debates as well as drawing upon the physical infrastructure and the faculty of the business school (Gordon Institute of Business Sciences, 2014).

SOCIAL VENTURE PHILANTHROPY

Among the important players in the social entrepreneurship support ecosystem are social venture philanthropies (SVPs). These organizations use a venture capital model in making investments in social entrepreneurs and their ventures. Like venture capitalists, SVPs not only provide financial capital to their investees, but they also offer technical assistance, mentoring, access to their networks, and expertise on boards of directors. In doing so, they address the limitations of more traditional philanthropy that is short-term, categorical, and transactional (Wei-Skillern et al., 2007). These limitations place a hardship on social entrepreneurs because they require these entrepreneurs to continually reapply for financing, to pursue multiple sources of funding to support their mission and to accomplish societal transformations through arm's-length transactions. The holistic approach of SVP makes it possible for social entrepreneurs to focus on the work of pursuing their mission and gives them the long-term support they need to achieve deep, lasting change.

Like commercial venture capitalists, SVPs put applicants for their investment through a stringent due diligence process. They are looking for strong leadership by the social entrepreneur and/or her or his management team. The strength of the concept and its potential for solving a social problem are important as well. SVPs want to feel confident that the prospective investee's opportunity is scalable, maximizing its ability to reach target beneficiaries with its mission. Of course, social return on investment (SROI) is the only return on investment (ROI) most SVPs are interested in. The due diligence process typically involves submission of a business model or plan and subsequent interviews and pitches to the SVP. The percentage of social ventures that receive SVP support relative to those that apply is very small. It is similar to the percentage of entrepreneurial ventures that receive commercial venture capital—2 to 4 percent (Timmons & Spinelli, 2007, p. 418).

Some SVPs are global in their reach. Ashoka, Acumen Fund, and Echoing Green are among the best known of this group. Others, like the Austin Social Venture Partners in Texas, are local or regional in scope. Most SVPs invest in nonprofit social ventures exclusively; however, a few—Acumen Fund and New Schools Venture Fund among them—also invest in for-profits.

BEING SYSTEMIC ABOUT SUPPORTING SOCIAL ENTREPRENEURS

As noted earlier in this chapter, some thought has been given to how providing support to social entrepreneurs might be treated more systemically; however, social entrepreneurship support ecosystems still tend to be just as fragmented and categorical as commercial entrepreneurship support ecosystems (Lichtenstein et al., 2004). Most assume that the social entrepreneur will be able to recognize the opportunities afforded by the ESOs and navigate the "non-system" on their own. The reality is that the system is opaque to most social entrepreneurs, and they may or may not learn about individual ESOs through word of mouth or by serendipity. In short, most support ecosystems lack a holistic strategy.

Lyons and Lichtenstein (2010) offer a remedy for this. They argue that communities should treat their social entrepreneurs and their enterprises as a "portfolio" of social business assets and manage that portfolio appropriately (Lyons & Lichtenstein, 2010, p. 258). For this purpose they recommend thinking of the goings-on of these social entrepreneurs and enterprises as a pipeline of social entrepreneurship activity—a pipeline, like all pipelines, with manageable volume and flow.

In Lyons and Lichtenstein's pipeline, the number of social entrepreneurs and their enterprises operating in the community expresses volume. Flow is manifested by the advancement of individual social entrepreneurs, or an entrepreneurial team, up a ladder of skill development. As the entrepreneur's skills increase, he or she is better able to restructure their enterprise to move it through the stages in its life cycle. So, flow is constituted of progress in social entrepreneurship skill development and smooth advancement through the business life cycle stages. Volume is a measure of the quantity of social entrepreneurship activity, and flow is the measure of its quality. Considered in another way, flow is about the development (improvement) of the community's social entrepreneurs and enterprises; while, volume is about more of that higher quality social entrepreneurship activity (Lyons & Lichtenstein, 2010).

Using skill level and stage in the life cycle as coordinates, all of the social enterprises in the community can be "mapped" (see Figure 12.2). This precise segmentation of social entrepreneurs and enterprises permits strategic intervention by the community to boost volume and maintain flow, recognizing the limited resources available to do so. In part, strategic intervention includes making appropriate matches between social enterprises and ESOs through tactical referrals (Lyons & Lichtenstein, 2010).[2] In this way, the ecosystem is rationalized. It becomes more transparent to social entrepreneurs, ESOs, and community-wide policy makers, and it offers a systemic,

---

2 For more detail on this pipeline approach to fostering community-wide social entrepreneurship see Lyons, T.S., & Lichtenstein, G.A. (2010). A community-wide framework for encouraging social entrepreneurship using the pipeline of entrepreneurs and enterprises model. In A. Fayolle & H. Matlay (Eds), *Handbook of Research on Social Entrepreneurship*. Cheltenham, UK: Edward Elgar.

Life Cycle / Skill Level	Stage 0 Pre-venture	Stage 1 Existence	Stage 2 Early Growth	Stage 3 Expansion	Stage 4 Maturity	Stage 5 Decline
D	4	4	0	1	2	0
C	7	9	0	2	2	3
B	12	15	3	4	5	8
A	25	10	5	8	6	6

FIGURE 12.2   Mapping Social Entrepreneurs and Enterprises in Community X

Source: from Lyons, T.S. & Lichtenstein, G.A. (2010). A community-wide framework for encouraging social entrepreneurship using the pipeline of entrepreneurs and enterprises. In A. Fayolle & H. Matlay. *Handbook of research on social entrepreneurship*. Cheltenham, UK: Edward Elgar. Reprinted with permission.

systematic, and strategic solution to the challenge issued by Bornstein, above, to "build a framework of social and economic supports" for social entrepreneurs.

VOICES FROM THE FIELD

Erica Dorn, Consultant for Fair Resources in the San Francisco Bay Area and Bernoulli Finance in New York City

Erica Dorn is a New York City-based consultant in the sustainable food and fiber shed space and a social entrepreneur. She spends much of her time consulting in the San Francisco Bay area for an organization called Fair Resources and in New York with Bernoulli Finance, both of which work with mission-aligned food and farm businesses to make positive changes in the food system. In addition, she sits on the board of directors of Slow Money NYC, an impact investing organization in sustainable food systems. She considers herself a "localist," as opposed to social entrepreneurs who are focused on having global impact. One might say that she is the embodiment of the old environmentalist axiom, "think globally; act locally."

Having previously worked for Accion, a microenterprise program, in New York City, in addition to her current activities, Dorn is very well versed in support systems for both commercial and social entrepreneurs. Her experience has taught her that the most significant needs of social entrepreneurs are the following:

1 Data-driven decision making and reporting—It's critical for social enterprises to be able to track their activities and have reporting mechanisms in place that allow for leadership and board decision making, and external reporting to funders. For many smaller social enterprises this can mean hiring an external Data Consultant, like datakind.org, or a CFO for hire (Non-Profit Finance Fund) that can serve as a balance check on the institution's metrics for measuring impact and help the institution best communicate their impact.

2 Leadership and Accountability—are key values that social entrepreneurs must embody. Social enterprises need significant leadership and human capital development in order to reach desired impact. Because social enterprises don't often have the resources to provide high-level benefits to their employees they must instead create well-aligned HR systems to ensure employee satisfaction. Hiring can be tricky within nonprofits because there are often conflicts that arise from perceptions of mission-drift and conflicting mission vs. financial incentives. It's important to have an internal "employee satisfaction" mission in addition to the external mission to achieve social change—progress begins from within.

3 A strong board of advisors and networks—to provide accountability and strategic advice—because of limited funding the entrepreneur must leverage networks to supplement for areas where they lack expertise/strength.

4 Willingness to fail—It's extremely important that a social entrepreneur be honest about the outcomes of their efforts. Many times, social enterprises only report on the positive impacts that they have and very rarely admit when something did not reach the desired outcome. This is often a result of the funder/entrepreneur relationship and stunts real change and progress.

It is these needs, in particular, that social entrepreneurship support ecosystems must address.

With these needs in mind, Erica believes that the primary role of a support ecosystem is to create accountability. As she puts it, "As in all forms of human development, an eco-system to support social entrepreneurs is extremely important. In particular for a social enterprise, internal and external stakeholders provide a necessary balance that allows an entrepreneur to flourish. Starting with a strong board of advisors, a social entrepreneur is able to create trust and transparency; these two qualities allow the entrepreneur to become increasingly clear about their path to achieving mission." Clearly, she emphasizes the human development aspects of social entrepreneur support over all others.

According to Dorn, the essential parts of an effective support ecosystem for social entrepreneurs should include:

1   incubators/hubs;
2   engaged advisory boards;
3   leadership development organizations (e.g., BALLE and the Unreasonable Institute);
4   foundations and individual funders;
5   volunteers;
6   external outcomes reporting (e.g., *Yes! Magazine* and Triple Pundit), which "plays a critical part in the social enterprise ecosystem—providing visibility and accountability."

However, she qualifies this by saying that, ultimately, it is the quality of the network of these forms of support that is most important to the development of the social entrepreneur.

Dorn makes the following observations about the strengths and limitations of the social entrepreneurship support ecosystem in New York City by way of example:

> Over the past decade and increasingly in the last five years the ecosystem to support social entrepreneurs has grown significantly with the existence of incubators and shared workspaces in New York City. New York is also home to the majority of large and family foundations that ultimately fund social enterprises and, due to this access, is an ideal city to incubate and grow social enterprises. Organizations like Acumen Fund and Echoing Green provide a vehicle for social entrepreneurs to be funded, find networks, and receive training. Impact Hub and the CSI provide a work and training space for social entrepreneurs as well as far-reaching networks and access to valuable and effective stakeholders. There are non-New York based organizations like the Unreasonable Institute and SKOLL that provide benefits to social entrepreneurs based in New York City as well.
>
> What makes New York a great place for social entrepreneurs is not merely the organizations targeted at serving social enterprises but also the incredible TA (technical assistance) providers that serve traditional businesses that have relevant applications to social enterprises, like General Assembly that provides business and tech-focused training and classes.
>
> However, the perception of New York is that it caters to traditional businesses and, therefore, has not been as prone to social innovation as other parts of the United States. New York is more commonly perceived as a playground for artists, fashion designers, and, on the flip side, the financial sector. This perception, in addition to the cost of living, has created the stigma that New York is not the ideal space for social innovation; yet, this is highly debatable. Cities like Detroit and San Francisco are branded as social innovation cities—Detroit because of the

cost of living and sheer need for innovation and experimentation to solve the vast social issues that have arisen from the fall of the auto industry, and San Francisco due to its proximity to Silicon Valley that has access to a large pool of tech savvy professionals that can "code for good"

These are compelling arguments, but New York has its social innovation assets as well, as do all cities.

CONCLUSION

Social entrepreneurs need not work alone. There is an emerging ecosystem of community support that exists to help them. This ecosystem provides financial, physical, human, and social capital as well as technical assistance aimed at meeting the needs of social entrepreneurs. It does this through the work of incubators, accelerators, coworking spaces, networks, social venture philanthropists, and others.

In order for a social entrepreneurship support ecosystem to be efficient and effective, it needs to be operated as a system, where the different components are networked together in a way that makes them transparent to the social entrepreneurs who can benefit from them. This can be accomplished in a centralized way, such as through Lyons and Lichtenstein's (2010) portfolio/pipeline model, or in a decentralized fashion, an example of which might be the CSI's efforts to reach out to other social entrepreneurship support organizations through its Community Animator.

No matter what organizations populate a community's support ecosystem and how they are organized their work is vital. Social entrepreneurship is becoming increasingly crucial to maintaining the equity and stability required for healthy communities and societies. Social entrepreneurs may be remarkable in their abilities to bootstrap and manage risk, but they cannot and should not be expected to do this without support. It is in the best interests of local communities and of nations to invest in social entrepreneurship support ecosystems.

QUESTIONS FOR "CONNECTING THE DOTS"

1   A recent study by the Global Entrepreneurship Monitor (GEM) project found that a major impediment to more people launching their own businesses is self-efficacy. Do you think this is also true for social entrepreneurs? Can support ecosystems help to address this issue? If so, how?

2   Does your community have a social entrepreneurship support ecosystem? If so, "map" it by listing the various support organizations in it. Are these organizations networked in any way? How would you improve on this ecosystem?

If your community has no such ecosystem, design your own. Where would you start in getting your ideal ecosystem implemented?

3 As is noted in this chapter, agency has been favored over context in entrepreneurship education. Arguably, this is no less true for entrepreneurship research. In your opinion, what is the proper relationship of agency and context in entrepreneurship? Do you believe that this relationship takes on greater importance in social entrepreneurship? If so, why?

REFERENCES

American Entrepreneurship Today NY. (2014). CSI – NY marks 1st anniversary. New York: AET LLC. http://ny.americanentrepreneurship.com/aetstories/entrepreneur-Supporting-organizations/centre-for-social-innovation-marks-1st-anniversary.html. Accessed October 15, 2014.

Bornstein, D. (2007). *How to change the world: Social entrepreneurs and the power of new ideas*. Oxford, UK: Oxford University Press.

Bromberg, J. (2014). CSI advances social enterprise. *Convene*, September 19. http://convene.com/centre-social-innovation-csi-advances-social-enterprise. Accessed October 15, 2014.

Cunniffe, E. (2013). Social enterprise, squared. *Nonprofit Quarterly* (June 26). PIC Net. https://nonprofitquarterly.org/policysocial-context/22526-social-enterprise-squared.html. Accessed October 15, 2014.

Dabson, B., Malkin, J., Matthews, A., Pate, K., & Stickle, S. (2003). *Mapping rural entrepreneurship*. Battle Creek, MI: Corporation for Enterprise Development for the W.K. Kellogg Foundation.

Duran, D. (2014). NYC coworking space more than just tables & chairs. *Drive the District*, July 4. http://www.drivethedistrict.com/2014/07/04/nyc-coworking-space-more-than-just-table-chairs. Accessed October 15, 2014.

Edward Lowe Foundation. (2002). *Building entrepreneurial communities*. Cassopolis, MI: Edward Lowe Foundation.

Feldman, M. P. (1994). The university and economic development: The case of Johns Hopkins University and Baltimore. *Economic Development Quarterly*, 8 (1): 67–76.

Florida, R. (2002). *The rise of the creative class*. New York: Basic Books.

Furnish Green. (2014). A trip to the Centre for Social Innovation. April 24. http://Furnishgreen.com/a-trip-to-the-centre-for-social-innovation. Accessed October 15, 2014.

Gordon Institute of Business Sciences. (2014). Network for Social Entrepreneurs (NSE). Pretoria, South Africa: University of Pretoria. http://www.gibs.co.za/programmes/the-centre-for-leadership-and-dialogue/overview.aspx. Accessed September 4, 2014.

Impact Entrepreneurs. (2014). Forge Portland: A new co-working space for nonprofits and social Enterprises. Portland, OR: Portland State University. http://impactentrepreneurs.wordpress.com/2014/04/11/forge-portland-a-new-co-working-space-for-nonprofits-and-social-enterprises. Accessed September 2, 2014.

Impact Hub. (2014). Is there a social network for social entrepreneurs? Yes! 7 to investigate. http://westminster.impacthub.net/2014/05/13/is-there--a-social-network-for-social-entrepreneurs-yes-6-to-investigate. Accessed September 4, 2014.

Kauffman Foundation. (2014). ID8 Nation. http://www.kauffman.org/what-we-do/programs/entrepreneurship/id8-nation. Accessed August 27, 2014.

Korosec, R. L., & Berman, E. M. (2006). Municipal support for social entrepreneurship. *Public Administration Review*, May/June, 448–462.

Koven, S. G., & Lyons, T. S. (2010). *Economic development: Strategies for state and local practice.* Washington, DC: International City/County Management Association.

Lichtenstein, G. A., & Lyons, T. S. (1996). *Incubating new enterprises.* Washington, DC: The Aspen Institute.

Lichtenstein, G. A., & Lyons, T. S. (2010). *Investing in entrepreneurs: A strategic approach for strengthening your regional and community economy.* Santa Barbara, CA: Praeger/ABC-CLIO.

Lichtenstein, G. A., Lyons, T. S., & Kutzhanova, N. (2004). Building entrepreneurial communities: The appropriate role of enterprise development activities. *Journal of the Community Development Society*, 35 (1): 5–24.

Lyons, T. S., & Lichtenstein, G. A. (2010). A community-wide framework for encouraging social entrepreneurship using the pipeline of entrepreneurs and enterprises model. In A. Fayolle & H. Matlay (Eds.). *Handbook of Research on Social Entrepreneurship.* Cheltenham, UK: Edward Elgar.

Mission*social. (2014). About mission*social. http://www.missionsocial.com. Accessed September 2, 2014.

nyc.socialinnovation.org. Join Us. nyc.socialinnovation.org/join-us. Accessed November 26, 2014.

Panzanzee. (2014). Panzanzee is Chicago's social enterprise incubator, co-working space and continuous community. http://panzanzee.com. Accessed September 2, 2014.

Porter, M.E. (1985). *Competitive advantage.* New York: Free Press.

Propeller. (2014). Incubator. http://gopropeller.org/incubator. Accessed on September 2, 2014.

Rominiecki, J. (2012). Creative spark: Incubators and coworking spaces ignite innovation. *Associations Now.* The Center for Association Leadership. http://www.asaecenter.org/Resources/ANowDetail.cfm?ItemNumber=233930.

Social Enterprise Trust. (2014). http://www.socialenterprisetrust.org. Accessed September 2, 2014.

Social Venture Network. (2014). About SVN. http://svn.org/who-we-are/about-svn. Accessed on September 4, 2014.

Stiles, A. (2013). Social innovation builds its dream home in New York City. *Fast Company*, May. www.fastcoexist.com/1681964/social-innovation-builds-its-dream-home-in-new-york-city. Accessed on October 15, 2014.

Timmons, J. A., & Spinelli, S. (2007). *New venture creation: Entrepreneurship for the 21st century*, 7th Edition. Boston: McGraw-Hill Irwin.

Wei-Skillern, J., Austin, J. E., Leonard, H., & Stevenson, H. (2007). *Entrepreneurship in the social sector.* Thousand Oaks, CA: Sage.

Zaleski, A. (2014). SocEnt Baltimore: Old Goucher coworking for social entrepreneurs. http://technical.ly/baltimore/2014/04/30/socent-baltimore-coworking-space. Accessed September 2, 2014.

The Future of Social Entrepreneurship

AIM/PURPOSE

This final chapter highlights the future opportunities for social entrepreneurs, including features, areas, and sectors where innovative solutions for systemic change and impact are needed.

LEARNING OBJECTIVES FOR THIS CHAPTER

1. To become aware of some of the latest ideas and innovations seen in the field of social entrepreneurship.
2. To discover some of the key challenges going forward in social entrepreneurship.
3. To understand new approaches and behaviors when resources for social entrepreneurs are scarce.
4. To be aware of the future need for "catalytic innovations" for social impact and be introduced to the concept of bricolage behavior in bringing innovations to the marketplace.
5. To look briefly at some future trends in social entrepreneurship.

The future for social entrepreneurship is replete with possibilities and innovations to solve many of society's most intractable problems. What is of particular importance is the recognition of the ever-evolving nature of the attention curve for businesses addressing social ills. There follow comments by a few experts about what they believe will be the future of social entrepreneurship:

> The future is about shifting from fail-safe models to safe-fail models—to be successful, we need to throw up as many balls in the air as possible.
> (Shrashtant Patara, Vice-President, Development Alternatives Group)

Taking on harder problems battled by more people will separate the high-quality enterprises that scale from the mediocre ones.

> (Bindu Ananth, President, IFMR Trust)

The sector will see some sort of consolidation, as more enterprises compete for limited resources. Mergers and acquisitions and stress on transparency and better managerial practices will be upcoming trends.

> (Yashveer Singh, National Social Entrepreneurship Network)

There aren't real failures in social enterprise, there are temporary setbacks. We need to build a support system for entrepreneurs who initially face hurdles, which will give them staying power and the ability to follow through.

> (Joe Madiath, founder and ED, Gram Vikas)

Along with the experts' perspectives, consider Figure 13.1, which uses the Gartner Hype Cycle to depict the changing views on social entrepreneurial approaches.

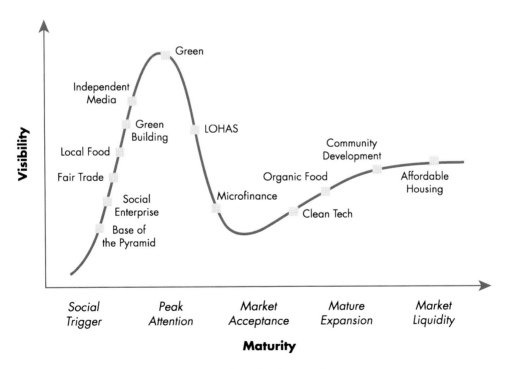

FIGURE 13.1 Attention Curve: The Capital Market for Good

Source: from the report, Impact Assets Issue Brief no. 2, *Risk, return and impact: Understanding diversification and performance within an impact investing portfolio.*

The initiating event is a social trigger, which occurs when some new opportunity is discovered to create both social and financial value. New social businesses are created and some level of acceptance of their purpose finds its way into society. This initial success may or may not be based in a new technology. The social trigger allows for others to observe a different perspective and, as a result, see how to do things differently in order to apply them to various existing and/or unaddressed problems.

Attention follows and an emerging market sector is created. Typically, this attention follows a curve upward until a level of peak attention is reached. The most common recent example is the way everything has gone "green." After initial acceptance the sector generally experiences a down cycle representing a time at which social entrepreneurs must show their mettle. While significant attention often brings a flow of new money and new entrants, the new ideas have to actually work or they disappear. It is here that the concepts of bricolage and catalytic innovation dominate. Survival of this stage results in market acceptance. The idea proves itself to be either sustainable or unsustainable. If the concept proves itself, a more mature period of expansion and development occurs, usually supported by outside smart money. Finally, the acceptance of the idea becomes so commonplace that market liquidity develops as a viable and commonplace investment opportunity.

KEY CHALLENGES GOING FORWARD IN SOCIAL ETREPRENEURSHIP

Tracey and Phillips (2007) have identified three key challenges inherent in social entrepreneurship: managing accountability, managing the double bottom line, and managing identity. Table 13.1 depicts the sustainability equilibrium across both social value creation and economic value creation. On the left side of the continuum, traditional nonprofits emphasize mission motives, stakeholder accountability, and the tendency to reinvest income in social programs or operations. On the right side, traditional for-profit firms possess profit-making motives and face accountability to shareholders, to whom they redistribute profits.

Toward the middle, the social enterprise entrepreneur shares much in common with the traditional for-profit entrepreneur (Austin, Gutierrez, Ogliastri, & Reficco, 2006; Chell, 2007; Smith & Barr, 2007); however, there are important differences in terms of opportunities exploited and the type of values sought. The social entrepreneur tackles social problems (such as hunger or poverty) and measures success in terms of the accomplishment of social value. Using innovation and resourcefulness, the social entrepreneur ultimately seeks to better the human condition (Dees, Emerson, & Economy, 2001), and in some cases may also engage in creating economic value. However, in this case, economic value is simply a means to an end

Table 13.1
Sustainability Equilibrium across Social and Economic Value Creation

Social/Environmental Value Creation					Economic Value Creation
Traditional Nonprofit	Nonprofit with Income-Generating Activities	Social Enterprises (e.g., cooperatives, limited liability companies)	Socially Responsible Business (e.g., B Corps)	Corporation Practicing Social Responsibility	Traditional For-Profit
Value creation achieved through: ■ grant writing ■ fund-raising activities ■ volunteers ■ in-kind donations	Value creation achieved through: ■ grant writing ■ fund-raising activities ■ volunteers ■ in-kind donations ■ for-profit ventures	Value creation achieved through: ■ grant writing (PRI) ■ for-profit ventures	Value creation achieved through: ■ patient capital ■ for-profit ventures	Value creation achieved through: ■ for-profit ventures	Value creation achieved through: ■ for-profit ventures
Examples: ■ Boys' and girls' club ■ Local food banks	Examples: ■ Goodwill Industries ■ Habitat for Humanity (ReStore Initiatives) ■ Salvation Army (thrift store)	Examples: ■ Organic Valley ■ CoolPass L3C	Examples: ■ Stonyfield Farm ■ Better World Books	Examples: ■ Campbell Soup Company ■ Abbott Laboratories	Examples: ■ Fidelity National Financial, Inc. ■ Allied World Assurance Company Holdings Ltd.

Source: adapted from Alter (2007).

rather than an end in and of itself (for an excellent discussion of social and economic value in social entrepreneurship, see Austin, Stevenson, & Wei-Skillern, 2006). As a result, the social entrepreneur leverages the innovative aspects of entrepreneurship but applies it for the common good rather than for individual gain.

THE FUTURE NEED FOR CATALYTIC INNOVATIONS FOR SOCIAL IMPACT

Effective social change and its long-term impact must rely on new approaches and methods. Christensen, Baumann, Ruggles, and Sadtler (2006) assert that social-sector organizations must develop fundamentally new approaches that are scalable and sustainable, with the ability to influence system-changing solutions. This is known as catalytic innovation, derived from Christensen's model of disruptive innovation, with an emphasis on creating social change.

Innovations can generally be separated into two distinct categories: sustaining and disruptive. Sustaining innovations include nearly all product and service innovations, whether incremental or breakthrough, that provide, for example, increased quality, better or more features and functions, and other changes targeted to existing customers of the organizations (Christensen & Bower, 1995). Disruptive innovations do not fulfill existing customers' needs as effectively as sustaining innovations. They tend to be less complex, more accessible and convenient, and less costly, thereby attracting new or different customer groups (Christensen & Bower, 1995). These types of innovations are likely to be attractive to markets that are not adequately served by existing product and service solutions.

Catalytic innovations, a subset of disruptive innovations, provide 'good enough' solutions to social challenges that are not effectively addressed using traditional approaches (Christensen et al., 2006). Catalytic innovators, whose primary focus is on social change, share the following five characteristics (Christensen et al., 2006):

1   Creating systemic social change through scaling and replication: These innovators are often new entrants that continually improve their offerings to expand their market reach. High transferability from one location to another enables the innovation to be scaled up and to be sustained across marketplaces.
2   Meeting a need that is either over-served or not served at all: New entrants to the market provide less expensive, less functional alternatives to a segment of the market over-served or not served at all by the dominant provider.
3   Offering products and services that are simpler and less costly than existing alternatives, and are considered "good enough": These innovations bring new benefits to people in ways that existing firms are not generally willing to undertake. Maintaining the status quo prevents traditional, dominant players

from trying new approaches that might cannibalize their current offerings. Catalytic innovators are thus able to attract new markets with alternatives and solutions that are affordable and effective enough to reduce the problems.

4   Generating resources, such as donations, grants, volunteers, or intellectual capital, in ways that are unattractive to incumbent competitors: Catalytic innovators tend to be creative in their approaches to identifying needed resources, and these may come from nontraditional sources.

5   Often ignored, disparaged, or sometimes encouraged by existing providers for whom the business model is unprofitable or unattractive, and who therefore retreat or plan to retreat from the market segment: The dominant provider often distances itself from the new entrant and moves toward a more lucrative market segment. This enables the catalytic innovator to capture the opportunity present in serving its intended market.

One of the ways that social entrepreneurs can engage in catalytic innovation is their ability to engage in bricolage behavior. Bricolage behavior is a set of actions driven by the search for existing and often scarce resources that can be combined and/or recombined to create novel and interesting solutions that affect their respective markets. By incorporating the role that catalytic innovation has on the relationship between entrepreneurial bricolage and growth in social impact, we are better able to understand the process by which social entrepreneurs adopt and utilize existing resources for the future development, growth, and sustainability of their own ventures.

Social entrepreneurs whose environments are typically resource constrained and often present new challenges without providing new resources (Baker & Nelson, 2005) tend to engage in bricolage behavior. As previously mentioned, underlying social entrepreneurship are multiple tangible and intangible benefits and rewards that are heightened by a sense of accountability to the constituencies served as well as the impact and outcomes that are created. Social entrepreneurs assess their success and influence in terms of their social impact, innovations, and outcomes, and not simply in terms of size, growth, return on investment, or processes.

Bricolage may be integral in developing novel innovations and, through this, furthering social change. As posited by Desa (2007):

> Since social ventures often operate in resource constrained environments yet are required to develop and deploy complete modular packages to scale their social impact, it appears that bricolage can be very applicable to understanding social venture development. The reasons for using bricolage are particularly relevant to social entrepreneurship: to create within penurious environments, to create despite limited knowledge, or to build upon their existing acts of creation.
>
> (Baker & Nelson 2005; Baker, Miner, & Eesley, 2003; see Figure 9.2)

FIGURE 13.2 Bricolage within Resource-Poor Environments
Source: adapted from Desa (2007).

The degree to which social entrepreneurs engage in bricolage behavior may determine their success in developing catalytic innovations for the marketplace. Bricolage notions of making do and using whatever is on hand link with a fundamental social shift toward developing smart, sustainable projects that are integral to social change. This represents a shift from consumption-based to conservation-based ways of doing things better through an improved understanding of existing resources—their form, function, and fungibility—thereby developing clever, creative means of developing products and services aligned with market needs. Bricolage enables these entrepreneurs to use creative approaches to attract and distribute resources, identify over-served or unserved market segments, and offer products and services that are simpler, less costly, and "good enough"—all characteristics of catalytic innovators (Christensen, Baumann, Ruggles, & Sadtler, 2006).

FUTURE TRENDS IN SOCIAL ENTREPRENEURSHIP

Disruptive Social Venture Models

There is a need for social entrepreneurship to develop disrupting business models and structures in a way that motivates other social entrepreneurs. The firm FrontlineSMS: Medic is disruptive, especially given its forthcoming field diagnostics tools, which could fundamentally shift the medical diagnostics industry. Frontline-SMS makes use of open-source software to support health services around the world. Better World Books is changing the way in which nonprofits and for-profits with similar goals work together, and provides a user experience that is compelling and coherent enough that it could eventually be a major player in the e-commerce space. It has reused or recycled over 40 million books and raised over US$9 million for literacy (over US$5 million for non-profit literacy programs and over US$3.6 million for libraries) and over US$1.8 million for student groups. The company capitalizes on the intrinsic value of books to fund and support literacy initiatives, locally, nationally, and globally, through its partnerships with well-established and widely respected organizations working on four continents: Room to Read, Books for Africa, Worldfund, and the National Center for Family Literacy (Fast Company, 2007).

VOICES FROM THE FIELD

A Quadruple Bottom Line for Social Ventures?

Despite a whole new generation of social ventures, both for-profit and not-for-profit, there are limitations in their potential to reform. For one, there are a number of areas, such as transportation and energy, where they often simply do not have jurisdiction. In addition, given the scale of social problems, they are limited by the pace at which they can grow. For example, Pratham, India's largest education NGO, founded in 1994, touches 1 million people today. However, Pratham estimates that there are over 100 million children who cannot read to its standard. Further, the role of government cannot be dismissed. Only the government, with its formidable revenue generation and reach, can provide widespread access to education, security, infrastructure, and healthcare—services that may not be commercially viable through the private sector.

However, in some countries, such as India, the disconnection between citizens and their governments has reached an all-time high. This is no surprise. For example, among the 543 elected members across thirty-six political parties of the fifteenth

Lok Sabha district there are 150 individuals with criminal records. The first parliament of India in 1947 still holds the dubious distinction of being the most educated parliament in the history of an independent India. In 2008, according to the Transparency International survey on corruption, 61 percent of Indians surveyed admitted to paying a bribe to a public official in the past year. As a result, most middle- and upper-income Indians and businesses would rather avoid government involvement at all possible costs. The use of "middlemen" to register property, obtain a license, or incorporate a company has become all too common. Reliance on the private sector for education, security, water, garbage disposal, power, and healthcare has become the norm. India remains one of the few democracies where the urban middle class have a lower voter turnout than the rural poor, despite urban polling stations being significantly more accessible. Politicians have become ubiquitously despicable.

Over the years there has been many a politician at the local and national level who has made an attempt to drive reform with integrity and transparency. However, such individuals usually represent lone cries in a wilderness of miscreants, which tends to render them dysfunctional or simply drives them away.

Source: Hans Taparia, July 27, 2010 (used with permission)

Social ventures are today evaluated by the "triple bottom line," a phrase that refers to their profits, social impact, and environmental impact. To sustain change over generations, a fourth bottom line is needed: political impact. While it may seem a distraction from their original charters, social ventures are in a unique position to gently but definitively support fresh local political talent. Successful social ventures tend to command high degrees of respect in the locales in which they operate. They also develop deep insights on the people in these communities. Large developing nations have no shortage of respected, high-integrity prospective candidates. They just need to be inspired and supported. More often than not, social ventures steer clear of the "politics" of their locality. But this defeats their purpose. By encouraging and supporting the right talent at a local legislative level, social ventures would be ensuring that their programs stood the test of time— through good governance. Most importantly, social ventures and those involved with them are constituents too. They must play a role in shaping their governments.

Internet Action beyond Donations

The number of online portals targeting the social sector has been growing and the scope of these destinations has been expanding rapidly. First, there are sites of general content that specialize in social giving (Guidestar), provide information (OneClimate, TakePart), and even offer comprehensive databases of nonprofit organizations and job opportunities (Idealist). Organizations that seek donations focus on giving either to nonprofit organizations (Network for Good) or to specific projects around the world (GlobalGiving, Jolkona Foundation). Different approaches include community project funding (CitizenEffect, Startsomegood) as well as portals that combine ways to give for particular causes (Care2, focusing on environmental issues). Social investing has also been manifesting through the Internet portals with international reach (Kiva, Microplace).

More sites are being created that provide information on volunteer work sought by nonprofit organizations (HandsOnNetwork, DoSomething). Pro bono work has also been catching up, with new companies bringing more opportunities to an older tradition dominated by the legal services (Taproot Foundation, LexMundiProBono).

There has also been a surge of Internet-based initiatives that give users the opportunity to donate to their preferred cause, or save for higher education, by earning dollars or points through either purchases or exposure to advertising (for exposure to many of these new initiatives, look up the firms UpPromise, OneCause, CauseWorld, SupportYourCause, SocialVibe, Bloson).

Recent Developments

In March 2010, co-founder of Facebook Chris Hughes announced that he will launch Jumo, a new social networking platform designed to help members find and connect with causes, nonprofit organizations, and individuals working on issues that they care about. Hughes plans to differentiate Jumo by focusing on creating longer term relationships between people and causes. He has also noted that the site will be designed to take advantage of content that has already been created elsewhere and will offer robust tools for sharing content.

VOICES FROM THE FIELD

A Facebook Founder Begins a Social Network Focused on Charities (by Jenna Wortham; used with permission)

Chris Hughes, one of the founders of Facebook and the chief digital organizer for Barack Obama's presidential campaign, knows a thing or two about building online communities. Now he is applying his expertise to a new venture called Jumo, which aims to connect people with nonprofits and charitable organizations. The site, which is being unveiled on Tuesday, aims to "do what Yelp did for restaurants," Mr. Hughes said, indexing charities "to help people find and evaluate them."

Individual charities, projects like building a school in rural Africa, and broad issues like gay rights will all have dedicated pages on Jumo.

Relevant news articles, Twitter posts, and YouTube videos will be added to the pages, and users can add their own feedback and comments. Users can also find their Facebook friends and follow their adopted projects and issues on the site. The idea is to take the principles that helped Mr. Hughes organize a network of volunteers into a successful political force and apply them to a much broader universe of causes and issues.

Mr. Hughes is not the first entrepreneur to venture into this territory. Causes, a Facebook application, and the website Global Giving are among the many existing ways to find and support charities online. But Mr. Hughes said that Jumo would not be primarily about soliciting donations. Instead, he said, the site would first try to deepen ties between its users and their favorite causes. "The more connected that individual is to an issue they care about, the higher probability there is they will stay involved over a longer period of time," Mr. Hughes said. To start, the Jumo site was seeded with more than 3,000 issues and groups. But "anyone with a social mission can create a page," said Mr. Hughes, who thinks Jumo could become a simple way for smaller charities to establish a social media presence. Jumo will allow only organizations that have been certified as tax exempt to solicit donations, as a way to discourage fraud. Jumo is itself a nonprofit, and will rely on payments from users and sponsorships from organizations that want better promotion on the website.

One challenge for Jumo will be figuring out how willing Internet users are to share details about their donations, which they can choose to display on their Jumo profile pages, said Susan Etlinger, an analyst at the Altimeter Group, a consulting firm. "The same dynamics of other social networks may not transfer to this activity," she said.

But Chris Bishko, director of investments at Omidyar Network, a philanthropic investment firm that contributed to the $3.5 million in grants that Jumo raised before its release, said that it was not such a long shot. "One thing we've learned with Internet companies is that if you can lower the barrier and lower friction, then activity follows where it didn't exist before," he said. As an example, he pointed to the flood of donations via text message that followed the earthquake in Haiti last January: "We saw what people were willing to do."

Another issue for Jumo is social network burnout. Will people who are spending time on Facebook and elsewhere be willing to add another site to their line-up?

Mr. Hughes said Jumo was not intended to compete with Facebook. Instead, he predicts that Facebook will become a ubiquitous backbone for the social Web, and that people will also use niche sites focused on specific interests and communities. Jumo will send out e-mails and updates tailored to its users to help them stay engaged, he said. It is not yet clear how much the Internet and social media can help push people to move beyond just "following" and "liking" things, but a social network like Jumo could be a crucial first step, said Steve MacLaughlin, director of Internet solutions at BlackBaud, a global provider of technology and services to nonprofits. "It's still not clear whether or not followers translate to volunteers and donors," said Mr. MacLaughlin. "But people that are more engaged with nonprofits are most likely to become a donor or support them in another way." The financial impact could be tremendous, he said. Of the $300 billion that was donated to charities and nonprofits in 2009, only 6 percent was submitted online.

> Source: http://www.nytimes.com/2010/11/30/technology/30jumo.html?_r=1# (accessed November 30, 2010) (used with permission)

One-to-One Business Models: TOMS Shoes but Also Eyeglasses

In TOMS Shoes: Start-Ups Copy "One-for-One" Model (by Kristi Oloffson; used with permission)

The business model for TOMS Shoes—giving away one pair of footwear to the needy for every one sold—seems risky in a recession where small companies are loath to add extra costs, but several start-ups are nonetheless following suit.

Small companies have long been charitable, but few incorporate any form of philanthropy into their business models from inception since it can take several years for a start-up to become profitable, experts say. But businesses following TOMS' so-called "one-for-one" giving model are pinning their hopes on consumers' consciences, saying the strategy can benefit more than just people in need by being an effective marketing tool. Eighty percent of 1,057 US adults surveyed in July said they'd favor a brand that's associated with a good cause over another that's similar in price and quality, according to Cone LLC, a strategy and communications agency in Boston. And 19 percent said they would switch to a more expensive brand to support a cause.

TOMS, which is credited by many as being among the first to take up the one-for-one strategy, has given away about 1 million pairs of shoes to children in need worldwide since it launched in 2006. The privately held Santa Monica, California company says it is profitable, but wouldn't disclose sales figures or how much it spends annually on its charitable donations. In TOMS' case, it passes the cost of its donated footwear on to consumers by charging nearly double what the shoes would typically cost, according to a company spokeswoman. Customers generally pay anywhere from $44 for shoes to $98 for TOMS' boots.

Still, most start-ups taking up the one-for-one concept are doing so on a smaller scale, and finding ways to absorb costs without laying it on the consumer—a risky proposition in a recession riddled with cost-conscious customers. New York retailer

Warby Parker makes a financial donation to Restoring Vision, a nonprofit in San Rafael, California for every pair of glasses it sells. Its contributions have so far amounted to roughly 10,000 pairs of glasses valued at slightly less than the $95 it charges for its own eyewear, says Neil Blumenthal, one of four recent business-school graduates who founded the company in January. Warby Parker's one-for-one initiative is funded through savings it gains from skipping channels that most other eyewear companies don't, he says. For example, the start-up operates entirely online, eschewing expenses associated with leasing and managing a storefront. The company also designs its own eyewear rather than outsourcing the job to brand-name designers, says Mr. Blumenthal.

Figs, a small necktie retailer founded six months ago in Santa Monica, California, donates one school uniform to a child in Africa for every tie it sells. Founder Heather Hasson says the uniforms cost less than what it spends on manufacturing its neckwear. The company has donated about 1,000 school uniforms so far. Similarly, Out of Print in Brooklyn, New York, donates one book to Books for Africa, a twenty-two-year-old nonprofit in St. Paul, Minnesota, every time it sells one of its T-shirts, which feature the covers of mostly out-out-of print books. Just a portion of the seven-month-old retailer's sales is needed to cover the cost of the donated books, says Jeff LeBlanc, co-founder, adding that he hopes to give away 20,000 books by the end of the year. Books vary between new and used, he says.

A one-for-one initiative may require investing time and money to make consumers aware it exists, says Tom Lumpkin, chair in entrepreneurship at Syracuse University. But entrepreneurs may be able to get the message across using social media and other low-cost resources and by including it in a company's overall advertising message. "In Toms' case, the one-for-one element is the primary hook in their promotion," says Mr. Lumpkin. "If that were not there, you could argue that TOMS would be just another shoe store."

Mr. Blumenthal says he and Warby Parker's three other founders have been spreading awareness of their company's one-for-one efforts mainly through their personal networks. "People underestimate the power of word of mouth and what makes something viral," he says.

Start-ups that engage in one-for-one giving are also likely to grow at a much slower pace than businesses that are not as charitable. "Your [profit] margins are a little bit less," says Figs' Ms. Hasson. But "you can actually help out some people who really, really need it."

Source: http://online.wsj.com/article/SB100014240527 487041160045755 22251507063936.html'intMode (used with permission)

Public–Private Partnerships

> Most difficult and important social problems can't be understood, let
> alone solved, without involving the nonprofit, public, and private sectors.
> We cannot even think about solving global warming, for example,
> without considering the role of global petrochemical firms such as
> Exxon Mobil Corp. and BP p.l.c., national agencies such as the EPA and
> the Department of Energy, supranational governmental agencies such
> as the United Nations and the World Bank, and non-profit groups
> such as Greenpeace and Environmental Defense.
>
> (Phills, Deiglmeier, & Miller, 2008, p. 43)

It is rare today to find complex, adaptive public problems that do not require
solutions in which stakeholders from nonprofit, public, and private sectors must
collaborate. Ours is increasingly a shared-power world; that is, "a highly networked
policy environment where many individuals, groups, and organizations have partial
responsibilities to act on public problems, but not enough power to resolve the
problem alone" (Crosby & Bryson, 2005, p. 22).

For example, the Obama administration has championed public–private collaboration as a strategic way to address the complex mandates of its numerous federal
agencies, viewing it as a key requirement to advance change (Natsios, 2009). The
US State Department's special representative for Global Partnerships, Ambassador
Elizabeth Frawley Bagley, defines public–private partnership as "a collaborative
working relationship among, not only governmental, but also non-governmental
stakeholders where goals and structuring governance, as well as our roles and
responsibilities, are mutually determined and decision-making is made among the
players" (Keegan, 2010, p. 34). Ambassador Bagley also highlights the challenges
of training professionals adequately, changing organizational cultures so that
people recognize the value of collaboration and assessing effectively the quality
and impact of these collaborative efforts (Keegan, 2010; Natsios, 2009).

Collaboration across sectors is difficult. The interests and vested interests in each
sector are quite different. Assumptions, expectations, priorities, language, pace,
access to resources, and other differentiating features in each sector strongly diverge
(Ansell & Gash, 2008). Effective performance in a shared-power world requires
in-depth learning to develop frameworks and habits of collaboration as well as
knowledge and skills to manage it. In response to this need, demand for guidance
and training for individuals in public–private collaboration is growing exponentially
(Natsios, 2009; Keegan, 2010).

Furthering Entrepreneurship Education in the Area

As a multidisciplinary field, social entrepreneurship also presents a unique opportunity for graduate education to address the need to better teach systems thinking and innovation (AACSB, 2010). Business schools and their MBA programs constitute a unique environment in which faculty members are asked both to contribute to academic research and to teach courses focused on theoretical frameworks and practical skills to future managers and business leaders. Bennis and O'Toole (2005) argue that the MBA degree is losing its appeal and value. Furthermore, the value of an MBA degree has been significantly affected by the recent global Great Recession (AASCB, 2010). At the same time, new forms of innovation, ones including inherent ethical and social components, are emerging as a solution to the current crisis (*The Economist*, 2010). Under these pressures, many business schools have shown a greater commitment to reinvent MBA education by developing social entrepreneurship as an integral part of their graduate business education model. Social entrepreneurship is a proactive redirection of the MBA experience and education, and a demonstration that MBA coursework can serve as a framework to create economic, social, and environmental value. With over 350 professors teaching and researching social entrepreneurship in more than thirty-five countries and approximately 200 social entrepreneurship cases (Brock & Ashoka, 2008) and fifty textbooks (which include social entrepreneurship and social intrapreneurship), the field is undeniably gaining momentum across universities and programs worldwide. This trend is evidence of "a new enthusiasm" for socially and environmentally responsible management among managers and business school students (Marcus & Fremeth, 2009, p. 4). The Aspen Institute's Center for Business Education (2008) survey indicates that MBA students are thinking more broadly about the primary responsibilities of a company and considering "creating value for the communities in which they operate" to be a primary business responsibility. The Aspen Institute's biennial *Beyond Grey Pinstripes* (BGP) reports a dramatic increase in the number of programs with required courses on business and society issues, from 34 percent in 2001 to 63 percent in 2007. Finally, the number of social venture competitions (see Table 13.2) has also increased substantially, giving aspiring social entrepreneurs the opportunity to vet and receive feedback on their latest approaches to solving society's problems.

Table 13.2
Social Entrepreneurship Case and Business Plan Competitions

University	Name of Case and/or Business Plan Competition
Yale University	Global Social Venture Competition (case), National Energy Finance Challenge (case), Net Impact Green Challenge (case), Philadelphia Green Economy (case), Social Impact Case Competition (case), Yale–Harvard Debate on Leadership and Ethics (case), Y50K Entrepreneurship Competition (case)
Stanford University	Challenge for Charity (C4C—business plan), The Executive Challenge (business plan)
University of Notre Dame	Invention Convention Youth Business Plan Competition (business plan), Social Venture Business Plan Competition (business plan), Baylor U Case Competition in Ethical Leadership (case), Johnson School HABLA Case Competition (case), Kellogg Biotechnology Case Competition (case)
University of California, Berkeley	Education Leadership Case Competition (business plan), Intel + UC Berkeley Technology Entrepreneurship Challenge, Gap Inc. Scholars in Corporate Social Responsibility (case), Global Social Venture Competition (business plan), Levi Strauss Small Grants Program (business plan), Social Enterprise Education Design (SEED) Fellowship Program (business plan)
New York University	Annual Social Venture Competition (business plan), Reynolds Foundation Graduate Fellowship in Social Entrepreneurship (business plan)
IE Business School	NETI—Best Social Project (business plan), Social Entrepreneurship Business Plan Competition (business plan)
Baruch College	Baruch College Invitational Entrepreneurship Competition: annual two-semester-long team event that provides an opportunity for New York City college students to develop new social ventures
Columbia University	Global Social Venture Competition (business plan), Student Competition (case)
Cornell University	Base of the Pyramid Narrative Competition (case)
University of North Carolina, Chapel Hill	UNC's Business Accelerator for Sustainable Entrepreneurship (BASE—business plan), Bonding with the Blues MBA Case Competition (case), Sustainable Venture Capital Investment Competition (business plan)
Simmons College	Silverman Business Plan Competition (business plan)

University	Name of Case and/or Business Plan Competition
Duke University	CUREs Nonprofit Business Plan Competition (business plan), The Duke Start-up Challenge (business plan)
Duquesne University	Annual Case Study Competition (case)
University of San Diego	MBA Business Plan Competition (business plan)
Babson College	Babson Innovation Competition (business plan), The Green Collar Venture Competition (business plan), Green Tower and e-Tower Rocket Pitches (business plan)
University of California, Davis	Big Bang! Business Plan Competition (business plan)
University of Colorado at Boulder	Cleantech Venture Challenge (business plan), Leeds Net Impact Case Competition (case), Rocky Mountain Real Estate Challenge (business plan), ULI Hines Urban Design Competition (business plan)
Monterey Institute of International Studies	Thunderbird Sustainovation Challenge Case Competition (case
University of Oregon	New Venture Championship (business plan)
University of South Carolina	Page Prize for Sustainability Issues in Business Curricula (case)
University of British Columbia	Net Impact Case Competition (case)
Carnegie Mellon University	City High Case Competition (case), International Operations Case Competition (case)

Redefining the Meaning of an Exit Strategy for Social Ventures

Mission Accomplished, Nonprofits Go Out of Business (by Stephanie Strom, April 1, 2011, used with permission)

A few nonprofit groups have recently announced plans to wind down, not over financial problems but because their missions are nearly finished.

Most notable, perhaps, is Malaria No More, a popular nonprofit that supplies bed nets in malaria zones. Its goal is to end deaths from malaria, a target it sees fast approaching.

The charity has announced plans to close in 2015, but it is keeping its options open in the unlikely event that advances against malaria are reversed.

"We never planned to be around forever," said Scott Case, a co-founder of Priceline and vice chairman of Malaria No More. "We have thought of this more as a project than as an institution-building exercise, and the project is nearing its completion."

So far, the number of organizations opting to go out of business for mission-related reasons is too small to call a trend. It is still far more common for a nonprofit to close its doors because of financial pressure, which is increasing as governments continue to pare their budgets and donors maintain tight grips on their giving. Still, the novelty of organizations going out of business once their work is done has attracted attention.

"I don't think it's going to be a widespread phenomenon because there are a lot of groups taking on problems like alcoholism and domestic violence that aren't problems that go away," said Jan Masaoka, editor in chief of Blue Avocado, a blog for nonprofits. "But I do see that in some cases there is an opportunity for organizations to wind down gracefully and with their job done."

Out2Play, an organization started by Andrea Wenner in 2005, plans to close its doors in 2012. The group has put up roughly 120 playgrounds used by about 80,000 children in public elementary schools around New York City and is fast running out of locations, in part because the Bloomberg administration liked the idea so much that it took on some schools itself. "When I first wrote the business plan, I thought about expanding it to other cities or into other types of institutions, like housing projects or hospitals, and we talked about those ideas and others when the board began seeing the end in sight," Ms. Wenner said.

Ultimately, though, the board decided that the model worked best for the purpose it had served and that anything else would require more than a simple tweak.

"For example, in a housing project, you would still need someone to take kids to the playground and supervise them," Ms. Wenner said.

In the end, said Robert Daum, chairman of Out2Play's board, "we just decided to declare victory and go home. Money is a scarce resource, and there are lots of other good causes out there, so there is no point in hitting up our friends and contacts for gifts simply to perpetuate the organization." Out2Play is working to complete roughly forty more playgrounds before it closes. It plans to leave behind an endowment to cover some of the maintenance costs associated with the playgrounds, Ms. Wenner said.

"Right now, I think of it as very exciting because there's a great sense of accomplishment that goes along with it, but I'm sure on the final day, I'll have a strange feeling, probably bittersweet," she said.

Executives who have closed nonprofits say a feeling of pride overcomes any potential regrets. "Knowing that we were going to close helped us work with extreme urgency and intensity and not slack off for a minute," said David Douglas, a founder of Water Advocates, a charity that closed late last year. Over its five years, Water Advocates raised more than $100 million. Its goal was to increase awareness of water issues, as well as to pull together the efforts of a wide range of organizations. The open knowledge that Water Advocates was destined to go out of business helped it to encourage greater collaboration among those various groups.

"We weren't trying to attract attention to ourselves, which allowed us to focus on the issue itself, and we were always looking at ways to hand off things to other nonprofit groups," he said. "And we weren't competing for money, which also helped us build relationships."

British philanthropy circles have recently been talking about the decision to close the Otto Schiff Housing Association, a nonprofit set up in 1933 to provide assistance to displaced Jews. In its latest incarnation, the organization operated a number of homes for victims of Nazi persecution. "Our client group was clearly diminishing by virtue of demographics, and the homes were increasingly unsuitable for use because they were aging," said Ashley Mitchell, who was brought in to revamp the association. Otto Schiff identified two other nonprofit groups, Jewish Care and World Jewish Relief, to take on its operations and began selling off the homes.

"We thought maybe those assets would sell for £8 to £10 million," Mr. Mitchell said, equivalent to $13 million to $16 million. "The last ones will be sold in a month, and I hope they will have raised a gross of £60 million," or roughly $97 million, much more than expected. About 85 percent of that money is going to the organizations taking on Otto Schiff's services, and the remainder will be left in a foundation and spent out over the next five years or so, Mr. Mitchell said.

"We had an operational imperative to do this because of the maintenance requirements of the homes, but it also made sense because our client base was dwindling," he said. In some ways, that is the argument Mr. Case makes for closing Malaria No More. Roughly 80 to 85 percent of the population at risk of contracting malaria had received bed nets and other interventions by the end of last year, he said, and there has been a significant drop in mortality caused by malaria over the last decade. "It's not just Malaria No More's work, of course, but it does mean we are getting close to our goal," he said. He said operating with the knowledge that the group would close had shaped how it operated and perhaps made it more effective. "It meant that we worked to increase public awareness of malaria as an issue rather than promote our brand," Mr. Case said. "And it meant we didn't have to worry as much about protecting the brand, so we could be edgier and think outside the box more."

What will happen to Malaria No More's employees is perhaps Mr. Case's biggest concern. But Martin Edlund, who has worked for the organization since its founding in 2006, said that he was more excited about the significance of its ending. "We talk around here about malaria being the first great humanitarian success story of the twenty-first century, and I comfort myself at night knowing that if I have that accomplishment on my résumé, I'm not going to have any trouble finding another job," he said.

Source: http://www.nytimes.com/2011/04/02/business/02charity.
html?_r=3&page wanted=1&src=twrhp (used with permission)

CONCLUDING THOUGHTS

The field of social entrepreneurship creates a unique opportunity to continually integrate, challenge, and debate many traditional entrepreneurship assumptions in an effort to develop a cogent and unifying paradigm. As the field continues to mature, we look forward to seeing how social entrepreneurs mobilize and utilize existing resources to "catalyze" innovations that address societal problems. The social entrepreneur of tomorrow will most likely not only find creative solutions, but also engage her or his own pre-existing knowledge and relationships to encourage stakeholders to take notice of these innovations and the impact they can have in driving long-term systematic change for broader social, political, and economic well-being.

QUESTIONS FOR "CONNECTING THE DOTS"

1 Given the number of possibilities and innovations for solving many of society's most pressing problems, what solutions in your own community would make the most immediate social impact?

2 Provide several examples of bricolage behavior from your own experience.

3 Provide examples of "catalytic" innovations from profiles of social entrepreneurs. How is their work "catalytic"?

4 Consider one of the future trends in social entrepreneurship. Which of the innovations resonates with you? Why?

Case Study 13.1

The World Resources Institute's New Ventures

Introduction

New Ventures is the World Resources Institute's (WRI) center for environmental entrepreneurship, providing business development services to small and medium-sized enterprises

(SMEs) in emerging environment-related markets. New Ventures addresses the key barriers to "green" entrepreneurial growth by building in-country support networks for environmental enterprises, increasing the pool of available and invested capital for these enterprises, and strengthening a global network that facilitates business linkages and knowledge sharing among environmental enterprises. WRI believes that environmental SMEs will play an important role in developing sustainable business, and its New Ventures program seeks to expand the potential of these enterprises in six key emerging markets including Brazil, China, Colombia, India, Indonesia, and Mexico. These countries are home to 46 percent of the world's population, are responsible for 12 percent of its GDP, and house 25 percent of the protected biodiversity areas on the planet. The six Local Centers are recognized as premier centers for environmental enterprise development in their local markets. New Ventures addresses the challenges faced by environmental SMEs in these six countries and supports their growth by:

- providing business advisory services;
- connecting enterprises to investors that can provide growth capital;
- facilitating access to global markets and buyers;
- building a global platform to create efficiencies for SMEs to learn from each other;
- creating a strong local support community to help take business models to scale;
- driving more financial capital into environmental SMEs by addressing barriers to investment.

Over the past ten years, New Ventures at WRI has:

- directly supported the business development of over 255 environmental SMEs;
- facilitated the transfer of over $203 million in SME investment;
- established six Local Centers with robust in-country presence and knowledge;
- expanded expertise in key sectors, including clean energy, water, sustainable agriculture, and green transport solutions;
- raised the profile of environmental SMEs in global and national media such as the *Financial Times*, the *Los Angeles Times*, CNN International, BBC Mexico, and *Hindustan Times*.

One of the companies that New Ventures works with, Vidrios Marte, was the first to bring technology for energy-efficient glass used in construction to Mexico. The company has succeeded in both saving energy—the glass it manufactures reduces energy consumption by up to 40 percent—and building a strong business model, with sales tripling over the past five years. Vidrios Marte is also currently recognized as one of the "best places to work" in Mexico.

Maraton Kencana, another company in WRI's portfolio, produces boutique furniture and accessories from natural raw materials such as coconuts, sea shells, and banana bark that have been discarded as waste by other industries. By using these materials, Maraton Kencana avoids using wood from Indonesia's endangered tropical forests while simultaneously reducing its materials costs. The company provides employment for over 150 local people, and has expanded into markets in Europe, South America, and the United States.

Future Strategy

Objective 1: Build and scale in-country support networks for environmental SMEs in key emerging markets. New Ventures has successfully engaged strategic partners and stakeholders to build a strong support community for SMEs with high growth potential and positive environmental and social impacts. In-country activities include:

- establishing coaching networks to mentor companies in business development;
- creating investor networks to provide access to capital;
- building the operational capacity of the six Local Centers to offer customized and ongoing business mentoring services for enterprises at various stages of development;
- engaging institutional buyers to understand the potential for creating new markets and supply-chain demand for environmental products and services.

New Ventures' Local Centers will continue to identify and select environmental SMEs that combine high growth potential with benefits to the community and the environment. Enterprises chosen for the New Ventures portfolio receive a minimum of forty hours of business mentoring and training services that assist the entrepreneurs in developing materials such as a business plan, PowerPoint presentations, and a one-page profile.

Local Centers will also work to build and strengthen in-country networks and partnerships that support the growth of the environmental SME sector. These networks include stakeholders such as investment funds, financial institutions, business incubators, universities, and government agencies. New Ventures Mexico, the oldest and most mature Local Center, currently has the Sustainable Minds Network for business mentoring and Las Paginas Verdes, a green business directory. New Ventures Mexico works closely with the Secretary of the Economy on public policy to allow for the growth of environmental SMEs, and also sustains relationships with a number of local funds and investors.

Objective 2: Increase investment in environmental SMEs to create viable enterprises providing products and services for tomorrow's consumers, institutional buyers, and MNCs. The first component of this strategy focuses on facilitating investment in individual companies within the New Ventures portfolio on both a local and a global level. On a local level, New Ventures will be showcasing selected New Ventures enterprises in the six countries of operation through in-country investor events or forums and meetings. On a global level, New Ventures will be creating and launching a "New Ventures Global Portfolio" composed of specific companies from the six New Ventures countries with strong financial performance and with the potential to raise capital from international investors. New Ventures DC will proactively showcase the "Global Portfolio" to global investors. Through the formation of a "Global Portfolio," New Ventures will develop a stronger case for approaching global investors as a means to increasing the pool of available capital.

The second component of this strategy focuses on increasing capital flows to the environmental SME sector as a whole. Three initiatives, focused on New Ventures' six countries of operation, are intended to provide investors with information and mechanisms to help them make better investment decisions and channel more funds into environmental SMEs. The target audience includes "direct" investors in SMEs, such as local banks, development organizations, and angel and venture capital firms, as well as "indirect" investors: those investing in funds that invest in SMEs, such as institutional investors and multilateral development banks.

- research: analyzing the investment potential of key environmental SME sectors and the barriers to their growth;
- investment strategies: working with financial institutions and investors to pilot innovative financing mechanisms to support environmental SMEs;
- metrics: developing sector-wide tools and standard metrics to enable environmental SMEs to inform investors of their financial, environmental, and/or social potential and performance.

Objective 3: Strengthen the global New Ventures network to share best practices and develop business partnerships among environmental SMEs. In the first ten years of operation, New Ventures concentrated on launching its enterprise acceleration centers in six of the world's most vibrant emerging economies. Going forward, New Ventures recognizes the importance of leveraging this global presence along with the insights gained throughout its ten years of operation to create dynamic opportunities for South–South and North–South collaboration. It will facilitate sharing of best practices between entrepreneurs, investors, and other organizations (NGOs, universities) through global or regional forums with the aim of creating business partnerships or valuable deals between entrepreneurs and investors or buyers.

Source: Interview with Ella Delio, Global Director,
New Ventures, World Resources Institute

THOUGHT QUESTIONS

1 Critique the business model of New Ventures' program. What are the potentials and risks associated with the six markets New Ventures is in?
2 In what ways can New Ventures further scale in-country support networks for environmental SMEs in key emerging markets?
3 How can New Ventures attract additional investment in environmental SMEs?
4 Recommend a variety of ways that New Ventures can disseminate best practices and develop business partnerships among environmental SMEs.

REFERENCES

Alter, K. (2007, November 27). *Social enterprise typology*. Virtue Ventures LLC.

Ansell, C., & Gash, A. (2008). Collaborative governance in theory and practice. *Journal of Public Administration Research and Theory, 18*(4), 543–571.

Aspen Institute (2008). *Where will they lead? 2008 MBA student attitudes about business & society*. Washington, DC.

Association to Advance Collegiate Schools of Business (AACSB) (2010). *Business schools on an innovation mission: Report of the AACSB International Task Force on Business Schools and Innovation*. Tampa, FL.

Austin, J., Stevenson, H., & Wei-Skillern, J. (2006). Social and commercial entrepreneurship: Same, different, or both? *Entrepreneurship Theory and Practice, 30*(1), 1–22.

Austin, J., Gutierrez, R., Ogliastri, E., & Reficco, E. (2006). *Effective management of social enterprises: Lessons from businesses and civil society organizations in Iberoamerica*. Cambridge, MA: Harvard University.

Baker, T., & Nelson, R. E. (2005). Creating something from nothing: Resource construction through entrepreneurial bricolage. *Administrative Science Quarterly, 50*, 329–366.

Baker, T., Miner, A. S., & Eesley, D. T. (2003). Improvising firms: Bricolage, account giving and improvisational competencies in the founding process. *Research Policy, 32*, 255–276.

Bennis, W. G., & O'Toole, J. (2005). How business schools lost their way. *Harvard Business Review, 83*(5), 96–104.

Brock, D. D., & Ashoka Global Academy for Social Entrepreneurship (2008). *Social entrepreneurship teaching resources handbook*. Retrieved from http://ssrn.com/abstract=1344412.

Chell, E. (2007). Social enterprise and entrepreneurship. *International Small Business Journal, 25*(1), 5–26.

Christensen, C. M., & Bower, J. L. (1995). Disruptive technologies: Catching the wave. *Harvard Business Review*, January–February, 43–53.

Christensen, C. M., Baumann, H., Ruggles, R., & Sadtler, T. M. (2006). Disruptive innovation for social change. *Harvard Business Review*, December, 39–55.

Crosby, B. C., & Bryson, J. M. (2005). *Leadership for the common good: Tackling public problems in a shared-power world*. San Francisco, CA: Jossey-Bass.

Dees, G., Emerson, J., & Economy, P. (2001). *Enterprising nonprofits: A toolkit for the social entrepreneur*. Hoboken, NJ: John Wiley.

Desa, G. (2007). Social entrepreneurship: Snapshots of a research field in emergence. Paper presented at the 2007 International Social Entrepreneurship Research Conference (ISERC), Copenhagen, June 18–19.

Economist, The (2010, April 17). The world turned upside down. A special report on innovation in emerging markets. *The Economist*, pp. 3–12.

Fast Company (2007). Profits with Purpose. Better World Books. 45 social entrepreneurs who are changing the world. Retrieved from http://www.fastcompany.com/magazine/121/profits-with-purpose.html#.

Keegan, M. J. (2010). Leading the Global Partnership initiative: Insights from Ambassador Elizabeth Frawley Bagley. *The Business of Government*, Spring, pp. 33–36.

Marcus, A. A., & Fremeth, A. R. (2009). Green management matters regardless. *Academy of Management Perspectives, 23*, 17–26.

Natsios, A. S. (2009). Public/private alliances transform aid. *Stanford Social Innovation Review*, Fall, pp. 42–47.

Phills, J. A., Deiglmeier, K., & Miller, D. T. (2008). Rediscovering social innovation. *Stanford Social Innovation Review*, Fall, pp. 28–39.

Smith, B., & Barr, T. (2007). Reducing poverty through social entrepreneurship: The case of Edun. In C. Wankel & J.Stoner (Eds.). *Innovative approaches to reducing poverty*. Charlotte, NC: Information Age Publishing.

Tracey, P., & Phillips, N. (2007). The distinctive challenge of educating social entrepreneurs: A post-script and rejoinder to the special issue on entrepreneurship education. *Academy of Management Learning and Education*, 6(2), 264–271.

Index